REIMAGINING INDIAN EDUCATION

Issues, Perspectives and NEP 2020

Editor

Ajit Mondal

SHIPRA

₹ 595
ISBN: 978-93-91978-75-4

2024
First Published in India

Reimagining Indian Education: Issues, Perspectives and NEP 2020

Published by:
SHIPRA PUBLICATIONS
LG 18-19, Pankaj Central Market
I.P. Ext., Patparganj, Delhi 110092, India
+91 11 47322068; 96500 28065, 9810522367
info@shiprapublication.com
www.shiprapublication.com

Preface

In today's knowledge-based society, education is seen as a key driver of development of any nation. Knowledge and skill are also the driving force for economic growth and social development of any nation in the 21st Century. Today's education system requires equipping them with relevant skills. The present system of human resource development necessitates transformation and orientation so that it can prepare youth with desired levels of knowledge, skills and competencies to harmonise education with employment across the globe. The Sustainable Development Goal 4 (SDG 4) also aims at ensuring inclusive and equitable quality education where relevant skills, including technical and vocational skills, for employment, decent jobs and entrepreneurship have also been attached markedly. The need of the hour therefore is to make the education system reorient in a manner that it conforms to the requirements of the empowering the students for livelihood and making them employable. The development of 21st century skills is thus a stated priority in curriculum at all levels of education across the globe. Every student in the 21st century needs to be able to think critically, solve problem, collaborate, communicate, innovate, be globally aware, and be technically literate. Other desirable 21st century skills include entrepreneurial skills, digital literacy, life skills, self-direction, personal and social responsibility, and character and citizenship. Accordingly, all the schools, colleges and universities have to prepare students for the workforce of the future.

India recognizes the requirement to revamp education system in tune with the demands of the 21st century. Accordingly, the National Education Policy (NEP) 2020 has put emphasis on the aim of education not only towards cognitive development, but also building character and creating holistic and well-rounded individuals equipped with the key 21st century skills. To this end, Government of India has made a series of policy reforms in the landscape of education since the enactment of the new policy. The NEP 2020 proposes the revision and revamping of all aspects of the education in terms of curricular structure, evaluation, regulation and governance to create a new system that is aligned with the aspirational goals of 21st century education. These reforms include access to equitable and quality education, changes in curriculum and pedagogy, equitable use of technologies, and rethinking how teachers are selected, trained, and assessed, re-imagining Vocational Education, restructuring higher education institutions (HEIs), catalyzing Quality Academic Research etc. The entire educational system in India is in the process of being restructured. The transformation and reorientation of the entire education system in alignment with the aspirational goals of 21st century education is indispensable but challenging endeavour.

The volume titled 'Reimagining Indian Education: Issues, Perspectives and NEP 2020' is an anthology of research-based articles focusing all the emerging issues in the landscape of Indian education in the context of the 21st century. Most of these articles deal with the changing paradigm of our education systems and recognize the challenging areas in the policy reforms embedded in the NEP 2020 in the context of various cultural and contextual milieus and federal governance in the country. This volume is full of deliberations in the form of a book to address various issues of Indian education with a futuristic perspective in the light of the 21st century. The key areas of each chapter can thus be delineated here.

Chapter titled "Nutrition and Education: Issues, Challenges and Opportunities for Holistic Development of Children" written by Madhumita Bandyopadhyay, Nassif Muhammed Ali, Anupam Gupta, Meenakshi Khandari and Anupriya Kholia captures a study of three different schemes; PM Poshan, Saksham Anganwadi and Poshan 2.0 in terms of their implementation in Haryana, Uttar Pradesh and Punjab for removing malnutrition and improving the quality of life of people of different age groups including children, adolescent girls and adult women – especially pregnant and lactating mothers – ensuring the holistic growth and development cannot be fulfilled by focusing on the children alone. Rather, it should also address mothers as well as prospective mothers in order to have a direct impact. The study explores the positive impact that three schemes are having on increasing enrolment, retention and bringing down the dropout rates in school on the one hand and improving the health and nutrition of pregnant and lactating women, adolescent girls and infants on the other. However, the study has not only indicated the importance of all these schemes targeting children even before their birth, but it also found a close association between their nutrition, school preparedness and ensuring strong foundation and holistic development at their preparative stage of life with its far-reaching impact on their educational attainment in the context of 21st Century.

Dr Sangeeta Angom in her Chapter titled "Exploring Access and Equity Concerns of Higher Education in India" has tried to explore the role of public as well as private higher education in the context of access and equity in India. The study has produced policy implications and contributions of the private and public sectors to frame the thinking of expansion of higher education with equity. She has pointed out the observations made in the new National Education Policy 2020 that the rapid expansion of higher education system has brought several pertinent issues, like inequitable access to quality education, low standards of undergraduate education, low quality and research output, rigid separation of disciplines, outdated teaching methods, unmotivated student, inadequate infrastructure and facilities, limited teacher and institutional autonomy, fragmented educational ecosystem, suboptimal governance and leadership of HEIs, and ineffective regulatory system. She concludes that various initiatives have taken for expansion of higher education and promotion of greater regional and social equity, yet considerable challenges remain. Access to higher education is still less than minimum international threshold levels and the distribution of institutions is skewed. Enrolment in public universities is largely concerned in the conventional disciplines whereas in the private self-financed institutions, the students' enrolment is overwhelmingly in the market-driven disciplines. State has to play a very important role in terms of providing framework and that framework will decide the way in which equity and equality is addressed.

Partha Roy and Dr Abhijit Guha in their Chapter titled "Web Technology in the 21st Century: Teaching-Learning Process" have intended to investigate how to use web technology in the classroom. In this regard, the researchers have found out and analyzed descriptive forms about the modern Web Technology and its effective impact on the teaching-learning process. They have concluded that Web Technology, which is also emphasized by NEP 2020, is a new viewpoint and helps to cope with a more dynamic environment in which Web Technology must be incorporated into the teaching and learning process for better academic outcomes in the 21st century. The study primarily captures the application of Web 1.0 Web 2.0 and Web 3.0 in teaching-learning process in general but they have analysed the scenario of radical transformation in the domain of teaching-learning process with the help of Web 3.0 technologies. Today, sharing technology with others is not only desirable, but also essential for the 21st centuries' citizens.

Chapter titled "Soft Skills in the 21st Century: Educational Needs and Practices" written by Swarup Chandi and Dr Puja Sarkar (Bal) is a discussion about the idea of soft skills, and why it is important, and what should be done to nurture the soft skills in individuals or students. It has also focused on the various initiatives that may be taken by academic as well as corporate organizations to betterment of their people on soft skills. In today's world, only hard skills or domain knowledge are not sufficient to cope with the changes happening within ever-changing globe. Some additional knowledge or skills, those are called soft skills or transversal skills, or 21st century skills are highly necessitated.

Dr Shnaoli Chakraborty Acharya in her chapter titled "Towards A More Orderly Transition: Innovations in 21st Century Teaching Skills" seeks to answer to the fundamental questions about what information and abilities teachers should possess and in which educational environment they will apply such knowledge and skills. It puts emphasis on improving the quality of teacher instruction by developing 21st century skill competencies. She has explored the essential skills for the 21st century learners. She has also examined the various aspects of 21st century talents, categorised into three main categories: Learning, Literacy and Life skills. Lastly, it entails the desired competencies of 21st century teachers.

Chapter titled "Curriculum Framework and Credit System for Undergraduate Programmes and NEP 2020", written by Susanta Rajbanshi and Dr Swati Gupta gives an overview of reconstruction and reformation of curriculum framework and credit system for undergraduate programmes in the context of the National Education Policy 2020. In consonance with the NEP 2020, University Grants Commission has formulated a new revised curriculum and credit system as "Curriculum and Credit Framework for Undergraduate Programmes (CCFUP)". This illustrates the main features of CCFUP, Programmes, Curriculum and courses, credit evaluation system and awarding degree under CCFUP. After discussing all the aspects of CCFUP, the study has attempted to make a critical SWOC (strength, weakness, opportunities and challenges) analysis.

Dr Smritikana Ghosh in her Chapter titled "A Holistic Perspective on Education: An Overview" has tried to clarify and gain an understanding of the concepts that underpin the holistic approach to education. She has explained the theoretical foundation of holistic education and its characteristic features. The principles, benefits and model of holistic education have been captured in this study. It has also entailed the methods, challenges and implications of holistic education. This approach takes into account the requirements of the child as a whole, which means that the requirements of the child's body, intellect, heart, and spirit are all taken into account. Students are able to gain information, skills, and attitudes that will serve them throughout their lives when they get an education that emphasises a holistic approach.

Nilay Mondal and Professor Khagendranath Chattopadhyay in their chapter titled "Reflective Teaching Practice in India from the Perspectives of National Professional Standard for Teachers (NPST)" is an appraisal on the concept of reflective teaching practice in India and how the draft National Professional Standard for Teachers (NPTS) emphasized reflective teaching practice. The 21st century education system demands quality of every aspect of education. The teachers and their methods of teaching are the very important factors of education. The choice of teaching method by teacher impacts the teaching-learning process greatly. Reflective teaching is a process that can enhance the quality of teaching and creates a positive learning environment for learners. The draft "National Professional Standard for Teachers" was developed by NCTE in the light of the NEP 2020 to ensure the quality of teacher education in Indian Education System. This chapter has explored the concept of reflective teaching, reflective activities for teachers, and the reflective process embedded in the NPST.

In the chapter titled "Holistic and Multidisciplinary Approach to Higher Education and NEP 2020", Basanti Mahanta and Professor Bijan Sarkar has concentrated on the holistic approach to higher education from the lens of National Education Policy 2020. The researchers have also analysed how a multidisciplinary and holistic approach can play an important part in the child's 'All Round Development' in respect of global education. The NEP

2020 envisages bringing back more holistic education in India in the 21st century. The UGC (2022) in 'Guidelines for Transforming Higher Education Institutions (HEIs) into Multidisciplinary Institutions' academic collaboration between institutions, through HEI clusters, leads to multidisciplinary education and research in different modes. This chapter has critically analysed the key concerns, learning strategies of holistic and multidisciplinary education in the context of NEP 2020. It has also outlined the roadmap for multidisciplinary education and research universities. The benefits and limitations regarding holistic education in Indian context have also been pointed out here.

The chapter titled "Developing, Nourishing and Bolstering Skills through Envisaging NEP 2020" written by Parnab Ghosh is primarily a qualitative analytical study and it has tried to find out the different aspects of skill development and their implementation in the context of the NEP 2020. He has explored what and how the NEP 2020 has proposed to promote skill development in India. This chapter starts with the background and genesis of skill development programme in India. It has also analysed the prior initiative and perspective of skill-based education programmes in India. The policy recommendations on skill development of the nation at all levels of education have been captured. He has concluded that the NEP 2020 is a comprehensive framework that aims to transform the Indian education system. The policy recognizes the importance of promoting skill development among students, teachers, and other stakeholders as well and proposes various measures to achieve such objectives.

The chapter titled "Learning Management System (LMS) in Education: An Overview" by Azharuddin Molla and Dr Rajab Ali Biswas made an in-depth description of Learning Management System (LMS) — a platform for digital learning. This chapter entails the concept and the interrelated aspects — Curriculum Planning, Content Management, Learners Participation and Instant Evaluation of LMS. It also delineated common features, types and historical background of LMS. In the last section, they have pointed out implications of LMS in the domain of education in the 21st century. In the current scenario, technological advancements have made it possible to spread any type of information rapidly with the help of networks. Similarly, the exchange of various types of information has become faster and easier in the field of teaching-learning and training. Just as teachers have harnessed technology to use various types of information in education; students are also taking the help of technology. In terms of classroom teaching, technical material is being provided directly both online and offline. LMS is the essential tool for managing all these issues.

Dr Ajit Mondal in his chapter titled "Policy Reforms in Teacher Education Envisaged by the NEP 2020: Prospects and Challenges" has mainly examined the policy reforms in teacher education envisaged by the National Education Policy 2020. The areas of concern over those reforms have also been addressed in this chapter. Before examining the policy reforms in Teacher Education, he has presented the current status of teacher education in India which will be revamped based on the policy recommendations. This chapter has also analysed the changing role of teachers in the light of the systematic reforms in Teacher Education embedded in the NEP 2020. It entails recognition and promotion of teachers, upgrading working conditions for teachers, continuous professional development of teachers, teacher educators and school principals, professional standards for teachers, teachers' recruitment and deployment with the objective of providing quality teachers in the school system. Its last section contains challenges to implementing the policy reforms envisaged by the NEP 2020.

The chapter entitled "Intellectual Property Rights (IPRs): NEP 2020 and Initiatives of UGC" written by Dr Arindam Bhattacharyya and Aditi Ray has mainly investigated the vision of National Education Policy 2020 on Intellectual Property and mission of the policy for the promotion of Intellectual Property Rights. It has also addressed UGC's several initiatives for the regular practice of intellectual property rights here for its better implementation. NEP 2020 envisages the promotion of quality research within the higher education institutions (HEIs) and simultaneously the higher apex body of Indian higher education, the UGC should play a significant role in implementing multidisciplinary research culture mandated in NEP 2020. It is important to promote more collaboration between HEI and industry through better clarity on Intellectual Property Right (IPR) policy. Educational institutions should also play a pivotal role in disseminating IP knowledge and creating IP professionals and policymakers. But the policy has crafted the multidisciplinary approach to higher education without paying attention to the overall infrastructural conditions in the HEIs across India.

Dr Mousumi Boral in her chapter titled "Research and Publication Ethics in Social Sciences" has critically captured significance of maintaining ethical standards in social science research and explored ethical issues related to data collection, integrity in data analysis and reporting findings in social science research. This chapter has also address issues such as selective reporting, data manipulation, and plagiarism. She has also elaborated positivist and non-positivist approaches related to health issues in social science research and pointed out the ethical challenges specific to research methods: quantitative and qualitative methods. Its last section deals with publication ethics and the strategies how to combat the ethical misconduct at the time of publication. She concluded stating that adequacy of funds is highly necessary for access, data collection, quality, collaboration, and dissemination especially in social science research. Currently, a gap exists between research and policy, with limited translation and implementation of research findings. Social science researchers need to be involved in policymaking processes to ensure the incorporation of research findings and recommendations.

Professor (Dr) Neeru Snehi in her chapter titled "Catalysing Research and Innovation in 21st Century Indian Higher Education" focuses on one of the major aspects of improving quality namely enhancing research and innovation in higher education institutions. She has analysed the policy implications related to research and innovations embedded in the National Education Policy 2020. She has tried to show the multiple pathways of enhancing research capacity in Indian universities and colleges. Lastly, this chapter entails some strategies to enhance research in higher education institutions in the context of the NEP 2020. She has concluded that higher education system in India is under transition and is attempting to align itself with the vision of NEP 2020.

Professor (Dr) Ujjwal Kumar Halder in his chapter titled "Social Science Research: Theories, Paradigms and Methodologies" deals with the understanding about social sciences and social science research. He has explained the relevant theories and paradigms in social science research. He has primarily analysed the significant paradigms or schools of thought in social science research, such as Positivism: Post-positivism, Interpretivism, Anti-positivism, Critical Theory, Structural Functionalism, Conflict Theory, Symbolic Interactionism, Rational Choice Theory, Feminist Theory, Social Learning Theory, Human Capital Theory, Social Exchange Theory, etc. In the last section, this chapter shows the contribution of theories and paradigms in social science research and contribution of social science research in developing theories and paradigms. Lastly, he has elaborated the significant methodologies in social science research.

I am highly indebted to all the authors for their contributions to this volume. The entire liability of originality and genuineness of the chapters in this book rests upon the chapter authors. We shall also feel rewarded if students, researchers, teachers and policy makers find this helpful. All the chapters will definitely help to have better insight into education for the 21st century. What actually Indian education system needs and where challenges remain for reorienting our present system in tune with the requirements of the 21st century have been adequately addressed in this book.

Dr Ajit Modal
Department of Education
West Bengal State University, Kolkata

Contents

1

Nutrition and Education

Issues, Challenges and Opportunities for Holistic Development of Children

Madhumita Bandyopadhyay, Nassif Muhammed Ali, Anupam Gupta, Meenakshi Khandari, Anupriya Kholia

Introduction

The importance of holistic development of children and the imperativeness of ensuring its access across the population have already been discussed far and wide. This question becomes all the more crucial in developing societies like India. It is in this light that the current paper focuses on a study of three different schemes: PM Poshan, Saksham Anganwadi and Poshan 2.0, which are being implemented across India for eradicating malnutrition and improving the quality of life of people of different age groups including children, adolescent girls and adult women – especially pregnant and lactating mothers. Based on secondary and primary data, an attempt has been made to find out how these schemes are being implemented in different states and a national narrative has been developed based on the findings. The paper concludes with a few points that underline the way forward. The importance of taking into consideration the health and nutrition of the children as well as the need for facilitating their growth in a healthy manner is underlined in the following observation:

> The period from birth to eight years old is one of remarkable brain development for children and represents a crucial window of opportunity for education. UNESCO believes early childhood care and education (ECCE) that is truly inclusive is much more than just preparation for primary school. It can be the foundation for emotional wellbeing and learning throughout life and one of the best investments a country can make as it promotes holistic development, gender equality and social cohesion (UNESCO, 2023).

The report further states that despite the evidence of its importance, early childhood care and education "is still often given low priority in education policy and investment and, where it does exist, may exclude marginalized groups" (UNESCO, 2023). It should be noted here that ensuring the holistic growth and development cannot be fulfilled by focusing on the children alone. Rather, it should also address mothers as well as prospective mothers in order to have a direct impact. Thus, the current paper is based on a study of the three different schemes of PM Poshan, Saksham Anganwadi and Poshan 2.0 in terms of its implementation as well as the way forward. While PM Poshan scheme is being implemented by the Ministry of Education for children enrolled in pre-school (3-6 age group) and elementary schools (6-14 age group enrolled in I-VIII grades), the Saksham Anganwadi and Poshan 2.0 schemes are being implemented by the Ministry of Women and Child Development. These schemes are envisaged to improve the nutrition, health and living conditions of its target groups which include women, adolescent girls and children from all sections of the Indian population.

The Study

The study is an attempt to assess the present status of these schemes since its inception taking into consideration the Covid-19 pandemic and its impact and to find out the extent to which it could be possible to address the objectives set before these schemes. Attempt was also made to study the quality of services that were provided, as well as the effect it had on the nutrition and education of the target groups and other aspects of their life. The study was therefore undertaken with the following objectives:

- To assess the present status of implementation of these schemes since their inception including the period of Covid pandemic.
- To find out whether these schemes are able to address the objectives set before these schemes.
- To find out the quality of the service provided by these schemes and best practices and appropriate initiatives adopted by the states;
- To assess the impact of these schemes on the nutrition and education of children (from 3 to 14 years) and adolescent girls (14-18 years).

Methodology and Mechanism of Conducting Study

The study has followed a triangulation of multiple methods, including secondary source-based content analysis and statistical analysis and an extensive field investigation to find out the actual implementation status of these schemes at the institutional level. Information both qualitative and quantitative has been collected with the help of secondary data, research studies and various other documents through desk research. In addition, two webinars and two face-to-face workshops have been conducted to develop a better understanding of the implementation of these schemes and also to collect information from various states.

Three different states were taken up for the field study, to gain a national picture as well as to enable a comparative analysis. The field visits have been conducted in the states of Haryana (Jhajjar and Nuh Mewat districts), Uttar Pradesh (Ghaziabad and Baghpat districts) and Punjab (Mohali District). In total 10 blocks across five districts from three states were covered under the study. From these states, altogether, 10 schools and 10 Anganwadi centres were visited by the research team to prepare case studies of these schools and to find out the institutional mechanisms of implementing these schemes.

Nutrition, Health and Quality of Life: An Overview of Literature

According to the National Council for Educational Research and Training (NCERT), the early years (0 to 8 years) are the most significant period of growth and development, in the life of a child. This is because it is during this period that the foundation for the holistic development of the child is laid. It is also the period when the foundations of the child's future learning are set up. In other words, children who are provided with quality early childhood education, and participate in it, are bound to demonstrate significant gains in all spheres of life as opposed to children who have no access to these. Strong foundation in thc early years has a lasting impact on children's development and is considered to be critical inputs in improving the enrolment and participation of children in formal schooling. The Integrated Child Development Service (ICDS) scheme is a multi-sectoral endeavour that aims at integrated delivery of a package of services for children of 0–6 years of age, pregnant and lactating mothers and adolescent girls from disadvantaged sections belonging to the poorest of the poor families (PIB, 2021). The key objectives of this scheme are to improve the nutritional and health status of children in the age group 0–6 years; to lay the foundation for proper psychological, physical and social development of the child; to reduce the incidence of mortality, morbidity, malnutrition and school dropout; to achieve effective coordination of policy and implementation among the various departments to promote child development; and to enhance the capability of mothers to look after the normal health and nutritional needs of their children through proper nutrition and health education. The above objectives are sought to be achieved through a package of services comprising supplementary nutrition and growth monitoring; immunization; health check-ups; health referral services; non-formal pre-school education and health and nutrition education to be provided at all Anganwadi Centres (AWCs) (PIB, 2021).

According to Sandhyarani, M.C., & Rao, C.U. (2013), Anganwadi workers play the role of bridge between the community and the ICDS. It also plays an active role in bringing the services to the doorstep of the beneficiaries. The Department of Women and Child Welfare has to look into the matter of remuneration and very importantly provide accurate knowledge with regard to the responsibilities of Anganwadi workers through organizing all the Anganwadi workers under one roof. Thus, the Anganwadi workers will be enhanced with the knowledge and their doubts will be cleared and they can deliver the services in a better manner.

Strauss and Thomas (1998) have underlined the economic value of preventing child malnutrition. According to, Behrman and Deolalikar (1987), improvements over time have been found to be driven primarily by technological and institutional changes that shift food demand and care practices. In the Indian scenario, one factor that has been making positive changes is the pre-school daycare centres funded through the government's

Integrated Child Development Services (ICDS) programme. The quality of services delivered at ICDS centres is highly contentious. Programme gaps exist in almost all areas of ICDS delivery, and even basic amenities are often lacking (Chudasama et al., 2014; Gupta et al., 2013). Workers have limited education, training, job security and infrastructure (Ramachandran et al., 2010; Sharma et al., 2014), and they report significant stress and dissatisfaction (Mohanan et al., 2012). If motivated to do so, caregivers can influence the prevalence of child underweight through two main channels: first through the direct provision of food and other services to the child at the centre, and secondly through effective communication with mothers either when they drop off or pick up their child from the centre or by making home visits. A World Bank report by Gragnolati et al. (2005) found both to be limited, with many missing meals and almost no effective communication between workers and mothers. A more recent household survey in 100 Indian districts indicates that although 96 per cent of locations were served by a functioning ICDS centre, only 50 per cent of them actually provided food on the day of the survey and just 19 per cent of the mothers reported that the workers provides nutrition counselling (Saxena, N. C., 2012).

Previous studies of ICDS programme impacts have used cross-sectional observations and found mixed results: Deolalikar (2005) found evidence of lower underweight prevalence among boys in locations with ICDS centres in the early 1990s, but Lokshin et al. (2005) find strong selection effects with ICDS centres more likely to be located in places that also benefit from other advantages. Focusing on Chandigarh, Thakur et al. (2011) found that programme enrolment was not associated with a lower prevalence of underweight children, but using national data and matching methods to address geographic and household-specific selection effects. Kandpal (2011) and Jain (2015) found significant gains in child height, and Mittal and Meenakshi (2015) found reductions in the prevalence of underweight. Randomized trials at ICDS centres have focused on introducing additional services, such as increasing take-home rations (Avula et al. 2011).

Thakur et al. (2015) and Desai et al. (2012) have studied the Anganwadi workers and their roles. The former noted that the AWWs had inadequate knowledge regarding the services rendered under ICDS, they had discontent regarding their remuneration, delay in receiving their funds and other supplies, they were overloaded with record maintenance burden, they complained of problems relating to infrastructure (Thakur et al., 2015). The latter (Desai et al., 2012) underlined that suggested that AWWs are overworked and ASHA (Accredited Social Health Activists) should be utilised so that the Anganwadi workers can focus on their services better. They highlighted that "the Anganwadi workers and helpers, who are the basic functionaries of the ICDS are not treated at par with government employees but are called 'social workers' or 'voluntary workers'. They are not paid salary but only honorarium". Manhas, Dogra and Devi (2012) have revealed that the implementation of services under ICDS is not up to satisfactory standards and still more efforts are needed for improving the quality of services for the successful achievement of expected targets. Various studies in the recent past had reflected the unsatisfactory implementation of growth monitoring practices by Anganwadi workers under ICDS (Singh, et al., 2017). Another study found that there are extremes of observations in different studies. On the other hand, (Tripathy et al., 2014) commented that the knowledge, attitude and practice of Anganwadi Workers with respect to growth monitoring, supplementary nutrition and immunization are satisfactory.

Nutrition and Education

Studies like Sood (2010), Rosso (1999), Alderman et al. (1997, 2001) etc. have already underlined the complex interrelationship between nutrition, social and economic factors, health and education. The incidence of malnourishment among children in India has been associated with many factors ranging from parental knowledge of infant feeding, hygiene and care of sick children; and gender-related socio-economic issues (UNICEF, 2004: 9). The risk of malnutrition decreases with an increase in family income. A mother's nutritional status, educational level, age and working status also impact on the nutritional and health status of her children. In India, malnourishment of children is strongly linked to socio-economic status, with a much higher incidence of malnourished children found in SC and ST groups. It is also

Table 1.1: *Additional Items Provided by the States and UTs for Mid-day Meal Scheme*

Best Practices	*Name of the State/UTs*
Eggs, bananas, any other fruits	Andhra Pradesh, Telangana, West Bengal, Odisha, Puducherry, Tamil Nadu, Jharkhand, Lakshadweep, Rajasthan, A&N Islands, Daman & Diu
Milk	Puducherry, Uttar Pradesh, Gujarat, Kerala, Karnataka, Madhya Pradesh
Dining halls	Tripura, West Bengal, Uttar Pradesh
Additional share Honorarium CCH & Cooking cost	Bihar, Uttarakhand, Puducherry, Lakshadweep, Haryana, Tamil Nadu, Karnataka, Chandigarh, Punjab, Kerala, Chhattisgarh, West Bengal, Jharkhand, Gujarat, Madhya Pradesh, Goa, Mizoram, Odisha, Dadra & Nagar Haveli, Daman & Diu
Kitchen Garden	Assam, Kerala, West Bengal, Tripura, Sikkim, Arunachal Pradesh, Nagaland, Lakshadweep
Additional foodgrains	Gujarat, Kerala
Tablet Based Monitoring	Bihar
MDM to Classes IX & X	Andhra Pradesh, Karnataka, Tamil Nadu, Telangana
Fabricated Kitchen	Maharashtra
Eating Utensils	Bihar, Gujarat, West Bengal, Uttar Pradesh, Madhya Pradesh

Source: Annual Report, 2017-18, GoI, MHRD, P, 58

prevalent among the Other Backward Castes (OBCs). In addition to nutritional disadvantage, they also tend to suffer from poor living conditions, and often have poor access to health care and schooling.

The turning point in initiatives for improving children's health and nutrition happened with the introduction of another Scheme, 'National Programme of Nutritional Support to Primary Education' commonly known as the Mid-day Meal Scheme, which was launched on the 15 August 1995 on a nation-wide scale by the Department of Elementary Education and Literacy, Ministry of Human Resource Development, Government of India. In one of its many directions in the litigation the Supreme Court directed the government to fully implement its scheme of providing cooked meals to all children in primary schools. This landmark direction converted the mid-day meal scheme into a legal entitlement, the violation of which can be taken up in a court of law. The direction and further follow-up by the Supreme Court have been a major instrument in universalising the scheme. Subsequently, it was decided to provide food to children with a specified calory calorie intake of 450 kcal at the primary and 700 kcal at the upper primary levels respectively. The protein intake was also fixed at 12 gm at the primary and 20 gm at the upper primary level. The main aim of the Mid-day Meal Scheme was to provide hot cooked Mid-day Meal to each and every child attending Government/Government-aided Schools, EGS and AIE centres and NCLP including Maqtabs and Madarsas. According to Govinda and Bandyopadhyay (2008), "…although the implementation of the SSA and the Mid-day Meal Scheme have had varied impacts at the grassroots level, it is claimed that, with the implementation of SSA and cooked Mid-day Meal Scheme, the number of out of school children has been reduced to less than 5 per cent of the total population in the 6-14 years old age group, i.e. from 44 million in 2001-2002 to 7 million in 2006." However, the implementation of the scheme suffers from a number of inadequacies and faces significant challenges in improving the coverage and quality of services (*see* Blue, 2005; Afridi, 2005; Khera, 2006).

Programmes like the Mid-day Meal scheme are also successful in other developing countries. A good example is Somalia, where the poorest enrolment rates among children in primary grades in the world was recorded (UNICEF 2015). Omar M. et al. (2019) and Wang & Fawzi (2020) have noted that school feeding schemes are very beneficial for the overall growth of children and adolescent girls particularly from low- and middle-income countries.

In the Indian context, the status of these schemes varies from state to state. In a recent article, while examining the impact of caste- and religion-based ideologies on nutritional policy, specifically the MDM programme in Karnataka, Joshi & Karpagam (2022) found that the inadequacy of providing nutritional food to all children is closely connected with the existing social issues like caste and religion-based discrimination, which has impacted the nutritional level among children severely. The findings of the study conducted by Pratichi Trust in Birbhum district of West Bengal (Rana et al., 2005) and that of Si & Sharma (2008) in Odisha suggest that the mid-day meal has made a positive intervention in universalisation of Primary Education by increasing enrolment and attendance in general and specifically with respect to girls and SC and ST students.

During the lockdown following the Covid 19 pandemic, several challenges and issues emerged due to the closure of Anganwadi centres and schools. The delivery of hot cooked meals to beneficiaries was interrupted. This was further accentuated by the lack of availability of food in the local market, labour shortages, transport interruptions, limited access to markets, supply chain disruptions etc. (Upadhyay MK et al., 2020).

It is in light of this that a study was undertaken, in order to assess the implementation of the policies, along with the best practices adopted by the individual states and the challenges faced by them. The study adopted a comparative method by conducting detailed fieldwork in the states of Haryana, Punjab and Uttar Pradesh. Both Haryana and Punjab adopted the mid-day meal scheme in the year 1995, whereas Uttar Pradesh adopted it voluntarily as early as 1953 (James, 2013). The status of implementation of the schemes in these three states respectively has been discussed in the following sections. This would include a broad spectrum of children from pre-primary to elementary level as well as adolescent girls along with pregnant and lactating women. Since the study involves three different schemes meant for different target groups, it makes sense to approach each of these schemes separately, even as at the ground level, these are very much interlinked.

The PM Poshan scheme replaced the national programme Mid-day Meal Scheme in September 2021. While previously, early childhood care and education (ECCE) or pre-primary education was covered under the 'Poshan Abhiyan' programme (launched in 2018 by the Government of India to reduce the level of malnutrition and related problems such as stunting, low birth weight, etc.), under the new regulation, it was brought under the PM Poshan scheme.

Systemic changes in this direction have also been proposed in the National Education Policy 2020 (MHRD, 2020). As per this, the pre-primary education in the formal education system has been restructured to ensure a strong foundation for children below six years. The existing scheme components have been re-organized under Saksham Anganwadi and Poshan 2.0 scheme, with an intent to addressing various gaps and shortcomings in the on-going nutrition programmes and in order to improve and accelerate the implementation of nutrition and child development outcomes. Saksham Anganwadi and Poshan 2.0 addresses the issue of nutrition among adolescent girls (14 to 18 years of age) as well as that of pregnant and lactating women, along with ECCE. In the above context, the present study has been conducted to understand the status of the implementation of these schemes which are dealing with child development holistically in the names of PM Poshan,

Table 1.2: *Nutrition and Food Norms under the PM Poshan Scheme*

S. No.	*Items*	*Primary*	*Upper Primary*
Nutrition norm per child per day			
1.	Calorie	450	700
2.	Protein	12 gms	20 gms
Food norms per child per day			
1.	Food grains	100 gms	150 gms
2.	Pulses	20 gms	30 gms
3.	Vegetables	50 gms	75 gms
4.	Oil & fat	5 gms	7.5 gms
5.	Salt & condiments	As per need	As per need

Source: PM Poshan Shakti Nirman, MoE (https://dsel.education.gov.in/pm-Poshan-scheme)

Saksham Anganwadi and Poshan 2.0 schemes. Towards studying these schemes in terms of both implementation status as well as the way forward, they have to be taken up one after the other. In light of this, it is worthwhile to focus first on the PM Poshan scheme.

As noted above, the PM Poshan scheme was undertaken by the Union government in place of the existing mid-day meal programme (Table 2) for providing one hot cooked meal in Government and Government-aided schools, in 2021. The main features of the scheme are:

- It covers primary (I-V) and upper primary (VI-VIII) school children who are entitled to 100 grams and 150 grams of foodgrains per working day respectively, to ensure a minimum of 700 calories.
- It also covers students of Balvatikas / Anganwadis/ Pre-school (children in the 3-5 years age group) accessing pre-primary education/ECCE.

Implementation Status of Schemes-- A National Picture

One of the methods employed in this study, as noted above, was the workshops or webinars that were organized with the states in order to find out the challenges that they faced in the course of the implementation of these schemes as well as the solutions that they have found to tackle these issues in terms of best practices. These workshops or webinars therefore provided the states with a platform to voice their concerns as well as share their initiatives with the rest of the country. The results that these interactions brought out will also be crucial in defining the way forward. This section therefore discusses these outcomes.

Challenges: Some states like Sikkim, J&K, Mizoram and Meghalaya faced challenges in implementing PM Poshan properly due to geographical barriers. The same reason makes infrastructural development like water supply, electricity and transportation rather difficult in these states.

Similarly, Goa has also cited limited transport as a challenge. The lack of proper storage spaces due to underdeveloped infrastructure was raised as a concern by both Mizoram and Uttarakhand. Social factors, more specifically

Table 1.3: *Challenges Faced in the Implementation of PM Poshan Scheme*

Challenges (PM Poshan)	*States*
Overall Implementation of the Scheme	Sikkim, J&K and Mizoram
Social Factor	Andhra Pradesh, Karnataka
Infrastructure	Meghalaya
Transportation	Sikkim, Mizoram, Meghalaya, Goa, J&K
Funding and	Karnataka, Meghalaya, Sikkim,
Human Resource	Andhra Pradesh, Uttarakhand
Storage	Mizoram, Uttarakhand
Salary	Meghalaya

Source: Workshop on an Evaluative Study of Saksham Anganwadi and POSHAN 2.0 Scheme in India 19-20 December 2022.

those pertaining to caste and religion, are faced by Andhra Pradesh and Karnataka. The deficiency in funding was the most common concern that was raised by several states.

Best Practices: Even as the scheme has recently been initiated, some of the states have been quite innovative in initiating and implementing the scheme. The cases of Andhra Pradesh and Meghalaya were notable in this regard.

Andhra Pradesh

- Standard Operating Procedure (SOP) manual developed, and all stakeholders including cooks have been trained.
- Mobile App and Dashboard for monitoring: In this practice, firstly, the user captures the food items served to children, using the existing mobile app and uploads the photograph. Secondly, the solution has to verify, as per the categorization given by the department, if the food item served is Good/ Bad then the AI solution categorizes and sends the result to the user and results are also displayed on the web UI for every school.
- Four tier Monitoring system of HMs, Educational Assistants in Village and Ward Secretariats, Self-help Groups and field officials.
- Involved village and ward volunteers in dry ration distribution.
- The state government provides MDM to 7,94,749 children of Classes IX and X. Rs. 122.53 Cr. budget has been released in 2022-23.
- The state is providing eggs to those who are non-vegetarian and bananas to those who are vegetarian for five days in a week per child with an additional budget.

Meghalaya

- Community Participation: In some schools, parents and the community contribute vegetables, fruits, firewood etc. to schools for cooking meals for the children.
- Uses of Tiffin box: In this practice students come in the morning, write their name on the tiffin box and put it on the rack. The cooking staff would

then duly serve the food in the same boxes. Other Government schools which have space limitations to seat the children together for meals have also been instructed to follow this system.

- Food diversity in Meghalaya schools: Schools are being given the flexibility to provide a diverse range of food. These vegetables and greens are grown in the school gardens or sourced from local farmers.

Empirical Evidences from the Field

The impact that poverty has on school education has already been discussed. The PM Poshan scheme aimed at improving the base and foundation of the extant mid-day meal scheme, by furthering its provisions and extent. The improved cost per child outlay, increased stress on the improvement of infrastructure and the provision of a kitchen garden within the school, are some of the key areas that were improved under the paradigm of the new policy.

Haryana

According to fourth joint review mission report on mid-day meal in Haryana (2013), Haryana implemented the mid-day meal scheme in 1995 "in the 44 educationally backward Community Development blocks of six districts of the State at primary level". This was implemented in the form of free foodgrains at a rate of three kilograms per child (National Programme of Mid-Day Meal in Schools (MDMS)), Annual work plan and budget 2019-20 Haryana). The scheme was extended across all middle schools during the year 2008-09 and was upgraded in order to provide cooked meal as per the guideline of the Government of India (Ibid.).

Implementation and reception: At the ground level, however, we could see that the scheme has reached across the schools at urban and rural spaces. We found that freshly cooked meal is being prepared and systematically served to children and that children are consuming it. While the nutritional components of the food served was being decided at the state level, the menu itself was decided by the respective schools. Our discussions in the classrooms also revealed a general impression that children liked the meal served. In a few rare cases, the parents asked children to carry their lunch from home to avoid the crowd at the school.

Cooking staff and helpers: While there were adequate staff for cooking in the schools in Haryana, teachers did raise the issue that adding the burden of 'managing' the mid-day meal on teachers is not ideal. They were of the opinion that it should be a separate posting. As far as the cooking staff and helpers were concerned, their issue was that their salary was not given on time. As far as the amount of salary was concerned, with Rs. 7000 per month, Haryana was paying their cooks and helpers well, at least in comparison to that of Uttar Pradesh and Punjab.

Infrastructure: The schools were also found to be rather spacious with enough space for children to play and adequate number of classrooms. The kitchen sheds were properly built with ventilation and were separate from the classrooms. However, most of these did not have electric lights or exhaust fans. For that matter, the lack of unhindered electricity was obvious for a school in Haryana, where students and teachers had to wait till 12 pm to be able to use the smart classrooms and other amenities like fans.

The children were also provided with a proper hall for having the meal. However, in most cases, children had to sit on carpets, and sometimes even on bare floor. The limitations of these halls also meant that children had to be seated in batches, which subsequently led to some shortages in the quantity of the food as well. The location of the school, especially with regard to its proximity to open drainages was another concern in terms of infrastructure in Haryana. Needless to say, this raises a lot of threats for students, teachers and the other staff. In short, there is still room for improvement as far as infrastructure is concerned.

Quality and Quantity of Food: The quality of the food served was really good. The food was cooked freshly and served hot. It was tasty as well and the students were allowed to have their fill, except in certain cases as mentioned above, where sometimes it falls short for the elder kids who eat in the second batch. Some of the students also noted that they do not eat before leaving for school in the morning. Even those who ate, barely had tea and biscuits in most cases. This factor has to be taken into consideration with regards to the quantity of food provided for children at school. It has to be ensured that children are provided with adequate food, especially since for a lot of them, the lunch at school is the first meal of the day. Another important fact to read alongside this fact is the contents of the meals provided. On the day of the visit, the meal provided was sweetened rice porridge (kheer). This is basically a dessert and not a proper healthy meal. This becomes more crucial when we read this alongside the fact that many kids do not even have proper breakfasts. The ideal case scenario then, would be to firstly ensure that the menu for each day consists of the nutrients essential for children and that it is a balanced diet. Secondly, schools could also provide light snacks or even kheer earlier in the day. One of the cooking staff at the school, who doubled as an SMC member (her children also studied in the same school) pointed towards this issue, saying that the school must provide some kind of snacks for the children a little earlier in the day.

Funding and grants: While the fund allocations for the scheme are happening at the state and district levels, it has been noted that there are often delays in its distribution. The schools in Haryana noted that many a time the teachers have to spend out of their own pockets to get vegetables and products like oil and ghee required for the meals. This is because only the basic foodgrains are provided to the schools for free and the rest of the products have to be managed from the fund provided. But the concern is that the fund does not often come through in time. There were instances where the grant was delayed for four months. On the other hand, while the fund allocation per child has been increased under the purview of the PM Poshan scheme, teachers noted that it needs further revision, and should be increased to Rs. 8 (for Primary school children) and Rs. 10 (for Middle school children).

Uttar Pradesh

According to James (2013), the Mid-day Meal scheme was initiated in Uttar Pradesh in 1953. She adds that this was "...a scheme on voluntary basis to give boiled gram, ground-nut, puffed rice and seasonal fruits." The scheme was further implemented across the state in 1995 like most of the rest of the country. In recent times, the government of Uttar Pradesh has made further changes in order to maximize the reach as well as benefits of the scheme. One of the major steps towards this direction was increasing the honorarium of the cooks by Rs. 500 per month. The state government also provided aprons, gloves and head covers to all the cooks. Fresh and seasonal fruits are also being distributed to provide additional nutrition to children. The state also developed a short film titled "Poshana" to train the cooks and helpers. A committee called *Maa Samuh* has also been created in each school, consisting of six mothers that regularly visit the schools and supervise the food that is being cooked and served (Mid-day Meal Authority, Uttar Pradesh).

Implementation: While looking at the ground reality of the implementation and reach of the scheme, we have understood that the food is being distributed systematically. However, just as in Haryana, it has been the opinion of the teachers that the mid-day meal duty is burdensome for teachers. It takes a lot of time and management, and this hinders their teaching time and concentration. That there are schools already facing staff shortages adds to this concern. However, the food that is being distributed is being consumed by children except for a few rare cases where the parents do not want their children to sit on the floor and eat amongst a crowd.

Infrastructure: From the field visits, it appeared that the minimum requirements were all met in terms of infrastructure, even though one of the schools was very close to a railway level-crossing. There were separate kitchen sheds and storerooms in the schools. However, on a closer inspection, it became evident that there was a lot of room for improvement. The storerooms needed better maintenance. The kitchen shed was rather small and congested. While the kitchen had a small window, it was not enough to provide the room with proper ventilation, and there were no exhaust fans either. The storeroom was found to be in a very dusty and unhygienic condition. And neither room had electric connectivity. As for the facility to seat the children for distributing the meal, they had to sit in the corridors on rugs or carpets.

Cooks and helpers: We found that the state was rightful in claiming that the salary for the cooks and helpers has been increased by Rs. 500/- However, it has to be noted that this takes their total salary to just Rs. 2000/- per month. Many states are already paying well above and beyond the said amount. Naturally therefore the cooks and helpers seemed rather unsatisfied with the condition.

Funding and grants: With regard to grants and funding, the cooks said that their salaries – while meagre – were still delayed. One of the staff told us that he/she has not received salary for nearly three months. As far as the fund for procuring food materials is concerned, while the head teachers said that it is adequate, they also noted that an increase in the funding, even if slight, would help the schools provide additional nutrition to the students in the form of fruits, milk etc.

Punjab

Punjab adopted the mid-day meal scheme in 1995, following the adoption of the same at the national level. However, according to the National Programme of Mid-Day Meal in schools (MDMS) Punjab (2020-21), the state could not distribute cooked meal scheme from the start owing to certain reasons that included the "paucity of funds involved in the conversion of foodgrains to cooked meal". This started changing in the year 2002-03, when the cooked meal was provided to the children of primary classes in one block of every district of the state. The scheme was spread across all the schools from September 2004.

Implementation: The food distribution in Punjab was rather effective in terms of children's consumption and reach. Our discussion with the students also leads us to believe that the children were quite happy with the food. The SMC members were also of the opinion that the mid-day meal was really helpful in ensuring better enrolment and attendance at the school. However, just as the other two states taken up here, in Punjab also teachers were of the opinion that the scheme ends up becoming burdensome for the teachers and that it detracts them from their primary task, which is teaching. Managing food materials, their quantity and distribution every day is, according to them, quite a chore. "We have to do this at our respective homes as well, and now we have to do it at school too," one of the female teachers who was in charge of the scheme in her school told us.

Infrastructure: While the infrastructure of the schools in Punjab was quite good, it has been noticed that there were some issues. One of the schools had a pond adjacent to it that caused structural issues to the school's walls, in addition to the threat to children's safety. The pond also meant that there were a large number of flies and mosquitoes which posed further health hazards. In another instance, the school hardly had any space and had to run two grades together in one classroom. One of the classrooms on the upper floor had to be converted into a kitchen, which further caused threat of hazards due to fire, smoke etc. The students also had to sit in the classrooms or the open yards in order to eat their food. There were no exclusive halls for the said purpose.

Cooks and helpers: The cooks in Punjab are paid slightly better as compared to their counterparts in Uttar Pradesh. However, it is hardly on par with the labour that they do or the kind of salary that the same amount of work would fetch them in other institutions. They raised their concerns in this regard and also pointed out that sometimes it feels like charity considering the meagre salary. They were happy about the work that they were doing, but felt that a better pay would be of great help to them.

Quality and Quantity: There were no concerns regarding the quantity of the food. All the children claimed that they ate to their fill. They also enjoyed the food that was distributed at the school. What was interesting to note though is that both the Primary schools we visited in Punjab also had LKG and UKG classes. However, these kids were sent home by 12 pm and they were not provided with any meal.

Funding and grants: The teachers in Punjab noted that with the initiation of the PM Poshan scheme, the cost per child has been increased and that this has been really helpful in covering the costs of the meals and distributing them properly. The concerns they had was more regarding the appointment of teachers as in-charges for the scheme.

Saksham Anganwadi and Poshan 2.0: An Overview of Literature

Present Nutritional Status of Children and Women

One of the composite indicators for child malnutrition in children under five years who are underweight (weight-for-age). In 2019, nearly 0.08 million of children under the age of five years died in India. Hunger, starvation and malnutrition are prevalent at varying levels among young children, particularly in poor families. As per the National Family Health Survey (NFHS-5) (2019-21), 32.1 per cent of children below five years are underweight, 35.5 per cent are stunted and 19.3 per cent are wasted in the country. However, there has been some improvement in the nutritional status of young children. As per the NFHS-4 data, the national average of children under five years who are underweight has reduced from 35.7 per cent as reported in NFHS-4, 2015-16 to 32.1 per cent in NFHS-5, 2019-21. Malnutrition is common in India as a whole, but the situation is especially alarming in the states of Bihar, Orissa, Madhya Pradesh, Rajasthan and Uttar Pradesh.

When it comes to women's health, the national data (NFHS-5) reveals that the percentage of women with low body mass index (BMI) is recorded 18.7 per cent in 2019-21 which has declined around four per cent since NFHS-4 (2015-16). Cases of anaemia among women are still quite high. Around 57.2 per cent of non-pregnant and 52.2 per cent of pregnant women aged 15-49 years are found anaemic respectively. Data reveals that adolescent girls who are anaemic within the age group of 15-19 are at high risk as their percentage has increased by almost five per cent since 2015-16. In addition, it should also be noted that around 12 per cent of women across the country are not using institutional services for birth. All the beneficiaries such as children, adolescent girls and women are covered under both schemes for the improvement of their nutritional status.

Initiatives of Government

The Government of India restructured the Integrated Child Development Services (ICDS) and Poshan (Prime Minister's Overarching Scheme for Holistic Nourishment) Abhiyaan into Saksham Anganwadi and POSHAN 2.0 in the financial year 2021-22. The restructured scheme seeks intended to address the challenging situation of malnutrition among children up to the age of six years, adolescent girls (14-18 years) and pregnant and lactating women. The achievement of the Sustainable Development Goals lies at the fore-front of this programme design. It shall contribute to the SDGs, specifically, SDG 2 on Zero Hunger and SDG 4 on Quality Education. The Mission will focus on the fundamental importance of nutrition and early childhood care and education for the well-being, growth and development of children into healthy and productive adults.

The current scheme consists of different sub-schemes including ICDS, Poshan Abhiyaan, Scheme for Adolescent Girls (SAG) and National Creche Scheme with following objectives:

- To prepare a comprehensive strategy to address the challenge of malnutrition, the Supplementary Nutrition Programme under Anganwadi Services.
- Scheme for Adolescent Girls and Poshan Abhiyaan been aligned under Poshan 2.0 as an Integrated Nutrition Support Programme.

Objectives of Poshan 2.0 are as follows:

- To contribute to the human capital development of the country.
- Address challenges of malnutrition.
- Promote nutrition awareness and good eating habits for sustainable health and wellbeing.
- Address nutrition related deficiencies through key strategies.
- AYUSH systems shall be integrated under Poshan 2.0 for wellness and nourishment.

Components:

- Nutrition Support for Poshan through the Supplementary Nutrition Programme (SNP) for children of the age group of 06 months to 6 years, pregnant women and lactating mothers (PWLM).
- For Adolescent Girls in the age group of 14 to 18 years in Aspirational Districts and North Eastern Region (NER).
- Early Childhood Care and Education (3-6 years) and early stimulation (0-3 years).
- Modern and upgraded Anganwadis under the purview of Saksham Anganwadi and Poshan Abhiyaan.

The scheme is open to all eligible beneficiaries and the only pre-condition is that the beneficiary has to be registered at the nearest Anganwadi centre with Aadhaar identification. The beneficiaries of the scheme will be adolescent girls in the age group of 14-18 years who will be identified by the states concerned.

Implementation Status

In the context of Saksham Anganwadis one of the major challenges was the flood in Assam. There was a lack of nutritional supplements and distribution in the states of Assam, Himachal Pradesh and Jammu and Kashmir. There was also a lack of

Table 1.4: *Challenges Faced in the Implementation of Saksham Anganwadi and Poshan 2.0 Schemes*

Challenges	*States*
Flood	Assam
Nutrition supplements	Assam and Himachal Pradesh, J&K
Medical facility	Assam and Andhra Pradesh
Training	Assam, Meghalaya
Lack of coordination	Daman & Diu and Dadra & Nagar Haveli
Internet Facility	Jammu and Kashmir
Social Factor	Andhra Pradesh
Implementation of the Scheme	Karnataka, Nagaland
Language Barrier	Mizoram

Source: State Presentations at the Workshop on an Evaluative Study of Saksham Anganwadi and POSHAN 2.0 Scheme in India, NIEPA, New Delhi 19-20 December 2022

training regarding the schemes of Saksham Anganwadis and Poshan 2.0 in Assam and Meghalaya. Medical facilities like weighing machines, first aid boxes etc. were not provided by the government due to limited funds. Lack of coordination was raised as a unique issue between Daman & Diu and Dadra & Nagar Haveli.

The language barrier was raised as a major concern by the state of Mizoram in implementing Poshan 2.0. In Assam and Meghalaya, there was a lack of training of Saksham Anganwadis and Poshan 2.0 staff regarding the schemes, whereas in some states like Karnataka and Nagaland, the overall implementation of the schemes was lagging.

The data indicate that women need more attention under Poshan 2.0 scheme, and more priority has to be given for the age group of 15-49 which is the reproductive age group for women and also includes the adolescent girls. Because of the low nutrition level of majority of women, there is a chance of children also becoming underweight, suffering malnutrition and anemia (NFHS 5, 2022, Fig 1.1).

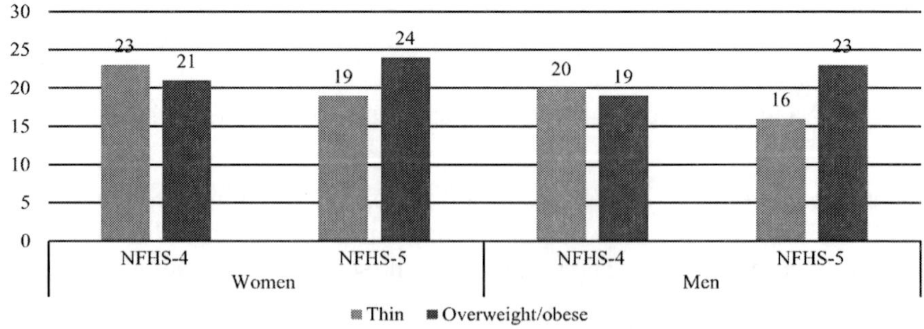

Figure 1.1: *Change in Percentage of Men and Women Affected by Malnutrition During NFHS-4 and NFHS-5*

Source: IIPS (2017): "National Family Health Survey-4, 2015-16" and IIPS (2021): "National Family Health Survey-5, 2019-21."

The data on nutritional statistics from NFHS-4 to NFHS-5 indicate that the situation has improved in the case of men as well as women. However, there is a gender gap in both survey periods. More women are found overweight as compared to men.

Empirical Evidences from the Field

Even though the UN's Sustainable Development Goal number 2 was to achieve food security and thereby end hunger and improve nutrition by 2030, according to the State of Food Security and Nutrition in the World 2022 (SOFI) the world is moving further away from its goal of ending hunger, food insecurity and malnutrition in all its forms by 2030 (Upadhyay, 2022). It is in this context that the Indian government launched the Poshan Abhiyan in 2018 towards eradicating hunger and malnutrition.

Following the global crisis posed by the Covid pandemic that derailed this scheme, in 2021, the Union Government merged several schemes "... like the Supplementary Nutrition Programme under Anganwadi Services, Scheme for Adolescent Girls and POSHAN Abhiyaan and re-aligned them as 'Saksham Anganwadi and POSHAN 2.0' for maximising nutritional outcomes (Upadhyay, 2022)."

Haryana

Implementation and reception: It has been observed in Haryana that the beneficiaries are availing the amenities and that the reception is good both from children as well as pregnant and lactating women. The staff in Anganwadis maintained a prompt list of infant children and it was also seen that they were regularly attending the Anganwadi. It was observed that the majority of pregnant women from the locality were reportedly aware and conscious regarding their health. They were also conscious of the amenities available through the Anganwadis. Vaccinations and medication were also being done in a time-to-time manner and updated thoroughly.

Staff and helpers: The Anganwadi supervisors and staff were quite satisfied with their roles and remunerations. They were aware of the limitations raised by the circumstances and the importance of the roles they were playing. They were also adept at the duties and responsibilities. Interestingly however, some of these staff were not aware of the latest developments at the policy level and had not even heard of the Saksham Anganwadi programme. This indicates the lack of updation and capacity building of these staff. This is something for the district and state level officers to address and act upon. While some of these staff were appointed on a contract basis, many of them have been working in the same position for 15 years and more.

Infrastructure: The infrastructure of the Anganwadis in Haryana was rather well equipped and placed within the school compounds as per the Saksham Anganwadi programme instructions. This enabled a complementary relationship between these two institutions in most cases. The Anganwadis also had separate spaces which were large enough for kids to play. The rooms were also large enough and, in many cases, were equipped with toys, charts and TLMs as well as weighing machines and height checking scales, to assess the growth of the children.

Quality and quantity: The Anganwadis in Haryana also served hot cooked meals to the children. These were nutritious and tasty. The quantity provided was also adequate and quite tasty as observed during data collection from sample schools.

Funding and grants: Regarding funds, there is a concern that it is not distributed smoothly and efficiently. Many a time the staff have to spend out of their own pockets and wait till the fund is passed months later. During our visit, it was found that no fund has been credited since the month of September 2022. However, in such trying scenarios, it was heartening that the Anganwadis sometimes get help from community organizations and even the adjoining school.

Uttar Pradesh

Implementation and reception: The visit to Uttar Pradesh raised a lot of concerns regarding the implementation of the schemes. It was observed that many parents and children have only registered at the Anganwadis to obtain the free rations provided there and that they do not cooperate with the institution otherwise. Many children are sent to private institutions for their ECCE development. However, it must also be noted that even as many children did not turn up, the Anganwadis were rather over-crowded.

Staff and helpers: With overcrowded Anganwadis found in some sample areas, it was obvious that the staff were over worked and weighed down by their various responsibilities. In addition, they were also sometimes tasked with additional duties like house visits during Covid times etc. In comparison to this, their salary was too less and with the meagre salaries, they sometimes had to spend their own money to manage the day-to-day affairs of the Anganwadis.

Infrastructure: The Anganwadis in Uttar Pradesh also had a lot of space constraints. The buildings were old and in various stages of disrepair. This also caused a lot of space limitations. The TLMs provided were also in rather poor condition. There were no proper kitchens or bathrooms and no support from schools either.

Quality and quantity: These Anganwadis did not have any cooking facilities. Nor did they provide freshly cooked meal to the beneficiaries. Only dry rations were provided, and this also often meant that children sat through the three hours on empty stomachs.

Funding and grants: Since there was no cooking facility, the only funding situation was that of the salary of the staff. However, even this has been pending far way too long. The dry ration, however, is supplied directly by the government agencies.

Punjab

Implementation and reception: In Punjab, the situation of the Anganwadi depended on where it was located. In areas where the migrant population was higher, there seemed to be a clear gap in communication between the staff and the beneficiaries. However, by and large, children were attending the Anganwadis and availing the benefits of the institution. However, many women usually do not associate with the Anganwadis with regards to their pregnancy, rather it was their mothers-in-law who visited the institution and took home the dry ration that is distributed. In fact, they were quite opposed towards their daughters-in-law visiting the Anganwadis. The general reception of the benefits and building of awareness, is therefore lacking and much of the population are not interested in the facilities either.

Staff and helpers: The Anganwadi staff in Punjab were of the opinion that things are alright, at least in terms of their remunerations. However, these did not get credited on time. They were aware of their roles and responsibilities and maintained records and registers well on their part, even though the community cooperation was much less.

Infrastructure: The case of infrastructure is also quite varied as in some locations they were well equipped with newly constructed buildings with attached kitchens and bathrooms whereas in some other situations, they were operating within Gurudwaras. This disparity has to be sorted and addressed as well.

Quality and quantity: Just as in Uttar Pradesh, Punjab also does not have the provision to give cooked meal to the beneficiaries. Rather dry ration is distributed. However, even this is supplied by the government agencies in bulk and not on time or as per requirements. We could observe that they had not received the supplies for a few months.

Funding and grants: Similar to UP, there are no fund provisions other than that of the salary, which again, is not often done promptly.

Comparative Analysis

When we juxtapose the empirical information gathered from the three states – Haryana, Uttar Pradesh and Punjab – we can find that there is a lot of variation in the implementation and running of the schemes. It can however be underlined that there are both concerns as well as achievements in the implementation of the schemes in all the sample areas across the three states. When it comes to the PM Poshan scheme, we find that the lack of funding is a major issue for all three states. The available funds are also not released in time, forcing the teachers and concerned staff to pay from their own pockets. This brings us to the next issue which is the added burden on teachers due to the mid-day meal duty that they have been assigned. The teachers of all the sample areas were unanimous in pointing out that there should be separate staff for managing the schemes on day-to-day basis. As far as the infrastructure is concerned, the sample area in Haryana is rather well equipped (even though there were concerns regarding hygiene and sanitation) as compared to that in Punjab (where space limitations seemed prevalent) and Uttar Pradesh, where existing facilities were not being maintained properly. Haryana also deserves plaudits for the higher honorarium that they provide their cooking staff as compared to the meagre ones in Uttar Pradesh and Punjab. It has to be noted, however, that the students were happy with the meals they were provided, and the parents also agreed that it motivates the children to attend school regularly and the parents to ensure that this happened. It was also found that the food that was provided was fresh, nutritious and tasty.

Lack of funds and their timely distribution was found to be an issue in the implementation of Saksham Anganwadi and Poshan 2.0 schemes as well, in all three states. In terms of infrastructure, Haryana once again has well equipped Anganwadis, as opposed to those in Uttar Pradesh which did not have the facility to cook and were therefore forced to distribute dry rations to the beneficiaries. In the area under study in Punjab, some Anganwadis were located within the compounds of Gurudwaras and this meant that there were space constraints. The Anganwadi workers who were interviewed in Haryana were quite updated and maintained the details of the beneficiaries promptly. Whereas those in Punjab and Uttar Pradesh were burdened with overcrowding and sometimes even the reticence on the part of mothers to associate with the institution. Within these limitations, however, the workers seemed to be trying their best to impart their duties. Even with low wages, they were aware of the important roles that they were playing.

Conclusion

From the analysis above, it is clear that the said schemes – PM Poshan, Saksham Anganwadi and Poshan 2.0 are up and running in all the states in the country. Further, it has also been established that these schemes have been creating a significant impact on the lives of their beneficiaries that include primary school students, adolescent girls, pregnant and lactating women, infants etc. as per respective schemes. However, it is also true that both the schemes have much more ground to cover, in order to reach its benefactors universally and address the targets that they set out to counter.

In terms of implementation and the amenities that have been made available at the ground level, it can be seen that several schools and many states have initiated exemplary best practices that show the way forward for other states and schools. The strict monitoring system for PM Poshan in Andhra Pradesh as well as the rotation of teachers in charge every week are good examples. On the other hand, the name tagged tiffin boxes used in schools in Meghalaya, where there is a lack of space for distributing the meal, is also a praiseworthy innovation. Andhra Pradesh has also extended the scheme in order to bring the students of Classes IX and X under the purview of the scheme. Similarly, in the case of Anganwadis, it can be seen that the Anganwadis in Haryana have all been integrated within the school compounds. These work as organically connected units with the Anganwadis receiving help and support from the schools as well. While the staff here are also more aware of their responsibilities and duties, the beneficiaries are more cooperative, and the community is also supportive.

There is however room for improvement as mentioned above. States have been facing several challenges. While some of these are unique, some challenges are common across several states. One of the biggest concerns raised by the staff – both in Anganwadis and schools – was that of the meagre remuneration that they receive. A few states have increased their own respective dividend and thus increased the salaries of the cooking staff. But most of the states have not been able to do that and the staff are therefore severely underpaid. Add to this the fact that even these salaries are also not distributed on time, and it becomes clear that this is probably the most crucial concern that has to be addressed. Similarly, the grants and funds from the governments are also not distributed on time and this adds further pressure on the respective staffs in terms of effectively carrying out their responsibilities.

Generating more awareness and engendering a more welcome attitude on the part of the communities would also be an important step in the right direction, since it has been noted that despite the earnest efforts of the staff, quite often women and families are not very supportive of the institutions and programmes.

Another important proposition that has come out of this study is that in states that have difficult terrains and higher altitudes, there has to be higher outlay for the transportation of goods and other materials. In states like Meghalaya, Mizoram, Nagaland etc., it has been reported that the difficult terrains cause the transportation charges to be double or triple of normal transport charges. Addressing this, therefore, is necessary in order to broaden the reach of these schemes.

To sum up, there is no denying the positive impact that these schemes are having an increasing enrolment, retention and bringing down the dropout rates in school on the one hand and improving the health and nutrition of pregnant and lactating women, adolescent girls and infants on the other. It should, however, be added that there is still a long way to go towards these schemes reaching and fulfilling their goals and committed and systematic efforts have to be made in order to achieve them. The study has not only indicated the importance of all these schemes targeting children even before their birth, but it also found a close association between their nutrition, school preparedness and ensuring strong foundation and holistic development at their preparative stage of life with its far-reaching impact on their educational attainment in the context of 21st Century.

Acknowledgement: Authors acknowledge the contributions made by other team members: Dr Vaishali, Raunak Katiyar, Ganesh Khetwal, Rohit Kumar and Muhammed Sahal, in conducting and completing the study.

References

Afridi, F. "*Child Welfare Programs and Child Nutrition: Evidence from a Mandated School Meal Program*". Job Market Paper, 2005, University of Michigan, Ann Arbor.

Alderman, H., Behrman, J. R., Lavy, V. & Menon, R. "Child Nutrition, Child Health, and School Enrollment: A Longitudinal Analysis. Policy Research Working Paper no. 1700", January, Policy Research Department, Poverty and Human Resources Division, 1997, The World Bank Washington, D.C.

Alderman, H., Behrman, J. R., Victor, L. & Menon, R. "Child Health and School Enrollment: A Longitudinal Analysis". *The Journal of Human Resources*, Vol. 36 No. 1, 2001, pp. 185-205. (http://www.sitemaker.umich.edu/fafridi/files/afridi_job_market_paper.pdf)

Avula, R., Frongillo, E.A., Arabi, M., Sharma, S., & Schultink, W. (2011). "Enhancements to nutrition program in Indian integrated child development services increased growth and energy intake of children." *The Journal of Nutrition*, 141(4), 680-684.

Behrman, Jere R., and Anil B. Deolalikar. "Will developing country nutrition improve with income? A case study for rural South India." *Journal of Political Economy* 95.3 (1987): 492-507.

Best Practices, Mid-day Meal Authority Uttar Pradesh, Accessed at: https://www.upmdm.org/bestpractices.html

Blue, J. "The Government Primary School Mid-day Meals Scheme: An Assessment of Program Implementation and Impact in Udaipur District". 2005, Seva Mandir, Udaipur.

Chudasama, R.K., Kadri, A.M., Verma, P.B., Patel, U.V., Joshi, N., Zalavadiya, D., & Bhola, C. (2014). "Evaluation of integrated child development services program in Gujarat, India." *Indian Pediatrics*, 51, 707-711.

Deolalikar, A.B. (2005). "Poverty and child malnutrition in Bangladesh." *Journal of Developing Societies*, 21(1-2), 55-90.

Desai, G., Pandit, N., & Sharma, D. (2012). "Changing role of Anganwadi workers, A study conducted in Vadodara district." *Healthline*, 3(1), 41-44.

GoI "Government of India, Ministry of Human Resource Development, Department of School Education & Literacy Department of Higher Education", Annual Report 2017-18, 2018, pp. 47-58 https://www.education.gov.in/sites/upload_files/mhrd/files/document-reports/MHRD%20AR-2017-18%20English.pdf

GoI "Government of India, Ministry of Human Resource Development, Department of School Education & Literacy Department of Higher Education", Annual Report 2018-19, 2020, pp. 57-66 https://www.education.gov.in/sites/upload_files/mhrd/files/document-reports/annual_rpt_eng_1819.pdf

Govinda, R., & Bandyopadhyay, M. (2008). Access to Elementary Education in India. Country Analytical Review.

Gragnolati, M., Shekar, M., Das Gupta, M., Bredenkamp, C., & Lee, Y.K. (2005). "India's undernourished children: a call for reform and action."

Gupta, A., Gupta, S., & Nongkynrih, B. (2013). "Integrated child development services (ICDS) scheme: a journey of 37 years." *Indian Journal of Community Health*, 25(1), 77-81.

IIPS (2021): "National Family Health Survey-5 2019-21."

Iips, I. (2017). National family health survey (NFHS-4), 2015–16. International Institute for Population Sciences (IIPS), Mumbai, India, 791-846.

Jain, J. and Shah, M. "Antyodaya Anna Yojana and Mid-day Meals". *Economic and Political Weekly*, 26 November, Vol. 40 No. 48, 2005. pp. 5076-5088.

Jain, M. (2015). India's struggle against malnutrition—is the ICDS program the answer?. World Development, 67, 72-89.

James, G. (2013). Fighting "classroom hunger" — Achievements of "Mid-Day Meal Scheme". *Yojana.*

Joshi, S. & Karpagam, S. "Mid-day Meals in Karnataka: Scientific Evidence in the Face of Social Conservation," *Economic & Political Weekly.* Vol. LVII No. 23, 2022.

Kandpal, E. (2011). "Beyond average treatment effects: distribution of child nutrition outcomes and program placement in India's ICDS." World Development, 39(8), 1410-1421.

Khera, R. "Mid-Day Meals in Primary Schools: Achievements and Challenges," *Economic and Political Weekly*, 18 November, Vol. 41 No. 46 pp. 4742-4750, 2006.

Lokshin, M., Das Gupta, M., Gragnolati, M., & Ivaschenko, O. (2005). "Improving child nutrition? The integrated child development services in India." *Development and Change*, 36(4), 613-640.

Manhas, S., & Dogra, A. (2012). "Awareness among Anganwadi workers and the prospect of child health and nutrition: A study in Integrated Child Development Services (ICDS) Jammu, Jammu and Kashmir, India." *The Anthropologist*, 14(2), 171-175.

Meenakshi, J.V. (2015). "Utilization of ICDS services and their impact on child health outcomes Evidence from three East Indian states," (No. id: 7646).

Mid-day Meal Authority Uttar Pradesh, "*Pradhānamantrī Poṣhaṇ Shakti Nirmāṇ (Madhyāhna Bhojana) Yojanā — Ek Parichay*" Accessed at: https://www.upmdm.org/

Mittal, N., & Meenakshi, J.V. (2015). "Utilization of ICDS services and their impact on child health outcomes-evidence from three East Indian states" (No. 247).

Mohanan, Monika, Aloysius H. Sequeira, and M.S. Kumar. "Employee engagement and motivation: A case study." *KHOJ-Journal of Indian Management Research and Practices* (2012).

National Program of Mid-day Meal in schools (MDMS), Annual work plan and budget 2019-20, Haryana Accessed at ; https://pmposhan.education.gov.in/Files/PAB/PAB-2019-20/States/Haryana/1_Haryana_final%20writeup%20of%20PAB%202019-2020.pdf

National Program of Mid-day Meal in schools (MDMS), Annual work plan and budget 2020-21, Punjab Accessed at ; https://pmposhan.education.gov.in/Files/PAB/PAB-2020-21/States/Punjab/1_Write%20up%202020-21%20(Final).pdf

Omar M.I., Muturi, W. & Samantar, S.M. "Influence of School Feeding Programme on Performance of Public Primary Schools in Bossaso District Bari Region," Puntland Somalia. *International Journal of Advanced Research,* Vol. 7 No. 4, 2019, pp. 1029-1051.

PIB, 2021 Press Information Bureau, Government of India, Ministry of Women and Child Development, "AIMS and Objectives of ICDS Scheme" (2021) Accessed at: https://pib.gov.in/Pressreleaseshare.aspx?PRID=1784152

Policy, N.E. (2020). Ministry of Human Resource Development, Government of India. English version.

Ramachandran, D., Canny, J., Das, P.D., & Cutrell, E. (2010, April). Mobile-izing health workers in rural India. In Proceedings of the SIGCHI conference on human factors in computing systems (pp. 1889-1898).

Rana, Kumar, et al. "Public-private interface in primary education: A case study in West Bengal." Economic and Political Weekly (2005): 1550-1555.

Report of 4th Joint Review Mission on Mid-day Meal Scheme Haryana, (17th March – 22nd March 2013), Ministry of Human Resource Development Department of School Education & Literacy, Government of India. Accessed at: https://pmposhan.education.gov.in/Files/Review/Reports/2013/Draft_Report_Review_Haryana.pdf

Rosso, J.M. D. "School Feeding Programs: Improving Effectiveness and Increasing the Benefit to Education. A Guide for Development and Human Development Program Managers". August, Partnership for Child Network, World Bank: Washington, DC, 1999.

Sandhyarani, M.C., & Rao, C.U. (2013). "Role and responsibilities of Anganwadi workers, with special reference to Mysore district." *Int J Sci Environ Technol*, *2*(6), 1277-96.

Saxena, N.C. (2012). Hunger and Malnutrition in India. *IDS Bulletin*, 43, 8-14.

Sharma, R., Webster, P., & Bhattacharyya, S. (2014). Factors affecting the performance of community health workers in India: a multi-stakeholder perspective. Global Health Action, 7(1), 25352.

Si, A. & Sharma, N. "An Empirical Study of the Mid-day Meal Programme in Khurda", Orissa, *Economic & Political Weekly*, 2008.

Singh, A.K., Nadda, A., Rochwani, R., Singh, P., Khan, Z.A., & Goel, R.K. (2017). "Study of knowledge and skills of Anganwadi workers regarding breastfeeding and infant and young child feeding practices." *Int J Med Sci Public Health*, 6, 1-6.

Sood, N. "Malnourishment among children in India: Linkages with cognitive development and school participation". *Consortium for Research on Educational Access, Transitions and Equity*, 2010.

Strauss, John, and Duncan Thomas. "Health, nutrition, and economic development." *Journal of economic literature* 36.2 (1998): 766-817.

Thakur, J.S., Prinja, S., & Bhatia, S.S. (2011). "Persisting malnutrition in Chandigarh: Decadal underweight trends and impact of ICDS program." *Indian Pediatrics*, 48, 315-318.

Thakur, K., Chauhan, H.S., Gupta, N.L., Thakur, P., & Malla, D. (2015). A study to assess the knowledge & practices of Anganwadi workers & availability of infrastructure in ICDS program, at District Mandi of Himachal Pradesh.

Tripathy, M., Kamath, S.P., Baliga, B.S., & Jain, A. (2014). "Perceived responsibilities and operational difficulties of Anganwadi workers at a coastal south Indian city." *Medical Journal of Dr DY Patil University*, 7(4), 468-472.

UNESCO. "What you need to know about early childhood care and education." Accessed at https://www.unesco.org/en/early-childhood-education/need-know

UNICEF, D. (2015). Annual results report (Education) 2015. New York: UNICEF.

UNICEF. (2019). The State of the World's Children 2019. Growing well in a changing world: children, food and nutrition. New York: United Nations Children's Fund (UNICEF).

Unicef. (2022). The State of Food Security and Nutrition in the World (SOFI) Report-2022.

UNICEF. "Somalia Annual Report 2015". Access at https://www.unicef.org/somalia/media/206/file/Somalia-annual-report-2015-eng.pdf

Upadhyay, M.K., Patra, S, Khan, A.M. "Ensuring availability of food for child nutrition amidst the COVID-19 pandemic: Challenges and Way forward." *Indian J Comm Health*. 2020; 32 (2-Special Issue): 251-254

Upadhyay, Aishwarya. "POSHAN 2.0: How Can India attain Zero Malnutrition Target?" *NDTV*, September 6, 2022. Accessed at https://swachhindia.ndtv.com/Poshan-2-0-how-can-india-attain-zero-malnutrition-target-70581/

Wang, D., Fawzi, W.W. "Impacts of school feeding on educational and health outcomes of school-age children and adolescents in low- and middle-income countries: protocol for a systematic review and meta-analysis." *Syst Rev* 9, 55 2020. https://doi.org/10.1186/s13643-020-01317-6

2

Exploring Access and Equity Concerns of Higher Education in India

Sangeeta Angom

Introduction

One of the recent changes in the education scenario of our country is the exponential growth of institutions. Despite unprecedented growth, the expansion of higher education has been extremely uneven and resulted in the neglect of quality, research and managements aspects. The rapid expansion of higher education system has brought several pertinent issues currently. Amongst other factors such as globalisation and internationalisation; one of the dimensions for such changes has been accomplished primarily through the opening and upgrading of private institutions or privatisation of higher education. Privatisation as one of the most burning topics currently is being debated in education sector worldwide. It is fast becoming a widespread trend. In the expansion of higher education, private sector has been playing an important role. Though privatisation has positive impacts on higher education in many aspects, however, concerns are also raised that privatisation harms educational equity and quality due to overemphasis on higher education as a tradable commodity. This issue can be further discussed in terms of their market-oriented courses and higher fee structure. Moreover, lack of policy measures towards mushrooming growth of private higher education and commercialisation of higher education especially the professional courses are becoming important factor for social exclusion rather than facilitating social inclusion in the country.

Indian higher education sector has been experiencing tremendous growth since independence in various frontages-increased access and participation, expansion of educational institutions as well as expansion of academic facilities and a growing private sector. The expansion of higher education sector is phenomenal in the post-independence period and became one of the largest systems in the world. There were only 20 universities and 500 colleges with 0.1 million students at the time India attained independence (UGC, 2011). Today, the system constitutes of 1,113 Universities, 43,796 Colleges and 11,296 Stand Alone Institutions with 41.3 million students and 1.5 million teachers. The enrolment ratio in higher education is increasing steadily and at faster rate during the last decades. The gross enrolment increased from mere 8.9 in 2002 to 27.8 in 2020. The country has entered massification of higher education with major share of expansion by the private institutions.

The revival and expansion of the higher education sector in this century has mainly relied on private institutions and household funding (Varghese et al., 2018). Despite unprecedented growth, the expansion of higher education has been extremely uneven and resulted in the neglect of quality, research and managements aspects. Moreover, higher education expansion is also found to be accompanied by various disparities such as regional disparities, social group disparities and gender disparities. In this context, Maiti and Jana (2022) rightly stated that the expansion of higher education is primarily driven by economic agenda, while the equity concerns are driven by social agendas like social justice. Thus, state policies play an important role in promoting equity in access to higher education.

It is also seen that the rapid expansion of higher education system has brought several pertinent issues currently. The main challenges and issues of concerns include inequitable access to quality education, low standards of undergraduate education, low quality and research output, rigid separation of disciplines, outdated teaching methods, unmotivated student, inadequate infrastructure and facilities, limited teacher and institutional autonomy, fragmented educational ecosystem, suboptimal governance and leadership of HEIs, and ineffective regulatory system (NEP 2020). Furthermore, the rapid changes in the system are also brought about by new technologies, globalisation, privatisation, and changed environmental factors. No doubt, various initiatives have been taken for expansion of higher education and promotion of greater regional and social equity, yet considerable challenges remain. Access to higher education is still less than minimum international threshold levels and distribution of institutions is skewed. Enrolment in public universities is largely concerned in the conventional disciplines whereas in the private self-financed institutions, the students' enrolment is overwhelmingly in the market-driven disciplines (UGC, 2011). There is a greater challenge continued with respect to quality and provision of relevant education. Majority of higher education institutions perform poorly in the area of quality on a relative global scale. The National Education Policy (NEP) 2020 aims to increase the GER from 26.8 per cent (MHRD, 2018) to 50 per cent by 2035. NEP also aims along with increasing enrolment to increase opportunities of access to students from socio-economically disadvantaged groups (SEDGs) and focuses on providing equal access opportunities by attending to their specific problems.

In this backdrop, this chapter develops an understanding of access and equity in higher education in which, firstly explores access and equity issues in three dimensions such as regional, social and gender in both public and private higher education and, secondly examines equity promotion policies and programmes of India. The chapter will have policy implications and contributions to frame about the thinking of expansion of higher education with equity in the context of NEP 2020. For addressing the first objective, the paper largely uses secondary sources that are All India Survey on Higher

Education (AISHE) reports. For the second objective, the article reviews of current knowledge about equity promotion policies in higher education in India and in other countries. The findings of research study on private universities in India are also used to understand the equity issues.

Understanding Access and Equity in Higher Education

Access and equity in higher education have been regarded as the basic and key responsibilities of any government. State policies play important role in promoting equity in access to higher education (Maiti and Jana, 2022). The term access is commonly used in association with development in higher education, it does not have a common definition. It has changed with history and may vary across countries due to different social realities and agendas, even among developing countries. According to Clancy and Goastellec (2007), three different principles have been used to frame access policies, namely inherited merit, equality of rights and equity, defined as equality of opportunity. Inherited merit is dependent on circumstances such as one's social group at birth and became untenable over time as demographic, economic, political, and ideological pressures forced a reconsideration of the idea of access toward a more inclusive concept, which accommodated larger numbers regardless of social origin. Hence inherited merit was replaced by equality of rights. Tham (2011) expressed that equality of opportunity became the accepted norm for defining access, as the nature of higher education is thought to privilege those with superior economic, social and cultural resources. It was also mentioned that the notion of equality has to take into account differences in the opportunity structure, with merit redefined as the distance between the academic levels reached by students and the diverse handicaps they face, be it in terms of personal characteristics, family, community or schooling experiences. Levy (2008) very rightly pointed out that it may also include those who are not academically able to gain admission into limited public institutions of higher learning, students from different socio-economic backgrounds and genders, as well as working and other non-traditional students.

While understanding access in the context of equity, one could well quote Skilbeck 2000's work that defined "Access" in terms of equality of opportunity embedded within its notions of equity in a broad and inclusive sense. It embraces a sense of justice and fairness as it seeks to provide opportunities for under-represented groups in society, such as those of low socio-economic status, women and girls, ethnic and other minorities, people with disabilities and others previous opportunity to enter higher education. Further, OECD defines equitable higher education systems as those that ensure that the only factors defining an individual's access to, participation in, and outcomes from higher education are that individual's innate ability and study effort. Equitable systems like this ensure that an individual's potential for achievement at higher education is not based on his or her personal and social circumstances such as socio-economic status, gender, ethnic origin, immigrants' status, place of residence, age or disability. UNESCO, 2017 pointed out that perspective on equity in accessing higher education has changed over time from equity norm of 'inherited merit' to norm of either the 'equality of right' or equality of opportunity approach access to higher education. Furthermore, it also mentions that 'equality of right' means that everyone should be treated in the same way independent of individual circumstances. Whereas equality of opportunity means that unequal treatment such as affirmative action is justified in order to redress severe social disadvantage attributable to past unequal treatment. In this context, equity means to be fair, and offering equal treatment to all sections of people where comparable conditions exist. It does not mean that there has to be precise equality of representation in all areas of higher education.

How to measure Access and Equity?

Tham (2011) very well discussed different ways of measuring access and equity. Measures of access and equity range from broad macro data on participation in higher education by different social groups, including entry measures, enrolment measures and output measures, to cohort analysis based on the socio-economic and educational backgrounds of parents. Another approach is to measure and analyse affordability issues, such as costs of tertiary education, living costs and financial aid (Murakami and Blom, 2008). Kinser (2009) measured it in terms of the types of institutions available and types of programmes offered; the number of students and their demographic characteristics; as well as the revenues and expenses of higher education institutions and the financing mechanisms for students. So, depending on availability of data, access and equity can be measured in numerous ways.

Access to Higher Education

For this study, access to higher education is assessed in terms of number of institutions, the enrolment numbers, Gross enrolment ratio (GER) and number of teaching staff. Among all the government documents, the 12th FYP for higher education sets out the vision, goals and objectives to be achieved. The vision was spelt as access will be coupled with equity and inclusion by bridging regional imbalances and disparities across disciplines and shall address spatial, economic, social and technological needs of the country.

Table 2.1: *Number of Higher Education Institutions and Average Enrolment per College*

Year	*Number of universities and university level institutions*	*Number of all types of colleges*	*College density*	*Average enrolment per college*
2016-17	864	40026	28	659
2017-18	903	39050	28	698
2018-19	993	39931	28	693
2019-20	1043	42343	30	680
2020-21	1113	43796	31	646

Source: Adapted from AISHE Reports of the respective years.

It is seen from the Table 2.1 that during the period from 2016-17 to 2020-21, the number of universities had increased from 864 to 1113 and the number of colleges had increased from 40026 to 43796. The college density per one lakh population also increased from 28 to 31. However, average enrolment per college has decreased from 659 to 646, this may be due to students opting to study undergraduate courses in the private universities. Though the number of colleges increased but the enrolment shows a decreasing trend with inconsistency in its growth trend.

Trend of Growth of Higher Education Institutions

The number of higher education institutions in both universities and colleges has increased steadily over the years since independence. However, the number of private institutions has increased tremendously since 1980. Based on Table 2.2, it can be seen that there are different types of higher education institutions namely Central universities, State universities, private universities, Government deemed universities, private deemed universities, stand-alone institutions, institute of national importance and open universities. There are four types of private higher education institutions presently operating in India. In the last eight years, we see major jump in terms of number of private universities and colleges. In terms of percentage share, state universities (36.2) are the maximum followed by the private universities (32.7). It was rightly predicted by Angom (2015) that private universities will grow more in near future. Seeing the current growth rate, number of private universities may surpass the public universities very soon. As of 2020-21, there are 365 state private universities, 80 private deemed universities. Private colleges share 78.6 per cent (Private aided 13.6 per cent and 65 Private unaided 65 per cent) of country's total number of colleges. There are also private colleges which are upgraded to deemed to be universities based on criteria determined by the UGC. The bulk of private providers are private colleges that do not confer degree directly but through their mother universities, i.e., affiliating universities. Government Colleges despite constituting only 21.4 per cent of total colleges based on actual response contribute 34.5 per cent of total

Table 2.2: *Number of Private Universities and Colleges, 2012-13 and 2020-21*

Categories of Institutions	*2020-21*	*2012-13*	*Increase in absolute number*
Central Universities	51 (4.6%)	42 (6.3%)	9
State Universities	403(36.2%)	292 (43.8%)	111
Government Deemed Universities	44 (3.9%)	47 (7.03%)	-3
Private Universities	365 (32.7%)	122 (18.3%)	243
Private Deemed Universities	80 (7.2%)	80 (11.9%)	0
Government Colleges	8903 (21.4%)	6938 (25.4%)	1965
Private Colleges	32697 (78.6 %)	20407 (74.6%)	12290

Source: AISHE, 2012-13 & 2020-21.

enrolment, Private (Aided) colleges constituting 13.6 per cent of total colleges account for 21.1 per cent enrolment, whereas the 65 per cent Private Unaided Colleges account for only 44.4 per cent of total enrolment.

Outcomes in India: Based on the availability of data, access and equity in Higher education with special focus on public and private universities and undergraduate colleges is being evaluated. This is being evaluated according to overall participation, the different pathways to education provided by the variety of programmes available in the country, access by gender, access by social group, PWD, minority groups and EWS, costs of programmes or fee structure, government policies in both monetary and non-monetary form for promotion of equity and access.

Increasing Participation

The increase in participation is being made possible as various types of private institutions such as colleges, private universities and private deemed universities provide a variety of alternative pathways to higher education in the country. Private higher institutions specifically offer various courses ranging from traditional degree or diploma to dual degree or integrated programme in attractive subjects such as management, engineering, computer applications, law, pharmacy etc. Some of the private universities do have proper placement cell and also arrange internship with some of industry or company for students to gain industry experience mostly at the final year of their study.

This chapter explores the trend for the rapid expansion in Indian higher education from the private sector perspective. India is home to the largest and most diverse higher education system in the world. Recently, the private sector presence in higher education has been witnessing growth in terms of number of universities and colleges. Enrolment in universities and colleges in India during the last eight years is given in Table 2.3.

During the last eight years, enrolment increased in both government as well as private universities. In 2012-13, state private universities had a share of 6.4 per cent of the total enrolment in the university departments, which went up to 14.75 per cent in 2020-21. Except for state private universities, there is a trend of decrease in percentage share of government universities. The growth rate for the last eight years in central and state universities is below three per cent while that in private universities is above 20 per cent which is of major concern. This indicates the importance of private higher education institutions contribution toward increased student participation in higher education in the country. The gross enrolment ratio (GER) in Higher Education (18-23 Years) based on 2011 population since independence and has reached up to 27.3 in 2020-21 from 21.5 as on 2012-13. Umakoshi (2004) rightly mentioned that the large majority of undergraduate students in India are in private colleges, although most such institutions are heavily subsidized by public funds and are subject to oversight by the public universities to which they are affiliated.

Table 2.3: *Growth of Enrolment in Public and Private Universities, 2012-13 to 2020-21*

	2012-13		*2020-21*			*Growth Rate*
Category	*Total*	*Per cent*	*Total*	*Per cent*	*Increase*	*(Per cent)*
State	23.9	41.02	27.78	30.8	2.12	2.8
Central	5.8	9.9	5.03	7.8	2.8	2.12
Private	3.7	6.4	14.75	16.3	11.01	21.63
#Government	63.38	45.8	89.63	41.1	26.25	2.2

Source: AISHE 2012-13 & 2020-21; # this column signifies total enrolment in both Central and State universities.

Regional imbalances in distribution of higher education institutions

Higher education in India is also characterised by extreme regional imbalances. This can be understood in terms of the geographical region wise distribution of colleges vis-a-vis the population in the age group 18-23, from 2012-13 to 2020-21. Referring to table state wise number of colleges per one lakh population shows the extreme regional imbalances. From 2012-13 to 2020-21, the percentage share of colleges from the southern region is the maximum at around 30 per cent currently though shows a decreasing trend. This is followed by the western states (24.1 %) and the northern states (24.2) in 2020-21. While the eastern and central region states have percentage share of below 10 per cent. The north-eastern region accounts for only 2.3 per cent of the colleges in India (Table 2.4). If we take universities share region wise in the country, then we find that 25.6 per cent of the universities are in the northern region. This is further followed by western (22.4%), southern (21%) and eastern (14.1%). The NE has the lowest number of universities which accounted only 7.1 per cent of the total.

It is also seen that college density varies from region to region with college density of southern being the highest and eastern being the lowest (*see* Table 2.5). However, there is an increasing trend of college density in the last eight years in all the regions. The average enrolment per college in Bihar and Delhi is high though college density is low. However, the states having high college density

Table 2.4: *Region wise distribution of college and its average enrolment*

		Percentage share of colleges from the total	
Sl No.	*Region*	*2012-13*	*2020-21*
1.	North	22.3	24.2
2.	South	32	29.9
3.	East	8.4	9.2
4.	West	25.3	24.1
5.	North East	2.4	2.3
6.	Central	8.1	7.9
All India		**35525**	**43796**

Source: Calculated from AISHE Report 2020-21 and 2012-13.

Table 2.5: *Number of colleges, college density and average enrolment per college of two states from each region in comparison*

		No. of colleges		*College per lakh population*		*Average enrolment per college*	
Sl No.	*States*	*2012-13*	*2020-21*	*2012-13*	*2020-21*	*2012-13*	*2020-21*
1.	***Southern Region***						
i.	Karnataka Hhigh college density)	3205	4233	44	62	436	392
ii.	Tamil Nadu (Low college density)	2372	2667	31	40	816	838
2.	***Northern Region***						
i.	Himachal Pradesh (High college density)	293	348	38	50	484	510
ii.	Delhi (high college density)	187	180	9	8	1311	1567
3.	***Eastern Region***						
i.	Odisha (High college density)	1069	1206	23	26	616	573
ii.	Bihar (Low college density)	675	1035	62	8	2018	1881
4.	***North East Region***						
i.	Sikkim (High college density)	12	23	15	30	461	578
ii.	Assam (Low college density)	529	595	15	16	908	795
5.	***Western Region***						
i.	Rajasthan (High college density)	2669	3694	32	40	661	467
ii.	Gujarat (Low college density	1880	2267	26	31	604	526
6.	***Central Region***						
i.	MP (High college density)	2280	2610	26	29	568	666
ii.	Chhattisgarh (Low college density)	602	870	20	27	509	546
All India		**35525**	**43796**	**25**	**31**	**715**	**646**

Source: Adapted from AISHE Report 2012-13 and 2020-21.

namely Karnataka, HP, Sikkim and Rajasthan have average enrolment per college below all India average of 646 in 2020-21. Both Rajasthan and Gujarat show decreasing trend in average enrolment per college.

Gender Imbalances in Higher Education

Gender inequality in terms of opportunities to higher education is continuing and enrolment is tilted in favor of men. While the GER for men was 22.7 and for women it was 20.1 in 2012-13. However, there is an improvement in GER for women in 2020-21 at 27.9 over that of men at 26.7. For students of SC and ST categories too, there is sign of improvement in GER of women in the last eight years from 15.0 in 2012-13 to 23.9 in 2020-21 for SC. For ST women too, there is appreciable improvement from 9.8 in 2012-13 to 19.1 in 2020-21. Region wise/state wise data shows that there is variation in terms of GER.

The best performing states and union territories in terms of GER for women in north, south, east, west, central and northeast are Chandigarh (77.0), Puducherry (61.1), West Bengal (22.3), Maharashtra (33.5), Madhya Pradesh (26.8) and Sikkim (44.0) respectively. The states and union territories having the least GER for women in those regions are Ladakh (11.9), Lakshadweep (7.2), Bihar (15.1), Dadra & Nagar Haveli and Daman & Diu (15.6), Chhattisgarh (21.3) and Assam (18.4) respectively. However, we see a different picture for GER of women state wise for SC and ST categories. For SC categories, the best performing states in terms of GER for women in those six regions mentioned earlier are Ladakh (266.7), Puducherry (45.6), Goa (39.0), Madhya Pradesh (25.8) and Mizoram (168.2) respectively. While the worst performing states in terms of GER for women in those regions are J&K (19.4), Karnataka (25.9), Bihar (9.7), Rajasthan (22.6), Chhattisgarh (20.4) and Tripura (15.8) respectively. Further, for ST categories, Uttarakhand (52.0), Tamil Nadu (38.2), Bihar (17.4), Goa (31.9), Chhattisgarh (16.2) and Sikkim (41.6) in those regions respectively. While the worst performing states and union territories in terms of GER for women in those regions are J&K (15.7), Lakshadweep (7.0), West Bengal (11.8), Maharashtra (14.4), Madhya Pradesh (16.1) and Tripura (12.4). Furthermore, in India GPI which indicates persistent equality between men and women enrolment in higher education is at 1.05 in 2020-21, a rise from 0.89 in 2012-13. For SC and ST categories too, it is at 1.07 and 1.02 respectively. This figure shows that there is equity between men and women in terms of enrolment at higher education.

As per Spatial analysis of NSSO data of rural-urban disparities in access to higher education and also based on Scaria's (2023) finding, it is learnt that majority of the students depend on public sector for higher education. However, the share of students enrolled in the private sector is relatively higher in urban areas compared to rural areas. Moreover, a greater number of males from urban areas go to private institutions compared to urban females, rural males and rural females.

Table 2.6: *Enrolment Share of Female in various Levels in 2012-13 and 2020-21*

(Figures in Percentage)

Universities	*PhD*	*MPhil.*	*PG*	*UG*	*PG Diploma*	*Diploma*	*Certificate*	*Integrated*	*Grand Total*
2012-13	41.7	56.4	48.7	45.9	26.5	28.9	54.5	37.5	44.9
2020-21	44.9	61	56.5	48.7	44.1	37.1	46.2	45	48.7
Growth rate (Per cent)	13.4	-6.8	6.8	5.4	11.9	8.2	-5.2	25.4	5.8

Source: Calculated from the data of AISHE Reports, 2012-13 & 2020-21

Private universities do attract more male students than the female students. However, the gender balance may be depending on the subjects offered and fees levied by the universities. Courses offered in the faculties of Technology and Engineering Studies, Faculties of Management Studies with high level of fee structures attract more male students. Courses offered in faculties like Law, Education, Pharmacy, Medicine are the areas which women either outnumber men or equal number with men (Angom, 2013 and Angom, 2021).

It is evident from above table that enrolment is skewed in favour of men in various levels of higher education except at the level of MPhil (56.4) and certificate (54.5) in the year 2020-21. In the year 2012-13 too, more women were enrolled than men in MPhil (61) and PG (56.5). Over the last eight years. The growth rate is highest at integrated level courses (25.4) followed by PhD level (13.4) and PG Diploma (11.9). There is negative growth rate at MPhil and Certificate level. This may be due to closing down of MPhil degree courses in universities. But for certificate level courses, this may be due to either closing down of the courses in many universities or number of students enrolled in these courses have decreased during the year.

Female enrolment share has increased in all levels in both public universities and private universities. However, percentage share of female enrolment

Table 2.7: *Enrolment Share of Female Level wise in three Types of Universities, 2018-19*

(Figures in Percentage)

	Central universities		*State public universities*		*State private universities*	
Universities	*2020-21*	*2012-13*	*2020-21*	*2012-13*	*2020-21*	*2012-13*
PhD	46	44.2	46.9	43.5	33	39.4
MPhil	46.6	44.1	64.2	51.5	68.5	54.3
PG	49.1	42.5	53.4	49.4	43.8	32.7
UG	43.3	47.3	47.6	41.8	33.7	27.5
PG Diploma	43	34.5	46.7	13.1	48	35.4
Diploma	29.6	23.9	37.8	12.3	24.9	17.5
Certificate	33.9	27.6	62.9	43.6	3.6	19.2
Integrated	43.9	44.8	49.5	39.3	43	32.5
Grand Total	48	46.3	51.8	42.1	35.3	28.4

Source: Calculated from data available at AISHE 2012-13 & 2020-21

in private universities (35.3 per cent) is much below than that of the public universities. In central universities, percentage share of female enrolment is maximum at the level of PG (49.1) while the least percentage share is at the level of Diploma course (29.6). While in State universities, the maximum and minimum percentage share of female is accounted by MPhil (64.2) and Diploma (37.8). In private universities too, MPhil course has the maximum number of female students (54.3) while Diploma has the minimum enrolment share of female at 17.5 per cent. The state public universities have 51.8 per cent share of female enrolment out of its total enrolment while private universities have only 35.3 per cent share of female enrolment. So, gender disparities are found wide in case of private universities. This may be due to its market-oriented courses for which male students are more preferred to be admitted by their parents.

The private universities are self-financed, so tuition fee is the only source of income for such universities. Generally, private universities do charge much higher tuition fee as compared to what is charged by the public universities for both general as well as professional/technical courses. For a typical undergraduate course like Bachelor of Arts (BA), a student in private university has to spend a minimum amount of Rs. 21,800 annually as tuition/semester fee. In a public university in Delhi, a student has to spend around Rs. 2,200 annually as tuition fee (Jamia Millia Islamia, 2019). For a technical course like BTech, in a private university in MP, a student has to spend around Rs.1,20,000 annually while in a public university in Delhi, a BTech student has to spend only Rs. 4,400 annually as tuition fee. Angom (2021) reveals in her study that the course fees for majority of the students from the sample universities were being supported by their parents only. However, very few sections of the students enjoy financial support in the form of scholarship (institutional/other national agency) or bank loan. There are evidences of paying high capitation fees by a student in a private professional college like medical colleges for obtaining MBBS course as high as Rs 45-50 lakhs per course. This creates an equity issue for low-income students.

Social Group Inequalities

This is explored in terms of GER, percentage of enrolment social group wise all India and social group enrolment university wise and level wise.

Table 2.8: *Social group wise Enrolment and Share of Female, 2012-13 and 2020-21*

(Figures in Percentage)

	All categories	*General*		*Scheduled Caste (SC)*		*Scheduled Tribes (ST)*		*Other Backward Classes (OBC)*	
Year	*% Female*	*% Out of Total*	*% Female*	*% Out of Total*	*% Female*	*% Out of total*	*% Female*	*% Out of Total*	*% Female*
2012-13	44.9	51.6	44.3	12.8	44.9	4.4	44.6	31.2	45.8
2020-21	48.7	44.1	47.8	14.2	49.2	5.8	50.6	35.8	49.2

Source: Calculated from data available at AISHE 2012-13 & 2020-21.

From the above table, it is confirmed that social disparities in enrolment in higher education continue to be still high. Enrolment shares of students from SC and ST category continue to be lower than 15 per cent though showing slight increase in the last eight years. Share of enrolment of female students from OBC is higher at 49.2, higher than the that of the students from general categories. This may be due to the quota system. It is observed that OBC is the most benefitted group from quota system.

Participation of students from 'Person with Disability' category and minorities

The share of students from person with disability (PWD) from socially disadvantaged groups such as the SCs, STs, OBCs and EWS is significantly lower than legally mandated five per cent reservation of seats in HEIs (NIEPA, 2020). As per AISHE, 2020-21 report, 79,035 PWD students enrolled in higher education, out of which 49,334 are male and 29,701 are female students. Social group wise distribution of PWD students is shown in Table 2.9. Female participation among PWD students is highest in General Category with 69 females per 100 males followed by SC Category 66. Share of PWD students from OBC is the highest while that from STs is the lowest. The growth rate of PWD students in higher education from 2012-13 to 2020-21 is 5.6.

Among Minority category, data on Muslims have been collected separately during AISHE. It is reported that as per the response received during the survey, 4.6 per cent students belong to Muslim Minority and 2.0 per cent are from other Minority Communities in 2020-21. There is an increasing trend in student enrolment of both Muslim Minority (4.2%) and other Minority Community (1.9%) from 2012-13 to 2020-21. Notable feature reported is that Muslim Minority and other Minority communities have more female students than male students in 2020-21. This is a positive development, however, there is still social disparities in enrolment at higher education.

Disparities in Enrolment in Public and Private Universities

There is growth of private universities in recent year in most of the parts of country, however majority of the students are currently dependent on

Table 2.9. *Social category wise distribution of PWD candidates*

Category	*% Out of total PWD*			*Female per 100 males*
	Male	*Female*	*All*	
Total	–	–	–	60
SC	8.2	8.3	8.3	61
ST	3.0	3.3	3.2	66
OBC	32.3	23.6	29.0	44
General	56.5	64.7	59.5	69
EWS	2.9	4.5	3.5	107

Source: Adapted from AISHE Report 2020-21

public sector for their higher education. It is also evident from the available data that share of enrolment in public sector is much higher than the private unaided institutions. Analysis of the Table 2.10 shows that percentage share of enrolment in public universities shows a decreasing trend during the period. OBC (37.8%) has the highest enrolment share in state universities and least share in central universities (4.6%). The share of enrolment of SC, ST and OBC shows an increasing trend in private universities. It is also evident from analysis of the enrolment shares of SC, ST and OBC in public and private universities that there are higher gender disparities in enrolment in private universities than that of the public universities. There is also increasing number of female enrolments in the universities over the years.

There are still gender disparities in enrolment at PG level in technical and professional subjects among SC category (*see* Table 2.11). For ST category, except in General degree in Arts, Science and Commerce and Pharmacy, there

Table 2.10: *Social Group wise Enrolment Share of Universities in 2012-13 to 2020-21*

	Central Universities		*State Public Universities*		*State Private Universities*	
Universities	*2020-21*	*2012-13*	*2020-21*	*2012-13*	*2020-21*	*2012-13*
All Categories	7.8	9.9	30.8	41.02	16.3	6.4
General	10	12	27.1	41.1	19.4	7.7
SC	5.1	10	34.2	42.9	10.9	3.4
ST	7.6	9.2	34.2	42.9	10.9	3.4
OBC	4.6	4.9	37.8	42.4	12.7	4.7

Source: Figures calculated from AISHE Reports 2012-13 & 2020-21.

Table 2.11: *Female Enrolment Ratio in PhD, MPhil and PG in Major Disciplines by Social Groups, 2012-13 and 2020-21*

	% of female in all categories		*% of SC-female*		*% of ST-female*		*% of OBC-female*	
Program	*2012-13*	*2020-21*	*2012-13*	*2020-21*	*2012-13*	*2020-21*	*2012-13*	*2020-21*
PhD	42	45.2	35.6	39.6	41.5	43.9	41.5	44.4
MPhil	56.4	55.12	49.1	56.6	48.6	52.1	62.9	68.9
MA	56.5	60.1	52.4	57.8	50.2	57.6	57.4	59.9
MBA	35.3	43.3	33.7	42.3	33.5	39.9	34.3	42.1
MSc	54.4	60.9	50.9	57.4	47.2	56.3	58.3	62.6
M.Com	55.6	66.5	50.5	60.4	44.7	55.8	56.4	63.4
MCA	40.6	43.1	36.5	43.1	36.2	40.8	41.2	45.4
MTech	34.4	32.1	28.2	33.3	26.6	28.6	32.9	34.7
ME	42.1	35.9	38.2	35.9	28.6	27.2	46.3	39.9
M.Pharm	42.8	53.8	45.5	53.8	39.1	51.6	39.9	53.7
LLM	37.8	43.9	32.2	43.9	43.8	42.9	33.4	42.9
MSW	42.4	54.3	37.4	54.3	39.1	49.6	40.6	55

Source: Figures calculated from AISHE Reports 2012-13 & 2020-21

Table 2.12: *Female Enrolment Ratio in PhD, MPhil and PG in Major Disciplines of PWD, Muslim, OMC and EWS Category in 2020-21*

Programme	*PWD*	*Muslim*	*OMC*	*EWS*
PhD	27.5	44.8	58.1	44.1
MPhil	30.5	54.9	64.0	42.3
MA	39.2	61.8	65.9	64.3
MBA	23.3	36.3	47.3	45.2
MSc	41.2	62.4	72.9	61.1
M.Com	39.8	62.5	68.7	77.3
MCA	20.1	35.2	50	40.7
MTech	15.6	31.8	43.2	20.2
ME	7.7	25.7	54.5	29.7
M.Pharm	42.4	54.3	64.5	52.5
LLM	34.9	47.6	50.9	44
MSW	42.4	56.2	64	51.7

Source: Figures calculated from AISHE Report 2020-21.

is still disparities in technical and professional subjects. While for OBC too, except in general degree in Arts, Science, Commerce, Pharmacy and Social Work, there is gender disparities in enrolment in professional subjects at PG level. At PhD level, there is still gender disparities among ST, SC, OBC and for all categories. Further, to add here that Scaria's (2023) spatial analysis shows that more persons are enrolled for technical education compared in urban areas as compared to rural areas. Further, she finds that an intersection of space and gender shows that relatively more urban women enrolled in technical/ professional education as compared to rural men and rural women.

From the Table 2.12, it is seen that for PWD students, there are gender disparities in enrolment in higher education at PG in most of the major disciplines and at the level MPhil and PhD. For Muslims, there is gender disparities in enrolment at PhD and PG degree in Technical and Professional subjects. However, female students from Other Minority Class (OMC) are doing better than male as except for Master in Technology, enrolment ratio is skewed towards female at PG, MPhil and PhD. There are still gender disparities in enrolment at PhD, MPhil, M.BA, MCA, MTech, ME and Law among EWS students.

The analysis of the data from AISHE 2021 on Female Share in Enrolment and Pass-outs at UG Level Discipline Wise, 2020-21 shows that enrolment of female is little ahead of male in science subjects. However, the enrolment ratio in some of the important disciplines such as commerce (48.5), engineering (29%), IT and Communication (39.2), Management (36.6), Law (33.7), Agriculture (29.9), Physical Education (29.9), Fine Arts (30.9), Paramedical Sciences (46.9), Hospitality and Tourism Management (21.7), Veterinary and Animal Husbandry (39.8) and Marine Science (16.9) is still skewed towards male. In terms of pass-outs in the year 2020-21, ratio female pass-outs in disciplines, namely, Engineering, IT & Com, Management, Law, Agriculture, Physical Education., Paramedical Science., Vetinerary & Animal Husbandry and Criminology needs improvement. Pass-outs in Marine Science is still so poor. This is also evident that majority of the students enrolled in Arts (35.3) as well maximum number of pass-outs is from the same stream (29.6) in higher education. Further, there are wide disparities in pass-out percentage of socially disadvantaged groups namely SC, ST and OBC at 11.4 per cent, 4.6 per cent and 30.05 per cent respectively. PWD female students pass-outs is still below 40 per cent. EWS female students are doing better at 49.9 per cent. Except at all level of MPhil, PG and UG, female pass percentage share is still below 50 per cent at other levels. Lowest pass percentage of female is reported at Diploma at 37.9 per cent.

Access and Equity Policies of India: Some Observations

Equitable access to education is the most debated topics worldwide today. There are studies conducted focusing especially on the effects of equity interventions on disadvantaged group across countries. As Sami (2020) revealed that few studies that look at several interventions implemented together are more effective than the individual interventions designed and implemented in isolation. It is further noted that the most effective equity promotion policies to overcome the barriers and increase opportunities for disadvantaged students at the tertiary level are those that combine financial aid with measures to overcome non-financial obstacles (OECD, 2008; Sami and Malee Bassett 2014). The findings of a survey conducted in 2018 for the Lumina foundation in 71 countries revealed that countries tend to use a mix of measures. Further, it was pointed out that the most frequently supported non-monetary programmes are affirmative action and reformed admission criteria, outreach and bridge programmes and retention programmes.

In India, the policies are mostly related to the policies of affirmative action and democratic inclusion besides monetary programmes. The most common non-monetary existing programme is the quota system for admission, while monetary programmes are grants/scholarships and student loan. Reservation policy or quota system is existing in India much before independence. This became a national policy as enshrined in the Constitution of India framed by Dr B.R. Ambedkar after independence. In India, reservation is all about reserving access to seats in the government jobs, educational institutions, and even legislatures to certain sections of the population. It is government policy backed by the Indian Constitution to provide reservation with aims to bring advancement of SC, ST or any Socially and educationally backward classes (OBC) or EWS as per Article 15 (4), Article 15 (5), and Article 15 (6), and secondly, to provide adequate representation of any backward class of citizens OR economically weaker sections (EWS) in the services under the State- Article 16 (4) and Article 16 (6). Reservation is becoming one of the means of uplifting disadvantaged groups. There are debates on reservation policy as some felt that it is a tool against social oppression and injustice against certain classes. Besides reservations, other methods like providing scholarships, funds, coaching, and other welfare schemes should be promoted and strengthened. Some would argue that though Indian constitution allowed reservation only for socially and educationally backward classes.

The UGC Regulations 2012 published in January 2013 on Promotion of Equity in Higher Educational Institutions defines equity as "a level playing field for all students in respect of the entitlement and opportunity for enjoyment of all legitimate rights". Various initiatives launched by the UGC towards enhancing access with equity through various fellowships, post-graduate scholarships, coaching schemes, residential coaching academies for minorities, support to institutions with relatively higher proportion of SCs, STs, minorities, capacity expansion for OBCs, support to persons with disabilities, empowerment of women, etc. are modelled and implemented by many universities in the country. Some of the notable schemes of the UGC for nurturing social equity for various beneficiary categories are Indira Gandhi Post Graduate Scholarships for Single Girl Child, Residential Coaching Academies for Minorities, Rajiv Gandhi National Fellowships for SCs & STs, and Maulana Azad National Fellowships for Minorities, Post-Doctoral Fellowships for SCs, STs, and Women etc. Many universities have adopted tutorials and remedial teaching for the weaker sections within the departments and special coaching for competitive tests, communication and soft skills are imparted from the Career Guidance Bureau. Besides, many universities have established their own centre for studies of social exclusion and inclusion.

Angom (2013) revealed that some of the private universities in India do offer financial assistance to students in some form of scholarships or stipends or others. For instance, in a university in Himachal Pradesh, students who stood first in a particular batch will be exempted from paying tuition fee for the batch. In another case, a private university in Gujarat provides free ship to top three ranking students in their semester examination. After examining these two cases, one could well understand that scholarships and free ship given to the students are on the basis of merit in most of the case. Further, Angom (2021) found in her study that 83.3 per cent of the sampled universities provide stipends or scholarships to the students who are either poor but meritorious or belonging to SCs /STs/ OBC or students from lower family income group. However, the criteria followed by the universities for providing such support vary from university to university. Besides, she also reveals that majority of the sample universities provide concession on tuition fee but to those students who belong to the SC, ST, and OBC categories.

Concrete Action Plans for the Present and Future of Equity and Inclusion

NEP 2020 policy aims to increase the GER from 26.8 per cent to 50 per cent by 2035. NEP also aims along with increasing enrolment to increase opportunities of access to students from socio-economically disadvantaged groups (SEDGs) and focus on providing equal access opportunities by attending to their specific problems. It is also noted that although there is an improvement in the enrolment ratio of SEDGs over the years, there still remain inter-group disparities in access to higher education opportunities. Disparities in access to HE has three dimensions, namely, regional disparities, group disparities and disparities between sexes (NIEPA, 2020). There are issues for concerns in higher education for providing equalising access opportunities due to three key disparities i.e., regional, social and gender. Such disparities also include disparities at the entry level, interaction at the academic level and outcomes and in facilitating inclusive campuses (NIEPA, 2020). These three key disparities have been discussed in the earlier sections.

NEP 2020 further addressed that there are certain facets of exclusion, that are particular to or substantially more intense in higher education. These must be addressed specifically, and include lack of knowledge of higher education opportunities, economic opportunity cost of pursuing higher education, financial constraints, admission processes, geographical and language barriers, poor employability potential of many higher education programmes, and lack of appropriate student support mechanisms. For this purpose, additional actions that shall be adopted by all Governments and HEIs are also highlighted by the policy documents.

Steps to be taken by Government

For SEDG's, there should be earmark government funds for education of SEDGs; setting clear targets for higher GER for them; provide more financial assistance and scholarships to SEDGs in both public and private HEIs; Develop and support high-quality HEIs that teach in local/Indian languages or bilingually.

1) Enhance gender balance in admissions to HEIs
2) Enhance access by establishing more high-quality HEIs in aspirational districts and Special Education Zones containing larger numbers of SEDGs
3) Conduct outreach programmes on higher education opportunities and scholarships among SEDGs
4) Develop and support technology tools for better participation and learning outcomes.

Policy envisages the following steps to be taken by all HEIs

1) Mitigate opportunity costs and fees for pursuing higher education
2) Provide more financial assistance and scholarships to socio-economically disadvantaged students
3) Conduct outreach on higher education opportunities and scholarships
4) Make admissions processes and curriculum more inclusive
5) Increase employability potential of higher education programmes
6) Develop more degree courses taught in Indian languages and bilingually
7) Ensure all buildings and facilities are wheelchair-accessible and disabled-friendly

8) Develop bridge courses for students that come from disadvantaged educational backgrounds
9) Provide socio-emotional and academic support and mentoring for all such students through suitable counselling and mentoring programmes
10) Ensure sensitization of faculty, counsellor, and students on gender-identity issue and its inclusion in all aspects of the HEI, including curricula
11) Strictly enforce all no-discrimination and anti-harassment rules
12) Develop Institutional Development Plans that contain specific plans for action on increasing participation from SEDGs, including but not limited to the above items.

Suggested Implementation Strategy to Promote Equity

Based on the above discussions, it can be noted that there is need to find out the various problems faced by the disadvantaged groups in access to higher education. So, identification of problem should be the first step and accordingly strategies should be adopted both at government and HEIs levels. Equity is not a destiny, but it is a choice. Since it is a choice, there are alternatives and there are policies that state can do something which is so important. It can be reflected here the findings of OECD study using data from 1973 to 2008 which clearly shows that education is emerging as simply an important factor for creating inequalities especially in the developing countries. This is in the context of knowledge economy which is not running normal. So, the progressive state action has played a major role. Evidence on inter generation mobility across countries has highlighted that parental education and influence on education progress of next generation has declined over a period of time. It is also observed that the state acted with a democratic sense and a political commitment has shown dramatic changes over the years. That is why, despite in terms of growth, an equity dimensions arise due to the absence of equity policy and the proper target.

Further, when higher education is distributed unequally, we are not only creating inequality in the present but also perpetuating inequalities in the next generation, therefore, scholars like Varghese (2023) felt that targeting is one of the interventions to promote equity policies. Such policy will be able to tell who benefits from higher education and who provides higher education. No doubt, the quota system has brought the biggest revolution in Indian higher education in changing the student composition and student diversity. However, institutions faced the challenge of interaction with the first-generation learners and also with those who are regionally deprived and socially deprived groups. This is because the policies seldom addressed the issues of what happens to them after entering college besides making policy of how to bring these groups of students to college and university. Moreover, one needs to take into account the schooling dimensions seriously. For addressing the equality issues, the policy should focus on creating an inclusive campus which is the biggest challenge for the institution. Furthermore, the market also plays a dominating role in increasing inequalities in access to higher education in India today. Because, privatization has brought wide state disparities in terms of density of colleges per lakh population and also gender disparities in the provision of professional and technical higher education. Angom (2021) reveals that market reforms in higher education have failed to reach the marginalized sections of the society.

As India implements NEP 2020, the following six strategies may have some resonance. These strategies have been suggested in line with NIEPA's (2020) NEP 2020 implementation strategies.

1) Firstly, to reduce regional disparities, there is need to prioritise the availability of quality higher education facilities in the underserved districts by designing a catchment area policy measure for students from SEDGs. There is also a need to expand both public and private institutions of professional and technical courses in disadvantaged areas. Besides, it will be a welcome step to increase budgetary allocation for scholarships and provision for scholarships as well as reservation policies by the private institutions.
2) Secondly, it is also suggested that there is need to have some strategies for increasing access for students from SEDGs in HE, such as, to implement and monitor the caste-based reservation policies, to organise outreach activities for increasing access to knowledge of college-going process, to identify student groups that are underrepresented in campus and coordinate with schools to establish pathways of access for students from underrepresented groups, to make campus safe place for women, and making institution building facilities friendly for person with disability (PWD) students.
3) Thirdly, for making campuses socially inclusive, there is need to adopt the strategies such as- to develop local context and diversity data-based campus diversity policy, to organise events and programmes of awareness about values of diversity and equity, and to promote feedback mechanism for students to promote their expression for any diversity issue or unequal treatment.
4) Fourthly, for increasing employability potential of higher education graduates equitably, both the system and institution should have equal efforts. At system level, it is suggested that the skill gaps need to reduce by improving cognitive skills and learning outcomes through high quality educational system. At the institution level, it is suggested that the SEDGs student support service needs the provision for subject and career choice, provision for soft skill and language training, creating inclusive internship programmes, strengthening existing government programmes for SEDGs students to improve competitiveness in selection tests etc.
5) Fifthly, to address the issues of SEDGs students relating to their difficulties in academic integration as they are coming from diverse socio-economic

background with various academic experiences, there is need to prove the academic support for creating inclusive classroom. Remedial coaching classes, therefore, must aim to address academic challenges faced by various equity groups and it must reach all needy students for addressing their academic adjustments difficulties.

6) Finally, for addressing challenges of social inclusion, classroom practices and nature of teacher-student interaction should be inclusive in nature. There is need for creating an environment where peer interaction is made healthy for academic growth, having sensitive administrative staffs on issues of diversity and equity, and having staff should behave with non-discriminatory attitude towards students from SEDGs. There should be provision for students to have equal opportunity to participate in co-curricular activities according to their interest while considering the special needs of differently abled students in such activities.

Institutions Initiatives

The universities must give special attention for organising various training programmes for capacity building among OBC students. Equal opportunity Cell and its functions may be further enhanced. Every university must ensure to have in their buildings the special facilities for physically challenged persons such as ramps, and entrances and toilet facilities etc. Universities must promote inclusive schemes and materialize the policy perspectives on equity to the maximum. In those institutions situated in minority concentration districts, women hostels should be provided. Every university must have in their website with the useful links to students' grievances portal, Internal Complain Committee, and Anti Ragging Cell within the student zone.

Conclusion

From the above discussion, it is learned that with the growth of higher education in India, inequality expanded. No doubt GER in higher education has increased with increase in the privatization of higher education. Further, when we look at the pattern of growth of higher education, it is evident that most of the institutions of higher education are run by private sectors and more than 60 per cent of enrolments are taking place in these private institutions. This further implies that some of the people are quite rich enough to go to private institutions. Inequality in access to higher education is happening when the market is deciding. Therefore, for bringing equality in access to education, both the state and market together has to do something when state's decisions are also highly influenced by market. Since, state has a dominant role in higher education provision, therefore, there is need to change the role of the state beyond funding and financing. Therefore, in conclusion it can be underlined that a state has to play a very important role in terms of providing a framework which will decide the way in which equity and equality are addressed.

References

ADBI *Working Paper 280.* Tokyo. Asian Development Bank Institute. Retrieved May 26, 2023. https://www.adb.org/publications/exploring-access-and-equity-malaysias-private-higher-education

Angom, S. (2013). A Study of Private Universities in India. *Unpublished Research Report.* New Delhi. NIEPA

Angom, S. (2015). Private Higher Education in India: Study of Two Private Universities, *Higher Education for the future. Vol 2 Issue 1,* Page no-92-111., Sage publication, January 2015

Angom, S. (2021). Indian Private University Acts and Regulations of Fee. *Unpublished Research Report.* New Delhi, NIEPA

Clancy, P. and G. Goastellec. (2007). Exploring Access and Equity in Higher Education: Policy and Performance in a Comparative Perspective". *Higher Education Quarterly.* 61(2), 136–154.

Government of India. (2013). Twelfth Five-year plan (2012-17). *Social Sector, Vol-III.* New Delhi: Planning Commission.

Government of India. (2015). All India Survey on Higher Education 2012-13, Final Report.

Government of India. (2020). National Education Policy 2020.

Government of India. (2023). All India Survey on Higher Education 2020-21, Final Report.

Illustration. Program for Research on Private Higher Education (PROPHE) *Working Paper 11.* Albany NY: University of Albany

Kinser, K. (2009). Access in U.S. Higher Education: What Does the For-Profit Sector Contribute? Program for Research on Private Higher Education (PROPHE) *Working Paper 14.* Albany: University of Albany

Levy, D. (2008). Access through Private Higher Education: Global Patterns and Indian Illustration. Program for Research on Private Higher Education (PROPHE) Working Paper 11. Albany NY: University of Albany

Maiti, A., and Jana, S.K. (2020). Diversity and Equity in Higher Education: A Study in India (eds) Handbook of Research on Practices for Advancing Diversity and Inclusion in Education 2020. Pp 263-280. Accessed on May 26, 2023. https://orcid.org/0000-0003-0838-9041

Murakami, Y., and A. Blom. (2008). Accessibility and Affordability of Tertiary Education in Brazil, Colombia, Mexico, and Peru within a Global Context. *Policy Research Working Paper 4517.* Washington DC: World Bank.

NIEPA. (2020). NEP 2020 Implementation Strategies. NIEPA, New Delhi

OECD. (2008). Tertiary Education for the Knowledge Society – OECD Thematic Review of Tertiary Education: Synthesis Report. Paris: Organisation for Economic Cooperation and Development.

"Policy and Performance in a Comparative Perspective." *Higher Education Quarterly.* 61(2), 136–154.

Salmi, J and D'Addio, A. (2020). Policies for achieving inclusion in higher education. *Policies Review in Higher Education.* Accessed April 17, 2023. https://cpce.udp.cl/cms/wp-content/uploads/2020/10/Policies-for-achieving-inclusion-in-higher-education.pdf

Salmi, J., and Malee Bassett, R. (2014). The Equity Imperative in Tertiary Education: Promoting Fairness and Efficiency. *International Review of Education. 60 (3),* 361–377. http://www.springer. Com/alert/urltracking.do?id=L56e01c1M101bee0Sb0db3d3

Scaria, S. (2023). Public Versus Private: Does Privatisation Enhances Gender Equity in Higher Education in India. Unpublished paper presented at International Seminar on

Diversity & Inclusion in Higher Education. Organised by CPRHE, NIEPA. 16 & 17 February 2023, New Delhi

Skilbeck, M. (2000). Access and Equity in Higher Education: An International Perspective on Issues and Strategies. A Report Prepared for the Higher Education Authority (HEA). Dublin: HEA.

Tham, S.Y. (2011). Exploring Access and Equity in Malaysia's Private Higher Education.

Umakoshi, T. (2004). Private Higher Education in Asia, (eds) P.G. Altbach & U. Toro. *Asian Universities*. (p. 34). Baltimore, Maryland: John Hopkins University Press.

UNESCO. (2017). Six Ways to ensure higher education leaves no one behind. *Policy Paper-10*. Accessed April 17, 2023. https://unesdoc.unesco.org/ark:/48223/pf0000247862

University Grants Commission. (2003). UGC (Establishment of and Maintenance of Standards in Private Universities) Regulations. New Delhi.

University Grants Commission. (2012). Promotion of Equity in Higher Educational Institutions Regulations, 2012

University Grants Commission. (2021). Inclusive and Qualitative Expansion of Higher Education. UGC. New Delhi

Varghese, N.V. (2023). State, Market and Equity in Higher Education, Key Note Speech. International Seminar on Diversity & Inclusion in Higher Education. organised by CPRHE, NIEPA. 16 & 17 February 2023, New Delhi

Varghese, N.V., Sabharwal, N.S. and Malish, C.M. (2018). *India Higher Education Report 2016*: Equity. New Delhi: Sage.

3

Using Web Technology in the 21st Century

Teaching-Learning Process

Partha Roy
Abhijit Guha

Introduction

Having web technology in the classroom is essential because it makes knowledge instantly available. Smartphones, computers, tablets, etc. as technology have already taken a commonplace for both students and teachers during learning. In order to provide students of all ages with relevant learning opportunities, it makes sense that efforts are being made to investigate how to use web technology in the classroom. In the classroom, web technology in a virtual classroom is utilized to create engaged students who are showing minimum interest in the learning objectives (Knowledgexpert, 2023). Web Technology integration also opens doors for individualized instruction to fulfil each student's specific needs as an individual learner within a larger classroom environment. In this regard the researchers find out and analyzed as descriptive forms about the modern Web Technology and its effective impact on the teaching-learning process. After the end of this paper, the researcher has come to the conclusion that Web Technology, which is also emphasized by NEP 2020, is a new viewpoint and helps to cope with a more dynamic environment in which Web Technology must be incorporated into the teaching and learning process for better academic outcomes in the 21st century.

Without the utilization of technology-related assistance, teaching and learning cannot function effectively in the 21st century as well as in the modern world. The entire educational system has undergone a complete transformation through the Internet. The teacher was the only resource for translating difficult knowledge into meaningful meaning, but now a days, the traditional positions have been replaced by Web Technology, which has created new opportunities for teachers' roles in areas like resource management and learning management. Teachers have access to a variety of media today to support and enhance the educational process. Instructors can even describe the learning objectives, choose the subject, choose the medium, decide on the stimulus situation, manage the teaching, conduct the evaluation, and then adjust the lesson plans in light of the evaluation's findings.

NEP 2020 also emphasized that, without the aids of modern technology, the educational process cannot be carried out in a methodical manner. The entire educational system has been technologically advanced. The new policy (2020) also makes it clear that technology may assist people and have chances that allow them to advance both personally and professionally. An independent organization named the National Educational Technology Forum (NETF) will be founded to provide a venue for the free exchange of ideas on the use of technology to enhance learning, assessment, planning, administration, and other aspects of secondary and higher education. By providing them with access to the most recent information and research as well as the chance to network and share best practices, the NETF aims to make it simpler for leaders of educational institutions, State and Central governments, and other stakeholders to make decisions about the introduction, deployment, and use of technology. (NEP, 2020) Some important points are given here —

(i) Educational theory and practice now have a scientific foundation for web technology. Using audio-visuals, charts, and models, smart classrooms, and e-learning rooms, it has changed a passive classroom into an active and dynamic classroom that has significantly motivated and raised the attention level of the pupils.
(ii) The teaching-learning environment at educational institutions has been modernized by the introduction of web technology. The students will be exposed to professionally made video or computer programmes.
(iii) Through planned lessons for drill, enrichment, or remediation, web technology has aided and augmented teachers' instructional programmes.
(iv) Online technology has given teachers well-integrated structured materials through the systematic organization of information and instructional materials. This allows the teachers to save a significant amount of time, which can then be used for creative work and quality improvement.
(v) Teachers' use of and training in web technology helps them advance their careers. It enables them to employ scientific techniques to address administrative and educational issues.

The teaching-learning process was enhanced, making it more efficient and process-focused. Knowledge has been improved and effectively transmitted for technologies like television, radio, computers, and LCD projectors, among others. So, technology is necessary at every single step of the teaching and learning process. It fulfills every requirement of contemporary needs of students to survive in 21st century with effective manner (Parankimalil, 2015; NEP, 2020).

Online content was pushed out to an audience in the Web technology (1.0) environment by a webmaster or curator. Information moved in only one direction. Collaboration and content sharing are concepts introduced by Web 2.0. By enabling people to upload blogs, wikis, movies, and images as well as participate in social media, it empowered the common user. Real-time activities are being emphasized in Web 3.0. Using Facebook live, online conferencing, YouTube, and other social media platforms, people broadcast videos. We were introduced to interactive video through devices like Google Cardboard and Oculus Rift, and we are now witnessing advancements in real-time virtual and augmented worlds. Every stage of the web's evolution builds on those before it to produce a more immersive experience. As educators, we face the difficulty of harnessing these platforms within our classrooms.

In the era of Web Technology (3.0), e-Learning will undergo an unparalleled transition towards a more mobile, semantic, and immersive web-based experience. Online course (SWAYAM-2014, MOOC-2006/2012, Swayamprabha-2017, etc.) instructors won't be referred to as faceless entities anymore, and critics of online education won't describe it as information dumps. Students will become engaged in a content-rich and intensely personal learning environment which will be both demanding and stimulating, and will accommodate to independent learning preferences.

Literature on Web Technology and its Application in Teaching-Learning Process

The evolution of Web Technology is effectively increasing the achievement of teaching-learning process. In this area the researcher wants to study narratively for understanding the major knowledge of web technology and its positive application in teaching-learning process. Review of related or selected literature helps the researcher to forward this study in a more reflective manner. There are various study describes below:

Owston, R.D. (1997) stated his paper on the World Wide Web technology to enhance the teaching and learning. He explained that the access of higher education system more effectively for web technology, learning make much flexible, home schooling, alternative schooling, extension courses more supportive for web. But also, there are various barriers based by teacher and students to accessible this web technology lack of knowledge, especially during online learning problem faced through technically. But it can say that web helps the teacher-students both as per interest from anywhere.

Naik, U. & Shivalingaiah, D. (2008), both researchers conducted a comparative study on Web Technology and its effectiveness. They reveal that the most people nowadays can hardly fathom life without the Internet. A web of data has replaced the web of papers. Three stages of Internet development are covered by the semantic wave. Web 1.0, the initial phase, was all about connecting information and entering the Internet. With the "I" in user interface and the "we" in a web of social involvement, Web 2.0 is about connecting people. Web 3.0, the next phase, has begun. It is about providing meanings, connecting knowledge, and putting it to use in ways that improve the relevance, utility, and enjoyment of our Internet experience.

An, Y.J. et al. conducted their research on Teaching with Web 2.0 Technologies and how it is Benefits, Barriers and Best Practices in modern era in 2009. Fourteen university professors with extensive experience teaching with Web 2.0 technologies took part in the study. Data for this study were gathered using a web-based survey. The findings of the study suggest that interaction, communication, and cooperation, knowledge creation, usability and flexibility, and writing and technological abilities are among the main advantages of adopting Web 2.0 technologies in teaching. Unease with openness, technological difficulties, and lack of time are the main obstacles faced by university teachers when implementing Web 2.0 technology in their lessons. The poll results also offered useful advice and pointers for using Web 2.0 tools in the classroom.

Simões, L. & Gouveia, L. (2009), in this study researchers analyzed that how the Web 2.0 environment helps the today's teaching conditions. Teachers can use Web 2.0 in their daily professional activities. The delicate subject of control over the learning process was also covered, with an emphasis on some possible problems that new technologies might pose for the settings of the classroom and school. Feldmann, B. (2014) published a paper titled 'Two Decades of e-Learning in Distance Teaching — Web Technology' at the University of Hagen. The way individuals learn and teach has changed substantially over the past 20 years as a result of technology. The shift began in the 1970s with an increase in the use of technology in the classroom, expanded in the early 1990s with the advent of the Internet, was followed by the development of learning management systems, and is presently being completed by the new and user-friendly possibilities of Web 2.0. The researcher performed a study survey on Web 2.0's effects on distance learners, focusing in particular on community usage, in order to learn more about the current preferences and expectations of the students. The findings of this study provided crucial new insights into the application of new technology, and in particular, into the demands and preferences of distance learners. These revelations help us gain a new perspective on key e-learning concepts that are applicable to more than just remote learning. (Feldmann, 2014)

Dominic. M., Francis, S. & Pilomenraj, A. (2014) completed their contemporary study on Web Technology and effectiveness of e-Learning. With technologies like big data, connected data, cloud computing, 3D visualization, augmented reality, and more, Web 3.0 is also known as the intelligent web or semantic web. These technologies turn passive learners into active learners during the learning process. This essay identifies the traits of the many web generations and how they affect the various e-learning generations, as well as the various problems with web 3.0.

Prabhu, D. (2016) wrote their article about Web 2.0 and Web 3.0 and its applications. They emphasized on the different features, tools, and benefits of Web 2.0. Especially, Web 3.0 technologies are discussed, including their need, foundations, structure, goals, components, and benefits. The user has no option to expand their involvement or interact with the UI on Web 1.0 sites, which are driven. Web 2.0 sites enable user engagement and interaction by providing an easy-to-use interface where users can update and publish already-existing content. Websites where computers will produce raw data on their own are referred to be Web 3.0 sites.

The Evolution of Web Technologies and relations the Sector of Education, related a study completed by Victor, S.R. & Mohammed, A.A. (2016). The limitations and disadvantages of this Web version are also discussed, along with recommendations for their integration into the current paradigm of educational practices and curricula. The following version, known as "Web 2.0", appeared to be a two-way channel, expanding the possibilities for what a user could accomplish with it. The newest version, known as "Web 3.0", which is in the works, has a more interactive and dynamic interface with highly advanced capabilities that give machines the ability to "think" and "perform" tasks by giving them the ability to comprehend and analyse data in order to meet the needs of the user. Therefore, it is crucial to understand how Education Technology has developed with Web 2.0, along with the improvements that may be made with Web 3.0, how it aids teaching and learning in a progressive manner.

Application of Web 2.0 in Enhancing Teaching and Learning of Technology Educational Courses in Tertiary Institutions in Rivers State, an article investigated by Deebom, M.T. & Amaso, T.F. (2017). The findings indicated that insufficient training facilities, limited bandwidth, and time constraints are the main issues with Web 2.0 applications in teaching and learning. It was suggested, among other things, that there should be in-service workshops training on Web 2.0 tools, that schools should have quick, high-bandwidth Internet access, and that they should have reliable power sources. Majid, I. & Verma, S. (2018) studied on the Web 2.0 Technological Tools in Teaching and Learning. According to the researchers, there is a digital wave that is spreading across. The educational industry has benefited greatly from digitization. Due to technology's ability to connect people almost anytime and anywhere, it has increased connectivity between teachers and students. Since several applications and technological advantages have only been made possible with the aid of the Internet and World Wide Web, Internet has today become the foundation of technology. Technology known as Web 2.0 has completely altered and revolutionized the educational sector that can be used throughout the teaching and learning process.

Three eminent researchers namely, Gupta et al., 2022 worked on how to Web 3.0 and its Reflections on the Future of e-Learning. Following this investigation of Web 3.0 applications, it has demanded simple, reasonable, and requiring little technical knowledge. Podcasting, weblogs, and other Web 3.0 features are simple for students or teachers to use. The Internet is always used by Web 3.0 as a transmission channel, which can be a useful way to create dynamic learning and teaching experiences.

Result and Discussion

In this present study different sources were consulted and read out thoroughly and rigorously to identify and extract the concepts as a result and for discussion.

Information Technology: The only purpose of information technology is to deal with the explosion of information. Information technology (IT) i.e., the microelectronics-based mix of computer and communications that is used to acquire, process, store, and disseminate spoken, graphical, textual, and numerical information. In other words, anything that transmits data, information, or perceived knowledge through any multimedia distribution mechanism and portrays it in any visual format is seen as falling within the umbrella of the information technology area. Information technology is a field of science, technology, engineering, and management that deals with handling information, applying it, and connecting it to social, economic, and cultural issues.

Communication Technology: Communication technology also consists of two words like communication and technology. The ability to communicate is essential to human existence. People's identity in modern society is changing into an information society, and communication is the exchange of information. It is the process and transmission of information from a sender to a receiver using a medium in which the communication information is understood by both the sender and the receiver. Communication skills refer to the knowledge, skills and understanding necessary to exchange information verbally or non-verbally. This is the processing of information related to accessing information, decoding information, and transmitting it to recipients via media and changers. Information in written, spoken, or gestural form transmitted by sound, action, or technological equipment is referred to as a medium or channel.

An electronic system used for intergroup communication is known as communication technology. It allows for easier communication between people or groups when they are not present at the same location physically. In addition to emerging computer technologies like email and electronic data exchange, it encompasses telephone, fax, radio, television, and video systems.

Instructional Technology: Today, it is widely acknowledged that instructional technology is a method or approach used in conjunction with the appropriate and necessary media and material to enhance the teaching-learning and evaluation process. It also refers to the application of a systems approach in the systemic design of a learning system. The phrase "instructional technology" should be interpreted to include any such elements that significantly contribute to a learner's personality development in a purposeful setting. Technology is permeating every aspect of the teaching and learning process; it is neither technology in education nor technology of education. Technology used in education has several facets. It consists of the following –

- The method of creating instruction.
- Using learning theories and styles to inform instructional design.
- Choosing the resources and tools needed to create and put into practice a design.
- The assessment of designs.
- The efficient use of teamwork.
- The application of technology to aid in the creation and delivery of teaching.

Technology and Teaching-Learning Process in the 21st Century

Today's students have quick access to a wealth of Internet resources, which motivates them to conduct research and develop more independence. Concepts are made easier to understand via simplification, such as through the use of an instructional film. It is essential to realize that there are many distinct learning styles and that not every one of them can be catered for by traditional education. For people who struggle in traditional classroom settings, having access to tools like online programmes might help them acquire credentials they otherwise might not have been able to. Technology is essential for holding children's attention so they can learn more efficiently since it may be difficult for them to remain interested in the lessons being taught. In the twenty-first century, technology may assist in giving students an education of a better quality. In the light of digital technologies and the rising relevance of employing technology for teaching and learning at all levels, from school to higher education, National Education Policy 2020 proposes the following significant initiatives:

1) It will be decided which institutions, such as NIOS, CIET, NETF, IITs, NITs, IGNOU, etc., would run a number of pilot studies concurrently to assess the advantages of combining traditional education with online education, develop e-content, etc.
2) Create digital infrastructure for betterment of the education and solve the problems easily.
3) Establish online teaching platform and tools such as SWAYAM, DIKSHA for e-learning and user-friendly assistive tools for monitoring progress of learners.
4) A dependable backup method for distributing digital information and distributing it to students shall be offered.
5) Establish virtual laboratories for instructors and students in SEDG to have appropriate access via appropriate digital devices.
6) To make assessment easily through National Assessment Centre or PARAKH, portfolio, rubrics, etc.

With the use of web technology, students may now obtain certificates online and extend their education by enrolling in schools that provide online courses. Instead of spending money on transportation or moving far away to attend college, they can learn from home. Employed professionals have the option of continuing their education without having to leave their full-time jobs. Since it has made education accessible to everyone, online learning has revolutionized the educational system. Technology is being used to alter how education is provided, whether it be through online learning or simply playing a video in a classroom. The evolution of teaching, which today involves more than just a lecturer in front of a blackboard, has been significantly influenced by technology. Education and how people learn and remember knowledge have been revolutionized. Its involvement in the future of education is essential to preserving the growth and development of the current economy.

Web 1.0 and Its Application in Teaching-Learning Process

The basic structure of the first Web was that a few number of individuals produced web pages, content, and web pages for a sizable audience of readers, enabling them to access facts, information, and content from the sources. Or you might say that Web 1.0 was created to make it easier for users to find information. This online version is frequently nicknamed "the read-only Web" since it lacks the crucial forms, images, controls, and interactivity we enjoy on today's Internet. The first instance of a global network was visible to users, providing a preview of potential future digital communication and information sharing. Applications at that time were also regarded as proprietary because a user could access a programme but not its source code to understand how it operated or modify it. This contrasts with the prevalent "open source" techniques used today. In essence, the Internet gave teachers access to a previously unheard-of audience. Theoretically, a teacher in a remote location may use the Internet to connect with pupils in neighbouring cities or perhaps even abroad. This new form of communication created possibilities we had no idea existed before thanks to specialized websites and electronic mail. It became possible to learn remotely (Simplilearn, 2022; Nufer, 2017).

Web 2.0 and Its Application in Teaching-Learning Process

Many of the arguments are heard from people who are against online learning as an educational technologist centre on the alleged lack of student individualization. These complaints frequently include terminology like "loss of face-to-face engagement" or "encouraging short attention spans". It views the virtual learning process as a depersonalized delivery technique that is no more effective than merely reading a textbook or going to the library, which is a widespread misconception about e-Learning. Although these criticisms may have been valid when Internet-based learning first began, web-based pedagogy currently includes a huge number of efficient delivery strategies that promote fruitful student participation. Here is a quick rundown of several Web 2.0 tools and features that can aid in the facilitation of learning:

1) *Skype/ Zoom/ BlueJeans/ GoToMeeting/ Google Meet* – Students can communicate with teachers and fellow students in real-time or in a synchronous setting using an Internet connection. These systems make use of multimedia technologies to enable webcam/microphone video conferencing between users. Moreover, these tools enable file sharing and online chat.
2) *Blogs* – Several teachers create specific blogs for their courses, similar to the threaded discussion boards in e-College, allowing students to share their research in an online classroom environment and reply to other students' remarks. The educator can then modify the curriculum to reflect the interests of the students.

3) *Wikis* – The idea of the wiki is another cooperative approach to communal constructionist learning paradigms, similar to course blogs. For academic purposes, a wiki offers a digital sandbox where students can expand on the ideas presented in class or conduct their own independent study to develop a theory that can be presented to the entire class. A wiki can be made available to a complete class, divided into smaller groups (think of the jigsaw learning technique), or even with individual student entries.
4) *Cloud-based document sharing* – Several students can collaborate on a single document using tools like OneDrive or Google Docs. The benefit is that each coworker can always instantaneously access the "latest" iteration. The cloud-based servers continuously track document changes, enabling users to see previously stored versions. These apps enable collaboration on spreadsheets, PowerPoint presentations, forms, and even drawings in addition to documents (Nufer, 2017).

They can also contain presentation, research, collaboration, audio, video, slideshow, photographs, music, drawing, writing, organizing, mapping, quiz and test generation, file storage, and web pages in addition to graphing and conversion tools. In order to keep up with the technology that permeates your kids' life, it is critical to stay updated on the most recent developments in education.

Using technology in the classroom may benefit you as a teacher in a number of ways by boosting the students' learning capacity and supporting the instructional objectives. The use of Web 2.0 tools in the classroom is growing, yet some teachers may find them intimidating if they lack technological confidence. The good news is that these products are frequently high user-friendly in design. Anyone may pick them up and utilize them. These resources are flexible, promote teamwork in addressing problems, offer value, raise student participation in learning communities, are reasonably priced, and require little of the instructors' time. Students may cooperate, produce global information, videos, and apps, as well as comment, learn, create, and actively participate in the learning process, with the help of web 2.0 technologies. While the student is the centre of attention, the instructor should act as their mentor and supervisor. Another aspect of Web 2.0 called interactivity allows students to publish, share, and critique one another's work.

The usage of Web 2.0 in education benefits both teachers and pupils. Teachers may provide educational opportunities for pupils utilizing Web 2.0 in a number of ways. There appears to be no end to the promise that wikis, blogs, and other virtual spaces provide for education. With the help of all of these resources, educators and students may use the Internet more as a platform than just a source of knowledge. Example — Google Classroom, Grammarly, Byju's learning app, Flickr, Google Ad Sense, Scribd, Wikipedia etc. (Simplilearn, 2022).

Web 3.0 and Its Application in Teaching-Learning Process

Web 3.0 has an impact on our understanding of the function and potential of technology as we engage with it, particularly in our virtual classrooms. It also has an impact on the visual design domains of our online world. You may have heard the term "semantic web" used to describe Web 3.0. Syntax describes the method of communication. The educational infrastructure now relies on the decentralisation of resources and data in Web 3.0. It enables students to amass knowledge from a variety of sources. To ensure access to a tamper-proof network, the knowledge is subsequently verified and saved on the blockchain network. The technology puts forth concepts like "Proof of Skill" that have the potential to significantly open doors for opportunities in the field of education. (Post & Perishable, 2022; Simplilearn, 2022)

Web 3.0 can make a difference in Education

Enhancing Teaching-Learning Processes – With the help of Web 3.0 technologies, education and learning will undergo a radical transformation. Using the most effective technologies, it claims to improve the teaching and learning process. Using technologies like AI, blockchain, and IoT, Web3 will make it easier for users to access the knowledge base from anywhere on the globe. Incorporating cutting-edge resources into engaging tasks will be made easier for teachers with the usage of technology. Increasingly complex kinds of online instruction will aid in the development of students' creative, analytical, and practical abilities since learners will be able to actively participate in the creation of information. Teachers can transport children to virtual locations while imparting any concepts by Metaverse. IoT (Internet of Things) and AI (Artificial Intelligence) can gain from a more engaging and interactive learning environment. Online instruction is made richer by the use of teleportation, holographic sharing, and immersive visual experiences. Enrolling in a training course will enable one to learn more about the Metaverse blockchain and Metaverse wallet, improving their knowledge of the subject.

Time-Saving – The teaching-learning process would be streamlined by decentralized web technologies to cut down on time-wasting. Less time will be needed for data collection and integration on the part of the learner. Without user input, modern technology will assess user preferences to provide the desired search results. Users may quickly and easily get information what they need. Teachers have access to a wealth of built-in features in a Web3 cluster that may be used to develop compelling, student-centred learning resources. By swiftly analyzing student performance over the previous years, teachers can use the tools to quickly compile a complete report on their students' growth.

Decentralized Education – A single organisation won't be the only credential keeper in a Web3 environment powered by blockchain technology. Students will be developing a strong portfolio of peer-to-peer mentoring, group projects, internships, and college courses. The system will display all of the micro-credentials, prizes, papers, and experience letters on something akin to a digital learning passport. The certificates and documents will be kept and verified on blockchain, making them secure and impervious to fraud.

DAOs against Universities – Through MOOCs, the process of schools, colleges, and universities sharing power and value with other entities has already started. Soon, educational DAOs will be implemented, completely overhauling the current system. In the financial sector, decentralized autonomous organizations are now often used. These groups will help students connect with others who share their interests and values. The participants obtain financial incentives for the contribution made by them to the organisation. They can simply support other team members or cooperate with them on group initiatives. As a working proof, the blockchain contains a record of every transaction.

Earning Opportunities – Web 3.0 is in favour of the 'earn as you learn' concept. The use of technology encourages students' creativity and gives them the platform they need to express it. Learners can easily make a good living as NFT creators. Before putting on their creative hats for such endeavours, they are not required to adhere to any predetermined methodology or meet any age or educational standards.

Personalized Learning – Students now have the choice to personalize educational content they want to access help by Web 3.0. According to their interests, students can study multiple subjects at once and lessen the load of uninteresting subjects that have historically followed them around.

No Boundaries – The education is shifted out of the four-wall classrooms as now with the help of current technologies pupils have the access to top-level education inside their homes. Students' chances of succeeding will rise as a result.

Low cost – The main accomplishment of Web 3.0 is that it enabled students to receive high-quality education at a lower cost despite the fact that everything is getting more and more expensive. By lowering the cost of investing, this will eventually boost profitability for the education sector.

Quality of Education – With the use of small electronic devices and a number of government initiatives that would not have been possible without the assistance of the technological advancements made possible by Web 3.0, children from underprivileged social groups can now have access to the highest quality education.

Democratization of Education – With the help of Web 3.0, anyone with a higher level of education may now launch their own educational institute for the cheapest price and cater to the largest possible audience of students. In the past, education was a very expensive industry that was governed by a particular elite group of individuals with the financial resources to run the enterprise. Everyone now has equal power. They each have an equal chance to establish a prosperous educational business if they have the necessary skills and capabilities.

Higher Education while Working – As a result of the introduction of multiple online learning programmes by Web 3.0, working professionals can now receive degrees through these programmes, and given the current market, many multinational corporations also recognize them (Aswal, 2022).

Conclusion

Today, sharing technology with others is not only desirable, but also essential for the 21st Century's Citizen. Yet, Internet and computer-based collaboration tends to be more common outside of schools than inside of them (Becta, 2008). Even if they are taught how to critically and properly use online information and services, students can access websites like Wikipedia and share files, photos, and podcasts. The process of teaching and learning must account for fresh viewpoints and the requirement to work in a more dynamic setting than most teachers were trained to handle. The difficulties of the vast quantity and diversity of digital information available as well as the continual development of new platforms for individualized learning have pushed the necessity for cooperation as the primary method of information retention. Such collaboration involves new techniques that must change the power dynamics of individuals engaged in educational activities, and it is not just between teachers and students in the school setting, it rather seeks their cohesive involvement. One of the most impressive and significant social networks promised benefits, saying that the control is now in the interaction process and not any longer within the primary responsibilities of the teacher.

References

An, Y. J., Aworuwa, B., Ballard, G. & Williams, K. (2009). "Teaching with Web 2.0 Technologies: Benefits, Barriers and Best Practices." *Association for Educational Communications and Technology,* 1-6.

Aswal, P. (2022). How Web3 Can Revolutionize the Education Sector? Retrieved from https://www.blockchain-council.org/web-3/how-web3-can-revolutionize-the-education-sector.

Becta. (2008). Implementing Web 2.0 in Secondary Schools: Impacts, Barriers and Issues. 1-39. Retrieved from https://dera.ioe.ac.uk/1538/1/becta-2008-ht-consolidated_trends_1of4_report.pdf.

Deebom, M.T. & Amaso, T.F. (2017). "The Application of Web 2.0 in Enhancing Teaching and Learning of Technology Educational Courses in Tertiary Institutions in Rivers State." *International Journal of Advanced Academic Research,* 3(4), 22-33.

Dominic, M., Francis, S. & Pilomenraj, A. (2014). E-Learning in Web 3.0. *I. J. Modern Education and Computer Science*, 2, 8-14. https://doi.org/10.5815/ijmecs.2014.02.02.

Epistemo, (2021). *Use of technology in 21st-century education - epistemo.* Retrieved from https://epistemo.in/blog/the-growing-use-of-technology-in-21st-century-education-2.

Feldmann, B. (2014). *Two Decades of e-learning in Distance Teaching – From Web 1.0 to Web 2.0* at the University of Hagen. Springer International Publishing, 446, 163-172. https://doi.org/10.1007/978-3-319-10671-7_16.

Gupta, A. K., Katiyar, D. & Goel, G. (2022). Web 3.0 and its Reflections on the Future of ELearning. *International Journal for Research in Applied Science & Engineering Technology*, 10(IV), 207-512. https://doi.org/10.22214/ijraset.2022.41293.

Knowledgexpert. (2023). Benefits & effects of using technology in the classroom. *KnowledgeXpert*. Retrieved from https://knowldgexpert.com/benefits-effects-of-using-technology-in-the-classroom.

Majid, I. & Verma, S. (2018). "Web 2.0 Technological Tools in Teaching and Learning. *International Journal of Education,* 10, 55-60.

Naik, U. & Shivalingaiah, D. (2008). Comparative Study of Web 1.0, Web 2.0 and Web 3.0. *6th International CALIBER 2008 Conference*, 499-507. https://doi.org/10.13140/2.1.2287. 2961.

National Educational Policy 2020. Retrieved from https://www.education.gov.in/ sites/upload_files/mhrd/files/NEP_Final_English_0.pdf

Nufer, S. (2017). A Brief History of Online Learning (and Where Do We Go From Here?). Retrieved from https://innovedtech.com/blog/2017/9/25/a-brief-history-of-online-learning-and-where-do-we-go-from-here.

Owston, R.D. (1997). "Research news and comment: The World Wide Web: A technology to enhance teaching and learning?" *Educational Researcher*, *26*(2), 27–33. https://doi.org/10.3102/0013189X026002027.

Parankimalil, J. (2015). Role of educational technology in the teaching-learning process. John Parankimalil. Retrieved from https://johnparankimalil.wordpress.com/2015/01/21/role-of-educational-technology-in-the-teaching-learning-process.

Post, E. & Perishable. (2022). what is web 3.0's impact on the education system? Advantages and technologies of web 3.0. *IIRF*. Retrieved from https://iirfranking.com/blog/education/what-is-web-3-0s-impact-education-system-advantages-technologies.

Prabhu, D. (2016). "Application of Web 2.0 and Web 3.0: An Overview." *International Journal of Research in Library Science*, 2(1), 54-62.

Simões, L. & Gouveia, L. (2009). Teaching on a Web 2.0 Environment. *VI Conferência Internacional de TIC na Educação - Challenges 2009, Universidade do Minho*, 1-11.

Simplilearn.Com (2022). *What is Web 1.0, Web 2.0, and Web 3.0? Definitions, Differences & Similarities*. Retrieved from https://www.simplilearn.com/what-is-web-1-0-web-2-0-and-web-3-0-with-their-difference-article.

Victor, S. R. & Mohammed, A. A. (2016). "Evolution of Web 3.0 Technologies in the Sector of Education." *Indian Journal of Applied Research,* 6(8), 212-214.

4

Soft Skills in the 21st Century

Educational Needs and Practices

Swarup Chandi
Puja Sarkar (Bal)

Introduction

In recent times, with the swift progression of technology and the emergence of diverse and collaborative workplaces, the significance of soft skills has escalated. It plays a crucial role in shaping an individual's social interactions, augmenting their professional efficacy, and elevating their career opportunities. In the contemporary era, soft skills, commonly referred to as interpersonal skills, are indispensable for achieving success. Soft skills refer to a set of personal attributes, including attitudes, and habits, that define an individual's character and influence their interactions with others. It has been found that in many studies, lack of soft skills leads to lack of motivation, noncompliance, erratic conduct, deceit, contention, and scepticism among learners. Further, soft skills are acquired behaviours that necessitate training and application in specific domain. It has been found in different literatures that, soft skills are comparatively hard to measure than hard or technical skills. However, these competencies can be attained through academic pursuits, professional endeavours, and personal encounters. The investigators discussed here the idea of soft skills, and why it is important, and what should be done to nurture the soft skills in individuals or students. It focused here on the various initiatives that may be taken by academic as well as corporate organizations to betterment of their people on soft skills. The present study is qualitative in nature.

Globalisation has become a buzz word in the twenty-first century. It expedites global trade and mobility (of people, things, services, societal systems, money, technologies, or cultural practices). It has also unified people of different nationalities, religions, and ethnicities in the workplace (Peter & Simatupang, 2019). Additionally, globalisation has increased the diversity and specialisation in the corporate sector. Due to this, the corporate sector is becoming more complex, and competitive. Business groups are working to acknowledge this transition as well. As a result, there is a greater appetite for individuals with specialist knowledge and abilities to administer the system. Majority employers tend to favour individuals who exhibit traits such as dependability, resourcefulness, ethical behaviour, effective communication skills, self-direction, a willingness to learn and work, and a positive attitude (Wats & Wats, 2009). Employers typically prioritise a well-rounded set of competencies in their workforce. Along with expertise and abilities specific to their field, possessing sufficient levels of attributes related to personality is viewed as profitable for advancing in one's career (Mitchel et al., 2010). The individual holds the belief that organisational goals and objectives cannot be attained solely through the utilisation of professional and technical skills. This is due to the fact that their personnel will also participate in various tiers of leadership and decision-making endeavours. Effective communication within the organisation, as well as with customers and other stakeholders, is a crucial requirement for employees. In this case, education plays a role in the development of such competencies and skills while maintaining the ability to develop hard skills and expertise in particular areas and these are called soft skills. Only education is a process which mainly organise such arrangements in the form of instruction, training, workshop, seminar through which people are skillfully competent in soft skills. Then they have availed the opportunities by the employer to join a corporate sector; through which, education fulfilled his duty and employers of the future labour market also get human resources with proper skills. In this perspective, it may be called, soft skills are bridging the gap between academics and the corporate sector. However, soft skills are as important in the perspective of employment as well as academics at present. Soft skills in business that allow individuals to interact harmoniously and efficiently with others, collaborate effectively, efficiently manage their time, and maintain a positive attitude towards the work environment and work processes. Similarly in academics, it also helps in the holistic development of individual's personality, motivates to work collaboratively with fellow students, solve a problem by oneself and stick to problem solving, not only that but also encourage creative thinking and critical thinking among them. Such skill makes them confident in interpersonal as well intrapersonal communication. Soft skills are indispensable not only in professional settings but also in daily life. The acquisition of these competencies is crucial for the cultivation of efficient human resources, which can subsequently contribute to the advancement of the nation (Staboulis & Lazaridou, 2020). Guglielmi (2015) conducted a study and opined that soft skills play a critical role in enhancing capacity building and expanding network building. Furthermore, it enhances one's knowledge, thereby augmenting their employability skills. Engelberg (2015) asserts that soft skills hold considerable importance as they contribute significantly to emotional intelligence, motivation, and temperament. Simultaneously, Cinque's (2015) states that possessing soft skills is crucial for enhancing one's employability and attaining personal fulfilment. The literature has identified several soft skills that are deemed significant in the workplace. These include communication, teamwork, motivation, problem-solving, enthusiasm, and trust (Chute, 2012; Ellis, Kisling & Hackworth, 2014; Rasul, Rauf & Mansor, 2013; Robles, 2012; Wahl et al., 2012). It has desirable characteristics for certain types of employment that do not rely on acquired knowledge; they include common sense, the ability to deal with people, and a positive, flexible attitude (Robles, 2012).

What are Soft Skills?

The concept of "soft skill" encompasses a wide-ranging and interdisciplinary construct that has been characterised in diverse manners, including but not limited to 21st century skills, non-cognitive skills, character skills, and life skills (Park et al., 2017). For the purpose of maintaining consistency with other fields such as economics, politics, and education, the researcher employs the term "soft skill" in this paper (Heckman & Kautz, 2012; Laker & Powell, 2011; Pellegrino & Hilton, 2012; Robles, 2012) to aid in facilitating the discussion.

In order to equip the next generation with the necessary skills to confront the complexities of contemporary society, it is imperative that the curriculum of the 21st century be designed accordingly. Conventional educational systems are structured to equip students with basic literacy skills but have not been adequately equipped to address the demands of contemporary society. According to Kwon (2008), soft skills have emerged as the primary determinant of career success in the contemporary era, with a marked preference for soft skills in career selection. According to Zhang (2012), these are a collection of beneficial behavioural attributes that depict individual's interactions within a societal setting. This pertains to an individual's way of thinking and belief. They are primarily influenced by personality traits rather than competencies. According to Park et al. (2004) and Robles (2012), "soft skills refer to adaptable personal attributes that manage our emotional, behavioural, and cognitive conditions, facilitating successful communication with others and the attainment of individual objectives". The aforementioned attributes pertain to individual temperament, specifically adaptability, perseverance, curiosity, and leadership. According to Heckman and Kautz (2012), "Soft skills as personality traits, goals, motivations, as well as preferences valued in the labour market, in school, and in many other domains". These entities are quite intangible, readily observable, but hardly quantifiable. They influence personality. In the current age of intense competition, significant efforts are being made to enhance it. According to Wikipedia (2007), "Soft skills refer to the cluster of personality traits, social graces, facility with language, personal habits, friendliness, and optimism that mark people to varying degrees. It complements hard skills, which are the technical requirements of a job." In this regard, Gates et al. (2016) opined that "Soft skills are a broad set of skills, behaviours, and personal qualities that enable people to effectively navigate their environment, relate well with others, perform well, and achieve their goals. These skills are applicable across sectors and complement the acquisition of other skills such as technical and academic skills." At present days, it is playing an important role in the holistic development of pupils and may perhaps help to govern their future employability and performance in any walk of their life they wish to go (Fallows & Steven, 2000; Washer, 2007). It is also crucial for enhancing one's employability and attaining personal fulfilment.

Various organizations, as well as experts, have made an effort to classify such attributes cum skills, which are summed up as soft skills. Such as the International Bureau of Education (IBE) has provided a framework regarding the soft skills, which are:

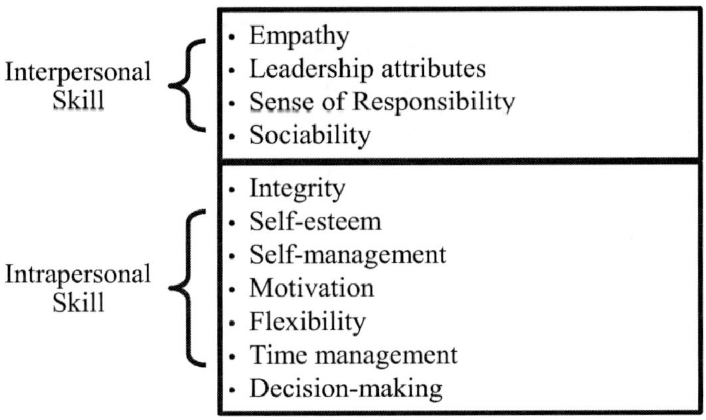

Figure 4.1: *List of Soft Skills*

Source: International Bureau of Education (IBE)

In this regard, the World Economic Forum (2016) again proposed a tripartite model based on economic demands and needs of education, which is as follows:

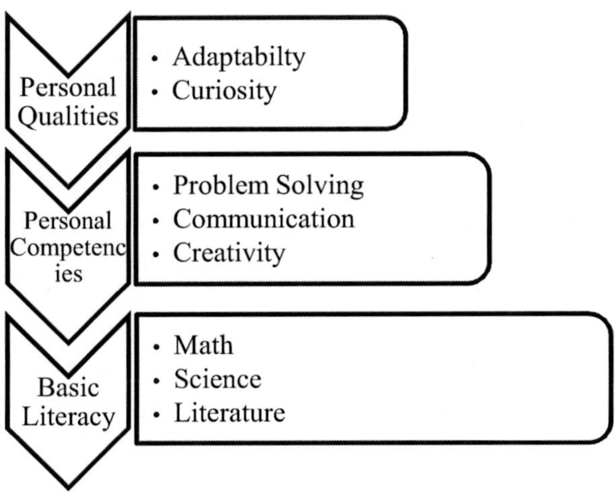

Figure 4.2: *List of Soft Skills*

Source: WEF, 2016

Keeping in mind Wikipedia's definition of soft skills, renowned career consultant Challa Ram Phani (2007) published an article under the headline "The top 60 soft skills at work", and gave a broad list of soft skills, that fall under the categories of personal qualities, interpersonal skills, and additional skills/knowledge. This broad list is shown in the Table 4.1:

Table 4.1: *Personal Qualities, Interpersonal Skills and Additional Skills/Knowledge*

Personal Qualities	*Interpersonal Skills*	*Additional Skills/Knowledge*
Cultural awareness	Communication skills	Responsibility
Common knowledge	Teamwork capability	Etiquette and good manners
Time Management	Negotiating skills	Courtesy
Problem Solving Skills	Conflict management	Integrity / Honesty
Critical and structured thinking	Empathy	Project management
Self-management	Sociability	Business management
Creativity		Work ethic
Self-esteem		

Source: Phani, 2007

In this regard, Whitmore (2012) has listed some skills-cum-personality attributes as soft skills and given proper justification regarding why they are important in the present days. These are—

1) *Critical thinking*: It refers to the capacity to engage in a systematic and analytical thought process aimed at effectively addressing a given problem or challenge. The act of thinking encompasses the resolution of issues, the formulation of deductions, the computation of livelihoods, and the making of determinations, all of which require the thinker to employ thoughtful and effective skills that are appropriate for the given context and type of thinking task. It is equally relevant in academics and corporate sector.
2) *Problem solving*: It is a multifaceted skill that involves the integration of various soft skills such as decision-making, leadership, and teamwork. The process of problem solving begins with the identification and definition of the pertinent issues. Subsequently, alternative solutions are formulated and evaluated, and the most suitable solution is implemented.
3) *Public speaking:* It was originally defined as the act of delivering a speech in person to a live audience. However, in modern times, it encompasses any form of speech delivery, both formal and informal, to an audience, including pre-recorded speeches transmitted over long distances through technological means. Effective public speaking is a valuable soft skill that necessitates exceptional communication abilities, enthusiasm, and the capacity to actively involve the audience.

4) *Professional writing:* It refers to writing for monetary gain or as an occupation. It encompasses any written communication produced within a workplace setting or context that facilitates effective communication among employees. This form of writing enables individuals to make informed decisions, provide guidance to clients, and bid on contracts, among other things.
5) *Teamwork:* It refers to the collective and coordinated endeavour of a group of individuals aimed at accomplishing a shared objective or executing a task with optimal productivity and efficacy. Having the ability to discern when to assume a leadership role and when to adopt a receptive stance necessitates a combination of intuitive and interpersonal skills. The amalgamation of various soft skills is a fundamental aspect of this particular soft skill.
6) *Digital literacy*: It refers to the capacity to proficiently employ information and communication technologies for the purposes of locating, assessing, generating, and disseminating information. This pertains to the grammatical composition, typing skills, and capability to write and generate visual, auditory, and graphic content through technological means. Originally, here the emphasis was placed on digital proficiency and independent computing systems. However, with the emergence of the Internet and the prevalence of social media, there has been a shift in attention towards mobile devices.
7) *Leadership:* It is an important soft skill in present day, which is characterized as a process whereby an individual is able to secure the assistance and support of others in the attainment of a shared and common goal. Effective leadership is frequently contingent upon the leader's capacity to devise strategies, attentively consider feedback, and integrate the concepts and contributions of their team members. Possessing a leadership skill set entails the capacity to motivate individuals and guide groups towards achieving their objectives.
8) *Work ethic:* It is a positive soft skill that manifests an attitude of determination and dedication towards one's work. The concept that works and effort possess an intrinsic capacity, attribute, or worth to confer ethical advantages and enhance individual traits and competencies. The possession of strong work ethics is a key factor in an individual's ability to excel in their professional endeavours. Instances of work ethic encompass traits such as commitment, trustworthiness, and discipline, among others.
9) *Creativity*: It is a valuable soft skill that enables individuals to generate novel and inventive solutions to a wide range of problems. The ability to engage in creative thinking facilitates ongoing learning and the exploration of new frontiers. The utilization of creativity can facilitate the process of ideation and problem-solving, by means of generating novel ideas through questioning and brainstorming.

Apart from that, upon examining several prominent studies (Voogt & Roblin, 2010, 2012, Scott, 2015, Chalkiadaki, 2018), it becomes evident that a distinct set of abilities, proficiencies, and characteristics are consistently mentioned in the literature pertaining to Soft Skills or 21st Century Skills. The aforementioned themes pertain to five principal domains that are predominantly linked to professional characteristics. These are:

- Communication skills, including language and presentation of ideas;
- Collaborative skills, including management of group activities and social interaction;
- Individual learning approaches, including critical thinking, metacognition and new skills acquisition;
- Individual autonomy, including flexibility, adaptability, and entrepreneurship; and
- ICT and digital literacy, including use of technology as tools for learning, communication, and collaboration.

Also featured are a number of core knowledge areas, including:

- Literacy,
- Numeracy, and
- STEM-associated fields of knowledge.

Finally, there are certain personal characteristics that are also widely regarded by experts as essential for achieving a fulfilling existence in the modern era. These include:

- Physical well-being and personal health;
- Social and emotional skills;
- Social citizenship; and
- Cultural and creative expression.

It has the potential to be utilised across a diverse range of occupations. Given their wide-ranging applicability, it is often regarded as valuable, although the notion of transferability is sometimes subject to scrutiny due to the fact that individuals acquire proficiency in specific contexts and may not be able to apply these skills in alternative settings. Soft skills encompass a variety of personal attributes and traits that enable individuals to effectively interact with others and navigate complex social situations. The term 'soft skills' is often used in opposition to 'hard' skills. These skills are typically more technical, occupation-specific, and can be taught with greater ease than soft skills. Both have complemented each other in individual's success in a particular field.

Why Soft Skills are Important in the Era of the 21st Century?

Due to globalization, today's world has been growing rapidly. In this situation, only hard skills or domain knowledge are not sufficient to cope with this change. Need some additional knowledge or skills, called soft skills or transversal skills, or 21st century skills. Various international and national organizations also accept the importance of soft skills, and even different countries take into account in mind regarding the importance of soft skills in the time of framing policy. In this regard, UNICEF stated that soft skills are currently gaining prominence due to their ability to enhance adaptability and resilience in a world undergoing rapid transformation. They facilitate navigation. Possessing key skills is crucial for securing employment, advancing in a career, and professional success. Corporations and institutions of higher education possess this understanding. The contemporary understanding of the significance of Soft Skills is on par with that of Hard Skills. Enhancing one's proficiency in both areas leads to improved performance in each. ILO also agrees with UNICEF. The National Education Policy for 2020 (NEP 2020) declares that the goal of education will not only be cognitive growth but also character building and generating holistic and well-rounded individuals with 21st century key abilities, i.e., soft skills, that supported the holistic development of learners. And here it has been acknowledged that soft skills are critical and should be emphasized together with other fields of knowledge needed in the 21st century. Incorporated with this NCERT stated that Soft skills referred to as non-technical skills, pertain to an individual's personal values and interpersonal abilities that influence their ability to collaborate effectively with others within a project team. The acquisition of soft skills is imperative for effectively navigating the external environment and engaging in cooperative endeavours with fellow professionals. The aforementioned competencies encompass proficient communication, adept leadership, and collaborative aptitudes; exhibiting adeptness in problem-solving, proactivity, and drive; evincing integrity and robust professional principles. The significance of soft skills cannot be overlooked in the contemporary knowledge-based society, as they are crucial for both academic and professional achievements. These skills enable individuals to thrive in their workplace and contribute to their success. Soft skills are necessary for effectively navigating the external environment and engaging in cooperative teamwork with fellow professionals. The Central Board of Secondary Education (CBSE) has acknowledged the significance of soft skills in contemporary times. The Central Board of Secondary Education (CBSE) has reaffirmed the discourse of the National Education Policy 2020 (NEP 2020) regarding the significance of soft skills. It has been emphasised that soft skills are essential competencies that an individual must possess for their comprehensive growth. This enables them to make valuable contributions toward the advancement and prosperity of their society, nation, and the world. The ability to confront the obstacles of a digitally evolving, globally engaged, collaboratively advancing, creatively developing, change-oriented 21st century society and to acquire competent human resources is facilitated by this skill.

After the above discussion, the importance of soft skills at present days has been realized and accepted as a crucial factor of success in any field. And here again, the investigator pointed out shortly the importance of soft skills. These are:

- It helps to shape an individual's personality by effectively dealing with the three domains, i.e. the cognitive, psychomotor, and affective domains of individuals.
- It encourages people to work together towards a common objective and enables individuals to express themselves more vividly.
- The acquisition of skills such as effective communication, time management, a positive work ethic, and the cultivation of interpersonal relationships can enhance an individual's employability.
- It helps to develop various traits of leadership in individuals.
- Assists individuals in developing informed decision-making skills.

How to Nurture Soft Skills among the People?

From the above discussion, it is observed that along with core knowledge or hard skills, the importance of soft skills is equally relevant nowadays. But this is not a new skill, just a collection of behavioural characteristics. All these characteristics as well as skills in children develop gradually with age. Therefore, necessary steps should be taken to develop these skills or qualities in them from an early age.

In the 21st century, it is proven that soft skills are a key factor for a human being, which has been discussed in the earlier section. So, we need to take various initiatives through introducing new training courses or adding a bit of additional knowledge or skills in the existing training programme for prospective individuals as well as for managers or administrators in this sector. And it needs to organize as early as possible for the education system and corporate world (Adheisat, 2022). Otherwise, the population will be limited to a number only, but those people will be of no use to the country and society and will become a burden on the country. But if they are given proper training and necessary steps are taken then it can be considered as a boon for any country. So, here the current investigator tries to generalize various initiatives, which have been recommended in various studies. The following initiatives are:

- *Frame a curriculum based on amalgamation of the needs of academia, corporation and society:* If the primary priority on the development of soft skills in the students, then the time of curriculum development should amalgamate the aims of education, corporate needs, and societal needs. As a result of which, various attributes from among the three aspects can be integrated here. After that, anything does not leave here, that is needed to get for an individual. It is the duty of the curriculum developer or course coordinator to do this. In this way also soft skill development can be done in the students.
- *Organize various co-curricular activities in the time of teaching-learning or period of fresher training programme:* Organize various co-curricular

activities (i.e., conduct impromptu debate, ask the cross-questioning, use SCAMPER (i.e., substitute, combine, adapt, modify, put, eliminate, reverse) mnemonic to ask questions during teaching-learning or training period of individuals, use brainstorming, etc. simultaneously in the time of curriculum transaction, which mainly promotes following soft skills, such as teamwork, resilience, perseverance, creative thinking, critical thinking, problem solving etc. (CBSE, 2020). Apart from that, students should encourage to join various systematic and tier-based leadership development, charitable endeavours, open pulpits, as well as various joint activities between student organizations. This type of activity helps to building leadership, cooperation, collaboration, empathy, respect, public speaking, and other virtues.

- *Additionally add the various short-term courses in parent programme:* In any parent programme at any level, various short-term compulsory or elective courses should be included. These directly or indirectly help to promote soft skills during the time of gaining domain knowledge or technical skills in a particular programme. Keeping in mind, at present in India, the two compulsory courses or papers, i.e., Ability enhancement course and Skill enhancement course have been added in Undergraduate and Postgraduate programmes by UGC. Where these papers or courses deal to promote efficiency or capability or skills of the 21st century in students.
- Schulz (2008) opined that there are two methods we can use to improve our soft skills. One way is enrolling for formal training, e.g. taking evening classes on rhetoric, languages, presentation skills, conflict or cultural management. The other way of acquiring soft skills we look at is self-training, usually based on books. As we saw earlier, changing personal traits often requires long-term practice, and therefore self-training might be more useful regarding the improvement of this category of soft skills. Additionally, during the last decade another method of self-training has become increasingly popular: Electronic Learning, usually abbreviated to e-learning.
- Apart from that, one needs to conduct various short-term courses for administrators as well as teachers. This will cover the recent initiatives, and strategies as well as various emerging skills regarding a particular profession and help them to realize how it is important for individuals. However, currently such courses are conducted in academic as well as corporate fields. Hope it will help to transmit this knowledge or skills to individuals.
- In addition, various seminars, workshops etc. related to soft skills can be organized for individuals as well as teachers, students, and administrative officials, where the awareness about soft skills among them can be made aware of its importance nowadays. But this effort will remain entirely on an unconscious level, unless it is brought to a practical level, it will achieve nothing.

Apart from that, the following teaching approaches may be used for the development of various soft skills in the students (Mawas et al., 2018). These are:

Problem Based Learning: It enables learners to engage in research, synthesise theoretical and practical knowledge, and utilise their competencies to devise a feasible solution to a specific problem (Savery, 2006). The utilisation of the 4Cs Principle (critical thinking, communication, collaboration and creativity) and teaching for transfer renders it an optimal approach for fulfilling the objectives of contemporary education in the twenty-first century (Scott, 2015). Furthermore, it serves as a source of motivation for learners to effectively allocate their time and resources while also publicly showcasing their work. Problem-Based Learning (PBL) is a pedagogical approach that fosters the development of flexible knowledge, problem identification and problem-solving skills, self-directed learning, and effective collaboration skills among students (Christiansen et al., 2013; Hmelo-Silver, 2004).

Flipped Classroom (FC): It plays a significant role in fostering the development of 21st century skills. This approach fosters self-directed learning, analytical reasoning, cooperative work, proficiency in technology, responsible online behaviour, innovation, and interpersonal competencies. The relocation of direct instruction beyond the confines of the classroom setting fosters an environment that promotes metacognitive learning and self-directed learning among students. It fosters critical thinking among students, thereby stimulating their inquisitiveness and expanding their intellectual horizons. The FC approach facilitates efficient collaboration among students through the use of social media platforms beyond the confines of the school environment. In addition, the classroom serves as a central location for engaging in constructive discourse with peers, engaging in introspection, and receiving guidance on writing tasks. The utilisation of technology for accessing educational content, engaging in interactive activities, and collaborating with peers promotes the development of students' digital literacy. This is due to the fact that learners leverage their personal devices as tools for learning and growth, rather than solely for social purposes. FC fosters a collaborative digital learning environment that instils fundamental values of respect and cooperation in the realm of online interactions among students. This is the reason why their proficiency in digital citizenship has improved. The acquisition of knowledge beyond the confines of the classroom environment has been shown to enhance the creative and innovative capacities of students. Through the transformation of the traditional classroom into an interactive and cooperative learning environment, students are able to enhance their social competencies.

Self-Directed Learning (SDL): It is a process whereby individuals take responsibility for their own learning by identifying their learning needs, setting learning goals, selecting appropriate learning strategies, and evaluating their learning outcomes (Knowles, 1975). The utilisation of SDL is conducive to the development of 21st century skills such as creativity and innovation. According to Herring (2012), self-directed learners exhibit traits of risk-taking and a dedication to continuous learning. These characteristics enable them to excel by distinguishing their abilities and utilising informal learning technologies at their disposal.

Computer Supported Collaborative Learning (CSCL): It is a pedagogical approach that promotes the development of students' ability to view situations from multiple perspectives, fosters an environment conducive to the cultivation of social and leadership skills, and offers a satisfactory learning experience that effectively mitigates anxiety (Garcia-Valcarcel et al., 2014). The field of Computer-Supported Collaborative Learning (CSCL) investigates the utilisation of technology as a means of providing scaffolding to facilitate collaborative efforts and promote advanced cognitive processes. Numerous research endeavours have been conducted to investigate the extent to which computer-supported collaborative learning (CSCL) facilitates the development of advanced cognitive skills, particularly those related to argumentation, such as the ability to provide justifications for a given idea, locate supporting evidence, and arrive at a sound conclusion (Linuma, 2015). In the end, it would be logical to say that in all cases one has to put in one's own effort to develop one's soft skills. Only then his self-development is possible.

Concluding Remarks

From the above discussion, it has been realized that soft skills are important in every sphere of our life in the present time. It helps us to shape our personality as well as all-around development. So, the present hours need to develop soft skills in the torchbearer of society. In this regard, needs have to play the different roles of various social institutions. But in reality, if it is observed, then it will be realized that these pictures are different. Even today in the educational institutions of our country, the so-called method of teaching and learning is used and there is emphasis only on the subjects of intellectual practice. Apart from this, there are some qualities or skills or to be clearer, there are some things, which are helpful in the formation and development of our personality and are relevant in the current era of globalization, but even today our society does not realize their importance. And even if there is, it is limited to the upper and middle strata of the society and is treated in the same way in the educational institutions adjacent to it. But for the rest of the society it is beyond imagination. After all, three national education policies (1986, 1992 & 2020) have been formulated till the 75th Independence Day of our country, at a certain time interval. In every educational policy, apart from the mentioned subjects, various other subjects and skills have been included in the curriculum as ancillary subjects to ensure the overall development of the personality and to ensure future employment. Not only that, the use of new and different perspectives and methods during the execution of teaching-learning tasks have also been mentioned. But in the field of education, the government in our country fulfills their responsibilities jointly, that is, the state and central governments jointly fulfill their responsibilities in the field of education. The state government oversees some parts of education, for example, certain states take specific decisions regarding school level education, while the central government mainly formulates and monitors various rules and policies related to higher education, but in both cases state and central governments mutually take the final decision. But due to various reasons disparity is still observed in different levels of education system. Wide gaps are currently observed among students with respect to various factors such as access to facilities as well as curriculum design, learning outcomes. Not only this, this discrimination is observed in different types of boards or educational institutions. At present, all these disparities should be removed as much as possible and human resources should be developed in accordance with the requirements of the era of globalization like the 21st century. In this regard, the government as well as policy makers and teachers all have to play a beneficial role. And it is hoped that they will be successful in this work and will be able to develop the future artisans of the society in a better way.

References

Adheisat, M. (2022). Family Educational Role in Developing Social Skills in Kindergarten Children of Jordan. *Journal of Positive School Psychology*, 6(5), 1236–1253.

Chalkiadaki, A. (2018). A systematic literature review of 21st Century Skills and competencies in primary education. *International Journal of Instruction, 11*(3), 1–16. Retrieved from http://www.e-iji.net/dosyalar/iji_2018_3_1.pdf

Christiansen, E. T., Kuure, L., Morch, A. and Lindström, B. (2013). Problem-based Learning for the 21st Century: New Practices and Learning Environments. Aalborg Universitetsforlag

Chute, M. (2012). A core for flexibility. *Information Services & Use, 32*, 143–147.

Cinque, M., (November 2015). Comparative analysis of Soft Skill identification and training – New perspectives.

Ellis, M., Kisling, E., & Hackworth, R. (2014). Teaching soft skills employers need. *Community College Journal of Research & Practice, 38*, 433–453. doi:10.1080/10668926.2011.567143

Engelberg, S. (November 2015). A developmental Perspective on Skills' Speech 'Soft Skills and their role'.

Fallows, S. and Steven, C. (2000). "Building employability skills into the higher education curriculum: a university-wide initiative", *Education+Training*, 42(2), 75-83. https://doi.org/10.1108/00400910010331620

Garcia-Valcarcel, A., Basilotta, V. and Lopez, C. (2014). ICT in Collaborative Learning in the Classrooms of Primary and Secondary Education. *Comunicar*, 21(42), 65

Gates, S., Lippman, L., Shadowen, N., Burke, H., Diener, O., & Malkin, M. (2016). *Key soft skills for cross-sectoral youth outcomes*. Washington, DC: USAID's Youth Power: Implementation, Youth Power Action.

Guglielmi, D. (November 2015). Employability: competencies to manage boundary less careers. Speech on Soft Skills.

Heckman, J.J., & Kautz, T. (2012). Hard evidence on soft skills. Labour Economics, 19(4), 451–464. https://doi.org/10.1016/j.labeco.2012.05.014

Herring, S. (2012). Transforming the workplace: Critical skills and learning methods for the successful 21st century worker. *Big Think.*

Hmelo-Silver, C.E. (2004). Problem-based learning: What and how do students learn? *Educ. Psychol. Rev.*, 16(3), 235–266

Knowles, M.S. (1975). Self-directed learning.

Kwon, S. (2008). Open up the ceiling on the common core state standard: preparing students for 21st century literacy –now. *Journal of adolescent and adult literacy*, 56 (4), 321-330

Laker, D.R., & Powell, J.L. (2011). The differences between hard and soft skills and their relative impact on training transfer. *Human Resource Development Quarterly*, 22(1), 111–122. https://doi.org/10.1002/hrdq.20063

Linuma, M. (2015). Learning and Teaching with Technology in the Knowledge Society: New Literacy, Collaboration and Digital Content. Springer.

Mawas, N. & Muntean, C. (2018). Supporting lifelong learning through development of 21st century skills. Conference: 10th International Conference on Education and New Learning Technologies, 7343-7350, 10.21125/edulearn.2018.1723.

Mitchell, G.W., Skinner, L.B., & White, B.J. (2010). Essential soft skills for success in the twenty-first century workforce as perceived by business educators. *Delta Pi Epsilon Journal, 52*(1), 43-53.

Park, D., Tsukayama, E., Goodwin, G.P., Patrick, S., & Duckworth, A.L. (2017). A tripartite taxonomy of character: Evidence for intrapersonal, interpersonal, and intellectual competencies in children. *Contemporary Educational Psychology*, 48, 16–27. https://doi.org/10.1016/j.cedpsych.2016.08.001

Pellegrino, J.W., & Hilton, M.L. (2012). Education for Life and Work: Developing transferable knowledge and skills in the 21st century. National Academy of Sciences.

Phani, C.R. (2007). The top 60 soft skills at work. http://in.rediff.com/getahead/2007/jan/08soft.htm

Ramot, P., & Simatupang, M.S. (2019). Teamwork soft skill development in facing the globalization. *International Journal of Engineering and Advanced Technology*, *8*(5C), 486–491. https://doi.org/10.35940/ijeat.E1069.0585C19

Rasul, M., Rauf, R., & Mansor, A. (2013). Employability skills indicator as perceived by manufacturing employees. *Asian Social Science, 9*, 42–46. doi:10.5539/ass.v9n8p42

Robles, M. M. (2012). Executive perceptions of the top 10 soft skills needed in today's workplace. *Business Communication Quarterly*, 75(4), 453–465. https://doi.org/10.1177/1080569912460400

Robles, M.M. (2012). Executive Perceptions of the Top 10 Soft Skills Needed in Today's Workplace. Business Communication Quarterly, 75(4), 453–465. https://doi.org/10.1177/1080569912460400

Savery, J.R. (2006). Overview of problem-based learning: Definitions and distinctions, *Interdiscip. J. Probl.-Based Learn.*, 1(1), 3

Schulz, B. (2008). The Importance of Soft Skills: Education beyond academic knowledge. *Journal of language and communication*, 146-154.

Scott, Cynthia, L. S. (2015). *The futures of learning 2: What kind of learning for the 21st century?* (ERF Working Paper No. 14). Paris: UNESCO Education Research and Foresight. https://unesdoc.unesco.org/ark:/48223/pf0000242996

Staboulis, M. & Lazaridou, I. (2020). Worldwide Approaches of Soft Skills Training as a Strategy Factor of ROI Growth. 4633–4639. https://doi.org/10.21125/edulearn.2020.1220

Voogt, J., & Roblin, N.P. (2010). *21st Century Skills* (Discussion Paper). Enschede: University of Twente.

Voogt, J., & Roblin, N.P. (2012). A comparative analysis of international frameworks for 21st century competences: Implications for national curriculum policies. *Journal of Curriculum Studies, 44*(3),299–321.doi:10.1080/00220272.2012.668938

Wahl, H. et al. (2012). Soft skills in practice and in education: An evaluation. *American Journal of Business Education, 5*, 225–232.

Washer, P. (2007). Revisiting key skills: A practical framework for higher education. *Journal of Quality in Higher Education*, 13(1), 57-67.

Wats, M., & Wats, R.K. (2009). Developing soft skills in students. *The International Journal of Learning,* 15(12), 1-10.

Whitmore, K. (2012). Which defense against what? A study to explore future concepts of security and defense. *International Journal of Future Studies, 8 (4) 1-19.*

Zhang, T. (2012). Preparing students for educated living: virtues of problem-based learning across the higher education curriculum. *New directions for teaching and learning, 24(95), 5-12.*

https://cbseacademic.nic.in/web_material/Manuals/21st_Century_Skill_Handbook.pdf

https://ncert.nic.in/textbook/pdf/kect108.pdf

https://www.education.gov.in/sites/upload_files/mhrd/files/NEP_Final_English_0.pdf

https://www.ilo.org/jakarta/info/public/pr/WCMS_776501/langen/index.htm#:~:text=The%20programmes%20focus%20on%20selected,interview%20and%20developing%20a%20CV.

https://www.unicef.org/rosa/stories/soft-skills-are-your-superpower

http://fishtreeblog.tumblr.com/post/102878026250/the-21st-century-skills-of-the-flippedclassroom

5

Towards a More Orderly Transition

Innovations in 21st Century Teaching Skills

Shnaoli Chakraborty Acharya

Introduction

Throughout history, teacher qualifications have been subject to significant expectations and criteria developed with various objectives, determining their social prestige, obligations, and spheres of authority. These expectations have always been influenced by the society's values, goals, ambitions, and economic structure of the time. However, with the advent of digitalisation, it has become essential to approach education and teachers from new perspectives. All individuals and organisations associated with education administration must reposition themselves and consider education's fundamental ideas and theories to adapt to the changing times.

Ongoing discussions are taking place regarding developing and updating teachers' skills. This is mainly due to changes in various areas, such as new forms of communication, classroom and school changes, diversity of educational resources, adaptability of curricula, management styles, learner profiles, and parent profiles. The question of what makes a teacher suitable and what gives education its purpose and relevance is being explored. Essential educational approaches and tenets are being identified to ensure that an entire employable generation reaches the desired level of economic development. The primary driving force behind modern teacher competencies is also being examined. Fundamental questions include what information and abilities teachers should possess and in which educational environment they will apply such knowledge and skills.

Teachers today face a unique challenge in assessing their students' abilities and providing them with the necessary skills for the future. Even though education has been entirely transformed by the new social structures of the 21st century, teachers are still being evaluated according to the competency standards developed for the previous century's talents. According to the Organisation for Economic Co-operation and Development (OECD), 21st century skills are crucial for keeping up with the knowledge-based society and securing employment in the 21st century economy (OECD, 2009). Educational reform is essential to meet society's growing social and economic needs. One of the main obstacles to achieving the required changes is the need for more context-specific knowledge on teaching methods and effective strategies for supporting teacher professional development. It is, therefore, crucial to improving the quality of teacher instruction by developing 21st century skill competencies.

Twenty-First-Century Learners: What are the Essential Skills to Learn?

The social constructivist educational philosophy (Vygotsky, 1962) laid the foundation for learning as an active process and knowledge within a social context. Learning is seen as a series of social processes that are inextricably shaped and influenced by an individual's context, and learning as an active process is rooted in social constructivism. Constructivist educational principles are still highly important for instructors worldwide, even though the perspective is based on and remains primarily a Western worldview (OCED, 2009). It has gained popularity in many nations. However, constructivist viewpoints should be taken seriously as they are commonplace in education. We must be aware of how such cultural variety and nuances affect ways of learning, for instance, in societies where verbal contact is not the primary method of knowledge transmission (Treviño, 2006). According to differences in socio-cultural practices, children (or, in this example, teachers) may learn more effectively through activities like observation, listening, or sharing responsibilities than through verbalisation or actions (Rogoff, 2003; Treviño, 2006).

In the 21st century, many complex problems and challenges require specific skills to be effectively addressed. Various individuals and organisations have suggested what is necessary to become practical problem solvers in this new world. The consensus is that traditional education systems, which rely on content-based knowledge transmission, are no longer sufficient for training the new generation of learners.

There has been much discussion about the significance of learning new skills and abilities to meet the challenges of our constantly evolving digital environment. Several organisations, including well-known tech companies, formed the Partnership for 21st Century Skills (P21) in 2002 to achieve this. According to Thrilling and Fadel (2009), P21 defined three fundamental subjects and seven twenty-first-century abilities people need to succeed in the modern world. Reading, writing, and maths are the core courses of education, but they also include themes relevant to the twenty-first century. Critical thinking and problem-solving, creativity and innovation, cooperation and teamwork, cross-cultural understanding, media literacy and communication, computing, information and communication technology (ICT), and self-reliance concerning learning and careers are the seven fundamental skills students must acquire.

The World Economic Forum (2015) put forth a complete list of 16 essential talents for a new vision in education for the twenty-first century, based on P21's classification. These abilities are broken down into four competencies, six character traits, and six core literacies. Literacy, numeracy, scientific, ICT, financial, and cultural/civic literacy are fundamental. The competencies include critical thinking, problem-solving, creativity, communication, and teamwork. Curiosity, tenacity and grit, flexibility, leadership, and social and cultural awareness are the character traits.

The Organisation for Economic Co-operation and Development (OECD) has provided a vision for the future of skills and education through its Learning Framework 2030. According to this framework, learners should acquire three transformative competencies to thrive in the future. These skills accept responsibility, resolve conflicts and challenges, and generate new value (OECD, 2018). The ability to learn new values is correlated with a person's flexibility, inventiveness, curiosity, and open-mindedness. Resolving conflicts and dilemmas requires integrated, interrelated, and relationally aware thought and behaviour. The ability to accept responsibility encompasses problem-solving, self-control, self-regulation, and self-efficacy. Future educators can influence people's personal and social well-being if they possess these qualities.

Numerous scholars and groups have recognised a comprehensive set of knowledge, skills, abilities, and other qualities (KSAOs) required for the twenty-first century. These competencies include technical skills like computing and ICTs, psychological attributes like self-control, curiosity, and adaptability, and subject knowledge like essential literacies. These KSAOs are imperative in the twenty-first century, and educational institutions must be adaptable and dynamic enough to foster them. A constantly expanding body of research supports the twenty-first century skill movement's fundamental tenets despite criticism of its content, rhetoric, and evidence base (Davies, 2018; Greenlaw, 2015; Lucas, 2019), a constantly growing literature documents its basic premises (Chu et al., 2021; Griffin et al., 2012). Global education systems seek to impart skills without a prescribed definition or approach (Joyces and colleagues, 2019). To cultivate 21st century KSAOs, educational practices must adapt systems and strategies based on shreds of evidence. The scientific literature guides practical approaches of instruction and support systems.

The Indian Context

"21st Century Skills" refers to psycho-social competence skills essential for thriving in the constantly changing global workplace. These skills are crucial for ensuring a successful career in the information age. The four Cs of 21st century skills — Collaboration, Critical Thinking, Communication, and Creativity — are necessary for sustained workplace success. Moreover, students graduating in the 21st Century are expected to possess the ability to generate new and innovative ideas, think critically, and solve problems from diverse perspectives. They should also be capable of working with people from different social and cultural backgrounds and have a 'learning to learn' attitude. The diagram below shows the varied dimensions of 21st century pedagogy:

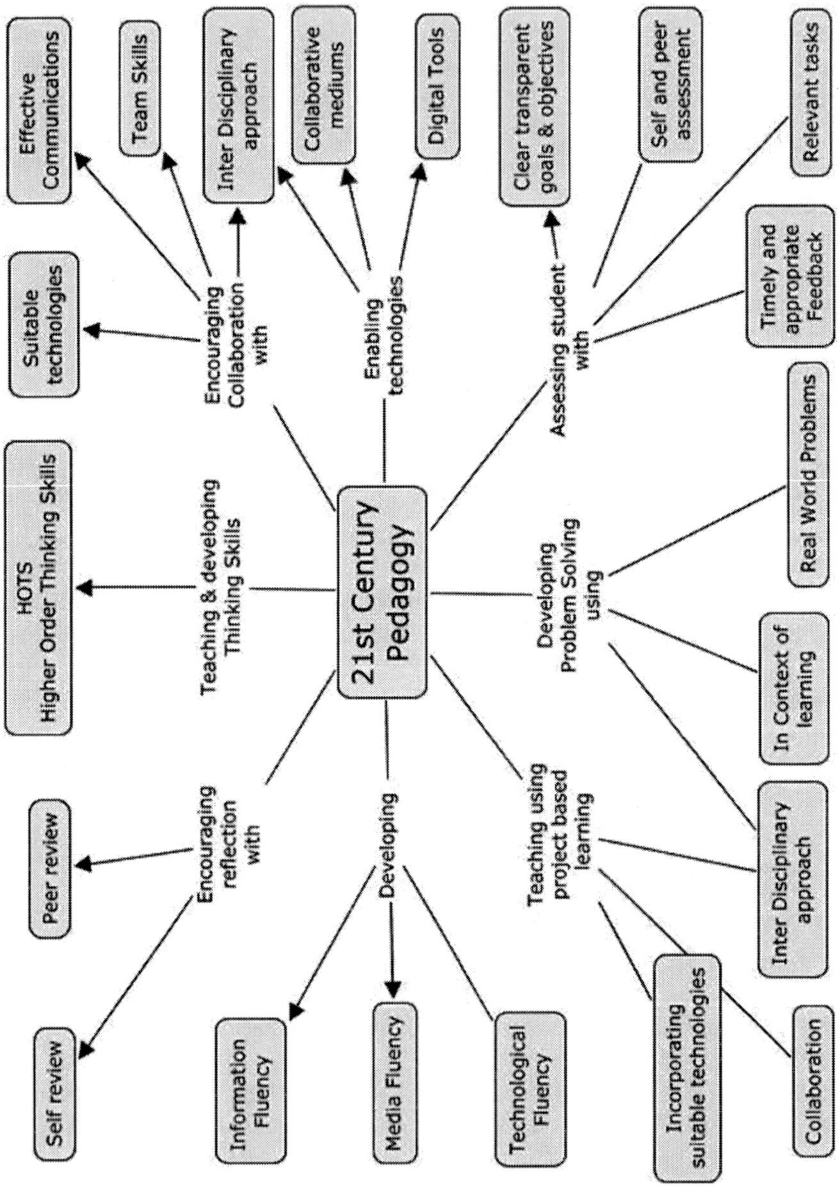

Source: www.bcourey.files.wordpress.com/

We, the educators are giving the students the necessary 21st century abilities to achieve in a dynamic and expanding global market. Futuristic leaders have been working to equip students for the twenty-first century in line with the times. Today's learners are multifaceted, tech-savvy, and highly motivated people thirsty for challenges, inspiration, inquiry, and creation. Education should include students' emotional, intellectual, social, and personal requirements in addition to being confined to the textbook. In the current era of information, learners ought to be able to think and operate with the following abilities. Let us examine the various aspects of 21st century talents, categorised into three main categories: Learning, Literacy skills and Life skills.

Learning Skills

The learning skills constitute the 4Cs — Critical thinking, Collaboration, Communication and Creativity. Teachers should promote critical thinking in their students since it involves analytical thinking, problem evaluation, and reasonable problem-solving. Students must comprehend the causes and mechanisms of events. Learning should connect with their cognitive capacities, motivate them to conclude a set of assertions and force them to evaluate things logically. With the knowledge provided, they ought to be able to characterise and assess data. In a formal learning environment, collaboration centres around working with peers and brainstorming sessions to generate diverse ideas. Collaborating will help students develop the ability to make judgements under challenging circumstances, apply those decisions in various ways, resolve conflicts and apply strategies as needed. Time management, essential for personality development, is linked to teamwork. They will also learn how to create reasonable and doable objectives. In order to be global citizens, students in the twenty-first century also need to be proficient communicators. To communicate effectively, they should be able to recognise the goal of a task, its medium, its recipient, and its environment. The curriculum needs to be designed with enough room for students to read, write, and listen intently while taking shifts or using technology. Reflective teaching and flexible curriculum design are enough to engage learners to participate in creative activities. Facilitators should teach learners to design, imagine, improvise, innovate, and create efficiently.

Literacy Skills

Information literacy, Media Literacy, and Technology Literacy could be considered as the literacy skills of the present era. Information literacy is a crucial skill for learners to master, enabling them to read, research, write, analyze, and manage information in digital teaching and learning environments. In the new normal, students must clearly understand how information is created and shared in the digital age. This is where media literacy comes into play, which involves the creation of social media profiles by teachers and school leaders to present themselves and their institutions in a more positive light to the world.

Additionally, researching using search engines and assessing online material are key components of the technology literacy skill set. Given the proposal for blended learning to continue post-pandemic education, students will inevitably need to learn how to use technology in the classroom for projects, PowerPoint presentations, and social media information sharing. Therefore, a modified curriculum is essential when online and blended learning are anticipated to take centre stage during the home-school transition period.

Life Skills

Three basic categories can be used to broadly classify life skills: accountability, ethics, and action. These abilities are critical to a child's overall development. Therefore, educators and administrators need to reconsider how they teach students these values—especially in the post-pandemic world of technological disruption. In order to thrive both within and outside of the classroom, face the difficulties of daily life on a personal and professional level, and develop into responsible global citizens, students need to have a firm grasp of ethical concepts. It is necessary to foster accountability so they can engage in activities on their initiative and learn how to assume ownership and responsibility in various circumstances. They must develop respect and understanding of diverse cultures and people and take risks adapting to diverse situations and places (C. Acharya, S., 2022).

Today's young minds are incredibly creative and productive, yet many cannot apply their skills in appropriate situations due to a lack of skill-based education. This has led to a general perception of the Indian education system that students are not receiving the necessary education to prepare them for the competitive 21st century workplace. Therefore, the education system must integrate skill-based teaching by encouraging students to generate new ideas and work on innovative solutions. Teachers are responsible for instilling the required skill sets in students and helping them become independent learners.

Teachers play a crucial role in helping students understand subject knowledge and the relevance of it in real-life situations. Therefore, it has become necessary for teachers to focus on developing 21st century skills throughout their careers. Unfortunately, unemployment rates have risen due to the lack of proper skills and knowledge among technical students and insufficient teacher training. Teachers are expected to facilitate a lifelong learning environment centred on the students by using competency-based approaches, participatory methods, new modes of assessment, and promoting the acquisition of skills, values, and attitudes.

In today's globalised era, language teachers are critical in honing students' language skills. English teachers can develop language skills by implementing skill-based activities in the classroom. Therefore, incorporating 21st century skills in their pedagogical approaches will equip students with essential skills. Developing critical thinking skills involves research and problem-solving in the language learning process. Creativity can be practised through writing and working on projects in the English language classroom. Communication skills are essential for goal-oriented transactions and require the meaningful conveyance of messages using fluent language. Collaboration is closely associated with communication and demands respect and understanding of social and cultural values in the workplace. Language teachers can implement various skill-based activities to develop 21st century classroom skills.

Desired Competencies of 21st Century Teacher

Education and training contribute to the economic and cultural aspects of the information society, where teachers play a vital medium. The must-have competencies of a 21st century teacher are as follows:

1) *Skilled in Technology Management* — Teachers should possess diverse skills to manage different types of knowledge. Their vocational development and training should qualify them to access, analyse, verify, and communicate information effectively while using technology where appropriate. They should possess strong pedagogical abilities that allow them to retain students' intellectual freedom of choice in the classroom and design and oversee learning environments. They should be able to successfully integrate information and communication technologies (ICT) into teaching and learning because they are confident in their ability to utilise them. They must also be able to guide and support students in networks where knowledge is generated and discovered. It is also essential that they have a solid grasp of the things they teach and that they view learning as a continuous process. They should be able to comprehend their experiences and adapt various teaching and learning tactics to the needs of their pupils, thanks to their diverse practical abilities.
2) *Community Engagement* — As professionals in their field, educators are expected to uphold social inclusion values and foster the potentiality in every learner. They must know human growth and development and possess self-confidence in relating to others. They should be able to work with students as partners and inspire them to become active and engaged members of society. Moreover, they must enhance students' collective intelligence and collaborate with colleagues to improve teaching and learning practices with new methodologies. Teachers must impart the importance of community outreach practices. It will help students integrate into their local communities and encourage them to take responsibility as global citizens. Teachers must understand the reasons behind social adaptation and exclusion to achieve this and teach to respect diverse cultures, promote cooperation, and uphold shared values. They must develop a strong inclination towards social harmony and education in all its aspects to work effectively. They are also responsible for implementing quality assurance systems through their expertise and proficiency.

3) *Skilled in Communication* — Teachers must possess excellent communication skills, and working well with others is vital to meet the profession's demands. Teachers must understand the impact of all stakeholders involved in the learning process to facilitate meaningful learning. Developing a collaborative working habit should align with a teacher's communication skills. The learning environment's ability to provide safe, flexible, innovative, and fruitful content depends on how well the teacher can lead the team. Therefore, teachers must understand and harness the entire team's potential, starting with themselves, to perform all roles effectively (Caena, 2017).
4) *Professionally Trained*— It is crucial for teachers to maintain professional development to increase educational performance and effectiveness. Professional training helps to increase their commitment to teaching, identity, and job satisfaction. They must keep up with their field's latest scientific, pedagogical, and technological developments, closely monitor society's constant change needs, and strive to provide the best education for their students. Serving society is a responsibility that teachers should take seriously. The following dimensions need to be considered while designing the teacher-training programmes for 21st Century Skills instruction in the classroom:
    a) It is essential to ensure that all teachers in the school who are involved in teaching students can deliver 21st century skills. This includes teachers of Computer Science, Art, Hindi (or any other language), Physical Education, and so on. It is important to note that teaching and learning 21st century skills should be integrated into all aspects of a student's course of study and should not be treated as standalone subjects. If some teachers cannot deliver these skills, careful consideration must be given to determine which teachers will be part of the initiative.
    b) To incorporate 21st century skills into their teaching methods, teachers of different standards and disciplines would require extensive training. This would include an initial intensive training programme and multiple update/review sessions throughout the school year. It is essential that the training is tailored to specific courses and grades.
    c) To effectively incorporate 21st century skills into their teaching, teachers of different standards and disciplines would require extensive training. This training would include an initial intensive session and multiple update and review sessions scheduled throughout the school year. Tailoring the training to the specific grade and course requirements is crucial.

Conclusion

It is crucial to take a realistic approach when considering teacher education. This is necessary to achieve the desired goal of changing the positions of teachers and the skills they need. A focus on literature shows that twenty-first century skills are now the guiding factors of teacher education in most countries. Clear syllabuses exist in practice with the usual methodologies to teach in the classroom. However, the new strategies should be documented with a strong emphasis on these skills, mainly information and communication technologies and the blended teaching mode. Teacher education reform should focus on pre-service teaching with rigorous internships or retrain in-service teachers with an emphasis on 21st century skills. However, as the pre-teaching training programme is also concerned with the successful teaching and recruitment processes of the would-be teachers, policymakers and practitioners must reframe the prescribed curriculum of teacher education programmes. Determining qualification standards without a robust implementation is meaningless; therefore, reconsidering the curriculum should be considered from this perspective. It is, thus, essential to have institutions collaborate to determine teachers' skills and organise teacher training.

Despite the challenges that have been outlined, the vital part of improving teacher practices lies in providing granular and specific feedback through the right tool. This feedback should be given regularly to promote self-analysis and continuous craving for improvement. To develop critical thinking among teachers, is imperative to get them educated through professional training that fosters ongoing reflection and continuous learning (Han & Brown, 2013). Students' 21st century learning can only be enhanced by 21st century teaching skills.

References

Caena, F. (2017). "Weaving the fabric: Teaching and teacher education ecosystems." In B. Hudson (Ed.), *Overcoming fragmentation in teacher education policy and practice*. Cambridge University Press.

Chakraborty Acharya, S. (2022). *Conceptualizing Educational Concerns in the New Normal: An Indian Perspective*, Mental Health Repercussions: Today and Beyond/ Ch. 1, Kanishka Publishers and Distributors, New Delhi.

Chu, S.K. W., Reynolds, R.B., Tavares, N.J., Notari, M., & Lee, C.W.Y. (2021). *21st-century skills development through inquiry-based learning: From theory to practice*. Springer International Publishing. https://doi.org/10.1007/978-981-10-2481-8

Davies, S. (2018, March 12). *A critical examination of calls for a '21st-century education'*. Uncommon Ground Media. https://uncommongroundmedia.com/21st-century-education-conundrum/

Greenlaw, J. (2015). Deconstructing the metanarrative of the 21st century skills movement. *Educational Philosophy and Theory, 47* (9), 894–903. https://doi.org/10.1080/00131857.2015.1035156

Griffin, P., McGaw, B., & Care, E. (Eds.). (2012). *Assessment and teaching of 21st-century skills*. Springer. https://doi.org/10.1007/978-94-007-2324-5

Han, H.S. & Brown, E.T. (2013). Effects of critical thinking intervention for early childhood teacher candidates. *The Teacher Educator* 48(2): 110–127.

Joynes, C., Rossignoli, S., & Fenyiwa Amonoo-Kuofi, E. (2019). *21st century skills: Evidence of definition, demand and delivery issues for development contexts* (K4D Helpdesk Report). Institute of Development Studies. https://opendocs.ids.ac.uk/opendocs/handle/20.500.12413/14674

Lucas, B. (2019). *Why we need to stop talking about twenty-first-century skills* (Seminar Series Paper #283). Centre for Strategic Education, Australia.

OECD. (2009). Creating effective teaching and learning environments: First results from TALIS. Organisation for Economic Co-operation and Development.

Organisation for Economic Co-operation and Development. (2018). *OECD Learning Framework 2030* (Position paper). OECD. http://www.oecd.org/education/2030-project/contact/E2030_Position_Paper_(05.04.2018).pdf

Rogoff, B. (2003). *The Cultural Nature of Human Development*. Oxford: Oxford University Press.

Thrilling, B., & Fadel, C. (2009). *21st-century skills: Learning for life in our times*. Jossey-Bass.

Treviño, V.E. (2006). Evaluación del aprendizaje de los estudiantes indígenas en América Latina. Desafíos de medición e interpretación en contextos de diversidad cultural y desigualdad social. *Revista Mexicana de Investigación Educativa* 11(28): 225–268.

Vygotsky, L.S. (1962). *Thought and Language*. Cambridge, MA: MIT Press.

World Economic Forum (2015). *New vision for education: Unlocking the potential of technology*. World Economic Forum. http://www3.weforum.org/docs/WEFUSA_NewVisionforEducation_Report2015.pdf

6

Curriculum Framework and Credit System for UG Programme and NEP 2020

Susanta Rajbanshi
Dr Swati Gupta

Introduction

India has an influential educational history all over the world. Starting from the Gurukul system of education to the British ruled education system, many upgradation and changes have been introduced, discussed, revised and implemented in the education system. After independence, National Education Policy 1968, 1986 and 1992 (POA) have taken many important initiatives to improve our education system. After 34 years, the government of India has taken initiative to change and revamp our education system by implementing National Education Policy 2020 (NEP 2020). NEP 2020 focused on the enormous change from the foundation level of education to research education. University Grants Commission has been playing an important role for reformation and reconstruction of the higher education system in the light of NEP 2020. The Ministry of Education and UGC have been framing different steering committees for making guidelines, curriculum, credit system, evaluation pattern for higher education. In consonance with the NEP 2020, University Grants Commission formulated a new revised curriculum and credit system as "Curriculum and Credit Framework for Undergraduate Programmes (CCFUP)". This study gives an overview of reconstruction and reformation of curriculum framework and credit system for undergraduate programmes. This study aims to illustrate the main features of CCFUP, Programmes under CCFUP, Curriculum and courses under CCFUP, credit evaluation system and awarding degree under CCFUP. After discussing all the aspects of CCFUP, the study attempts to make a critical SWOC (Strength, Weakness, Opportunities and Challenges) analysis.

National Education Policies in India always try to create a new path in our ongoing education system. The first education policy was promulgated in 1968 followed by the policy of 1986 which remained popular and effective in the Indian education system. It was revised in 1992 as Programme of Action (POA). Since that time, different sectors of the education system followed it (Pawan, 2020). After 34 years, the government of India has taken initiative to change and revamp our education system by implementing National Education Policy 2020 (Kumar, 2020). This policy mainly focuses on the student centric holistic development approach (NEP, 2020). National Education Policy 2020 revised the structure for school education as 5+3+3+4 instead of 10+2 traditional system (Govinda, 2020). If the whole education system is considered as a house then school education is the foundation of that house and higher education is the roof of the same house. India as a developing country should focus on school education as well as higher education to meet the global needs (James, Cobanoglu & Cavusoglu, 2021). Hence, University Grants Commission (UGC) mainly focuses on the reconstruction and reformation (UGC, 2008 and 2014) of higher education in India and for effective implementation of NEP 2020, the UGC has reframed and reconstructed curriculum framework and credit system for undergraduate programme (UGC, 2018) and brought "Curriculum and Credit Framework for Undergraduate Programmes (CCFUP)". Curriculum and Credit Framework for Undergraduate Programmes incorporates a flexible choice-based credit system (Aithal & Kumar, 2016), multidisciplinary approach, and multiple entry and exit options for Undergraduate Programmes (CCFUP, 2022). This will facilitate students to pursue their career path by choosing the subject/field of their interest.

Curriculum and Credit Framework for Undergraduate Programme (CCFUP)

Keeping in view of NEPs recommendation, the UGC has revised the Choice Based Credit System and released a new Curriculum and Credit Framework for Undergraduate Programmes in December 2022 (Kumar, 2022). This document /curriculum consists of 32 pages with the content of Introduction, Anchors to National Education Policy 2020, Curriculum Framework, Outcome based approach to higher education, Structure of Undergraduate Programme, Pedagogical Approaches, Learning Assessment and Acknowledgement. The new curriculum and credit framework recommends that "the undergraduate degree will be of either 3 or 4-year duration, with multiple exit options within this period, with appropriate certifications, e.g., a UG certificate after completing one year in a discipline or field including vocational and professional areas, or a UG diploma after two years of study, or a Bachelor's degree after a 3-year programme. The 4-year multidisciplinary Bachelor's programme, however, shall be the preferred option since it allows the opportunity to experience the full range of holistic and multidisciplinary education in addition to a focus on the chosen major and minors as per the choices of the student" (CCFUP, 2022). The New Curriculum Framework mainly focuses on: i) flexibility to move from one discipline of study to another; ii) opportunity for learners to choose the courses of their interest in all disciplines; iii) facilitating multiple entry and exit options with UG certificate/ UG diploma/ or degree depending upon the number of credits secured; iv) flexibility for learners to move from one institution to another to enable them to have multi and/or interdisciplinary learning; v) flexibility to switch to alternative modes of learning (offline, ODL, and Online learning, and hybrid modes of learning). Regulations for

Academic Bank of Credit (ABC) and guidelines for Multiple Entry and Exit (NCF, 2023) are already in place to facilitate the implementation of the proposed Curriculum and Credit Framework for Undergraduate Programmes (NEP, 2020; CCFUP, 2022).

Vocational Education and Training will form an integral part of the undergraduate programme to impart skills along with theory and practical. A minimum of 12 credits will be allotted to the 'Minor' stream relating to Vocational Education and Training and these can be related to the major or minor discipline or choice of the student. These courses will be useful to find a job for those students who exit before completing the programme. The following are the focused features of the curriculum and credit framework for Undergraduate Programmes (CCFUP):

- *Eligibility to Admission in Undergraduate Programme (UG):* The eligibility will remain unchanged and will be Senior Secondary School Leaving Certificate or Higher Secondary (12th Grade) Certificate obtained after successful completion of Grade 12 or equivalent stage of education.
- *Semester*: A semester comprises of 90 working days and an academic year is divided into two semesters (UGC on CBCS, 2018). The Undergraduate programme consists of eight semesters. A summer term is for eight weeks during summer vacation. Internship/apprenticeship/work-based vocational education and training can be carried out during the summer term, especially by students who wish to exit after two semesters or four semesters of study. Regular courses may also be offered during the summer on a fast-track mode to enable students to do additional courses or complete backlogs in coursework. The Higher Education Institutions (HEIs) can decide on the courses to be offered in the summer term depending on the availability of faculty and the number of students (CCFUP, 2022).
- *Duration of the Programme*: The duration of the UG programme is four years or eight semesters. Students who desire to undergo a 3-year UG Programme will be allowed to exit after completion of the 3rd year. If a student wants to leave after the completion of the first or second year, the student will be given a UG Certificate or UG Diploma, respectively, provided they secure the prescribed number of credits. Students who exit with a UG certificate or UG diploma are permitted to re-enter within three years and complete the degree programme. Students may be permitted to take a break from the study during the period of study but the total duration for completing the programme shall not exceed seven years.
- *Disciplines*: Curriculum of undergraduate programme mentions two types of discipline, i.e. major discipline and minor discipline. *Major Discipline is* the discipline or subject of main focus and the degree will be awarded in that discipline. Students should secure the prescribed number of credits (about 50% of total credits) through core courses in the major discipline. *Minor discipline* helps a student to gain a broader understanding beyond the

major discipline. For example, if a student is pursuing Education as a major discipline and obtains a minimum of 12 credits from a bunch of courses in Statistics, then the student will be awarded BA degree in Education with a Minor in Statistics.

- *Teaching Learning Components*: Teaching learning process goes through Lecture- Tutorial-Practical (L-T-P) method.
- *Credit Hours for Different Types of Courses*: The engagement of teacher and student related to a course is measured in terms of credit hours. A credit is a unit by which the coursework is measured. It determines the number of hours of instruction required per week over the duration of a semester (UGC on CBCS, 2014). Lecture-Tutorial- Practical method is used for instructing the students about the classes. The distribution of courses may have only a lecture component or a lecture and tutorial component or a lecture and practicum component or a lecture, tutorial, and practicum component, or only practicum component as required according to the nature of the courses (UGC on CBCS, 2018). One credit for lecture or tutorial work means one hour of engagement per week and one credit practical means two hours of engagement per week.

For example, a four-credit lecture/tutorial course in a semester means four one-hour lectures per week with each one-hour lecture counted as one credit. In a semester of 15 weeks duration, a four-credit lecture/tutorial course is equivalent to 60 hours of teaching. On the other hand, a one-credit practicum course in a semester of 15 weeks of duration is equivalent to 30 hours of practical work.

The following types of courses/activities constitute the programmes of study (CCFUP, 2022) –

1) *Lecture courses:* These involve lectures relating to a field or discipline by an expert or qualified personnel in a field of learning, work/vocation, or professional practice.
2) *Tutorial courses:* This involves problem-solving and discussions relating to a field or discipline under the guidance of qualified personnel in a field of learning, work/vocation, or professional practice.
3) *Practicum or laboratory work:* This type of work requires students to participate in a project or practical or lab activity that applies previously learned/studied principles/theory related to the chosen field of learning, work/vocation, or professional practice under the supervision of an expert or qualified individual in the field of learning, work/vocation or professional practice.
4) *Seminar*: This requires students to participate in structured discussion/conversation or debate focused on assigned tasks/readings, current or historical events, or shared experiences guided or led by an expert or qualified personnel in a field of learning, work/vocation, or professional practice.

5) *Internship*: In this, students are to participate in a professional activity or work experience, or cooperative education activity with an entity external to the education institution, normally under the supervision of an expert of the given external entity. A key aspect of the internship is induction into actual work situations. Internships involve working with local industry, government or private organizations, business organizations, artists, crafts persons, and similar entities to provide opportunities for students to actively engage in on-site experiential learning.
6) Studio activities: Studio activities involve the engagement of students in creative or artistic activities. Every student is engaged in performing a creative activity to obtain a specific outcome. Studio-based activities involve visual- or aesthetic-focused experiential work.
7) *Field practice/projects:* These are the courses requiring students to participate in field-based learning/projects generally under the supervision of an expert of the given external entity.
8) *Community engagement and service*: This type of courses students need to participate in field-based learning/projects generally under the supervision of an expert of the given external entity. The curricular component of 'community engagement and service' will involve activities that would expose students to the socio-economic issues in society so that the theoretical learnings can be supplemented by actual life experiences to generate solutions to real-life problems.

Awarding of Degree

Mainly five types of degree will be awarded at Undergraduate level i.e. UG Certificate, UG Diploma, 3-year UG Degree, 4-year UG Degree (Honours) and 4-year UG Degree (Honours with Research) (CCFUP, 2022).

1) *UG Certificate*: Students who opt to exit after completion of the first year and have secured 40 credits will be awarded a UG certificate if, in addition, they complete one vocational course of four credits during the summer vacation of the first year. These students are allowed to re-enter the degree programme within three years and complete the degree programme within the stipulated maximum period of seven years.
2) *UG Diploma*: Students who opt to exit after completion of the second year and have secured 80 credits will be awarded the UG diploma if, in addition, they complete one vocational course of four credits during the summer vacation of the second year. These students are allowed to re-enter within a period of three years and complete the degree programme within the maximum period of seven years.
3) *3-year UG Degree*: Students who wish to undergo a 3-year UG programme will be awarded UG Degree in the Major discipline after successful completion of three years, securing 120 credits and satisfying the minimum credit requirement.

4) *4-year UG Degree (Honours)*: A four-year UG Honours degree in the major discipline will be awarded to those who complete a four-year degree programme with 160 credits and have satisfied the credit requirements.
5) *4-year UG Degree (Honours with Research)*: Students who secure 75 per cent marks and above in the first six semesters and wish to undertake research at the undergraduate level can choose a research stream in the fourth year. They are to do a research project or dissertation under the guidance of a faculty member of the University/College. The research project/dissertation will be in the major discipline. The students who secure 160 credits, including 12 credits from a research project/dissertation, are awarded UG Degree (Honours with Research).

Table 6.1: *Minimum Credit Requirements to Award Degree under Each Category*

Sl. No.	*Broad Category of Courses*	*Minimum Credit Requirement*	
		3-Year UG	*4-Year UG*
1	Major (Core)	60	80
2	Minor Stream	24	32
3	Multidisciplinary	09	09
4	Ability Enhancement Courses (AEC)	08	08
5	Skill Enhancement Courses (SEC)	09	09
6	Value Added Courses common for all UG	06-08	06-08
7	Summer Internship	02-04	02-04
8	Research Project / Dissertation	–	12
Total		120	160

Source: NCFUP, 2022, UGC

Note: *Honours students not undertaking research will do three courses for 12 credits in lieu of a research project / Dissertation.

- *Letter Grades and Grade Points*: The Semester Grade Point Average (SGPA) is computed from the grades as a measure of the student's

Table 6.2: *Letter Grades and Grade Points*

Letter Grade	*Grade Point*
O (Outstanding)	10
A+ (Excellent)	9
A (Very Good)	8
B+ (Good)	7
B (Above Average)	6
C (Average)	5
P (Pass)	4
F (Fail)	0
Ab (Absent)	0

Source: Guideline for CBCS (CBCS, 2018) and NCFUP, 2022, UGC.

performance in a given semester. The SGPA is based on the grades of the current term, while the Cumulative GPA (CGPA) is based on the grades in all courses taken after joining the programme of study (CBCS, 2014, 2018). The HEIs may also mention marks obtained in each course and a weighted average of marks based on marks obtained in all the semesters taken together for the benefit of students. When students take audit courses, they may be given pass (P) or fail (F) grade without any credit (CCFUP, 2022).

SWOC Analysis

After giving an overview and discuss about of all the features of Curriculum and Credit Framework for Undergraduate Programme, this study focused on SWOC analysis which is mentioned below:

Strength

1. It is based on a student centric approach.
2. It focuses on continuous and comprehensive assessment.
3. It provides flexibility in duration for completing a programme.
4. Part completion of a programme with required obtained credit after particular duration.
5. Advantage to choose courses from intradisciplinary, interdisciplinary and multidisciplinary courses.
6. It bestows an opportunity to choose more elective courses and non-credit courses.
7. The learner may have an additional advantage to go to the field of research at undergraduate level.
8. It also provides an advancement to complete a programme partially by obtaining the required credits for UG certificate and UG diploma.
9. It provides an opportunity to transfer credits between universities by creating an account on Academic Bank of Credit.

Weakness

1) This curriculum and credit framework focuses less on core areas. In these systems students get the opportunity to acquire multiple knowledge but it may create less opportunity to go into the depth of a core area.
2) Initially at the implementation level students may be confused with this system, like choosing a subject, earning credit, award degree etc.
3) For giving the option to multiple exit and multiple entry the entire programme may take seven years.
4) The option to take courses according to their ability and pace is limited. There is no freedom for the first year student to take an advanced course or a third year student to take an introductory course.

5) Students are compelled to be inside the classroom for the entire five hour per day schedule leaving no scope for independent study.
6) There is no provision for the First semester students to engage in any orientation programme, which is essential for making them familiar with this new UG programme.

Opportunities

1) This new curriculum and credit system create opportunities for students to learn according to their own choice and pace.
2) It provides an opportunity to expose oneself in a multidimensional way.
3) Learners get the opportunity to complete their programme within the maximum limit of time.
4) Students get the opportunity to change institutions after completion of required credit.
5) Students have an opportunity to choose papers outside of their core area so that they can be specialized in multidiscipline.
6) Students have an opportunity to take extra credits more than the minimum requirement to complete the course which will give weightage for further opportunities.
7) Higher education grading is acceptable internationally so that students can compete for international opportunities.
8) Credit-transfer opportunity and possibility of taking different courses in different modes simultaneously learners to complete the total credit requirement within the minimum period.

Challenges

1) Students may face a dilemma in choosing the subjects due to their inexperience in predicting future demand.
2) Opportunity to take credits outside the core subject area may dilute the depth in core area of studies.
3) Lack of trained teachers may create a challenge for effective implementation of this curriculum.
4) Use of credit and transfer of credit instead of percentage can cause confusion.

Conclusion

The National Education Policy 2020 is the most important and effective education policy for 21st century and it aims to address the many growing developmental imperatives of our country. This policy proposes the revision and revamping of all aspects of structure of education, including its regulation and governance. The National Education Policy lays particular emphasis on the development of the creative potential of each individual. India is a diverse and multicultural country and most of the population belongs to youth. So it is very necessary as well as challenge for the government to create opportunity of quality education for youth. The aim of the government of India is to increase the 50 per cent Gross Enrolment Ratio in higher education including vocational education by 2035. Therefore, UGC has made different steering committees under its supervision; such one is *'Curriculum and Credit Framework for Undergraduate Programme'*.

After giving a critical analysis of this framework, this study may conclude that Undergraduate programmes create opportunities for holistic development. Hence students can learn according to their interest and own pace, enhance their psychomotor capacity through the ability enhancement and skill development courses and enrich themselves with intellectual, aesthetic, social, physical, emotional, ethical and moral qualities. Contrary to this framework may also lead to some challenges informing credit transfer on time, coordination among different departments/ colleges, completion of online courses on time etc. This framework breaks the boundaries of traditional arts, science, commerce streams by introducing a multidisciplinary approach. Most important opportunity and advantage of this framework is partial fulfilment of degree by obtaining required credit and which will be globally acceptable. After successfully implementing this curriculum and credit framework, the students will be able to identify, recognize and foster their unique capabilities in academic and non-academic spheres.

References

Aithal, P.S., & Kumar P.M. (2016). "Analysis of choice based credit system in higher education." *International Journal of Engineering and Modern Education.* (IJERME) ISSN (online): 2455 – 4200. DOI: 10.5281/zenodo.161046

Govinda, R. (2020). NEP 2020: "A critical examination." *Social Change*, *50*(4), 603–607. https://doi.org/10.1177/0049085720958804

James, W.B., Cobanoglu, C., & Cavusoglu, M. (2021b). *Advances in Global Education and Research*: Volume 4. In *Anahei Publishing eBooks*. https://doi.org/10.5038/9781955833042

Kumar, M.J. (2020). National Education Policy: How does it effect higher education in India? *IETE Technical Review*, *37*(4), 327–328. https://doi.org/10.1080/02564602.2020.1806491

Ministry of Human Resource Development. (2020). *National Education Policy.* Government of India, New Delhi. https://www.scribbr.com/citation/generator/folders/5xKQDhVsR1KtfeXblzvCzW/lists/7OrwxEVlt5wr5XU39JPrI/cite/report/

Pawan, K. (2020). An empirical study on NEP 2020 [National Education Policy] with special reference to the future of Indian education system and its effects on the stakeholders. *Zenodo (CERN European Organization for Nuclear Research)*. https://doi.org/10.5281/zenodo.4159546

UGC (2022). Curriculum and credit framework for undergraduate programme. University Grants Commission, New Delhi. https://www.ugc.gov.in/pdfnews/7193743_FYUGP.pdf

UGC (2008). From Chairman on examination reforms. D.O. No. F.1-2/2008(XI Plan), dated Jan 31, 2008: Annexure-II, Action *Plan for Academic and Administrative Reforms.* UGC guidelines on adoption of choice based credit system. *University Grants Commission* Bahadurshah Zafar Marg New Delhi — 110 002. http://collegesat.du.ac.in/UGC_credit_Guidelines.pdf

UGC (2014). UGC guidelines on adaptation of choice-based credit system, university grants commission, New Delhi. http://www.ugc.ac.in/pdfnews/9555132_Guidelines.pdf

UGC (2018). Minimum Course Curriculum for Undergraduate Courses under Choice Based Credit System, University Grants Commission, New Delhi. https://www.ugc.gov.in/pdfnews/8023719_guidelines-for-cbcs.pdf

UGC (2023). National Credit Framework. University Grants Commission (UGC), New Delhi.https://www.education.gov.in/sites/upload_files/mhrd/files/National_Credit_Framework.pdf

7

A Holistic Perspective on Education

An Overview

Smritikana Ghosh

Introduction

The purpose of giving children an education that takes a holistic approach is to equip them with the abilities they'll need to do well in school as well as in life in general. The purpose of this research is to clarify and gain an understanding of the concepts that underpin the holistic approach to education. One may use the phrase "holistic education" to refer to a wide variety of theoretical frameworks and teaching methodologies. The concept of completeness is emphasized, and every effort is made to ensure that important aspects of the human experience are not overlooked. The current cultural influences that are used in holistic education to teach young minds about what it is to be human include things like the media and music, to name just two examples of these influences. It shines light on life's most difficult challenges, how to overcome them, how to attain success, and what basics must be grasped from the beginning in order to accomplish all that is in store for us farther down the road.

The educational model of the contemporary era has undergone a transformation. On the one hand, traditional schooling had a habit of concentrating more on theory than on actual practice. On the other hand, many people are of the opinion that older, more conventional methods of teaching, such as the gurukul system, were better at combining theory and practice. An education that takes a holistic approach takes into consideration the complete kid. There is a focus on the intellectual development, emotional growth, physical development, and spiritual development of the person. This approach emphasises that each child is an individual with their own unique set of needs and intrinsic skills, and that the conditions necessary for optimum learning are those in which those criteria are fulfilled. The idea that children learn best when they are actively participating in activities that they find engaging and pleasurable is one that forms the basis of the holistic education philosophy. It is an excellent strategy for encouraging youngsters to think creatively and to express themselves in an uninhibited manner. In addition to this, a holistic education instills in its students a sense of civic duty and puts a premium on the importance of the natural and human-made environments in which they live. In the 1980s, the idea of "holistic education" began to take shape as a separate academic subject in the region of North America known as the United States. It was a reaction to the "mechanistic" or "Cartesian Newtonian" worldview that was prominent in traditional schools at the time. This worldview held that everything could be explained by mechanical processes.

According to Shriner et al. (2005), holistic education, which is distinct from paradigm-based education, explores and questions the assumptions that are established by mainstream curricula and cultural norms, both of which are seen as being too restrictive and compartmentalized. This is done in contrast to paradigm-based education, which does not research or challenge these assumptions. To put another way, the objective of an education that takes a holistic approach to learning is to alter the basic principles that are the foundation of the conventional educational system. According to Martin and Forbes (2004), what sets holistic education apart from other pedagogical systems is its emphasis on learning via direct experience, in addition to its attention on the relevance of connections and fundamental human values within the classroom environment. This is in addition to the fact that holistic education places an emphasis on the importance of the classroom environment. This is the defining characteristic that differentiates holistic education from other educational methods. Holistic education seeks to instil in students the knowledge and abilities that will allow them to thrive not just academically but also in other aspects of life. The basic pillars of the holistic education paradigm include the development of self-awareness, good relationships, constructive social behaviours, emotional maturity, and resilience, as well as an appreciation for beauty, transcendence, and the truth. The goal of a holistic education is to adapt the learning of human goodness, personal greatness, and the joy of life through challenges and successes in a society in which a child no longer gets suitable support from families, faiths, or traditional tribes. Holistic education attempts to make the learning of human goodness, personal greatness, and the pleasure of life through struggles and accomplishments more applicable.

Theoretical Foundation

The term "holistic development" refers to a broad method of education with a wide range of learning outcomes in mind. The primary objectives of educational institutions should be the cultivation of higher order skills as well as the encouragement of individuals' unique learning styles. A paradigm of education that places a focus on the empowerment of students and instructors in a range of different settings is referred to as "holistic development", and the phrase "holistic development" refers to that paradigm. The raising of educational norms to a higher level as a direct consequence of putting this plan into action is essential to the accomplishment of any nation-building mission. If you give it some thought, you'll eventually come to the conclusion that the more you know, the less you really understand. The more you learn, the less you realise you understand. A student is better prepared for success in any area of study when they have received an education that is holistic. Schools are adjusting their focus to assist kids acquire the life skills, attitudes, and self-awareness they will need to flourish in today's more complex environment (Sarkar, 2022).

Students benefit from increased growth in their social and emotional intelligence and are better prepared to deal with the challenges of real life when they get an education that takes a more holistic perspective. The New Education Paradigm 2020 suggests that classroom instruction should place less of a focus on academic learning and more on practical experience. Everyone, without exception, regardless of gender, ethnicity, financial background, or any other element, must have access to education of the highest possible calibre. According to the National Education Policy for the year 2020 (NEP, 2020), a holistic education encourages "the full cognitive, emotional, social, intellectual, and spiritual development of each learner". If people want to be successful in the world that we live in today, which is so technologically sophisticated, they need to have a broad variety of skills and the ability to think creatively outside the box. In the fast-paced digital world of today, an education system that is centred on technology is very necessary. Important for achieving success in a broad range of academic endeavours (both curriculum-based and extracurricular). For children, education may be made to seem more natural and engaging, which is the central concept of the holistic education approach. The objective of using a holistic approach to education is to guide students towards becoming successful leaders in all parts of their life by assisting them in making effective use of the skills they acquire while they are enrolled in academic programmes (Scholar Base, 2014).

The ability of a kid to learn may be hindered by a number of factors, including the prevalence of physical, mental, and emotional violence among children of school-age, the pressure to conform that comes from academic competition, the demands of extracurricular activities, and the expectations of society as a whole. We are not yet at the point as a community where we can let a youngster fly freely, so in the meantime, we make them observe the constraints that are established by their parents and educators. This problem is solved by using comprehensive instructional approaches. Teaching kids not just academics but also the abilities they'll need to flourish in today's society is one of the primary tenets of holistic education, which places an emphasis on the significance of doing so. The purpose of education seen from a holistic point of view is to cultivate the complete child into an individual who is self-reliant, self-confident, and contributing to society. The development of empathetic awareness and ecological consciousness is a primary focus of the programme. It takes into consideration the student's mental health, as well as their social and emotional well-being to the same extent.

It was important for schools and the field of social work in particular, to provide children the tools they would need to become productive members of society, and this was emphasised in the classroom. They should be able to rise to the occasion and have a good effect on the environment around them regardless of the challenges that they face. Children are at a greater risk of dying young because they do not have the capacity for resilience and optimism. Without a shadow of a doubt, one of the primary goals of the modern educational system is to assist students in becoming more self-aware of their limitations and in developing the skills necessary to compensate for those limitations. This has to begin at an early age in one's life. Parents and teachers have a duty to support their children in developing a healthy sense of self-esteem and a belief in their own capacity to accomplish their objectives in life. This is because they are the key influences in a child's life, and as such, they are in the best position to do so. The capacity to develop and sustain healthy relationships is impacted when an individual makes the decision to behave in a manner that is in line with their own wishes. In a holistic educational setting, the immediate social and emotional surroundings of a kid, as well as that child's physical and mental health, are all addressed as part of the curriculum.

Children do not automatically have the capacity to overcome challenges; rather, they need guidance and instruction in order to learn how to do so successfully. The phoenix, a legendary bird that is said to have arisen from the flames to bring song to the world, ought to be the subject of the lesson. This concept inspires younger generations to engage in introspection about the world that surrounds them and to look for the truths, realities, beauty, and meaning that exist within it. In today's schools, the significance of receiving an education that is balanced in all aspects cannot be stressed. The adoption of a more comprehensive worldview may be beneficial to one's personal life, interpersonal connections, and professional accomplishments. It's possible that a student's destiny will be determined by whether or not their school practices holistic education.

Characteristics of Holistic Education

- It encourages growth in all areas of a person's being.
- It's all about the connections (open, democratic, and egalitarian connections).
- Experiential learning (as opposed to just "basic skills") is the focus.
- It "acknowledges that cultures are made by people and can be changed by people," as opposed to just adhering to a culture that already exists.
- At its heart lies what has been described as a "profound respect for life and the unknown (and never fully known) source of life."

The National Education Policy 2020 is the product of extensive and in-depth deliberations, and it seeks to improve the standard of education in India in order to turn it into a knowledge powerhouse. The comprehensive National Education Policy 2020 has as its goal the reform of the Indian education system via the implementation of qualitative changes at the grassroots level. The NEP 2020 advises a combination of online and offline learning as a way to "avoid overexposure of school-going children to technology." The goal of the policy is to achieve excellence, justice, and inclusivity. Policymakers and academics encounter a myriad of challenges in putting the policy into action and turning the concept into reality; nevertheless, if they collaborate and pool their resources, they may be able to accomplish their aim.

Guiding Principles of Holistic Education

Holistic education's guiding principles were spelt out in detail in a statement published in 2000 called Education 2000: A Holistic Perspective (Flake, 2000).

- *Recognising Students* — Every single student is one of a kind and brimming with unique perspectives, capabilities, and ideas. To put it another way, it is critical to stress upon pupils the significance of valuing and accepting one another despite the fact that they are unique individuals. Everyone has an endless capacity for development, is creative by their own nature, and has certain physiological, psychological, cognitive, and spiritual needs and resources. This potential for growth and these creative tendencies are innate.
- *Human Development Education* — The purpose of education is to help individuals realise their full potential. Every student ought to grow into a whole human being while they are there. Relationships with oneself, one's family, one's community, one's global community, the earth, and the cosmos should be developed via education.
- *Educators' Changing Role* — As a result of their professional detachment from the spiritual, moral, and emotional difficulties that are inextricably related to the process of human growth, many contemporary educators have gotten buried in the rigouts of professional isolation. This may be seen in their inability to adequately address the needs of their students. Learning is not something that can be made but rather must be encouraged in the classroom, which is why holistic educators feel that instructors should serve more as guides than manufacturers of knowledge for their students. It is imperative that educators be allowed the autonomy to plan and carry out courses that are tailored to meet the needs of their specific student populations.
- *Experience's Primary Function* — The majority of learning occurs via hands-on and experiential activities. The student benefits from a dynamic and multimodal engagement with their environment, which also sheds light on the hidden messages that are concealed all around them. The state of knowledge is fluid. Instead of presenting a confined, fragmented, and predigested "curriculum" as the way to knowledge and wisdom, education should foster spontaneous, healthy development via experience.
- *The Power to Decide* — Both the children and their parents should be provided with relevant alternatives throughout the whole of each and every stage of the educational process. Only in an environment free of constraints can genuine learning take place. One must have the freedom to think for themselves, to voice their mind, and to grow as an individual. It is essential to provide children with genuine agency over their educational experiences. They should have a major influence over the courses they take and the disciplinary rules the school implements, consistent with the level of maturity both they and the school possess.

- *Global Citizenship Education* — Every one of us is a citizen of the planet. As a result, the primary objective of education should be to instil in pupils an appreciation for the diverse range of human experiences. The breadth of the human experience is incommensurable with the rules and presumptions of any one civilisation. As the new global society takes form, individuals from all over the world are coming into contact with one another for the very first time in the history of humanity. Teachers who see education from a more holistic perspective believe that it is high time for students to learn to respect the great range of human experiences and the unrealized potentials that lay dormant inside each one of us.
- *Participatory Democracy Education* — Every student should have access to an education that is founded on democratic ideals and that inspires them to be productive members of society and stewards of the environment, and this education should be delivered by their schools. It is not enough to provide individuals merely the right to vote for their leaders in order to have a truly democratic society; instead, it is important to equip voters with more agencies in civic concerns. A democratic society is not just one in which the "rule of the majority" is applied; rather, it is a society in which the views of the people are respected and in which issues that impact actual people are addressed. It is a culture that, where adjustments in social norms and cultural practices are merited, is open and accepting to beneficial changes in such norms and practices.
- *Learning and Enlightenment* — The belief that human beings are spiritual beings experiencing human experiences is held by many educators who subscribe to the holistic school of thought on education. The development of an individual's physical, emotional, and mental states run parallel to their progress in the spiritual realm. Signs of a spiritually developed and experienced person include the depth of creative experience, a great appreciation for the numinous wonder of existence, a sanctuary from the frenzied activity, pressure, and overstimulation of contemporary life, and a feeling of connectedness to both oneself and others.

Advantages of Holistic Education

- *Creates Balanced Individuals* — Students are encouraged to build a well-rounded view on life through learning from a holistic perspective, which incorporates all aspects of their lives, including their academic, athletic, social, and other endeavours. As a consequence of this, more people could be healthy and ready to make constructive contributions to the communities in which they live. Someone who has experience or training in a wide range of fields is called a renaissance man or woman.
- *It Prepares People for 21st Century* — In the 21st century, we are expected to be proficient in a variety of fields. Abilities in critical thinking and creative thinking are more likely to be appreciated in today's workplaces than they were in industrial countries of the past. The young of today need

an all-encompassing education that will provide them with the vast range of information and social skills essential for them to be successful so that they can meet the difficulties that lie ahead in the future.

- *Cohesive Communities* — Young people who are aware of and respect their connection to communities are better able to learn how to coexist with others and look out for their needs. The child and everyone else stand to profit from this.
- *Its Inspiring* — Young people who get an education that places an emphasis on developing the full person might reasonably anticipate being exposed to a wide range of academic fields, such as the arts, humanities, sciences, and so on.

Disadvantages of Holistic Education

- *Infrequently Used Past the Primary Years* — After the first few years, there is less of a need to pursue an all-encompassing strategy. Play-based learning and forest schools are two examples of holistic teaching methods that are used with young children. However, from the ages of eight and nine, pupils are subjected to growing pressure to prioritise reading and arithmetic at the cost of other aspects of the 'whole' kid. Play-based learning and forest schools are two examples of holistic teaching methods that are used with young children.
- *Many Parents may Disagree* — It is possible for educators to find that there is pushback against placing an excessive amount of focus on extracurricular activities, humanities subjects, and soft skills. It's possible that some parents may protest that their children are falling farther behind their peers who are the same age because of the tactics you use.
- *Fits poorly many school curriculums* — Low levels of student achievement are typical at a large number of schools. They typically have a lot on their plates, with reading, science, and mathematics occupying the spotlight most of the time. When working within these boundaries, it might be difficult for instructors to offer their pupils with educational experiences that cover a wider range of topics.
- *Time-consuming and costly* — There are a lot of different ways to get a well-rounded education, but most of them demand a large commitment of both time and money. Sending children to "summer camps" in order to provide them with a well-rounded education is one of the strategies that we use. This causes a significant financial burden for the parents. In a similar vein, extracurricular programmes in the arts and sports have a tendency to be pricey, which restricts their availability to families with sufficient financial means.

Model of Holistic Education

Students are able to accomplish their educational objectives by focusing on self-discovery as well as professional excellence, which are the foundations of holistic education. The higher education system relies on these two pillars to function properly. As a result of the fact that instructors are responsible for the intellectual, emotional, and spiritual development of their pupils, the educational system of today has to adopt an approach that is both diversified and comprehensive.

- *A Well-Rounded Education* — It is the responsibility of schools to encourage children's healthy mental, emotional, and behavioural development. Students need to develop skills such as critical thinking, empathy, and passionate caring, all while learning to be professionally oriented. Students may find that relaxing activities like yoga, pranayam, sudarshan kriya, and meditation benefit them. According to research conducted at Yale and Harvard, both meditation and Sudarshan Kriya are beneficial to the mental and emotional health of students.
- *Participation of All Senses* — Students need to make use of all of their learning capabilities, including their auditory, visual, and kinesthetic ones. Students can prefer learning via their senses. They could choose a sense in accordance with what the discussion is about. Some youngsters acquire knowledge more easily via auditory, visual, or kinaesthetic (touching and moving) channels. Consideration must be given to the degree to which it is tailored to the preferences, capacities, and capacities of the individual learner.
- *Concentrate on Skill* — The ideal educational system would assist pupils in learning both theoretical ideas and practical abilities. Education that focuses on practical skills is necessary in the modern society. In order to make education relevant and connected to the workforce, all academic content must be converted into skills that are in demand. The University Grants Commission's Learning Outcomes-Based Curriculum Frameworks serve as a framework for the capacity development of students enrolled in higher education institutions.
- *Motivation by a Higher Good* — Patten gale is the one who came up with the phrase "purpose-guided education". He also argued that its implementation would prioritise intrinsic motivation and help students become more interested in learning experiences by tying in students' ideas and life aspirations to course requirements. Patten gale is credited with inventing the term "purpose-guided education". We need to assess the ways in which we are cultivating an atmosphere in which young people may discover their life's purpose and be provided with the means to achieve it.
- *Concentrated Studying* — Pedagogical practices used in higher education institutions need to be brought up to date in order to make students' educational experiences more interesting, adaptive, and enjoyable. It is impossible to overestimate the educational benefit that comes from getting practical experience and participating in internships. When the professional and academic sectors collaborate, there is a greater potential for the creation of new learning opportunities for students.
- *Learning in Multiple Modes* — The education of the future will be more integrated. Technology is becoming an absolute must in the classroom. It

is possible that blended learning will revolutionise education as a result of developments in industry. Traditional classroom instruction is combined with online educational technology such as learning management systems and the ever-expanding capabilities of mobile devices in blended learning, which aims to make the educational process more engaging and comprehensive.

- *Educating the Whole Person* — The majority of people identify with their physical selves, yet we are so much more. Since it has an effect on our feelings, the environment might be thought of as our "first body". The body, the mind, the ideas, and the emotions all come before the self. The student, their family, their job, and the community all benefit from education that focuses on the whole person. The individual's self-confidence and character will both improve as a result of this.
- *Old and New Ways of Learning* — As teachers, it is our responsibility to examine the extent to which students can link their own personal experiences to both classic works of literature and cutting-edge technological developments. The teaching of history could become more important in the future. On solid ground, fruit can be grown. In education, there should be a healthy balance between the rationality of the West (scientific) and the tradition of the East (philosophical).
- *Learning without Stopping* — The process of education never ends. One study conducted by Forbes discovered that continuing one's education throughout one's life increases both one's happiness and one's health. Because of breakthroughs in medicine, the average human life expectancy is expected to rise to between 90 and 100 years in the not-too-distant future. Lifelong learning programmes have to be made available to students of all ages by educational establishments like colleges and universities. Continuous education might be an asset in meeting the criteria of several careers.

Because experiential learning broadens the number of ways in which students may engage with the many stakeholders of a variety of organisations, the holistic education model as a whole has the potential to help students develop sensitivity to the needs of multiple stakeholders. The overarching goal of NEP 2020 is to cultivate good human beings who are able to think and act rationally, demonstrate compassion and empathy, demonstrate courage and resilience, demonstrate a scientific temperament and creative imagination, and have sound ethical moorings and values that can be applied across generations and cultures to create a society that is more just and pluralistic.

Goal of Holistic Education

The NEP 2020 states that "it is essential that an identified set of skills and values are incorporated at each stage of learning" for the holistic growth and development of the pupils. According to Forbes (2003), the term "ultimacy" is the one that "best encapsulates the goal of holistic education". The pursuit of the highest state of being (such as enlightenment, the greatest stage of development, or the greatest moment in life, which is very seldom experienced by anyone) and having the most concern or participation (such as service to others) are two of the definitions of ultimacy that he offers. It's possible that these two meanings are compatible with one another. Those who subscribe to the concept of original sin contend that holistic educators have a different perspective on the need to shape and govern children than does the notion of original sin itself. Therefore, holistic educators feel that they have a unique viewpoint on development because they believe that people have an inherent inclination to do good and that growth consists largely of disclosing or exposing what is already there or inherent in the child (Grimes, 2007).

As a result of these beliefs, holistic educators believe that they have a distinct advantage over conventional educators. The ultimate objective, which is sometimes referred to as enlightenment or oneness with cosmic harmony, is a theme that appears repeatedly throughout holistic literature. According to Nielsen (2008), pupils are able to realise their maximum potential when they are actively engaged in an all-encompassing learning environment. Forbes promotes "ultimacy" in a study that was newly published, and the report "shows the philosophical coherence of what makes holistic education different from mainstream approaches to education". Ultimacy is often used by educators who pursue a "holistic" approach to teaching and learning in order to discover answers to fundamental concerns about the nature of humans and the desire for purpose in one's life.

Challenges of Holistic Education

The investment of time and effort that is necessary to put the approach into action is one of the most significant challenges that holistic education faces. To implement a holistic method of education, which emphasises the development of the whole kid rather than only concentrating on one subject at a time, may need a significant amount of time and labour. Due to the highly individualised nature of the instruction that is provided in this environment, it may be challenging to develop a curriculum that is applicable to each and every child there. In order to give kids with an education that is genuinely all-encompassing, teachers need to be very flexible in the way they approach instruction and have a solid understanding of the many learning styles and goals that each of their students has. In conclusion, the cost of a comprehensive education may be expensive since it requires a greater number of instructors and extra materials, both of which drive up overhead costs.

Four Holistic Education Pillars of Learning

Twenty-first century holistic education comprises four learning pillars for approach. UNESCO has recognised these four pillars with slight variations (Nava, 2001). These are:

- *Studying How to Study* — Learning how to ask questions is necessary for this. Questions are the means through which the conscious mind acquires knowledge. Instead of focusing on finding a solution, we will be investigating the problem at hand. Activating awareness is beneficial to developing attention, receptivity, perception, inquisitiveness, intuition, and creative ideas since it helps to open up new channels of observation. Learning how to study well needs independent control of one's own education, knowledge, and upkeep. It highlights science (Nava, 2001). The aim of traditional schooling and the practice known as "rote learning" is to have students "acquire itemised codified information or factual knowledge", however this kind of education is different. The idea is to "shake the very tools of knowledge", as the phrase puts it.

- *Learning How* — To affect this kind of transformation in society in this new century calls for behaviour that is both intelligent and responsible. It is vital to acquire skills like flexibility, teamwork, problem-solving, and sound judgement via hands-on experience if one is interested in obtaining a vocation and producing high-quality products and services. According to Schreiner (2005), learning by doing demands a level of tolerance for uncertainty as well as independence. This educational pillar encourages students to apply what they learn and has tight ties to both vocational and occupational training as well as education in the workplace. In conventional or industrial economies, the acquisition of skills training for 'doing' things or carrying out duties is just half of the tale. People's efforts are becoming more symbolic as a result of the digital economy. Learning to accomplish anything involves abilities that are based on behaviour. UNESCO (1996) states that human characteristics and interpersonal ties take precedence over material and technical factors.
- *A Course in Being* — Connecting with one's inner self, which exists beyond the everyday mental and emotional processes, is an essential part of learning to be comprehending the concept of group membership. The recently uncovered global dimension incorporates objectively held human values in addition to those held subjectively. Discovering oneself and being aware of oneself are necessary steps on the path to wisdom. This kind of learning is encouraged by holistic education (Nava, 2001), which acknowledges that people are spiritual beings who are looking for meaning in their lives. Because of this, "learning to be" might also mean growing more fully human via the accumulation of knowledge and experiences. This necessitates the development of a curriculum that emphasises critical thinking, independent judgement, personal commitment and responsibility, memory, logic, a sense of aesthetics, physical ability, communication and social skills, and universal human values.
- *The Art of Leaving Together* — In other words, in order to learn how to live an efficient life, you need to respect other people and collaborate with them. Putting aside preconceived notions, dogmas, prejudice, authoritarianism, and stereotypes is an effective method for preventing conflict, violence, and other negative outcomes. The concept of connectivity, or

the web of life, plays an important role in this study (Nava, 2001). This concept places an emphasis on learning via the discovery of others and the ongoing experience of working towards common objectives. In particular, it requires introspection and self-awareness, curiosity about the world and others, compassion and cooperative social behaviour in caring and sharing, deference to others and their cultures and values, the ability to engage with others and resolve conflicts through dialogue, and the capability to work effectively in teams UNESCO (1996).

Implications of Holistic Education

At each and every point in a child's academic career, the development of the complete child is given top priority. In every era, from the ancient to the mediaeval to the contemporary, it was necessary for a child to reach a certain age before they could begin their education. If you want your children to have successful educational experiences, you need to include them in every facet of the educational programme. This involves making an effort to develop their cognitive abilities as well as their physical capabilities. Children are better able to discover and completely develop their strengths when they are exposed to a wide range of learning situations (Mcilroy, 2022). This allows for children to also address any flaws that they may have. The process of teaching and learning may be beneficial to teachers since it can help them improve their skills in a variety of domains, including processing auditory and linguistic information, verbal fluency, physical dexterity, attention in the classroom, and other similar talents. Abilities that a student has in the social, physical, mental, and intellectual realms all contribute to their overall potential for academic achievement. Building a strong foundation in social and emotional skills is necessary in order to learn how to regulate and safeguard one's own feelings. Encourage them to express their emotions in a way that is productive and healthy. It is essential that children be presented with many opportunities to unearth, develop, and perfect their skills, as well as to focus on strengthening areas in which they are lacking.

- *Affectionate Support* — As part of an all-encompassing educational programme, there is a strong emphasis placed on the mental health of the students. In an environment that takes a holistic approach, educators strive hard to win the respect of each and every one of their pupils. Students who attend schools that use a holistic approach are more inclined to discuss their emotions with their teachers. When using this approach, the teacher may make a note of the specific set of qualities possessed by each individual pupil.
- *Making Connections* — The conventional method of teaching has a tendency to take on a more formal tone. In other words, the engagement that takes place between professors and students is more of a formal nature. On the other hand, when learning takes place in a more holistic setting, both

students and teachers feel more at ease while engaging with one another. This is due to the change in conditions in the surrounding area. As was said before, the traditional method of instruction takes place inside the four walls of a designated classroom. Students and teachers might easily grow distanced from one another in a setting like this one. Nevertheless, students and teachers in holistic classrooms gain from the unusual environment by growing more comfortable communicating with one another. This is an advantage that holistic classrooms provide. The atmosphere is looser and less stuffy than before. At this type of school, not only do the pupils, the teachers, and the parents get along better with one another, but the parents do as well. The investment that parents make in their children's education and development as whole persons increases, and they take a greater interest in their children's extracurricular and co-curricular activities as a result.

- *Body Growth* — In holistic classrooms, not only is the mental but also the physical health of the students a primary focus. As contrast to the more traditional educational environment of a classroom, holistic teaching methods include a range of approaches to education that are aimed at improving the students' physical health. Lessons that take place outside and a focus on maintaining a healthy body are both essential components of the entire curriculum. The extracurricular activities, such as sports and field excursions that are part of holistic educational models are included into the daily agenda.
- *Reduces Schoolwork* — A change in viewpoint among parents and educators in a setting that prioritises holistic education would naturally result in a reduction in the amount of academic pressure placed on students. The concept of themes is no longer considered to be the only thing that matters by teachers and parents. Everyone, including parents and teachers, is well aware of the many advantages that may accrue to students as a result of their involvement in extracurricular activities. Because students now have more time on their hands, it is possible for them to concentrate on other areas of interest, such as sports, and improve their performance in those areas.
- *Technology and Health Care* — A more comprehensive approach to education would be beneficial not just to the wellbeing of the nation but also to the development of its technical infrastructure. In interviews, Bill Gates has been quoted as saying that "Technology should be used as part of a well-considered, whole-person approach to education reform". This strategy should also include training for teachers, suitable curriculum, the engagement of parents, and programmes for children that address unmet requirements for essentials such as nutrition and health care. Clearly, the use of technology in the classroom has to be included within a larger and more comprehensive strategy.
- *Actively Teaches* — Students are deemed to be participating in "active learning" if they make a contribution of any kind to the instructional

procedure. Learning this requires participation in hands-on activities such as experiments, field trips, and group projects. In order for comprehensive educational techniques to be successful, active engagement from students is necessary. Students are inspired to take an active part in their own education and to cultivate a true enthusiasm for the subject matter that they are learning, which is one of the many reasons why holistic education is so beneficial.

- *Integrated Education* — Understanding human development in its whole is of the utmost importance, which is why a holistic approach to education is so beneficial. It takes into account the children's mental and physical growth as well as their abilities. The technique, on the other hand, does not rule out the possibility of classroom teaching in theory. Therefore, it is reasonable to assert that a holistic educational system incorporates everything and everything that has to be included into the process of learning.
- *Whole-person Education* — The same may be said of the word "holistic education", which, in common parlance, is understood to mean "education for the whole person". The phrase "holistic approach" is used to refer to a style of education that places an emphasis on the whole growth and development of a kid rather than only the intellectual growth of that youngster.
- *Free Speech* — One of the biggest benefits of a genuinely comprehensive education is the development of students' free speech abilities. Participating in activities that allow one to exercise one's right to freedom of expression is an essential part of being a student. Students are provided with the chance to use their own discretion and cognitively develop as a result. A successful career would be one that makes use of these qualities to their full potential.

Methods of Holistic Education

- *Group Educated* — Experiences like working in a team, in which members share their knowledge and points of view in service of achieving a shared goal, are the only way for a person's sense of self-worth and capacity to lead others to develop. The most beneficial feature of acquiring knowledge in a social setting is the degree to which individuals cooperate and connect to one another. Learning and working together with others bring out a person's hidden skills and potential.
- *Teacher Training Programs* — Consistent professional development opportunities for teachers contribute to the cultivation of compassion in the classroom. The mental health and social development of students have to be given main consideration in educational programmes for future teachers. As a direct consequence of this, pupils will have a greater sense of ease in expressing themselves to their respective teachers. In recent years, there has been a significant change in the obligations that are placed on educators. The conventional paradigm of education places the teacher in the role of the classroom's autocrat; the holistic model, on the other hand, positions teachers more in the role of guides and mentors than as tyrants.

It is more important than ever before for teachers in the classroom to assume greater and more substantial responsibilities. The holistic approach positions instructors more in the role of friends, mentors, and advisers to the students in their classroom.

- *After-school Clubs* — Students might potentially get a more well-rounded education via the usage of extracurricular activities at their schools, such as clubs and sports teams. Students are given the opportunity to relax and enjoy themselves outside of the confines of the classroom thanks to the aid provided by these groups. In addition to this, it illustrates to them that there is more to being successful than only achieving high grades in one's coursework.
- *Extracurricular activities* — It is possible for schools to integrate holistic education into the standard curriculum in a number of different ways, including via the use of extracurricular and co-curricular activities. It offers chances for education that take place in settings other than the conventional classroom. Examples of extracurricular activities include sports and the performing arts (music, dance, and theatre). Other types of cultural activities include reading and writing. Participating in extracurricular activities at school may help students develop skills such as leadership and the ability to work together effectively. Without acquiring these skills, a student's growth and development would remain unfinished. If students are not provided with chances to express themselves creatively via activities like music, dancing and the arts, it may be difficult for them to recognise their own skills and capabilities.
- *Parental Engagement* — There is a significant and positive association between the level of parental participation in their children's educational experiences and the level of success achieved by comprehensive instructional strategies. The importance of parents being actively involved in their children's education should be emphasised in schools as well as other types of institutions.
- *Learning Through Inquiry* — Students participate actively in a process of learning that promotes the study of ideas, high-level thinking, and inquiry that has obvious linkages to the actual world. This method of learning encourages students to study concepts, think deeply, and investigate. The term for this kind of educational approach is "active learning". Using this strategy might perhaps inspire students to ask more questions and engage more actively in their own education. Students, as a direct result of this, develop a deeper interest in any given subject, and they get more engaged in the process of figuring out how to solve difficulties.

Conclusion

It cannot be denied that a well-rounded education has the ability to have a formative effect on our nation. Pupils of today who have grown in all areas will offer themselves as tomorrow's thinking leaders once they have reached that point. The practice, which stretches back many decades, of providing its residents with a comprehensive education is one that has a long history in India. We need to collaborate in order to cultivate and continuously develop the ecosystem of holistic education in order for Indian institutions to compete on the international arena. Come relive the golden days of Nalanda and Takshashila Universites with me so that we may show the rest of the world our best educational traditions. Students are more likely to benefit from an environment that is interesting, inspirational, and encouraging if the educational system they are enrolled in adopts a more holistic approach. It is far simpler to say than to really achieve the goal of adopting a more holistic perspective in the classroom. It is a well-known fact that there are many challenges involved in the process of implementing more comprehensive pedagogical practices in educational institutions such as schools. Consequently, problems with inadequate infrastructure and finance, as well as challenges associated with the availability of appropriate training facilities for teachers, may be contributory causes. On the other side, there are many who believe that the significance of classroom lectures and textbooks is decreased when the attention is placed on the kid as a whole. This approach takes into account the requirements of the child as a whole, which means that the requirements of the child's body, intellect, heart, and spirit are all taken into account. Students are able to gain information, skills, and attitudes that will serve them throughout their lives when they get an education that emphasises a holistic approach.

The development of future citizens who will make meaningful contributions to society and the globe with true concern and awareness is the intended result of pursuing an education that takes a holistic approach. It integrates the fundamental concepts of connection and interconnection that are central to both environmental education and global education. The goal of holistic education, which is predicated on the concept of interdependence, is to make the world a place where humans and all forms of life may peacefully live with one another. It disagrees with the idea that consumerism should be one's primary focus in life in today's environment. Instead, it focuses on education that is founded on the fundamental realities of life and the natural world around us. The purpose of a holistic education is to bring together different aspects of society and the person. This vision of the long-term sustainability of education has to be brought back into focus as the primary goal of an education that takes a holistic approach. Educational institutions have to embrace more comprehensive methods to teaching if they want to maintain their relevance. Through comprehensive education, students have the opportunity to develop both their cerebral and physical identities concurrently. The only way to establish a healthy and powerful environment is via teaching and learning that assists kids in comprehending both the good and bad aspects of their surroundings. As a result, education is embedded inside the system. Many different kinds of social and cognitive activities are brought into the classroom by teachers, policymakers, and other stakeholders in order to encourage students' autonomy, openness to cooperation, and open communication.

References

Flake, C.L. (2000). *Holistic education: Principles, perspectives and practice).* Brandon, VT: Holistic Education Press.

Forbes, S. (2003). *Holistic education: An analysis of its ideas in nature*. Brandon, VT: Foundation for Educational Renewal.

Government of India (2020). *National Education Policy 2020*. New Delhi: Ministry of Education, Government of India.

Grimes, B. (2007). "Multidimensional classroom: development a comprehensive research base for Holistic education." Dissertation, England: University of Cambridge.

Martin, A.R. and Forbes, S.H. (2004). "What Holistic Education Claims About Itself: An Analysis of Holistic Schools" Literature. Paper presented at the American Education Research Association Annual Conference (San Diego, California, California, April 2004).

Mcilroy, T. (2022). Empowererd Parents. *Why is Holistic Development imporatant in the Early years?10 reasons*.

Nava, R.G. (2001). *Holistic Education: Pedagogy of Universal Love*. Brandon: Holistic Education Press.

Nielson, A.C. (2008). "The philosophy of regenerative education and living school." Dissertation, USA: University of California.

Sarkar, D. (2022). "NEP 2020 holistic education to reboot Society." *The New Indian Express*.

Scholar Base. (2014, March 5). Scholistic Approach to Learning. *Why holistic Education is important*.

Shriner, P., Banev, S., & Oxly, S. (2005). *Holistic education Resource Book*, Verlage: Waxmann

SRM University (2021). *NEP 2020 to provide Holistic, Student-centric, Flexible and Multidisciplinary Education*. Andhra Pradesh: SRM University AP.

UNESCO (1996). 'The four pillars of education,' in Learning: The Treasure Within: Report to UNESCO of the International Commission on Education for the Twenty First Century. Paris: UNESCO.

8

Reflective Teaching Practice

From the Perspectives of National Professional Standard for Teachers (NPST)

Nilay Mondal
Khagendranath Chattopadhyay

Introduction

The 21st century education system demands quality of every aspect of education. The teachers and their method of teaching are the very important factors of education. The choice of teaching method of teacher impacts the teaching-learning process greatly. Reflective teaching is a process that can enhance the quality of teaching and creates a positive learning environment for learners. Reflective teaching is an active process of examining one's own practice in order to improve the teaching-learning process comprehensively. It enables the entire teaching process active and meaningful. The draft "National Professional Standard for Teachers" was developed by NCTE to ensure the quality of teacher education in Indian Education System. National Professional Standard for Teachers (NPST) has mentioned reflective practice as an important quality standard for teachers.

Teachers are one of the vital resources in every educational institution. The quality of education is determined by the quality of the teachers and the teaching they provide. The role of teachers is important in providing learning experiences to lead their students in their future life. For this, the teachers are to be well equipped with the necessary skills and updated knowledge and empower themselves to meet new challenges. An ongoing concern for teacher educators and policymakers is equipping teachers with qualities that improve teaching and result in effective and successful learning. Among these qualities, reflection as a teaching strategy is very important for quality teaching as well as learning (Ayoobiyan & Rashidi, 2021). Yanuarti & Treagust (2015) also expressed reflective teaching practice is one of the main criteria to consider good teaching and learning practices. Teachers' reflection is part of teacher standards in India. NCF 2005, NCFTE 2009, NEP 2020, and NPST has emphasized reflective teaching practices as important criteria for teaching standard. In the 21st century Indian education system demands a quality teaching-learning process. And as an important draft, NPST has mentioned different quality indicators which are highly relevant for 21st century Indian Education. In this chapter, we discuss the concept of reflective teaching practice, its level, and types, and how the draft National Professional Standard for Teachers emphasized reflective teaching practice.

Conceptualising Reflective Teaching

The term 'reflection' is closely associated with the work of John Dewey and Schön (Akbari, Behzadpoor & Dadvand, 2010). John Dewey (1923, p. 118) defined reflection as "active, persistent and careful consideration of any belief or supposed form of knowledge in the light of the grounds that support it and the further conclusions to which it tends" (Vashistha, P., 2022). According to Zukrina, K. & Suwarish, M. (2021) reflective teaching practice is a process, where teachers look back at what he has done in the class and think of a better way by combining it with previous experience to change and improve teachers' behaviour, practice, and teaching. Larrivee, B. (2008) explained the term reflective practice as the on-the-job performance resulting from practising a reflective process consisting of decision-making and problem-solving. Here the researcher focused on decision-making and problem-solving as important considerations of reflective practice. Schön (1983) discussed two terms namely, 'reflective-in-action' and 'reflective-on-action' to explain how people reflect on their practice. He proposed that 'reflective-in-action' happens during an activity, i.e., on the spot reflection, on the other hand 'reflection-on-activity' takes place after an event, here the teacher thinks back, and reflects on the incident (Farahian & Rajabi, 2022).

Generally, the term reflective teaching refers to a process, where teachers revisit, and rethink their teaching practice in order to evaluate the effectiveness of their teaching in the class. They examine their overall performance as an effective teacher. In the teaching-learning process, reflective teaching is very essential as it deals with a better outcome for both teacher and students. Jack C. Richards (1990) published a three-stage process of reflection, which involves the event itself, recollection of the event, and review and response to the event. The first stage is an actual teaching process in the classroom, such as a lesson or other events of teaching. The next stage is the collection of the event that happens during teaching. Several methods are available during this stage including video or audio recording of the lesson, peer group discussion, or students' feedback. And in the final stage, the teacher critically evaluates his or her practices.

Types of Reflection

Valli (1997) described five different types of reflection. Within a teacher education programme, it would be helpful for prospective teachers and also it can be useful to decide for teachers what needs to be made. The five types of reflection have been explained below —

1. *Technical Reflection:* Technical reflection is concerned with externally imposed criteria. During technical reflection, the teachers judge their teaching performance based on those external guidelines. Those guidelines, standards, and evaluation criteria are set by an outside authority. Here research is the main source of knowledge. It is very much rule-governed.

2. *Reflection-in and on-Action*: Schön (1983) gave the terms 'reflection-in-action' and 'reflection-on-action'. 'Reflective-in-action' happens during the teaching-learning process, i.e., on-the-spot reflection; on the other hand, 'reflection-on-activity' takes place after classroom teaching, here the teacher thinks back and reflects on the incident. During reflection-in and on-action, prospective teachers are not directed to follow external rules.
3. *Deliberative Reflection*: In contrast to technical reflection, where research is the main source of knowledge, during deliberative reflection decision-making is based on a wide range of sources — research, guidance from expert teachers, experience, personal beliefs and values, and so on. Here multiple perspectives are followed not only a single voice. This teacher education programme focuses on developing decision-making capabilities. So, the quality of reflection would be judged by teachers' abilities.
4. *Personalistic Reflection*: Personalistic reflection involves allowing one's individual growth, connections with pupils, and upgrading pupils holistically (Minott, M., 2008). In personalistic reflection, teachers are concern not only for their student's academic achievement but also for all aspects of their students' lives — their personal interests, and their desire for the future. Teachers would be caretakers of their students, not just information givers. Here reflection quality is determined by the ability to empathize.
5. *Critical Reflection*: This type of reflection is influenced by political philosophers like Habermas (1974). Here school and knowledge are seen as political constructions. The aim of critical reflection is to improve the quality of life of marginalized people. The teacher considers the social, moral, and political dimensions of schooling. Critical reflection would help teachers to change or modify teaching methods and practice and school structure, that enhance social inequality and injustice.

Level of Reflection

Griffiths and Tann (1992) identified five levels of reflection. The five levels are —

1) *Rapid Reaction*: This is the level of the act-react process of teaching. This level is a part of 'reflection-in-action' from the work of David Schön (1983). At this level, teacher reflection is immediate and automatic. For example, if a child is giving a correct answer, a teacher may praise him/her automatically, but the reaction may not be the same for all teachers.
2) *Repair*: The second level is repair, i.e., thoughtful 'reflection-in-action'. At this level, teachers pause for thought during teaching and this is very quick. For example, if a teacher finds that a child shows an unexpected interest in a piece of work, then the teacher will decide whether to allow or carry on with normal work.
3) *Review*: This level and the following two are part of the 'reflection-on-action' of David Schön (1983), so thought and reflection is going on after

the teaching is completed. Review is often interpersonal and collegial. Review can happen any time during the day — during break time, or at the end of the day. At this level, the teacher will think about the progress of a particular child or particular group. And after review, if necessary, a teacher may modify the existing teaching-learning plan.

4) *Research*: During the fourth level, the observation becomes more systematic and sharply focused on the identified issue. The teacher may collect information during a week or month and analyze and evaluate that information. To gather information on a particular issue, the teacher may use a tick sheet, video, or reflective diary. After collecting the information, the teacher will reflect carefully on the reasons why the issue takes place.
5) *Re-theorising and Reformulating*: The re-theorising and reformulating level is more abstract and rigorous than other levels. It is a matter of months or years. At this level, the teacher critically read theories. The teacher's own theory regarding reflection will become changed. This is a long-term 'reflection-on-action'.

Classroom Activities that Promote Teacher Reflection

During the teaching-learning process, the teacher plays an important role to maintain the overall activities of a classroom. Spalding, A. (2020) mentioned some activities of a teacher that indicate reflective teaching. These are —

1) *The ratio of Teacher-Student Interaction*: Teacher-student interaction is one of the key indicators of reflective teaching. One-way or teacher-centred education reduces the interaction between student and teacher. A reflective teacher always encourages healthy interaction in and even outside the classroom.
2) *Type of Question*: It is important that what types of questions are asked by the teacher during the lessons. In a close-ended question, a student cannot explain the answer appropriately. A reflective teacher always asks students open-ended questions. An open-ended question is required for an effective teaching-learning process.
3) *Opportunity to Respond*: Student responses including asking them to answer the question, provide an opinion, or discuss a lesson, are essential for an effective classroom. And a reflective teacher always encourages students to respond in the classroom. They make every student active in the lessons.
4) Instructional vs. Non-instructional Time: During the lesson, a teacher should focus on time management. If students engage more time in the instructional process, they will learn more. So, a teacher should try to give more time to instructional activities than non-instructional activities like collecting students' work at the end of the lesson.
5) *Teacher talk vs. Student talk*: Depending on the learning content, teacher must determine the duration of student talk compared with teacher talk.

They decide how much talk is necessary from the teacher's or students' perspective, keeping in mind the nature of the topic.

6) *Growth vs. Fixed Mindset:* A fixed mindset teacher believes that student qualities such as intelligence, and abilities are innate and unchangeable. A reflective teacher should always be a growth mindset person and always promote a growth mindset among students. A growth mindset teacher believes that students' qualities can be developed by consistent efforts.

Characteristics of a Reflective Teacher

To become a reflective practitioner, a teacher needs to follow some important criteria. D.L. Jones (1990) mentioned three important characteristics of a reflective teacher.

1) *Open Mindedness:* An open-minded teacher should be an active listener and ready to listen to different sides to give attention to all possible alternatives and to find out the possibility of errors (Jones, D.L., 1990). A reflective teacher examines his or her various activities and tries to find out which are actually beneficial for learners' development. A reflective teacher should not be rigid in his or her own beliefs, always be ready to adopt new and effective practices.
2) *Attitude of Responsibility:* Moral and responsible actions of teachers are an essential element of teaching (Jones, D.L., 1990). A reflective teacher is responsible for his or her action in the school. A reflective teacher should always be responsible for students' holistic development.
3) *Whole-heartedness*: It refers to that "responsibility and open mindedness must be the central element in the life of reflective practitioner" (Jones, D. L., 1990). Pandey (2013) states that overcoming fear and uncertainties of the teaching process to critically evaluate their practices in order to improve. It refers that the reflective teacher to be totally involved in a subject (Nurfaidah, 2018)

Eby and Kujawa (1998) stated six important characteristics of a reflective teacher—

1) Reflective teachers are active
2) Reflective teachers are persistent
3) Reflective teachers are careful
4) Reflective teachers are skeptical
5) Reflective teachers are rational
6) Reflective teachers are proactive.

National Professional Standard for Teachers (NPST)

The draft "National Professional Standard for Teachers" was developed by NCTE to ensure the quality of teacher education in Indian Education System. This draft has identified several standards, which are in line with the fundamental principles given in the NEP 2020. These professional criteria are necessary for effective teaching-learning system. The professional standards ensure that teachers from different level of education would be highly competent, professionally trained and passionate.

NPST towards Reflective Practice

National Professional Standard for Teachers (NPST) as a part of NEP 2020 has mentioned reflective practice as an important domain of professional development as well as the professional standard. Here the researcher discusses important statements regarding reflective practice from NPST. It states that *"Reflect on own teaching practice and identify learning needs" (p. 41)*. The teachers are directed towards reflecting at their own teaching, which they practise in the classroom and from that they must identify the learning needs of the students. To improve the quality of learning, it is required to identify the learning needs and the teacher must try to solve the problems. This draft has mentioned four types of teachers according to their performance criteria, i.e., Beginner teacher, Proficient teacher, Expert teacher and Lead teacher. Here reflection as a sub-domain of professional development has identified different performance criteria according to different types of teachers.

- *Beginner Teacher*
  "Demonstrate understanding of reflective practices and able to reflect on own work" (p. 41)
  So, as a beginner teacher he/she just started to understand the concept and process of reflection and gradually he/she can reflect on own work in practical situations.
- *Proficient Teacher*
  "Use reflective practices to modify own teaching practice" (p. 41)
  So, here we can notice that the performance/criteria of a proficient teacher are not only just reflect their teaching but also, they can be able to modify their practice according to learning needs or situations. NPST here stressed on modification of teaching based on reflection.
- *Expert Teacher*
  "Support colleagues in reflecting on their teaching practice to improve teaching and learning" (p. 41)
  Here NPST has focused on how teachers are able to support their colleagues in reflective practice. So, as an expert teacher he/she must help his/her colleagues in the process of reflective practice.
- *Lead Teacher*
  "Coach and mentor colleagues in applying reflective practices." (p. 41)
  Lead teachers are the most experienced teachers. They have already completed previous three performances. Here the teachers have become

coach or mentor. They help their colleagues to apply reflective practice in real or practical situation.

Conclusion

In the present chapter, the researchers have attempted to strengthen the connection between teachers' reflective teaching practices and quality criteria as mentioned by NPST. The chapter explained what reflective practice entails, types and levels of reflective teaching practice and the important statements regarding reflection in the draft NPST. When teachers are critically and systematically reflecting on their teaching practices, then they can ensure effective and quality teaching. Reflective practices greatly impact teachers' professional development, and a professional teacher is always responsible for effective learning among learners. Reflective teachers are more aware of what happens in the lesson. With such awareness, they become more conscious about the teaching-learning process and try to offer more learning opportunity for learners that creates a quality teaching-learning system.

References

Akbari, R., Behzadpoor, F., & Dadvand, B. (2010). Development of English language teaching reflection inventory. *System*, *38*(2), 211-227. https://doi.org/10.1016/j.system.2010.03.003

Ayoobiyan, H., & Rashidi, N. (2021). Can reflective teaching promote resilience among Iranian EFL teachers? A mixed-method design. *Reflective Practice*, *22*(3), 293-305. https://doi.org/10.1080/14623943.2021.1873758

Davut Göker, S. (2016). "Use of reflective journals in development of teachers' leadership and teaching skills." *Universal Journal of Educational Research*, *4*(12A), 63-70. https://doi.org/10.13189/ujer.2016.041309

Dewey, J. (1933). *How we think: A restatement of the relation of reflective thinking to the educative process*. Houghton Mifflin.

Eby, J.W., & Kujawa, E. (1998). *Reflective planning, teaching and evaluation: K-12* (3rd ed.). Upper Saddle River, NJ; Merrill-Prentice Hall

Farahian, M., & Rajabi, Y. (2022). "An investigation into the level of reflection and barrier to EFL teachers' reflective practice." *International Journal of Research in English Education*, *7*(2), 81-100.

Griffiths, M., & Tann, S. (1992). "Using reflective practice to link personal and public theories." *Journal of Education for Teaching*, *18*(1), 69-84. https://doi.org/10.1080/0260747920180107

Hollins, E.R. (2011). "Teacher preparation for quality teaching." *Journal of Teacher Education*, *62*(4), 395-407. https://doi.org/10.1177/0022487111409415

Jones, D.L. (1990). The challenge of becoming a reflective teacher. *Kappa Delta Pi Record*, *27*(1), 16-18. https://doi.org/10.1080/00228958.1990.10518618

Journal editors | IGI global. (n.d.). IGI Global: International Academic Publisher. https://www.igi-global.com/dictionary/quality-teaching

Larrivee, B. (2008). Development of a tool to assess teachers' level of reflective practice. *Reflective Practice*, *9*(3), 341-360. https://doi.org/10.1080/14623940802207451

Mathew, P., Mathew, P., & Peechattu, P.J. (2017). "Reflective Practices: A Means to Teacher Development." *Asia Pacific Journal of Contemporary Education and Communication Technology*, *3*(1), 126-131. www.apiar.org.au

Minott, M.A. (2008). "Valli's typology of reflection and the analysis of pre-service teachers' reflective journals." *Australian Journal of Teacher Education, 33*(5). https://doi.org/10.14221/ajte.2008v33n5.4

Murray, E. (2015). Improving Teaching through Collaborative Reflective Teaching Cycles. *Investigations in Mathematics Learning*, *7*(3), 23-29. https://doi.org/10.1080/24727466.2015.11790343

National Professional Standards for Teachers-2021 Prepared by NCTE, Download from https://ncte.gov.in/WebAdminFiles/PublicNotice/Hindi_0_17_11_2021_637727482281976435.pdf

Njiku, J. (2018). Peer Observation and Reflective Teaching: Student-Teachers Learning to Teach Mathematics from their own Experiences. *LWATI: A Journal of Contemporary Research, 15*(3), 23-34.

Nurfaidah, S. (2018). Three attitudes of a reflective teacher. *Research and Innovation in Language Learning, 1*(1), 39. https://doi.org/10.33603/rill.v1i1.1084

Orlova, N. (2009). Video Recording as a Stimulus for Reflection in Pre-Service EFL Teacher Training. *English Teaching Forum*, 30-35.

Pandey, S.R. (2013). Reflective practice: A gateway to professional development. *Journal of NELTA, 17*(1-2), 40-49. https://doi.org/10.3126/nelta.v17i1-2.8091

Pant, P. (2022, October 27). *What is reflective teaching and its benefits*. Suraasa | Online Teacher Training Courses, Qualifications. https://www.suraasa.com/blog/reflective-teaching

Pellegrino, A.M., & Gerber, B.L. (2012). Teacher Reflection Through Video-Recording Analysis. *Georgia Educational Researcher*, *9*(1). https://doi.org/10.20429/ger.2012.090101

Qing, X.U. (2009). Reflective Teaching— an Effective Path for EFL Teacher's Professional Development. *Canadian Social Science*, *5*(2), 35-40.

Schon, D. A. (1983). *The reflective practitioner: How professionals think in action.* Basic Books, New York.

Spalding, A. (2020). *How to encourage reflective teaching in your school.* Professional Learning Resources & Blog | IRIS Connect. https://blog.irisconnect.com/uk/blog/5-benefits-of-encouraging-teacher-self-reflection

Valli, L. (1997). "Listening to other voices: A description of teacher reflection in the United States." *Peabody Journal of Education, 72*(1), 67-88. https://doi.org/10.1207/s15327930pje7201_4

Vashistha, P. (2021). "Education 4.0 Role of reflective teacher as a key transition." *Kalyan Bharati, 36*(8), 328-332.

Wagner, K. (2006). *Benefits of Reflective Practice.* ResearchGate | Find and share research. https://www.researchgate.net/publication/234744889_Benefits_of_Reflective_Practice

Wittek, L., & Habib, L. (2013). "Quality Teaching and Learning as Practice Within Different Disciplinary Discourses." *International Journal of Teaching and Learning in Higher Education, 25*(3), 275-287.

9

Holistic and Multidisciplinary Approach to Higher Education and NEP 2020

Basanti Mahanta
Bijan Sarkar

Introduction

The Government of India passed the National Education Policy 2020 (NEP 2020) on July 29, 2020. The new policy featured arguing a paradigm shift in education in India from the traditional approach to a multidisciplinary and holistic approach. Development of critical thinking and problem-working capacities results in creativity. A holistic and multidisciplinary education can help an individual's all-around development — intellectual, physical, emotional, aesthetic, moral, and social. The NEP 2020 envisages bringing back more holistic education in India in the 21st century. The present study has concentrated on the holistic approach to higher education from the NEP 2020 lens. The researchers have also analysed how a multidisciplinary and holistic approach can play an important part in the child's 'All Round Development' in respect of global education.

NEP 2020 promotes multi-correctional and holistic education with a broader ambition to foster balance and honesty of knowledge besides duly recognizing, relating, and nurturing the unique capabilities of every student, by sensitizing preceptors as well as parents to inspire each student's holistic development in both academic and non-academic disciplines. The policy also focuses on developing multidisciplinary education as it's known to make vibrant communities of scholars, thinkers, inventors, and scientists, by enabling scholars to come well-rounded individuals, who can suppose holistically for their life and the world. Yash Pal Committee Report emphasizes the need for multidisciplinary education. The report declared that there is a need to interpret pupils, particularly at the undergraduate level, to various disciplines (Yash Pal, 2009). Pathak (2020) in his study on 'Holistic Education, Critical Thinking, and Multidisciplinary Approach' has raised some serious questions, looked at the social dynamics of education, and proposed a set of possibilities from the social context of learning. He puts forward how the academic machinery works and has elaborated on the meaning attached to the concept from multiple perspectives, that is, of the students, teachers, parents, and the larger society. Quoting NEP 2020, Pathak has explained the need for integral education that would promote critical thinking. He further advocated that pedagogy must evolve to make education more holistic, inquiry-driven, learner-centred, flexible, experiential, discovery-oriented, and enjoyable. Yadav (2020) in her study on 'NEP 2020: Towards a holistic and multidisciplinary approach to Education' supported NEP 2020 for its completeness and stated that the application of the policy would bring about inclusion, holistic development of the pupils as well as provide the multidisciplinary approach to education. Aithal & Aithal (2020) in a study on the 'Analysis of the Indian National Education Policy 2020 towards Achieving its Objectives' have extracted the elements of a well-defined and futuristic education embedded in the new policy. The study suggests strict monitoring of quality through biennial accreditation based on self-declaration of progress through technology-based monitoring. Sundaram (2020) in her article on 'National Education Policy 1986 vs. National Education Policy 2020 – A Comparative Study' accomplishes that NEP 2020 has much scope for a multidisciplinary approach with digital learning, self-sufficiency in curriculum, and courses and covers the way for holistic development of student-centric learning. According to UGC (2022) in the report Guidelines for Transforming Higher Education Institutions (HEIs) into Multidisciplinary Institutions — Academic collaboration between institutions, through HEI clusters, leads to multidisciplinary education and research in different modes.

Aims of Holistic and Multidisciplinary Education in the Light of NEP 2020

A multidisciplinary and Holistic Approach in Higher Education aims to develop the following skills and overall personality building in the youth like –

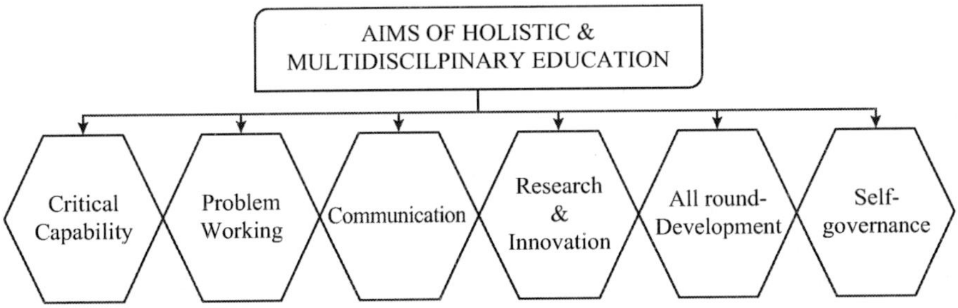

Source: Authors.

- *Critical capability*: With multiple discipline knowledge, a pupil can suppose beyond the horizon of a single discipline and suppose about the logical connections between different ideas.
- *Problem-working*: Quick and effective result to a problem, is the skill that employers search for in the present time. The knowledge of different subjects in a multidisciplinary approach will develop pupils' logic and logical experience to handle delicate situations.
- *Communication*: Knowledge is confidence and effective communication is the result of wide knowledge. With holistic and multidisciplinary education

scholars will be suitable to partake in ideas, express their passions and contribute to public progress.

- *Research and innovation*: To get better results in creativity, development of critical thinking, opinions making chops, and problem-working capacities, it is necessary to integrate the humanities and trades with Science, Technology, Engineering and Mathematics (STEM), which is imaged in the NEP 2020. Embracing the multidisciplinary and holistic approach to education will help to do better in research and innovation.
- *All-round development*: A holistic and multidisciplinary education would help the development of an existent. It isn't good to make constraints on subjects in which an existent isn't interested. Rather than give them the choice of subjects he wants and let to finish their studies at the undergraduate position. A holistic and multidisciplinary education helps to develop aesthetic, social, intellectual, physical, and moral experiences in an intertwined manner.
- *Self-governance*: With the choice of their subjects, pupils will come suitable to set their precedence and knowledge of geography for disciplined literacy.

Key Concerns of Holistic and Multidisciplinary Education in the Context of NEP 2020

Holistic and multidisciplinary education will help advance well-rounded individuals that possess critical 21st century abilities in fields crosswise the arts, humanities, languages, sciences, social sciences, and professional, and vocational fields. UGC (2022) declared in the report Guidelines for Transforming HEIs into Multidisciplinary Institutions that the NEP 2020 visualizes the establishment of one Education Department in colleges or universities or HEIs to contribute to a multidisciplinary and holistic education to contribute to research and development in three areas:

1) to conduct cutting-edge research in various aspects of education,
2) to support the actualization of all teacher education in multidisciplinary institutions, and
3) to contribute to multidisciplinary and holistic higher education across disciplines.

- Large multidisciplinary universities and colleges/associations will grease the move towards high-quality holistic and multidisciplinary education. Inflexibility in class and new and engaging course options will be offered to pupils, in addition to rigorous specialization in subjects. This will be encouraged by increased faculty and institutional autonomy in setting classes. Pedagogy will have an increased emphasis on communication, discussion, debate, exploration, and openings for cross-correctional and interdisciplinary thinking. Departments in Languages, Literature, Music, Philosophy, Indology, Art, Dance, Theatre, Education, Mathematics, Statistics, Pure and Applied bits of knowledge, Sociology, Economics,

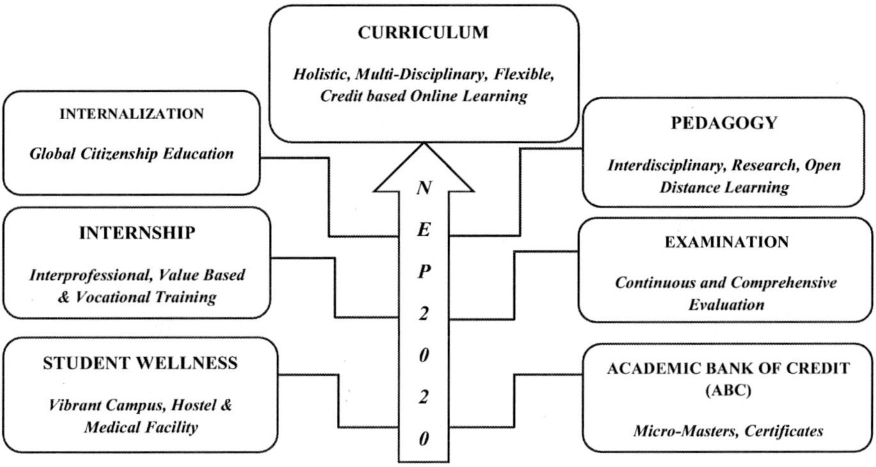

Figure 9.1: *Roadmap for Multidisciplinary Education and Research Universities*

Source: Authors

Sports, restatement and interpretation, and other similar subjects are demanded a multidisciplinary.

- Imaginative and flexible curricular structures will enable creative combinations of disciplines for study and would offer multiple entry and exit points, therefore, removing presently current rigid boundaries and creating new possibilities for lifelong literacy. Graduate- positions, master's, and doctoral education in large multidisciplinary universities, while furnishing authoritarian exploration-grounded specialization, would also give openings for multidisciplinary work, including in academia, government, and diligence.
- Flexible and innovative curricula towards the attainment of such a holistic and multidisciplinary education, the flexible and innovative classes of all Advanced Education Institutes (HEIs) shall include credit-grounded courses and systems in the areas of community engagement and service, environmental education and value-grounded education. Environment education will include areas similar to climate change, pollution, waste control, sanitation, natural diversity conservation, natural coffers and biodiversity administration, timber and wildlife conservation, and sustainable development and living. Value-grounded education will include the development of humanistic, ethical, indigenous, and universal moral values of verity (Satya), righteous conduct (dharma), peace (shanti), love (prem), force (ahimsa), scientific temper, citizenship values, and also life-chops; assignments in service and participation in community service programmes will be considered an integral part of holistic education.
- Model public universities for holistic and multidisciplinary education, at par with the Indian Institutes of Technology (IITs), Indian Institutes of

Management (IIMs), etc., called Multidisciplinary Education and Research Universities (MERUs) will be set up and will aim to attain the loftiest global ethics in quality education. They will also help set the loftiest ethics for multidisciplinary education across India.

- The structure and lengths of degree programmes shall be acclimated consequently. The undergraduate degree will be of either a 3 or 4-year duration, with multiple exit options within this period, with applicable instruments, an instrument after completing 1-time in a discipline or field including vocational and professional areas, or a certificate after 2-times of study, or a Bachelor's degree after a 3-time programme. The 4-time multidisciplinary Bachelorette's programme, still, shall be the favoured option since it allows the occasion to witness the full range of holistic and multidisciplinary education in addition to a focus on the chosen major and minors as per the choices of the pupil. An Academic Bank of Credit (ABC) shall be established which would digitally store the academic credits earned from colourful honoured Advanced Education Institutes (HEIs) so that the degrees from other Education Institutes (HEIs) can be awarded considering credits earned.
- Focus on research and innovation by setting up a start-up development centre, technology development centres, centres in frontier areas of research, greater industry-academic linkages, and interdisciplinary research including humanities and social sciences research. Given the situation of epidemics and pandemics, HEIs must take the lead in undertaking research in areas of infectious diseases, epidemiology, diagnostics, instrumentation, and other relevant areas. Higher education institutions will develop specific hand-holding mechanisms for promoting modernization among student communities.

Learning Strategies for Holistic Development

The holistic approach to education develops a learner's social and academic maturity to accept life's challenges, build their thoughts, and learn from their errors (Sarkar, 2022). Holistic education makes a student for lifelong learning. The educational focus moves toward the life skills, attitudes, and personal awareness the student will need in an increasingly complex world (Sarkar, 2022). Holistic development is the combination of enhancing the education model of empowering pupils' performance and schoolteacher strategies in different areas. Some learning strategies for holistic development are:

- *Team learning:* It increases tone-confidence and leadership quality and occurs when a person shares his or her knowledge and views to reach the destination of cooperation where an existent learns together to achieve the thing of a platoon task. The stylish part of platoon literacy is the strong collaboration and correlation between individualities. It shows the retired quality of the person while doing platoon literacy.

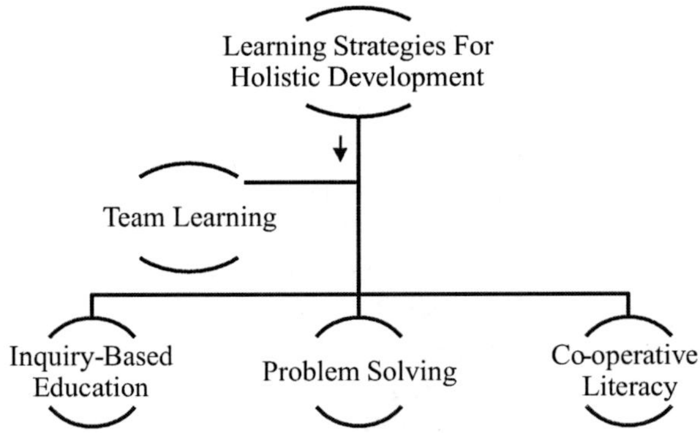

Figure 9.2: *Learning Strategies for Holistic Development*

Source: Authors.

- *Inquiry-based education:* This literacy process involves academics in the discussion of concepts, research findings, and a perceptive stance of inquiry that makes connections to the actual world. Literacy can support academics in this process by encouraging them to share existential literacy and pose questions. Students grow increasingly interested in inquiry-based learning as a result.
- *Problem-solving:* The problem-solving processes on any content and increasing their interest by involvement in inquiry-grounded literacy.
- *Transforming literacy:* It is the tool to enhance educational values' results and issues and produce educational literacy material, perfecting the conception and traits of literacy.
- *Cooperative literacy:* When working together, students contribute significantly to a large group or peer group. Partial plan conditioning improves an individual's cognitive and affective sphere capability by providing multiple opportunities and problem-solving skills for learning and development through group collaboration. Students improve their tone of voice and advanced academic skills through cooperative literacy.

Benefits of Holistic Education

Holistic education is based on a learning attitude that brings several profits to students, teachers, schools, and communities. Students are empowered to improve their educational outcomes and gain the life skills necessary to take on a successful professional career. According to Lemkow (1990), holistic education aims to bridge the gaps in a contemporary civilization that dichotomises mind and body, intellect and emotion, rationality and intuition, science and art, individual and society, and humanity and nature. The benefits of holistic education according to American University (2020) and HEI School (2022) are –

1) *Develops Well-rounded Adults:* Holistic education is designed to ensure people grow with an appreciation of all aspects of life academic, sporting,

social, etc. This helps ensure people are balanced and ready to contribute to society.

2) *Improved Academic Achievement:* Holistic education can ameliorate the academic achievements of all children, anyhow of background and circumstances, by feeding individual learning styles and furnishing a probative literacy context. According to the Learning Policy Institute, children's brain capacities are improved when they feel physically and emotionally safe and connected to others.
3) *Developed Creative Thinking:* In the 21st Century, we're anticipated to have multiple different careers. People's careers are more likely to bear critical and creative thinking experience than the manufacturing societies of history. To be ready for future challenges, youthful people need a broad range of knowledge and social chops that can be gained through a holistic class.
4) *Enhanced Mental and Emotional Well-being:* In a conformational ambient, where social and emotional literacy is emphasized along with academics, scholars have a better chance of arising with character-mindfulness, confidence, and a sense of social responsibility.
5) *Increased Problem-Solving Ability:* Pupils assigned with working on real-world problems in their communities' crop with strong critical-thinking chops. These hands-on systems give scholars chops that will apply to their adult careers, similar to the gathering, assaying, and reporting data and uniting with others.

Limitations of Holistic Education

Critics have cited several downsides to holistic education and some of the more prominent ones have been given below –

- *Underemphasize Academic Learning:* A holistic approach may limit children's time on academic aspects of literacy. We live in a competitive world where education systems are contending to have the most educated pool for calculation and knowledge of the future. In this environment, a nation with a holistic class may slip behind other nations that are ray-concentrated on calculation and knowledge alone.
- *Rarely used beyond early years of education:* This isn't important amenability to using a holistic approach beyond the early times. While in the early times, we had holistic approaches like play-grounded literacy and forestland seminaries, after about periods 8-9, youthful people are decreasingly dragooned into fastening more and more on calculation and knowledge to the detriment of other aspects of the 'whole' child.
- *Time-Consuming and Precious:* Numerous holistic literacy openings are time-consuming and precious. For illustration, we frequently shoot pupils to 'summer camps for holistic development. This costs parents a lot of plutocrats. Also, if we want our children to appreciate trades and sports, these are frequently expensive adulterous openings only open to the fairly fat.

- *Doesn't fit well with numerous academy Curricula:* Many schools have veritably structured literacy issues. They're frequently veritably crowded with calculation, wisdom, and knowledge as the most important rudiments. When we educate within these education systems, it's hard for preceptors to build holistic literacy openings in the classroom.
- *Many parents may disagree with it:* Teachers may find that teachers will dispute an overemphasis on social-emotional education, trades, humanities, and sports. You may come across parents who tell you that their children are falling behind other children of their age because of how you're tutoring them.

Conclusion

We need to understand what children need to bear from education, not only academic growth but also keep growing other than courses like extracurricular activities. Every parent's content to transfer their children to school and council for the need to learn some specialized things and betterment of the future and also fitting for holistic development in all-around (Social, Intellectual, Physical, Emotional and Mental) development that means holistic development Education is the inner part for only education system can change the actions and help scholars and help pupils to understand his/ her intellectual pressure and the teaching-learning process is the only way to make up the healthy and important atmosphere to understand the relationship between positive and negative environment. Also constructing self-dependence and team spirit and true communication in education, educationist, policymaker and stakeholder ensure that the class isn't only integrated with a theory based but also with a large number of conditioning and practices. The recent initiative of multidisciplinary education of the Government of India, contained in NEP 2020, is important. There are challenges of institutional restructuring as a large asset is required for a single discipline institution to adapt into a multidisciplinary institution. However, partially the curricular restructuring will allow multidisciplinary teaching in Indian higher education.

References

Aithal, P.S, & Aithal S. (2020) Analysis of the Indian National Education Policy 2020 towards Achieving its Objectives. *International Journal of Management, Technology, and Social Sciences*. 5(2):19–41. http://doi.org/10.5281/zenodo.3988767.

Bhushan, S. (2020). *Multidisciplinary Approach to Higher Education.* Commonwealth Educational Media Centre for Asia (CEMCA), 1-14. Retrieved from- https://www.cemca.org/ckfinder/userfiles/files/EdTech-Notes-Multidisciplinary-Approach-in-Higher-Education.pdf.

Channawar, S. (2022). Conceptual Framework for Holistic Development: NEP 2020, *Madhya Bharti UGC Care Group I Journal,* 82(24): 22-27. Retrieved from- https://www.researchgate.net/publication/368662624.

Gurchal, M.G. & Yamdagini, P. (2022). 252 Multidisciplinary and Holistic Approach in Higher Education Concerning NEP 2020, *International Journal of Advanced Research in Science, Communication and Technology (IJARSCT)*, 2(5): 66-69. Retrieved from- https://ijarsct.co.in/Paper3561.pdf

Kakodkar, P.V. & Manivasakan S. (2022). National Education Policy 2020 compliant multidisciplinary education and research universities for dental education in India – A road map, *Review Article on Medical Education* 3(1): 60-63. Retrieved from- http://www.journaljme.org/text.asp?2022/3/1/60/344280.

Lemkow, A.F. (2021). A Holistic Approach to Education for Sustainability: Ecofeminism as a Tool to Enhance Sustainability Attitudes in Pre-service Teachers, *Journal of Teacher Education for Sustainability*, 23(1): 6-21. Retrieved from- https://doi.org/10.2478/jtes-2021-0002

MHRD (2020). *National Education Policy 2020*. New Delhi: MHRD, Govt. of India.

Pathak, A. (2020). Holistic Education, Critical Thinking, and Multidisciplinary Approach– Are the educational ideals the National Education Policy has proposed merely fancy words? *The New Learn*. 2020. Retrieved from https://www.thenewleam.com/2020/08/holistic-education-criticalthinking-and-multidisciplinary-approach/

Priyadarshini, A. & Dave, D. (2021). Holistic and Multidisciplinary Education through Open and Distance Learning to Realise the Vision of National Education Policy-2020, *UNIVERSITY NEWS*, 59(07): 70-73. Retrieved from- https://www.researchgate.net/publication/349456236.

Sarkar, D. (2022). NEP 2020 holistic education to Reboot Society. *The New Indian Express*. Retrieved from http://www.newindianexpress.com/opinions/2022/jul/28/nep-2020holistic educationtorebootsociety2481715.html#:~:text=increasingly%20complex%20world.

Shukla, B., Joshi, M., Sujatha, R., Beena, T. & Kumar, H. (2022). Demystifying Approaches of Holistic and Multidisciplinary Education for Diverse Career Opportunities: NEP 2020, *Indian Journal of Science and Technology*, 15(14): 603-607.Retrieved from- https://doi.org/10.17485/IJST/v15i14.2296.

Sundaram, K.M. (). National Education Policy 1986 vs. National Education Policy 2020 – A Comparative Study, *International Research Journal on Advanced Science Hub (IRJASH),* 2(10): 127-131. Retrieved from- https://www.rspsciencehub.com/article_5948.html

UGC (2022). Guidelines for Transforming Higher Education Institutions (HEIs) into Multidisciplinary Institutions, 1-26. Retrieved from- www.ugc.ac.in.

Yadav, S. (2020). Towards a holistic and multidisciplinary approach to education under Shikshak Parva Initiative *Ministry of Education, PIB Delhi.* Retrieved from- https://pib.gov.in/PressReleaseIframePage.aspx?PRID=1656274

10

Developing, Nourishing and Bolstering Skills through Envisaging NEP 2020

Parnab Ghosh

Introduction

India is a country endowed with huge human resources lacking skilled individuals in global employment opportunities. The youths require necessary skills acquisition and competencies relevant to international standards. With the growing economic and industrial development, a shortage of skilled human resources has been observed but it should not be a constraint for our nation because of increased human resources. The NEP 2020 has envisaged this issue with great vitality. It has emphasized skill development or acquisition and enhancement, especially for the major population of the country i.e., youths. Various recommendations, measures, and initiatives have been taken by the Government of India since independence but all those resulted in lukewarm development. The NEP 2020 has stressed the practical implementation of its recommendations to a great extent to prepare our youths skilled and employable. This qualitative analytical study has tried to find out the different aspects of skill development and their implementation by accumulating and analyzing data acquired from secondary sources.

The National Education Policy NEP 2020 is a comprehensive framework that aims to transform the Indian education system. One of the key objectives of the NEP 2020 is to promote skill development among students. The policy recognizes the importance of developing skills that are relevant to the changing needs of the economy and society (Devi & Cheluvaraju, 2020). In this article, we will explore how the NEP 2020 is promoting skill development in India. The NEP 2020 places a strong emphasis on vocational education. The policy recognizes that traditional academic programmes may not be suitable for all students and that vocational education can provide an alternative pathway to success (Verma & Kumar, 2021). The NEP 2020 proposes to integrate vocational education into mainstream education, starting from the secondary level (Aithal & Aithal, 2020). This will enable students to acquire practical skills that are relevant to various industries and sectors. The NEP 2020 also recognizes the importance of technology in promoting skill development. The policy proposes to leverage technology to provide access to high-quality educational resources and training programmes (Shukla, Joshi, Sujatha, Beena & Kumar, 2022). This will enable students to acquire new skills and knowledge at their own pace and convenience. The NEP 2020 also proposes to establish a National Educational Technology Forum (NETF) to facilitate the use of technology in education. The NEP 2020 recognizes that collaboration with industry is essential for promoting skill development. The policy proposes to establish partnerships between educational institutions and industry players to provide students with hands-on training and exposure to real-world scenarios. This will enable students to develop skills that are aligned with the needs of the industry. The NEP 2020 also proposes to establish a National Research Foundation (NRF) to promote research and innovation in various fields, including skill development.

Background and Genesis of Skill Development Programmes in India

Skill Development in the Gandhian Concept of Basic Education: Modern history determines Gandhiji as the pioneer of skill development activities. Mahatma Gandhi was one of the earliest advocates of 'self-reliance' in contemporary history. To support the rural economy and encourage indigenous production to achieve self-sufficiency, he offered a unique and innovative model of development. His early endeavours were represented by the word 'Hind Swaraj' (1909), where he expressed his opinions on localism and involvement at the grassroots level, the function of the local community, and its capability to produce, generate, and offer a sustainable life to all members of a community. Later, he added these goals into the Constructive Programme (1941), in which he talked of building 'Poorna Swaraj' using the truth, nonviolent means, and the independence of every unit. The concept of self-reliance refers to initiatives that are financially self-sufficient, depend on one's resources, and have ways to a goal. During the Indus Valley Civilization, India had conventional production methods whether they are agricultural or non-agricultural.

Gandhiji's Constructive Programme: Through truthfulness and non-violent methods, with the independence of every modest unit without discrimination of race, colour, or religion, he was interested in creating an efficient civil society to ensure the advantages of independence could be transmitted to the people; for this, he wanted to set up a circle of grassroots administrators who would work for the innovative change of the country. He consistently centred his plans on the 'Khadi' which signified the first step toward financial liberty and equal treatment for every individual within the country as well as decentralization of production and supply of the necessities of life and other rural businesses as well. In this way, 'Poorna Swaraj' (Complete Freedom) could be realized.

Various attempts have been made to integrate vocational education as a part of school education, but the achievement has been very less in reality. The post-independent education commissions like the Mudaliar Commission (1952-53) have recommended giving importance to the vocational education but the result was not worthwhile to mention (Arun & Malik, 2022). Later the Kothari Commission (1964-66) suggested making skill-based vocational education a distinct stream of higher secondary education. This recommendation was taken with earnest care and importance but did not reach any remarkable height at all because of several reasons like poor public perception about vocational education as well as its social status and nature of employment lost significance in the major middle-class families. Ultimately the outcome went in vain (Prakash, 2021).

Prior Initiative and Perspective of Skill-based Education

Atal Innovation Mission (AIM)

The industrialization that traversed the globe in the previous century left India behind. However, India does have a special chance to contribute to the knowledge-driven revolution that is now spreading across the globe. To achieve this, the NITI Aayog has established the long-term national cornerstone enterprise AIM. The main goal of AIM is to build and support a top-notch innovative and entrepreneurial environment across the entire nation, as well as to provide such an ecosystem so that it can turn our current job searchers into future job creators.

AIM's Holistic Approach: The Atal Innovation Mission has initiated a holistic framework to achieve its goals:

1) A need for entrepreneurship prevails. The development of an inventive, problem-solving mindset in high school students is urgently needed at the educational level.
2) The number of startups is increasing both at the university and corporate levels. Many startup projects, both from the government and the business sector, have been successful in the nation.
3) However, there is an increasing need for top-notch incubators in different institutions around the nation to support and nurture startups and ensure their success. This assistance would be provided mostly by incubators.
4) With a total of 100 smart cities recognized across the nation, we must ensure that world-class incubators are present in every single one of them.
5) At last, there has been an evolution in views towards entrepreneurship (Seshadri, 2020).

Atal Tinkering Labs

1) The Atal Innovation Mission has created Atal Tinkering Laboratories (ATLs) in schools throughout India with the goal of "Cultivating One Million Children in India as Neoteric Innovators."
2) The goal of this programme is to cultivate in young minds a sense of wonder, imagination, and creativity as well as to instil skills like design mentality, mathematical reasoning, adaptive learning, physical computing, etc. (Seshadri, 2020).
3) ATL is a workspace where children can provide shape to their thoughts through hands-on DIY (Do It Yourself) mode and develop innovation skills.

4) Young children will have the opportunity to work with tools and equipment to comprehend STEM (Science, Technology, Engineering and Math) principles.
5) The ATL would include computers, 3D printers, sensors, open-source microcontroller boards, science, electronics, robotics, educational kits, and other "do it yourself" learning tools.

Children's imaginations are encouraged by practical knowledge and access to the newest tools and technologies as they learn to translate abstract concepts learned in class into practical solutions. It encourages school children to adopt an inventive, problem-solving approach. For our nation's children and young people, this is crucial. One can develop an attitude to become a prospective creator of employment of the future if one can start developing novel designs and solutions in the classroom.

National Challenges for Youngsters

In New Delhi, the "Ideate for India – Creative Solutions Using Technology" National Youth Challenge is unveiled recently.

1) The purpose of this nationwide challenge is to offer school children around the nation a forum and opportunity to develop creative solutions to issues they observe in their surroundings and their communities.
2) "Ideate for India" will equip and enable these students to go from being "users" of technology to "creators" of new indigenous technologies to address pressing local challenges by reimagining solutions.
3) All students in the country in grades 6 to 12 are eligible to participate in the National Challenge.
4) Students may express their opinions on any of the 11 central theme areas.
5) For the challenge, students must browse online videos, comprehend problem-solving techniques, and share a 90-second video outlining the issue and a possible fix.

To achieve the government's goal of "Transforming India," MHRD made great strides in the education sector's transformation. Education Quality Upgrading and Inclusive Programme (EQUIP), a five-year vision plan, has been made public by the Department of Higher Education Ministry. SWAYAM 2.0, Deeksharambh, and PARAMARSH are a few of this department's key projects. (Yojana Team, 2020).

Vision NEP 2020 and Mission-Skill Development of the Nation

The conventional system of education is unable to adequately satisfy demands for both quantity and quality of products. Because of this, most students who learn through this process are unable to find their jobs. Higher academic education, on the other hand, results in a class of people who lack skills yet want jobs. Lack of communication between institutions and the industry is the main cause of this. To produce human resources with the needed levels of competence and skill, it is necessary to restructure the current system (Prakash, 2021). To address the demand of each sector by providing standardized programmes of acceptable employability, formal institutes of vocational education must therefore be formed and strengthened. In independent India, this issue has received considerable study, but with very modest success.

Educational Reforms through New Education Policy

The National Education Policy's (NEP 2020) paradigm shift from the conventional teacher-centred to learner-centric approach involves supporting the holistic development of pupils by highlighting their creative potential. The strategy emphasizes the fundamental idea that education must foster the development of social and emotional abilities as well as cognitive skills, including the "foundational skills" of literacy and numeracy and "higher-order" skills like critical thinking and problem-solving.

School Education

Making ECCE Skill-based followed by NEP 2020

Early Childhood Care and Education (ECCE) needs to be standardized due to India's changing socio-economic situation. ECCE was first recognized in India with the Kothari Commission Report (1964–1966) and followed by the Right to Education Act of 2009, which excluded children between the ages of three and six from being part of a fundamental right to education. The NEP 2020, on the other hand, calls for a five-year foundational stage of education, including the first two years of primary school and three years of ECCE in the new 5+3+3+4 system (Garg, M., 2022). The NEP 2020 has recommended improving ECCE through –

1) Flexible learning_allows students the freedom and option to acquire knowledge at their own pace and by their intellect, ability, skills, and interests. (Singh, A.K., 2022).
2) Multifaceted learning indicates to development of 21st century abilities or the 5Cs: communication skills, critical thinking, creativity, cooperation, and character development that go beyond the conventional focus on education.
3) Play-based learning enables collaborative, enjoyable and engaging learning.
4) Activity-based learning guarantees that students actively engage with the subject matter and the course content.
5) Discovery learning encourages students to research new ideas by drawing on their prior learning and experiences. (Singh, A.K., 2022). This education system will help children of early age to attain optimal outcomes in the domains of cognitive and socio-emotional-ethical development as well as in life-long learning.

Major Initiatives taken for School Education before NEP 2020

1) *NISHTHA*: The National Initiative for School Heads' and Teachers' Holistic Advancement (NISHTHA) was established as a national mission to enhance outcomes for learning at the elementary school level (Yojana Team, 2020).
2) *DHRUV*: The Pradhan Mantri Innovative Learning Programme (DHRUV) was established to recognize and support gifted students in enhancing their knowledge and abilities. It will serve as a platform for showcasing the abilities of talented and deserving students and assisting them in achieving greatness in their particular fields of study, whether it be science, creative writing, the performing arts, etc. (Sharma & Thakur, 2022).
3) *Shagun*: Shagun, one of the largest integrated online junctions for school education in the world, is a comprehensive effort to improve the school education system by providing an interface for all online portals and websites related to various initiatives of the Department of School Education and Literacy. The newly constructed junction will include report cards for 15 lakh schools across the nation. The Portal aims to link 26 crore pupils and 92 lakh teachers. (Yojana Team, 2020). The general public can immediately comment on schools, which will boost public participation and confirm accountability and openness (Yojana Team, 2020).
4) *Unified District Information System for Education Plus (UDISE+):* The updated UDISE+ has been introduced to guarantee the quality, authenticity, and quick accessibility of data from every school in the nation. The Data Analytics portal provides details on the school's overall ranking (Yojana Team, 2020).
5) *Digital Infrastructure for Knowledge Sharing (DIKSHA) 2.0*: It was introduced in 2017 to give teachers access to a digital platform that gives them the chance to educate themselves, network with other educators, and learn (Yojana Team, 2020).
6) *Operation Digital Board (ODB)*: The goal is to have two smart classrooms in each secondary/senior secondary school by March 2023 (Sharma & Thakur, 2022).

Post NEP 2020 Initiatives on Skill-based Primary Education

Nipun Bharat Mission: The most encouraging development in early-stage education recently is the growing emphasis on Basic Education (derived from Gandhiji's concept) or Foundational Learning. The first six years of life are when the brain develops the fastest, and effective early care and education may truly transform education, as science has now established. Giving kids access to flexible, multifaceted, multilevel, play-based, activity-based, and inquiry-based learning is crucial. The most crucial strategy to guarantee that every kid has equal chances to study during the primary stage of schooling is to ensure that they start reading early on and well. A paradigm shift in the current educational system was advised by the National Education Policy 2020 (NEP 2020). NEP 2020 promotes a new curriculum and pedagogical structure organized into four levels, namely Foundational, Preparatory, Middle and Secondary (5+3+3+4), while also acknowledging the individual potential of each learner and supporting a scientific approach. With ground-breaking suggestions like low-stakes board exams, a focus on formative evaluations, experiential learning at all levels, inventive and activity-oriented pedagogies to foster children's critical thinking, creativity, and curiosity, and a crucial role for foundational learning, the Policy aims to transform the educational system and make it appropriate with the aspirations of the twenty-first century. The emphasis on the universal acquisition of core abilities by all pupils by the end of Grade III is one of NEP 2020's main suggestions. Children's aptitude for reading, meaningful comprehension, and the practical application of fundamental mathematical concepts are all accounted for by foundational learning. The policy indicates unequivocally that the entire policy will become inapplicable unless we take immediate action to improve foundational learning. The 'National Initiative for Proficiency in Reading with Understanding and Numeracy', or NIPUN Bharat, was introduced on July 5, 2021, by the Department of School Education and Literacy to address the aforementioned issues and achieve the goal of attaining foundational literacy as envisioned by the NEP (Sharma, R., 2022).

This mission is focused on ensuring that everyone has access to fundamental literacy and numeracy (FLN) skills. In the ensuing five years, every kid will be able to acquire the desired learning abilities in reading, writing, and numeracy because of this mission (Sharma, R., 2022). Foundational Literacy through NIPUN Bharat's mission aims to reduce drop-outs and improve the transition rate, create a conducive and friendly learning environment, nurture innovative pedagogies and experiential learning, and empower teachers through the NISHTHA training programme and holistic development of the child (Sharma, R., 2022).

Objectives of the Mission: The holistic development of learners, which includes –

- Goal-1: their physical and mental well-being,
- Goal-2: their capacity for effective communication, and
- Goal-3: their ability to become involved in their immediate surroundings (Sharma, 2022).

For achieving this, the necessities are –

- Competency improvement for successful learning results.
- Participation of every individual involved.
- Restructuring learning assessments.

The goal of *Vidya Pravesh* is to make early childhood care and education accessible so that students are comfortable in the classroom. Thus, the NIPUN

Bharat Mission will create a milestone by producing important learning results that will benefit and influence this nation's future (Chaturvedi & Awasthi, 2022).

Higher Education

NEP 2020 has stressed more holistic and multidisciplinary education. The initiatives are already taken by the government and UGC at different times before NEP 2020 and these plans have been vitalized once again as per their skill-based nature in the new education policy.

1) *Five-year vision plan 'Education Quality Upgradation and Inclusion Programme' (EQUIP)*: EQUIP is a vision plan that aims to implement strategic actions in the sector over five years (2019–2024) to overhaul India's higher education system.
2) *Institution of Eminence (IoE)*: Ten institutions from the public and private sectors must be designated as IoE. Over the next five years, each IoE will become eligible to receive Rs. 1000 crore (Yojana Team, 2020).
3) *SWAYAM 2.0:* Top-tier universities have started offering virtual degree programmes through SWAYAM with improved features and services. SWAYAM (Study Webs of Active-learning for Young Aspiring Minds) is an online digital platform that hosts several courses provided free of charge to students living in any area of the country by the greatest professors from universities, institutions, and schools. Only examinations and certificates require payment. MOOCs, or massive open online courses, are another name for these classes (Prasad & Singh, 2020). Though these programmes prevailed before NEP 2020 but proclaimed massively in the new education policy.
4) *SWAYAM PRABHA – DTH Educational Channels*: It is a project to telecast high-quality educational programmes through 32 DTH channels on a 24/7 basis to reach out to students/learners of India with wide reach and minimal cost. It aims to provide dedicated channels 'IITPAL' to support students of XI and XII standards who are interested in attending premier educational institutions in India. (Yojana Team, 2020).
5) *NPTEL*: This initiative was not introduced in the new education policy, but the convergent trend has been influenced to mention it in the perspectives of NEP 2020 in the discourse of skill development and skill enhancement. National Programme on Technology Enhanced Learning is a project of MHRD that was started in 2003 by seven Indian Institutes of Technology (Bombay, Delhi, Kanpur, Kharagpur, Madras, Guwahati, and Roorkee), along with the Indian Institute of Science, Bangalore, to provide quality education to anyone interested in attending the IITs. The main objective was to provide undergraduate and graduate-level management courses as well as web and video courses in all of the major engineering and physical science fields. It is the largest global online collection of engineering, and fundamental sciences, plus a

few humanities and social science courses (Ministry of Education, SWAYAM and NPTEL portal).

Implementation of Quality Improvement Programme

1) A student induction programme guide called *Deeksharambh* has been introduced.
2) Learning outcomes-based curriculum framework (LOCF) revision – A new curriculum based on LOCF for 16 subjects has been released to the UGC website to assist universities in revising their curricula (Yojana Team, 2020).
3) Learning resources based on ICT are employed to facilitate successful teaching and learning (Gupta & Shah, 2023).
4) The Scheme for Trans-disciplinary Research for India's Developing Economy (STRIDE) was established to encourage faculty members to conduct high-quality research and to produce new knowledge (Yojana Team, 2020).

PARAMARSH–This programme aims to mentor organizations seeking accreditation from the National Assessment and Accreditation Council (Yojana Team, 2020). However, a new field termed educational technology (ET) has evolved as a result of how technology is implemented in education. Any technology-mediated remedies must first work to address the country's enormous access gap to ICT infrastructure. A few significant issues with the country's adoption of technology in education were mentioned in the draft of National Education Policy (NEP) 2019. One such worry is the accessibility of local knowledge for troubleshooting and maintaining hardware and software at distant sites. It suggests using local skills to handle technology challenges in classrooms. In this approach, integrating technology into education has an impact on local jobs as well. One thing to be kept in mind is that NEP 2020 is more or less a conglomeration of different schemes or projects structured by the present Government in the centre.

NEP 2020 – A Pathway of Skill Development: The Perspectives

1) Through the NEP, students will be able to develop a "learning to learn" mindset that values critical thinking, creative problem-solving, and problem-solving skills.
2) Students will be given a platform to develop personally within a multidisciplinary education and innovation culture.
3) In addition to science and math, the curriculum and careers will also emphasize the arts, crafts, humanities, games, sports, languages, literature, culture, and values to promote students' holistic and all-around growth and help them to realize and free themselves.
4) Thus, New India will offer a solid foundation for an educational system by the year 2022, based upon the principles of five pillars – accessibility, equity, quality, affordability, and accountability to ensure continual learning (Sarangi, S., 2022).

Other Skill-Based Perspectives according to NEP 2020

1) *Students' Assessment Reforms:* NEP 2020 seeks to change the culture of assessment. It places a strong emphasis on reforming assessment to maximize each student's learning and development. Despite learning and development, it also emphasizes regular, formative, competency-based assessment, and the evaluation of higher-order skills as well.
2) *NEP 2020 outlines the skill-based assessments in key grades in India*: To assess students' development of foundational knowledge, higher-order thinking skills, and their application, the National Education Policy (NEP 2020), suggests a low-stakes annual school examination in grades 3, 5, and 8 across all schools (public and private).
3) *A Competency-based assessment framework*: NEP 2020 promotes core competency testing to decrease academic stress and the requirement for tuition by highlighting the need to upgrade progress reports and board exams.
4) *Establishing a national assessment or evaluation centre*: The creation of the PARAKH (Performance Assessment, Review, and Analysis of Knowledge for Holistic Development), a proposed national assessment centre, is essential for conducting continuous assessments of the educational system (Gavhane, S., India's National Education Policy 2020).
5) *Maxims of High-quality Assessment System (in suggestive mode)*:
   a) Creating consciousness among the stakeholders
   b) Reaching consensus amongst the stakeholders on what the basic and important competencies are
   c) Continuing to build capacity on different components of assessment.

Teacher Education

Significance of Skill-based Teacher Education

It's crucial for educators to build analytical and assessment abilities to foster 21st century skills like thinking critically. It's important to instil in kids the qualities we value most in 21st century abilities, such as cooperation, communication, creativity, and critical thinking (Sarangi, S., 2022). Students today are much more informed and do not only rely on textbook content for their study. In this case, the teacher needs to expand beyond the textbook. Teachers need to be more professional in how they interact with children and parents, maintain control over the classroom environment, and regulate behaviour.

Challenges of the Present Teacher Education System

- *Insufficient use of science and technology:* The most recent technologies have not been fully included in teacher education or training programmes to help students strengthen their teaching abilities.
- *Lack of control over teacher education institutions*: Due to the teacher education institutions' rapid growth, it is difficult to keep track of all of them. Some of these organizations sacrifice quality to save money.

- *Lack of life skill development*: The fundamental problem is that teacher education is memory-based, meaning that there is no active participation of students. As a result, there is a lack of life skill development among learners, which is crucial for their overall growth.
- *Co-curricular activities are lacking or inadequate in teacher education*: These activities are not well-planned. These tasks are occasionally neglected because of poor time management.
- *The issue with classroom management*: Classroom management is neither appropriate nor effective. The duty of conducting classroom observations is not taken seriously by student teachers.

Major Recommendations of NEP 2020 on Teacher Education

1) Teachers should provide a global framework for their lessons, and NEP suggests Continuous Professional Development (CPD) for this purpose (Sarangi, S., 2022). It means a teacher should improve himself or herself not only at the pre-service stage but should continue his or her personal professional growth and development in the in-service stage also.
2) Phased continuous development, as teachers advise students, is always long-term and comprehensive. The teachers teaching in rural schools in India should be given the same opportunity to participate in various activities as their urban counterparts, and the General Education Council should be given full authority to impartially evaluate the value of the teachers using the National Professional Standards established for the teachers in both rural and urban areas.
3) With the multidisciplinary and integrated approach of the curriculum in consideration, all aspects of the teaching and learning process of the Bachelor of Education degree (BEd.) need to be revised. Supporting and nurturing teachers during all stages of their careers is one of NEP's primary goals.

Teachers' Recruitment, Training, and Assessment as per NEP 2020

Improved recruitment and placement methods for teachers can directly support SDG 4's goal of guaranteeing inclusive and equitable access to high-quality education for everyone (Disale, R., 2022).

Criteria of Teacher Recruitment: Teachers are at the centre of the major changes to the educational system, according to the National Education Policy 2020 (Disale, R., 2022).

- The new education strategy suggests initiatives that encourage the smartest and brightest individuals to pursue careers as teachers at all levels.
- A teacher must pass the TET, conduct a demonstration class, succeed in the interview, and be bilingual to be hired by either private or public schools.
- Teacher Eligibility Tests (TETs) are going to be expanded to include candidates for all new stages of schooling (Foundational, Preparatory, Middle and Secondary).

- When hiring subject instructors, both TET and NTA test results in the relevant subjects shall be taken into account.
- It is to address the demand for teachers to teach the recently adopted classical languages and vocational and skill disciplines, the NEP 2020 also urges school complexes to engage local renowned persons or specialists as "master instructors" in various areas.

Training to prepare Skilled teacher

1) According to NEP 2020 (Disale, R., 2022), educators will get ongoing professional development along with training, encouragement, and support to help students learn the fundamentals of literacy and mathematics.
2) To guide all teacher education, a National Curriculum Framework for Teacher Education (NCFTE, 2021) will be developed on the recommendations of NEP 2020 on teacher education and training.
3) A variety of academic materials and pedagogy will be covered in the BEd. degree in addition to excellent practical skill-based training (Disale, R., 2022).

Independent Teacher-training Wing

Experts may be hired to serve as trainers for the teacher training programme, and they would instruct the district-selective teachers in a separate training wing. Other teachers from the district, tehsil, and block levels can then be trained by these instructors. This may be put into practice at the SCERT training facility offered by states and UTs (Disale, R., 2022).

Merit-based Assessment of Teachers

1) Strict, open procedures for hiring teachers will be used. Merit-based promotions with a framework for multi-source periodic performance reviews and potential advancement routes for becoming educational administrators or teacher educators will be the norm (Disale, R., 2022).
2) The National Council for Teacher Education will create a uniform set of National Professional Standards for Teachers (NPST) by 2022 (Sarangi, S., 2022).
3) Guidelines for teacher education programmes must also be prepared with the recommendations of NEP 2020, which calls for a reform of the assessment system by the 2022–2023 academic session.

Skill-based Research Education

Skills should be engaged in interdisciplinary research which will be helpful for the economic, intellectual, societal, environmental, and technological health and progress of a nation.

- *Upskilling Young People:* The government is committed to adopting thoughtful actions to define the nation's futuristic vision to stimulate youth participation in numerous initiatives, growth, and development. This can be done by teaching young people how to spark revolutions, as shown by initiatives like the National Education Policy.

- *Vocational Training and its Present Situation*: The *Samagra Shiksha Abhiyan* has developed several schools to educate and skill-training millions of young children in an integrated and holistic way. In the last six years, there has been a significant increase in the use of vocational education, and CBSE has been recognizing vocational training as a crucial element of holistic education. For schools and students, the applicable competency-based courses offered by CBSE show a variety of options. The following challenges encountered by the mission:
  a) vocational education is perceived to have a social status hierarchy;
  b) there are no vertical mobility pathways;
  c) mainstream education is not integrated at all levels;
  d) there are not enough institutions offering vocational training;
  e) the curriculum is not broad enough;
  f) the medium of instruction is inappropriate;
  g) there are not enough faculty to train the students;
  h) there is not enough attention paid to developing industrial sectors; and
  i) there is inadequate infrastructure.

Larger Goals, Expectations and Initiatives on Vocational Education

1) By 2025, the National Education Policy 2020 hopes to expose 50 per cent of students to vocational education through its integration into K-12 classrooms and postsecondary institutions.
2) The kid must remain at the centre of any intervention involving vocational education to address the learning outcomes.
3) The National Skills Qualification Framework (NSQF) includes vocational subjects in the curriculum, and efforts have been taken to deliver age-appropriate and personalized vocational education at the primary, secondary and higher secondary levels (Chawla, 2023).

Technology and Education

During the pandemic, the use of technology in education has gained popularity and given rise to a growing need for digital infrastructure or cyberspace to support universal skill learning. Along with continued development and effective policy changes to reduce the digital gap in India, the use of artificial intelligence in education has been a successful endeavour.

1) *Making a stable and sustainable future*
   To contribute to the general development of students, companies and communities, skill training has to be increased in light of the constantly shifting socio-economic situations. Therefore, any educational strategy must consider the words of Benjamin Franklin, who is credited with saying, "an investment in knowledge pays the best interest".

2) *Quality education involves the following:*
   a) Curricular Materials
   b) Linkages across levels of school education
   c) Synergy
   d) Innovative Pedagogy
   e) Assessment
   f) Capacity Building and Teacher Training
3) *Toward Sustainable Development*
   The Government's recent emphasis on improving school education is demonstrated by the numerous successful measures it has taken to raise educational standards. The implementation of new policies, support for multilingualism, encouragement of research, innovation, and other skill development programmes are illustrative examples of the Government's thoughtful steps towards a sustainable future and the accomplishment of the Sustainable Development Goal for Education (SDG 4) (Singh, A.K., 2022).

Artificial Intelligence-based Skill Development in Education Sector

Robot Teachers

Humanoid robot teachers can help real teachers deliver lectures to students, and robot teachers can use AI to make learning more engaging for pupils. AI-enabled robot teachers assist in resolving students' questions and can support human instructors in delivering classes and responding to students' frequently asked questions (FAQs).

Personalised Education

a) Al can assist in tailoring the instructional strategy to the unique needs of each student.
b) Al-based software can examine each student's learning style, preferences, and knowledge gaps. Thus, the adaptable teaching methodology may be customized for each learner.

Tutoring Al

Tutoring Al is crucial in helping students outside of the classroom by tutoring them and answering their questions. Chatbots and other systems that support AI help students find answers to their questions. In addition, Al has dealt with the problem of timely responses by providing prompt solutions to repetitive and often requested concerns.

Automated Grading System

a) AI-powered grading software employs machine learning algorithms to evaluate the answers and imitate the grading habits of human professors.
b) It assists in removing teachers' subjective evaluation methods (Dang & Sharma, 2022).

c) The automated grading technique is most frequently employed in optical mark recognition (OMR) criteria, which reads the darkened areas on test papers to evaluate multiple-choice questions (Dang & Sharma, 2022).
d) Software that supports AI can be used to detect plagiarism in a variety of papers and reports.

Natural Language Processing

a) Natural Language Processing (NLP) in educational content might assist students in making essential adjustments by recommending corrections to their documents.
b) Examples of NLP software include Turnitin, which helps writers to examine plagiarism with detailed reports.
c) NLP tools like Google Translate also assist in translating between different languages.

Administrative Tasks

a) AI can support instructors in executing their repetitious administrative activities, such as organizing courses, curriculum planning, recording attendance, assessing papers, sending report cards of kids directly to the parents, etc.
b) AI has increased teachers' effectiveness and made it simpler to complete administrative responsibilities.

Creation of Smart Content

AI-based software tools facilitate the creation of intelligent content, which can include videos, study aids, and digital textbooks. AI can improve many educational activities' efficiency and accuracy, which will ultimately lead to an improvement in the educational experience overall. AI may also be applied to train instructors and improve their skills with the aid of automated trainers and computerized examinations.

Enhancing Skills for Startup India

In the Union budget 2023-24, the Finance Minister talked about making India a knowledge-based digital economy. It means scientific digitization of the whole economy; the Government of India is moving towards 100 per cent digitization of government processes to make them more citizen-centric. Under this, a Digital Public Infrastructure will be developed for the farmers of the country. ICMR Labs will also be made available to private medical colleges and private sector research and development companies to promote health-based research. A new programme will be started through the Center of Excellence to promote research and innovation in pharmaceuticals. District Institutes of Education and Training centres will be developed for revolutionary change in the training of teachers. A National Digital Library will also be built. Under the Pradhan Mantri Kaushal Vikas Yojana, skilling and training will be given for artificial intelligence, coding, 3D printing, and the Internet of Things. A total of 30 Skill India international centres, 3 Centers of Excellence for Artificial Intelligence, and 100 labs for the development of 5G applications will be opened in the country. The government will also give stipends to 47 lakh youth so that everyone gets an equal opportunity (Thakur, A.S., 2023).

Closing Remarks

In conclusion, the NEP 2020 is a comprehensive framework that aims to transform the Indian education system. The policy recognizes the importance of promoting skill development among students, teachers, and other stakeholders as well and proposes various measures to achieve such objectives. By focusing on vocational education, integrating technology, and collaborating with industry, the NEP 2020 aims to equip learners with the skills and knowledge that are relevant to the changing needs of the economy and society. The new education policy has scaled up the whole education system to a learner-centric approach by moulding the system toward critical thinking, holistic approach, inquiry-based, discovery-based, discussion-based and analysis-based learning. Although the new education policy has some positive aspects, it also features several gaps and loopholes that are disconcerting. Along with its three-language formula comprising any two regional languages, it allows schools to select any medium of teaching skills but also suggests that it be the vernacular or any other local or regional language. The NEP 2020 is mostly open, yet it is still centralized. This will result in mediocrity and have the potential to stifle creativity and local sovereignty. A substantial amount will be needed to carry out all of NEP 2020's requirements. It is projected to represent six per cent of our GDP. It can be challenging to see how it will manage its finances when the present educational budget is below one per cent of the total GDP and our economy is currently in the doldrums. In addition to the government initiative, it puts education to philanthropy but at the same time, it encourages education for sale and does not provide any tools to fight against inequality or corruption (Fr. Victor Ferrao). For the new system to operate its choice-based modules and to make accessible vocational courses like woodworking, electric work, gardening, and ceramics, the school infrastructure will need to be updated and extended. In addition, it will be difficult to train and skill teachers, and there is little guidance in that direction. The choice-based system will also place a tremendous amount of pressure on parents and students, who will require guidance and counselling to make wise decisions so that the student's learning outcomes have a place in the job market, which is already contracting due to the growth of artificial intelligence, machine learning, and big data analytics (Fr. Victor Ferrao). Moreover, the emphasis on vocational education at the upper primary level may cause the withdrawal of a greater number of children from education after completing elementary education. The issue of multiple entry and exit points will tend to legitimise huge drop-out from the school education system. Furthermore, the integration of vocational education into formal education will lower the standard of education concerning learning outcomes and it will deviate from the objectives of vocational education in terms of providing quality training to individuals as well. The scope of achieving the skill development and employability agendas is the most difficult and crucial issue. This is due to the projection of the current situation, which states that since the 1990s, under the guidelines of neoliberal reforms, the private sector was also supposed to contribute to the essentiality of the state's provision of employment, but due to the absence of employability, the private sector has also left youth battling to obtain their fair share of the labour market (Vaishali, 2023). The economic perspective, or the practical component of acquiring a skill, is another important consideration in light of the rising unemployment rate, particularly among educated people. When compared to industrialized countries, the secondary data on youth with vocational training (i.e., 10%), which includes only two per cent with formal vocational training while the remaining eight per cent have non-formal vocational training, may appear depressing. It means that two per cent of people must have got training through ITIs, which are 90 per cent sponsored by the private sector, and that the remaining eight per cent of people who have obtained non-formal training are members of disadvantaged groups (Vaishali, 2023).

Four policy recommendations that should be taken into consideration right away could be made in the process of reimagining skill-based vocational education. To satisfy the quality standards specified for both academic and vocational education, increased public financing is required, with six per cent of the GDP allocated to education. The second step is to access the process of establishing skill-based training and vocational education and to concentrate on how well institutions are prepared in terms of having teachers and trainers available for students to attend such education. The third step is to improve the macroeconomic unemployment situation by determining the demand on the Indian job market and connecting the vocation (to be taught in educational institutions) to the appropriate industry where the prospective student could get training and a job offer in the future (Vaishali, 2023). The fourth policy recommendation is to take a practical approach to ensure that the child has ample opportunity to instil democratic principles through general education and subsequent learning by doing or hands-on training, which may be used to either succeed in studies or pursue a career based on the child's needs and interests. In the present-day scenario, the aforementioned suggestions and recommendations are very important and need to be followed and maintained as well.

References

Aithal, P.S. & Aithal, S., (2020), "Analysis of the Indian National Education Policy 2020 towards Achieving its Objectives"; *International Journal of Management, Technology, and Social Sciences* (IJMTS), Vol. 5, Issue. 2, pp. 19-20. http://doi.org/10.5281/zenodo.3988767

Arun, D.P., Malik, J.S., & Shelar, R. (2022), "Perceived Challenges of National Education Policy, 2020 by the students." *Indian Journal of Extension Education*, 58(2), p.73. https://doi.org/10.48165/ijee.2022.58214

Devi, L., & Cheluvaraju. (2020), "A Study on Awareness about the Impact of National Education Policy 2020 Among the Stakeholder of Commerce and Management Disciplinary." *European Journal of Business and Management Research*, 5(6) https://doi.org/10.24018/ejbmr.2020.5.6.640

Disale, R. (2022), Recruitment, Training, and Assessment of Teachers, Retrieved from www.yojana.gov.in

Editorial, Transforming Learning, February 2022, Retrieved from www.yojana.gov.in

Fr. Victor Ferrao, New Education Policy: A Critical Analysis; MGM University Aurangabad, India. Retrieved from: https://mgmu.ac.in/wp-content/uploads/NEP-Indias-New-Education-Policy_2020-final.pdf

Garg, M. (2022), Quality Education for All, February 2022, Retrieved from www.yojana.gov.in

https://www.nptel.ac.in

https://www.swayam.gov.in/nc_details/NPTEL

India Today Web Desk, explained: how will NEP 2020 change the education system in India, https://www.indiatoday.in/education-today/featurephilia/story/

Kumar, A. (2021), "New Education Policy 2020: A roadmap for India 2.0." *Advances in Global Education and Research*, Volume 4. P. 1-7. https://doi.org/10.5038/9781955833042

Maurya, A., & Ahmed, A. (2020). "The New Education Policy 2020 Addressing the Challenges of Education in Modern India." *International Journal of Multidisciplinary Education Research*, 12(5), p.31–38.

Prakash, V. (2021), Desirous of Jobs but Devoid of Skills; from Revisiting Issues and Concerns in Higher Education in the backdrop of National Education Policy 2020, Vidyavani Foundation, p. 301-304.

Prasad, K.D. (2022), Singh, B.P., Online Learning in Lockdown, June 2020, Retrieved from www.yojana.gov.in

Sarangi, S. (2022), Reinventing Teacher Education, February 2022, Retrieved from www.yojana.gov.in

Sharma, R. (2022), NIPUN Bharat Mission, February 2022, Retrieved from www.yojana.gov.in

Shukla, B., Joshi, M., Sujatha, R., Beena, T. & Kumar, H. (2022). "Demystifying Approaches of Holistic and Multidisciplinary Education for Diverse Career Opportunities: NEP 2020." *Indian Journal of Science and Technology*, 15(14), p.603–607. https://doi.org/10.17485/IJST/v15i14.2296

Singh, A.K. (2022), NEP 2020: Vision and Pathways, February 2022, Retrieved from www.yojana.gov.in

Vaishali, 2023. "Revisiting Vocational Education in Indian Schools in the light of the NEP 2020," from *National Education Policy 2020: Policy Reforms and Perspectives*, Atlantic Publishers & Distributors (P) Ltd, p. 189-190.

Verma, H., & Kumar, A. (2021). "New Education Policy 2020 of India: A Theoretical Analysis." *International Journal of Business and Management Research*, 9(3), p.302–306. https://doi.org/10.37391/ijbmr.090308.

Yojana Team (2022), Key Initiatives in Education, February 2020, Retrieved from www.yojana.gov.in

11

Learning Management System (LMS) in Education

An Overview

Azharuddin Molla
Rajab Ali Biswas

Introduction

Information and communication technology (ICT) mediated education is an essential pathway to acquiring knowledge and skills in the 21st century. Learners' achievement is linked with today's teachers' techno-pedagogical knowledge. Learning can be managed, administered and delivered in an effective way if education system utilizes ITC based educational technology. This chapter goes towards such management system. A learning management system (LMS) is a software application for the administration, documentation, tracking, reporting, automation, and delivery of educational courses, training programmes, materials or learning and development programmes. The learning management system concept emerged directly from e-Learning. Simply an LMS is a platform for digital learning. The main objectives of the study are to examine about the conceptual framework of LMS, to study the essential structural requirements i.e. the four factors of LMS and to discuss additionally about various types of LMS development options, customer types, licensing types etc. The present study is qualitative in nature based on secondary data collected from different books, research papers, and Internet. The data are carefully and critically interpreted and analysed to explain the objectives of the study. The use of LMS in teaching and learning process in higher education, specifically, recognized the knowledge and benefits of using LMS as perceived by students studying education programmes (Rahman, 2019). Learning management system can help in delivering teachers as well as students' training materials in a easily accessible way.

Online learning or electronic learning management system are most popular at present situation. The technological trends of e-learning are growing with a very rapid pace. Some of the emerging trends of e-learning are mobile learning, micro-learning, adaptive e-learning, Artificial Intelligence (AI), etc. All these trends help people get access to a world class learning experience. E-learning or the electronic learning is the type of learning carried out, facilitated or supported by some or the other electronic gadgets, media or resources. It facilitates the use of electronic media, like microphones and listening devices, like audio and video tapes. In this sense, e-learning may call for the services of the advanced electronic information and communication media (Back, et al., 2016).

A learning management system is digital application-based software. It can be used for the administration, documentation, tracking, reporting and delivery of e-learning, education courses and instructional or training programmes (Ouadoud, Chkouri, & Nejjari, 2018). LMS range from systems for managing, training and records of e-content to software for distributing online, blended or hybrid learning courses with the help of the Internet through collaboration with many software and website as well. At present (in 21st century) almost all of the higher educational instructions, like colleges and universities use LMS for delivering online courses as well as on-campus courses. Most of university students also have access to the Internet as their Institutions provide Internet access. Some students are also having access to Internet within their home as they used to the Internet Service Provider (ISP) (Adzharuddin & Ling, 2013). In commercials or corporate sector's training departments will use LMS for the delivery of online training, to automate record-keeping, employee registration etc. Most of LMS are web-based to facilitate access to learning content and administration. They are also used by educational institutions to enhance and support classroom teaching and providing courses to a larger number of learners (Kraleva, Sabani, & Kralev, 2019). The use of LMS in teaching and learning process in higher education specifically, recognized the knowledge and benefits of using LMS as perceived by students studying education programmes (Rahman, 2019). Learning Management System is a software that can be held to deliver teachers as well as students training materials in a way that make it easily accessible. A learning Management System (LMS) structure the control of a central login area of student and provide and admin are for huge management as well as course management (Parmley, 2018). "e-learning is organized within an integrated system. Different tools are integrated in a single system, which offer all necessary tools to run and manage an e-learning courses. All learning activates and materials in a course are organized and managed by and within the system. LMS typically offer discussion forums, file sharing, management of assignments, lesson plans, syllabus, chart, etc." (Dalsgaard, 2006). This chapter intend to conceptualise the framework of LMS, to examine the structural requirements of LMS, to delineate the various types of LMS, common features of LMS and the historical evolution of LMS. Its last section entails the use of LMS in education from the lens of the students and teachers.

What is Learning Management System?

A Learning Management System is a software application for the administration, documentation, tracing, reporting, automation, and delivery of educational courses, treading programme or learning and development programme. It can be used to support traditional face-to-face instruction, as well as blended/hybrid and distance learning programme. LMS is a focused online delivery of learning, online content, including courses, both synchronous and asynchronous based.

An LMS is a web-based system that provides an infrastructure to deliver our content, monitor participation, access student and facilitate communication through a number of built-in tools (Naveh, Tubin & Pliskin, 2010). LMS is a software application for the administration, documentation, reports and delivery of any educational matters, training, courses, programs or learning and development programs (Rahman, Daud & Ensimau, 2019). According to Parmley (2018), LMS is primarily a software helping in delivery of teacher's learning materials in a way that makes it easily accessible to his/ her students. LMS configures the content and provides a central login area for students and also supplies and admin area for user management as well as course management. Oakes (2002) defines of LMS as a tool for "learner and organization, focused its concerned with the logistics of managing learners, learning activities and the competency mapping of an organization". Technically the term of LMS is "a software application for the administration, documentation, tracking, reporting and delivering by e-learning education courses or training programmes" (Ellis, 2009). "Learning Management System is a software-based application which helps us to administrate, document, track, report and evaluate the teaching learning process, training programs, virtual classes, and e-Learning programs" (Chaubey & Bhattacharya, 2015). A Learning Management System is "a software environment that enables the management and delivery of learning content and resources of students. It provides an opportunity to maintain interaction between the instructor and students and to assess the students by providing immediate feedback on the online quizzes" (Martin, 2008). In a nutshell, a LMS can thus be stated as a software application for the administration, documentation, evaluation and delivery of any educational contents, training, courses, learning or developmental programmes. Immediate feedback provision also remains for the assessment of the students' activities. The following Fig. 11.1 exhibits the cardinal components of Learning Management System.

Learning Management System is basically divided into four independent aspects, but these aspects are interrelated to each other (Halder & Saha, 2023). They are – Curriculum Planning, Content Management, Students / Learners Participation and Instant Evaluation –

1) *Curriculum Planning:* The first aspect of LMS is curriculum planning. In this stage curriculum planning should be taken by the authorities, to know about overall courses to be studied and to develop specific course of study on the basis of the content related to specific course. And then authority should plan a schedule of time to complete the course within given time and acquisition of appropriate learning management software.
2) *Content Management:* Content management is a significant aspect of LMS. In LMS there is a need to develop a specific content management platform for the sake of access, manage, store, content materials through unique login ID.

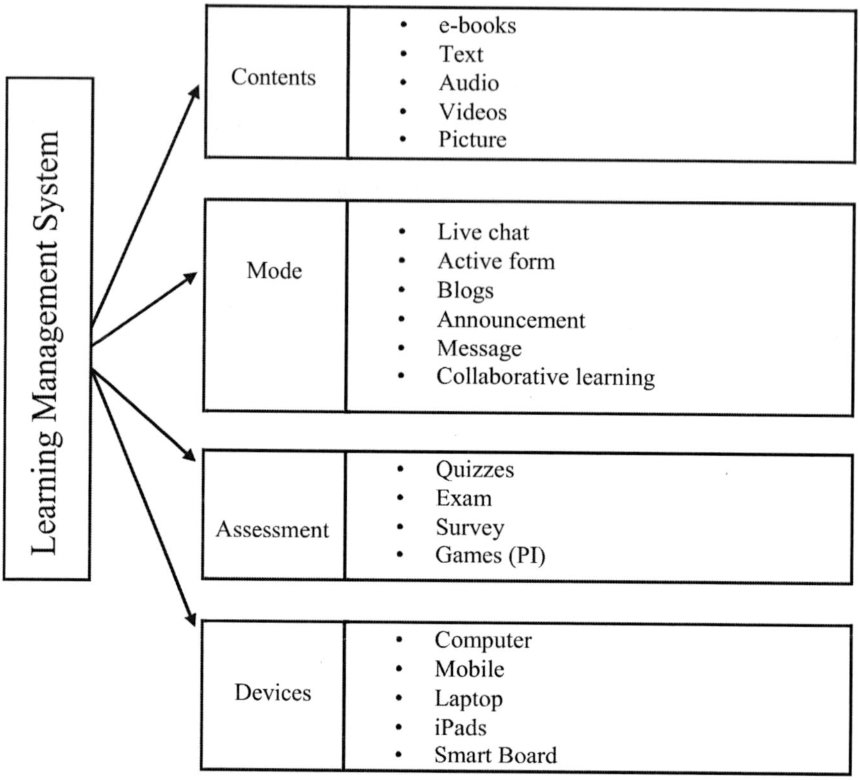

Figure 11.1: *Components of Learning Management System (LMS)*

Source: Authors

3) *Students / Learners Participation*: Active participation of students in learning is key feature of teaching. LMS provides the opportunity to the student active engagement in learning through chat, group messaging, gamification etc.
4) *Instant Evaluation*: LMS provides instant evaluation of student's response. It also identifies the overall performance of the students as well as predicts student's future performance.

The four interrelated aspects of LMS are captured in detail in the following Fig. 2.

Common Features of Learning Management System

A learning management system is useful for both teachers and students. This application has a lot of features. The features of LMS are listed below.

1) *Course and Content Management:* With the use of a learning management system (LMS), new teaching-learning materials can be created, classes and content can be copied and reused, materials can be modified according to

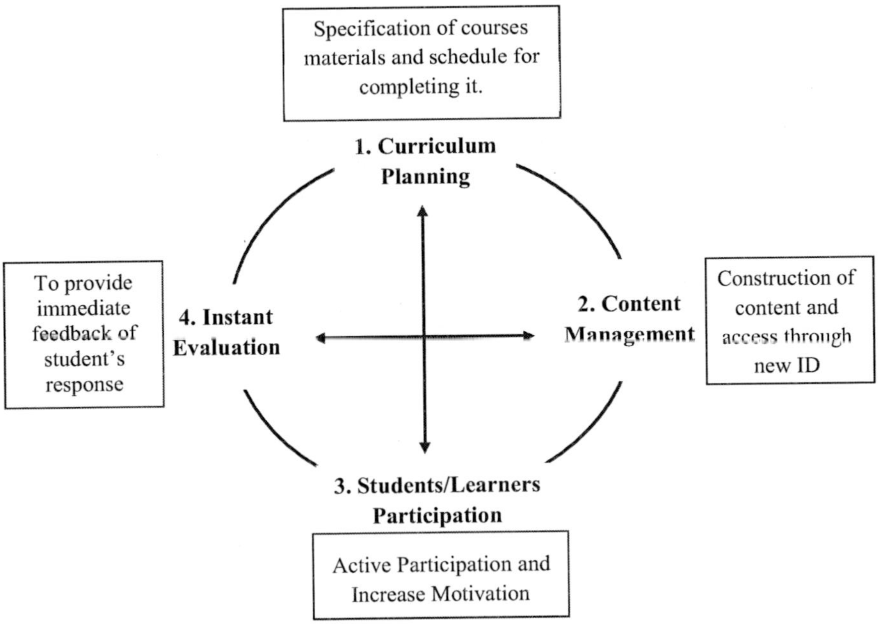

Figure 11.2: *Overview of Learning Management System*

Source: Authors

requirements, and participants can be managed. Content is uploaded and made available in the form of audio, video, PowerPoint, PDFs, graphics, photographs, other media.

2) *Learning Paths:* Learning routes are all about gaining an elementary knowledge of a subject before moving on. They lead students down a route of courses where they learn about increasingly complex ideas. A learning route must be established in order to master a subject, not just in the classroom but also online.
3) *Assessment and Certification:* The teacher can assess each learner's performance and generate a score with the help of an LMS. The learner's performance can also be recorded, transcripted and maintained. Teachers can generate certificates of achievement for students either automatically or manually through an LMS (Halder & Saha, 2023).
4) *Analysis and Report:* Teachers may construct reports for learning outcomes, completion rates, across the organization education efforts, examination assessment, and a variety of customizable reports and data fields through the LMS application. The capacity to improve initiatives is provided by this instrument.
5) *Notification Alert:* With the use of alerts and notifications, you can keep your students on task and informed of any programmed updates you make. Automated alerts and reminders can be sent in real time to desktop and

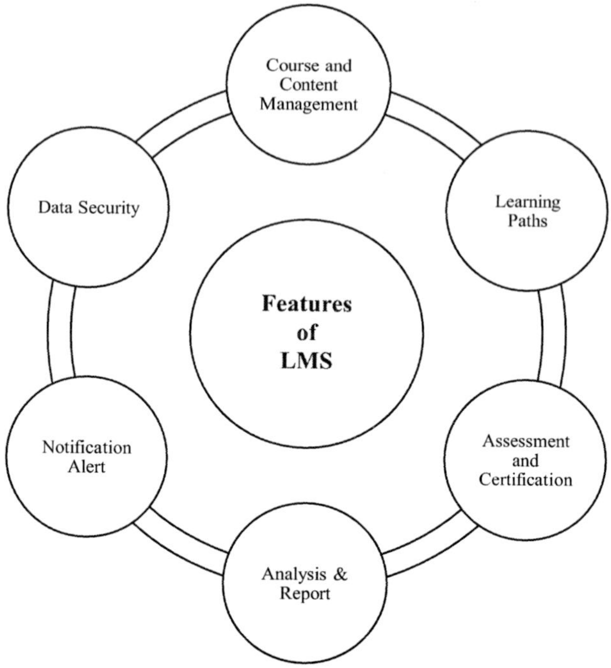

Figure 11.3: *Common Features of Learning Management System*

Source: Authors.

mobile devices regarding critical dates, upcoming activities, exam dates, course upgrades and additions, schedule changes, and other teaching or training related activities (Halder & Saha, 2023).

6) *Data Security:* The security features of learning management systems can guard your data from malware and unauthorized access from outside sources. Data encryption, multi-factor authentication, user roles and permissions, automated data backups, IP blockers, and audit reports are a few of the more important features.

Components of Learning Management System

Designing any types of application requires certain number of components. Similarly, the components required for developing an online teaching-learning application are mainly of five components (Esther, 2018). These are –

1) *User Interface:* Generally user interface refers to the users of an application. There are three categories of users to use the online LMS application; one category is those who will learn using it, another category of users are those who will teach and those who will manage this application as admin. All types of users will take the help of any Internet web browser to operate this system. Users will use Hypertext Markup Language (HTML) to enter their details to use Cascading Style

Sheet (CSS) for design specific web pages. Also use a variety of high level languages to provide written content.

2) *Web server:* Web server is basically used to host any type of web application. It is managed using the individual's domain name. A web server is a combination of software and hardware. Internet users transfer various types of information through it. This information is stored as necessary.
3) *Server-side Programming:* A server side programme is one such technique that works as any type of web development technique. This programme helps to create a web server script and create a customized response for each user on the website. The same web code helps describe and manage any type of script. The HTP (Hypertext pre-processor) language is used as a server-side design language for user feedback. It (HTP) was primarily used because its code is easily accessible and reusable.
4) *Database System:* A database system is any type of information organized in a structured way. Information is stored electronically within the computer. Technically any data storage is managed by a Database Management System (DBMS). User can use it anytime by using specific code. There are different database systems according to different platforms. Some of the most popular database systems are – Oracle, MySQL, MS SQL Server, PostgreSQL, MongoDB, IBM D B2, Redis, Cassandra, MariaDB, OrientDB, SQLite, Neo4j, etc.
5) *Data Access Layer:* A data access layer is managed by computer software which helps the user to easily manage the process of data delivery, data storage etc. It is most commonly used in Microsoft Access. It is a personalized system where procedures are divided into several classes, the classes are divided into bullet procedures. Classes are used to create database connections with web pages.

Historical Background of Learning Management System

The modern LMS is mostly cloud-based and widely influenced by computer applications. The first invention of learning management system can be noted in 1924 with the invention of "Teaching Machine" by Sydney Pressey. It is used to administer and check MCQ automatically. The next invention was "Problem sylinder" by M. E. Lazerte in 1929. It was presented a problem of a student and tested whether the solution steps taken by the student were right. And a significant change has occurred in 1990 launched by SoftArc, the first ever LMS software for MacIntosh platform. An open-source internal network was introduced called Moodle developed by Martin Dougiamasin 2002. It is a three users' platform. The administrator makes courses for teachers and manages the general settings. Now in recent days, various LMSs are invented for fulfilling several purposes for blended learning, distance education, flipped classroom and other e-learning projects in schools, universities, workplaces and other sectors.

Table 11.1: *Historical Background of Learning Management System*

Invention and Year	*About the Invention*	*Initiated by*
Teaching Machine (1924)	Teaching Machine resembled a typewriter with a window that could administer questions. One window was used to show the question and the other one to fill in the answer.	Sydney Pressey
Problem Sylinder (1929)	Problem sylinder is a device which provided instruction without the need for an instructor's involvement. It not only tested learners' knowledge with multiple choice questions but also *tested* the response of the learner whether the response is right or wrong.	M.E. Lazerte
Adaptive teaching system, SAKI (Self-Adaptive Keyboard Instructor) (1956)	It automatically adjusted questions for learners according to their performing level. It offered modified practice questions based on the learner's performance as their performance improved over time	Gordon Park and Robin McKinnon-Wood
PLATO (Programmed Logic for Automatic Teaching Operation) (1960)	PLATO was a computer-based training programme that facilitated self-paced learning, allowing learners to monitor their own learning progress.	Dr Donald Bitzer
The HP-9100A (1970)	It could process and solve engineering problems ten times faster than existing machines. The HP-9100 laid the foundation for the way connections are established today through the Internet, and essentially covered the way for the regular use of the LMS. Hewlett-Packard introduced the first ever desktop. From that day on LMS started taking totally new face.	Hewlett-Packard
TCP/IP (Transmission Control Protocol/Internet Protocol) (1982)	Transmission Control Protocol or Internet Protocol. When you have direct access to the Internet, your computer is provided with a copy of the TCP/IP program. It's the basic communication language or protocol of the Internet. TCP/IP had made online learning possible, and this still has a huge influence in present days	Robert Elliot Kahn and Vint Cerf

Invention and Year	*About the Invention*	*Initiated by*
SoftArc (1990)	The first ever LMS software for MacIntosh platform was launched by SoftArc in 1990. SoftArc is based on a probabilistic model of the error generation and propagation process in a processor. LMS First class, the first e-learning software, was launched by SoftArc for the Macintosh platform.	SoftArc
Ekko (1991)	Ekko initiated by NKI Distance Education Network was the first fully featured LMS.	NKI Distance Education Network
MySQL (2007)	Interactive Learning Network was the first online learning system to influence a rational MySQL database.	CourseInfo
Moodle (Modular Object-Oriented Dynamic Learning Environment) (2002)	The first open-source LMS is Moodle. With Moodle learners could start learning as soon as they downloaded the application onto their desktops. Modified learning was made possible by allowing learners choose the content they desired to store or export.	Martin Dougiamas
The messaging standard, SCORM (Sharable Content Object Reference Model) (2007)	The messaging standard, SCORM (Sharable Content Object Reference Model), was introduced, specifying the parameters on content packaging and metadata. It is a staple feature of today's LMS.	Microsoft Corporation
Private cloud (2008)	The idea of a platform for deploying clouds was born in 2008. This enabled LMS to exist entirely online without needing to be installed on an internal network.	Eucalyptus
2010 to present year	Developed various advanced level of LMS like- Blackboard, MOOCs, Google Classroom etc.	

Source: Authors

Most Popular Learning Management System

1) *Blackboard*: Blackboard is one of the popular digital learning platforms. This digital platform provides services through SaaS (Software-as-a-Service) as well as non-SaaS models. This software provides many services related to teaching, learning and instruction; so, we can say

that blackboard is an online services provider software. Feature of this software are learning management, data analysis, communication, collaboration with teachers and students, web conferencing, teacher can deliver homework easily, conduct assessment or test and track grades. This platform can also provide teaching/instruction through online and blended modes. The blackboard learning ap provides the content in more than 30 languages.

2) *Schoology*: Schoology is another popular online learning platform that provides all the features of student's need. It is free version online packages of the learning management system (LMS). Schoology can help student's offline classes and engage with their teachers outside the class as well. This platform will design of lessons, communicate with students, and collaborate with teachers. Most advantages of it focus on building of knowledge and connection to students with learning community and administrators. Schoology make it easy to communicate and share instructional materials with teachers from other schools.
3) *Google Classroom*: Google Classroom is most popular cloud-based LMS that is the part of Google apps. It can enable student's access this platform through computer, tablets and smartphone. Google Classroom is suitable for academic teaching-learning instruction only. Users (teachers and students) can create Google Dots to manage assignments, YouTube videos as well as attach files from Google drive. It can help users provide feedback through interact on the documents. Teachers can create online classrooms for the teaching-learning content. Online test can be created to assess student's progress. This online platform is able to interconnect many Google products like Google docs, Google spreadsheets and Google slides.
4) *Canvas:* Canvas is open and most effective web-based learning platform. It can be run digitally, teachers create and present online learning material and measure student learning outcome. Students enroll the Canvas virtual classroom and receive feedback about student's interaction skill development and learning achievement. Canvas includes digital course creation and management tools. It can be freely accessible.
5) *Edmodo:* Edmodo is a free digital learning management portal that can provide classroom learning environment, content materials, self-communication and assessment with social media. Student as well as parent can get quick feedback to discussion of question and stay connected with students, planners and teachers. It is sliding different as compared to Google classroom. Edmodo is a type of "class folder" where a large file must be placed. Nasrullah, et al. (2021) was conducting a study on 'Putting Edmodo into Classroom: Portraying LMS Manifestation.' The major finding of the study exposed that Edmodo could help to communicate and collaborate in higher level of education. Teachers and students interact through this application and they send feedback as well.

6) *LearnDash:* LearnDash is a word process LMS. It can be used in various sectors, for example different companies, colleges – universities, training organizations and entrepreneurs for creating online courses.

Types of Learning Management System

Due to the rapid growth of technology in current situation, many LMS are being used on the field of digital learning. It is difficult to say which of these is the best but depend on the institutional or student's objective the appropriate elements is determined. Some of the more popular LMS are –

1) *Installed LMS*: Installed LMS is a type of LMS that is locally hosted. Like traditional applications and LMS software, it has to be installed on premises and user's server. Installed LMS are also called 'on-premise LMS'. This type of LMS gives us the power to customize every feature of a software and store a person's database locally, significantly removing any security risks. This flexibility, unfortunately, comes with a cost. Hosted on your server, your team is in charge of setting up, maintaining, and upgrading the learning platform and system. You are also expected to fix any unforeseeable downtime issues, making it a very expensive LMS option.
2) *SaaS – LMS*: One of the important types of LMS are SaaS (Software-as-a-Service). SaaS LMS are also known as web-based application system. This type of LMS was developed for the reduction of cost and easily accessible to learning environment system. Most important benefit of this application is that it can be easily accessible from any device and any web browsers with minimum costs. This application also can save time, power and it can easily access, upgrade and storage lot of data system. EdApp is a common and good example of SaaS or web-based LMS. Most of importance feature of EdApp is – no need to install anything on your devices, or even pay for a big, clunky setup. It can be accessed fully free. That means the user has no limited fees trial, and it can be used free forever.
3) *Open-source LMS*: One of the major types of learning management system is easy access by user. Anyone can use it to add and delete specific features. Any users with minimum technical knowledge can create free online courses and customize the content. Even it can change its entire system for the convenience of users. Since its inception it has gained particular popularity, because no fees are required for this. However, due to technological advancement, these types of LMS need to be customized in a newer way. Since it is accessible to everyone, so various types of malicious programmes including viruses can cause problems here. Although due to the lack of specific guidelines for new users, its use has decreased at present.
4) *Closed-source LMS:* The opposite of open-source is an application based LMS which is a closed source application. It does not directly provide any access code to users. User has to pay some amount of money to use

this application. So, it has very little use in traditional teaching-learning system. But it keeps the user free from various complications or dangers technically. Because its programming is managed in such a way that permission is required for uploading or upgrading anything. Such applications are particularly effective in managing advanced institutional management.

5) *Integration-capable LMS:* Integration refers to the interrelationship of each other. Creating a new type of application integrates with other applications in the case of LMS. These applications include various software like – zoom, google meet. Can be used by saving time and without spending any money. It requires specific code to use, but can be further accessed multiple times without any code.
6) *Mobile LMS:* Mobile is the most user-dominant LMS in the learning world in the present situation. This delivers the content to the user very easily and quickly. Instructors and trainees can easily communicate simultaneously through the use of mobile phones or tablets. Any type of course can use this platform for electronic device; the learning process can be done anytime from anywhere.
7) '*EdApp*': It is a universally accepted and trusted mobile training app, which combines smart phone technology and specific learning techniques to create a convenient platform for learners. This application has about 80 micro learning platforms, which can be accessed seamlessly with the help of mobile (Panda, 2020). To create any type of course and writing content requires separate configuration. A complex and boring subject can be presented to students in an interesting way through smartphone.

Implications of LMS in the Domain of Education

Currently, online learning and teaching process is widely used. Especially in the higher education system where the students are getting the learning material easily, the teacher can easily complete the teaching process and impart the content to the students. The system through which this service is managed is the Learning Management System. LMS has more impact on learning outcomes. The uses of LMS can be broadly divided into four main areas, namely, students, teachers, administrators and assessment. LMS serves the following functions:

1) Students can easily access the learning content.
2) Content – Documents, audio, video, images, etc. can be collected by students.
3) This requires technical devices and an application of LMS.
4) Students can manage the process by creating and verifying content themselves.
5) Various applications can self-assess by using software.

6) The pre-recorded topics in an LMS application can be used by the student as per their convenience.
7) Teaching and training can be done in less time and less cost.
8) Institutional management requires a technical host to manage an LMS, which is technically called CMI.
9) Various applications of LMS are available in the market for checking the learning level of students.

Conclusion

In the current scenario, technological advancements have made it possible to spread any type of information rapidly with the help of networks. Similarly, the exchange of various types of information has become faster and easier in the field of teaching-learning and training. Just as teachers have harnessed technology to use various types of information in education; students are also taking the help of technology. In terms of classroom teaching, technical material is being provided directly both online and offline. LMS is the essential tool for managing all these issues. Students in higher education institutions can get different types of updates regarding their courses. Also, the provider can store various types of educational information (text, audio, video, image of any kind) digitally and use it as needed. Among the main components of education, it can be considered as the most significant component at present. LMS is particularly effective in making the subject matter interesting in classroom teaching. Hence there is talk of imparting technical knowledge to students institutionally or government initiatives. Note that in the National Education Policy 2020, students are mandated to impart technical knowledge from the sixth standard (Gandhi, 2021). LMS has directly helped classroom management during the recent pandemic situation. Recently various universities are conducting their various courses or programmes directly through LMS. For example, Chandigarh University is offering near about 150+ courses through Blackboard LMS (Panda, 2020).

References

Adzharuddin, N.A., & Ling, L.H. (2013). "Learning Management System (LMS) among University Students: Does It Work?" *International Journal of e-Education e-Business e-Management and e-Learning*, Vol.3, p.233, 2013.

Back, D.A., Behringer, F., Haberstroh, N., Ehlers, J.P., Sostmann, K., & Peters, H. (2016). "Learning management system and e-learning tools: an experience of medical students' usage and expectations." *International Journal of Medical Education*, Vol.7, pp.267-273. https://doi.org/10.5116/ijme.57a5.f0f5

Chaubey, A., & Bhattacharya, B. (2015). "Learning Management System in Higher Education." *International Journal of Science Technology & Engineering* – IJSTE, Vol. 2 (3).: https://www.researchgate.net/publication/288737185

Dalsgaard, C. (2006). "Social Software: E-learning Beyond Learning Management System." *European Journal of Open, Distance and E-learning.*

a. https://old.eurodl.org/?p=archives&year=2006&halfyear=2&article=228

Esther, O. (2018). "Learning Management System: A Tool for Effective Teaching Process." *The International Journal for Science and Technology*. https://www.researchgate.net/publication/328047933

Ellis, R.K. (2009). Field guide to Learning Management System. American Society for Treading and Development (ASTD), Learning Circuits.

Gandhi, R. (2021). "Review on the Key Features of the National Educational Education Policy 2020 in the Context to Pre-school Education and its Expected Impact." *International Journal of Management, Technology and Social Science*, 6(1).

Halder, S., & Saha, S. (2023). "Learning Management System and Learning Content Management System in Education." *The Routledge Handbook of Educational Technology*, pp.294-304.

Ilyas, M., Kadir, K.A., & Adnan, Z. (2017). "Demystifying the Learning Management System (LMS): Journey from E-Learning to the Strategic Role." *European Journal of Business and Management*, Vol.9(9).

Iqbal, S., & Qureshi, I.A. (2011). "Learning Management Systems (LMS): Inside Matters." *Information Management and Business Review*, Vol. 3 (4), pp. 206–216. https://doi.org/10.22610/imbr.v3i4.935

Ismail, J. (2002). "The design of an e-learning system: Beyond the hype." *The Internet and Higher Education*, Vol.4(3–4), pp329–336. https://doi.org/10.1016/s1096-7516(01)00069-0

Kraleva, R., Sabani, M., & Kralev, V. (2019). "An Analysis of Learning Management Systems." *International Journal on Advanced Science Engineering and Information Technology*, Vol. 9 (4), Aug 2019.

Martin, F. (2008). "Blackboard as the Learning Management System of a Computer Literacy Course." *MERLOT Journal of Online Learning and Teaching*, Vol. 4(2), pp. 138–145. https://jolt.merlot.org/vol4no2/martin0608.pdf

Malik, H.A.M., Abid, F., Kalaichelvi, R., Bhatti, Z. (2018). "Challenges of Computer Science and IT in Teaching – Learning in Saudi Arabia." *Sukkur IBA Journal of Computing and Mathematical Science*, 2(1), pp. 6.

Middleton, D. (2010). "Putting the Learning into e-learning." *European Political Science*, Vol. 9 (1), pp.5–12. https://doi.org/10.1057/eps.2009.37

Naveh, G., Tubin, D., & Pliskin, N. (2010). "Student LMS use and satisfaction in academic institutions: The organizational perspective." *The Internet and Higher Education*, Vol. 13 (3), pp. 127–133. https://doi.org/10.1016/j.iheduc.2010.02.004

Nasrullah., Rusmanayanti, A., Rosalina, E. and Ningslh, R.P. (2021). "Putting Edmodo into Classroom: Portraying Learning Management System (LMS) Manifestation." *Journal of English Education and Teaching* (JEET), Vol. 5 (3), pp. 317-329. file:///C:/Users/Raju/Downloads/Putting_Edmodo_Into_Classroom_Portraying_Learning_.pdf

Oakes, K. (2002). "E-learning: LCMS, LMS — They're not Just Acronyms But Powerful Systems for Learning." *Training & Development*, Vol. 56 (3), pp. 73-75.

Ouadoud, M., Chkouri, M.Y., & Nejjari, A. (2018). "Learning Management System and the Underlying Learning Theories: Towards a New Modeling of an LMS." *International Journal of Information Science & Technology* — IJIST, Vol. 2 (1), 2018.

Panda, S. (2020). "Analyzing Effectiveness of Learning Management System in Present Scenario: Conceptual background and Practical Implementation." *International Journal of Innovative Research and Advanced Studies* (IJIRAS), Vol. 7 (9), 2020.

Parmley, L. (2018). What is an LMS? (Definition and Examples). Course Method. https://coursemethod.com/lms-definition.html

Parmley, L. (October, 2018). What is an LMS? (Definition and Examples). Course Method. https://coursemethod.com/lmsdefinition.html

Rahman, M., Daud, M.Y., & Ensimau, N.K. (2019). "Learning Management System (LMS) in Teaching and Learning." *International Journal of Academic Research in Business and Social Sciences*, Vol. 9 (11), pp. 1529–1535. https://doi.org/10.6007/ijarbss/v9-i11/6717

Selim, H.M. (2007). Critical success factors for e-learning acceptance: Confirmatory factor models. Computers & Education, Vol. 49(2), pp. 396–413. https://doi.org/10.1016/j.compedu.2005.09.004

Tretinjak, M.F. (2018). Moving teaching from blackboard to the learning management system—Helping absent students learn from home. 2018 41st International Convention on Information and Communication Technology, Electronics and Microelectronics (MIPRO), 500–502.

https://appinventiv.com/blog/top-web-app-database-list/

https://www.techtarget.com/searchcio/definition/learning-management-system

https://www.softwaretestinghelp.com/learning-management-system/

https://en.wikipedia.org/wiki/Learning_management_system

https://www.learnupon.com/blog/lms-features-overview/

12

Policy Reforms in Teacher Education Envisaged by the NEP 2020

Prospects and Challenges

Ajit Mondal

Introduction

Teaching is a form of social action and inquiry, and has evolved over the last two hundred years. Understanding of and practices related to teaching and teacher education have undergone paradigmatic shifts, from its conception as a vocation and craft, to the idea of a profession with specialized knowledge, prolonged preparation and professional ethics (Sarangapani et al., 2021, p. 11). Today's preparation of teachers i.e. teacher education is a significant segment of the whole education system. If the future of any nation depends on activities within her classroom under the care of teachers, at first teacher education system should be overhauled at any cost. "Teacher Education is a continuous process, and its pre-service and in-service components are inseparable" (Government of India, 1986, Para 9.4) and the teachers play a crucial role in the enhancement of quality in education and the key catalyst of implementation of educational programmes. The national policies on education in 1968 and 1986 addressed the issues related to teacher education and teachers. Now it is pertinent to examine the policy reforms in teacher education envisaged by the new policy. The areas of concern over those reforms have also been addressed.

The Government of India approved the National Education Policy 2020 (hence after NEP 2020) on 29 July 2020, 34 years after the last National Policy on Education in 1986. The NEP 20 proposes a series of policy reforms at all levels of education system of the country including teacher education (TE). It recommends shifting the TE system to locate only in multidisciplinary higher education institutes and firmly seeks to establish integrated teacher education (ITE) in those public multidisciplinary institutions by 2030. This shift means that the stand-alone teacher education institutions (TEIs) will be phased out, since a four-year integrated bachelor's degree shall be the minimum qualification for all future aspiring school teachers. There are other reforms embedded in the NEP 2020 too, including revitalization of the regulatory system "in order to raise standards and restore integrity, credibility, efficacy, and high quality to the teacher education system" (p.42). Before throwing light on the policy perspectives with reference to teacher education and teachers, we should have an outline of the current scenario of the teacher education sector in India.

Mapping the Current Status of Teacher Education in India

The National Council for Teacher Education (NCTE) was established as a statutory body by an Act of Parliament (Act No. 73 of 1993) with a view to achieving planned and coordinated development of teacher education throughout the country, the regulation and proper maintenance of norms and standards in the teacher education system and for matters connected therewith. The NCTE Act came into force w.e.f. 01 July 1995 and the NCTE came into existence on 17 August 1995 with its Head Office in New Delhi (NCTE, 2022, p.1). The Research Group, Azim Premji Foundation in the document *'Issues in Education: Teachers and Teacher Education'* in 2021 has remarked the landscape of teacher education institutions in India in the following way –

> India has one of the weakest teacher education systems in the world. It is marked by a large number of stand-alone institutions run by private entities, offering single programmes. Most teacher preparation programmes build very little perspective or capability on curriculum and classroom processes; what exists is out-dated and distanced from the reality of the school and the children the teachers are expected to serve. The average quality of teacher educators is poor. Stand-alone institutions struggle to build the kind of varied faculty and resources that good teacher education needs. This has also led to both intellectual and professional isolation of teacher education from the rest of higher education. The sheer number of such institutions, their uneven geographical spread and their poor outcomes are clearly indicative of the fundamental weakness of our system (p. 13).

As per the 27th Annual Report 2021-22 of the National Council of Teacher Education (NCTE), as on 31 March 2022, there are a total of 16,333 teacher education institutions (TEIs) in India. There are fifteen teacher education programmes ranging from DPSE (Pre-primary) to M.Ed. including D.P.Ed., B.P.Ed., and M.P.Ed. The following Table 12.1 shows the programme-wise total teacher education institutions in India.

According to the Research Group, Azim Premji Foundation in the document 'Issues in Education: Teachers and Teacher Education' published in 2021, there are 17,503 Teachers Education Institutions (TEIs) in India with an intake capacity of preparing 18,86,028 teachers (including a small number of teacher educators) every year. Around 1,452 public TEIs are run by the government, including about 600 District Institutes of Education and Training (DIETs). The remaining, nearly 15,464 (around 92%), are privately-run. The majority of TEIs are in the private space with roughly 11 private TEIs for every one public TEI (public TEIs 1,452: private 15,464). In Uttar Pradesh, this ratio is 1:55. The distribution of private TEIs is skewed as well with 54 per cent of all the private TEIs in the country present in the four states of Uttar Pradesh, Rajasthan, Maharashtra and Tamil Nadu. Only 12 states/UTs have at least one TEI in each district.

Table 12.1: *Programme-wise Total Recognized Courses of Teacher Education in India*

Sl. No.	*Name of Teacher Education Course*	*Total Number of Courses Recognized as on 31 March 2022*
1.	DPSE (Pre-Primary)	204
2.	D.El.Ed. (Elementary)	10495
3.	D.El.Ed. (Elementary) (ODL)	06
4.	Diploma in Arts Education (Performing)	18
5.	Diploma in Arts Education (Visual)	10
6.	B.El.Ed. (Elementary)	106
7.	B.Ed. (Secondary)	9361
8.	B.Ed. (ODL)	42
9.	B.Ed. (Part-time)	11
10.	B.Ed. M.Ed. (Integrated)	31
11.	B.A. B.Ed./B.Sc. B.Ed. (Integrated)	786
12.	M.Ed.	1254
13.	D.P.Ed.	166
14.	B.P.Ed.	632
15.	M.P.Ed.	181
16.	Others	75
Total Number of Recognized Courses		**23378**

Source: 27th Annual Report 2021-22, p. 28, NCTE, GoI., 2022

The report of the Research Group of Azim Premji Foundation, 2021 highlighted that a large proportion of private TEIs, i.e., 62 per cent offer B.Ed. and D.El.Ed. programmes prepare teachers for the elementary and secondary stage of schooling. Table 12.2 indicates the share of teacher preparation programmes under the regime of the private TEIs.

The TET qualification, an essential requirement for employment as elementary school teachers, can be considered as one indicator of the quality of teacher education. In September 2016, 3,37,609 appeared for the examination (Central-TET) and 43,130 qualified. Thus, out of a potential cohort of qualified teachers, only 10.4 per cent are eligible for appointment as elementary teachers. There is, thus, a huge amount of wastage in the teacher education system in India (Azim Premji University, 2021, p. 19).

As per NCTE Regulations 2014 and Regulations 2019, there are currently 16 teacher education programmes across India. During 1947-48, only 235 Teacher Education Institutions existed both at elementary (184) and secondary (51) stages. At present 16,917 Teacher Education Institutions and Universities

Table 12.2: *Stage-wise Teacher Preparation Programmes under Private TEIs*

Sl. No.	*Stage of Teacher Preparation Programmes*	*Number of Private TEIs*
1.	Elementary and secondary stage	15113
2.	Pre-primary stage	140
3.	Physical education	734
4.	Teacher educators	1144

Source: Azim Premji University, 2021, p. 16

have been preparing school teachers. The growth of TEIs has become more than 80 times since Independence but State sponsored teacher education system has not been established adequately to prepare teachers who can impart quality education in schools after passing 75 years of Independence.

In the Report of the Justice Verma Commission (JVC) set up by the MHRD, Government of India under the chairmanship of Justice J.S. Verma, at the behest of the Hon'ble Supreme Court on 13 May 2011, made a significant observation on the current gloomy picture of Indian teacher education system in the following way –

> Historically, teacher education was largely in the public sector and teacher education institutions were regularly monitored for maintaining quality. With privatization and liberalization in the field of education, the share of self-financing teacher education institutions in the sector of teacher education has become inappropriately large. Currently, 85 per cent of teacher education institutions are in the private sector while more than 80 per cent of elementary school children are in the State schools. This necessitates the need for an appropriate regulatory framework to ensure quality standards in teacher education. The NCTE, even as a statutory body, has not been able to control the proliferation of sub-standard teacher education institutions due to its inability to enforce the prescribed norms and also inability to continuously supervise the institutions recognized by it. This has led to commercialization of teacher education (MHRD, 2012, p. 5, Para 1.5.1).

Consequently, this commercialization of teacher education has badly impacted the success of the universalization of school education through the Samagra Shiksha Abhiyan (SSA). The Report of the Justice Verma Commission (JVC) has also stated that –

> Currently close to 90 per cent of pre-service teacher training institutions are in the private sector. On the other hand, around 80 per cent of children, enrolled in State schools, is the direct responsibility of the State as per the RTE Act. A market demand for a large number of teachers in the growing sector of school education over the past decade has led to the proliferation of sub-standard private teacher education institutions. The proliferation of sub-standard private teacher education institutions and the current state of teacher education curriculum and transaction are both serious impediments to fulfilling the objectives of the NCF, 2005 and the RTE Act, 2009 (p. 21, Para 2.9).

After publication of the report of Verma Commission in August 2012, the NCTE has had seven years till the arrival of new policy in July 2020 to check the utter corruption in teacher education system but failed. The NEP 2020 has endorsed by referring to the observation of the Verma Commission Report (2012) –

> A majority of stand-alone TEIs — over 10,000 in number are not even attempting serious teacher education but are essentially selling degrees for a price. Regulatory efforts so far have neither been able to curb the malpractices in the system, nor

> enforce basic standards for quality, and in fact have had the negative effect of curbing the growth of excellence and innovation in the sector. The sector and its regulatory system are, therefore, in urgent need of revitalization through radical action, in order to raise standards and restore integrity, credibility, efficacy, and high quality to the teacher education system (Government of India, 2020, p. 42, Para 15.2).

Whatever the new policy has talked about the stringent action against substandard stand-alone TEIs, it hints at the utter failure on the part of past and present union government as well as state governments. Moreover, the role of the NCTE as a statutory body in teacher education is questionable. Its functions remain only as a revenue collector at the cost of offering recognition to TEIs and teacher education institutions are functioning as 'commercial shops'. Until robust and vibrant State sponsored teacher education system is established, only the reliance over the self-financing teacher education institutions revitalization through radical action in the sector of teacher education is a distant dream. Now let's have a glance at the policy recommendations of the NEP 2020 in teacher education sector including about teachers.

NEP 2020: Transforming Teacher Education

Teacher education is an essential part of education system of any nation in generating a pool of school teachers for moulding the next generation. The National Education Policy 2020 addressed the issues and concerns of teachers and teacher education and made an array of recommendations to impart quality education through quality teachers at all levels of school education. The policy intended to bring multidisciplinary perspectives within the activity of teacher preparation. Future teachers will acquire "knowledge, formation of dispositions and values, and development of practice under the best mentors. Teachers must be grounded in Indian values, languages, knowledge, ethos, and traditions ... well-versed in the latest advances in education and pedagogy" (Government of India, 2020, p. 42, Para 15.1). To this end, the policy proposed a number of reforms in the form of recommendations. All stand-alone TEIs will gradually be moved into multidisciplinary colleges and universities by 2030. The policy recommended that –

> The 4-year integrated B.Ed. offered by such multidisciplinary HEIs will, by 2030, become the minimal degree qualification for school teachers. The 4-year integrated B.Ed. will be a dual-major holistic Bachelor's degree, in Education as well as a specialized subject such as a language, history, music, mathematics, computer science, chemistry, economics, art, physical education, etc. (Government of India, 2020, p. 42, Para 15.5).

Besides this programme, the policy also suggested that –

> The HEI offering the 4-year integrated B.Ed. may also run a 2-year B.Ed., for students who have already received a Bachelor's degree in a specialized subject. A 1-year B.Ed. may also be offered for candidates who have received a 4-year undergraduate degree in a specialized subject (Government of India, 2020, p. 43,

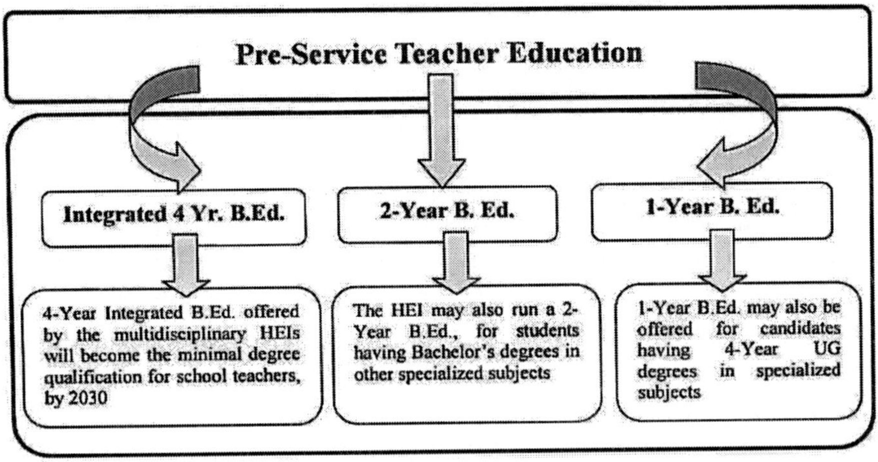

Figure 12.1: *Pre-Service Teacher Education Programmes under the NEP 2020*

Source: Government of India, 2020 & Compiled by the Author

> Para 15.5) or who have obtained a Master's degree in a specialty and wish to become a subject teacher in that specialty (Government of India, 2020, p. 23, Para 5.23).

In short, this policy proposed mainly the following three types (approaches) to in-service teacher education programmes captured in the Figure 1:

In addition to that, if any multidisciplinary higher education institution offers the 4-year in-class integrated B.Ed. programme and acquires accreditation for ODL, such institution can also run "high-quality B.Ed. programmes in blended or ODL mode to students in remote or difficult-to-access locations and also to in-service teachers who are aiming to enhance their qualification, with suitable robust arrangements for mentoring and for the practicum training and student-teaching components of the programme" (Government of India, 2020, p. 23, Para 5.23).

All B.Ed. programmes irrespective of duration will comprise "training in time-tested as well as the most recent techniques in pedagogy, including pedagogy with respect to foundational literacy and numeracy, multi-level teaching and evaluation, teaching children with disabilities, teaching children with special interests or talents, use of educational technology, and learner-centred and collaborative learning" (Government of India, 2020, p. 23, Para 5.24).

All B.Ed. programmes will also strengthen the practicum training by emphasising "the practice of the Fundamental Duties (Article 51A) of the Indian Constitution along with other Constitutional provisions while teaching any subject or performing any activity" and by appropriately integrating "environmental awareness and sensitivity towards its conservation and sustainable development" (Government of India, 2020, p. 23, Para 5.24).

This policy also recommended that –

> Special shorter local teacher education programmes will also be available at BITEs, DIETs, or at school complexes themselves for eminent local persons

> who can be hired to teach at schools or school complexes as 'master instructors', for the purpose of promoting local professions, knowledge, and skills, e.g., local art, music, agriculture, business, sports, carpentry, and other vocational crafts (Government of India, 2020, p. 24, Para 5.25).

> Shorter post-B.Ed. certification courses will also be made widely available, at multidisciplinary colleges and universities, to teachers who may wish to move into more specialized areas of teaching, such as the teaching of students with disabilities, or into leadership and management positions in the schooling system, or to move from one stage to another between foundational, preparatory, middle, and secondary stages (Government of India, 2020, p. 24, Para 5.25).

To attract the excellent and efficient students towards teaching profession objective and transparent selection, the policy recommended "suitable subject and aptitude tests conducted by the National Testing Agency, and shall be standardized keeping in view the linguistic and cultural diversity of the country" (Government of India, 2020, p. 43, Para 15.7).

The NEP 2020 suggested all the multidisciplinary universities and colleges to establish education departments to perform twofold functions – offering B.Ed. programmes and carrying out cutting-edge research in various aspects of education in collaboration with other departments such as psychology, philosophy, sociology, neuroscience, Indian languages, arts, music, history, literature, physical education, science and mathematics (Government of India, 2020, p. 42, Para 15.4).

Besides the teaching of cutting-edge pedagogy, the teacher education programmes will include grounding in sociology, history, science, psychology, early childhood care and education, foundational literacy and numeracy, knowledge of India and its values/ethos/art/traditions, and more (Government of India, 2020, p. 43, Para 15.5).

In-service continuous professional development for college and university teachers will continue through the existing institutional arrangements and ongoing initiatives; these will be strengthened and substantially expanded to meet the needs of enriched teaching-learning processes for quality education. The use of technology platforms such as SWAYAM/DIKSHA for online training of teachers will be encouraged, so that standardized training programmes can be administered to large numbers of teachers within a short span of time (Government of India, 2020, p. 43, Para 15.10).

A National Mission for Mentoring shall be established, with a large pool of outstanding senior/retired faculty – including those with the ability to teach in Indian languages – who would be willing to provide short and long-term mentoring/professional support to university/college teachers (Government of India, 2020, p. 43, Para 15.11).

There is no dearth of policy reforms in the NEP 2020 for revitalizing the whole gamut of teacher education system in India. This policy has also incorporated a number of issues related to the changing role of teachers in the 21st century. These need to be examined here.

Recognition and Promotion of Teachers

Teachers are the frontline providers of quality education and considered to be the most vital single factor in the system of education. A teacher is just like the backbone of the society and acts as an architect of the nation's development. Teachers, thus form the very heart of the education process, and represent an indispensable vehicle towards a progressive, just, educated, and prosperous society (NCERT, n.d.). Considering the vital role of teachers, the policy proposed some provisions under the caption of the 'Career Management and Progression' (CMP). To incentivise and recognise the outstanding teachers, the following provisions have been prescribed –

1) Recognition and promotion will rest upon the teachers in terms of their outstanding work. Salary will be hiked for performing their best work.
2) A robust merit-based structure of tenure, promotion, and salary structure will be developed, with multiple levels within each teacher stage (Government of India, 2020, p. 22, Para 5.17).
3) Promotions and salary will be enhanced only on the basis of appraisal instead of length of tenure or seniority. To this end, a system of multiple parameters for proper assessment of performance will be developed for the same by State/UT Governments that is based on peer reviews, attendance, commitment, hours of CPD, and other forms of service to the school and the community or based on National Professional Standard for Teachers (NPST) developed by NCTE (Government of India, 2020, p. 22, Para 5.17).

However, the policy restricted the career advancement-related incentives of teachers within a single school stage (Foundational, Preparatory, Middle and Secondary).

Upgrading Working Conditions for Teachers

The policy intended to revamp the service environment and culture of schools with a primary objective of maximizing the ability of teachers to do their jobs effectively (Government of India, 2020, p. 21, Para 5.8). To this end, the policy recommendations comprise ensuring decent and pleasant service conditions at schools, adequate and sound infrastructure, safe, and effective learning environment for teachers and students, including children of all genders and children with disabilities and sensitization of teachers through in-service training towards safety, health and environment at workplace in schools (Government of India, 2020, p. 21, Para 5.9). Moreover, teachers will not be involved any longer in non-academic tasks. Particularly, teachers will be engaged in mid-day meal related work for a rationalized minimum time (Government of India, 2020, p. 21, Para 5.12). This policy failed to devise pathways how teachers can be exempted from the engagement with varied administrative work, arrangement of mid-day meals, voting duties, household surveys. Teachers are still acting as the vehicles of such works.

CPD of Teachers, Teacher Educators and School Principals

Pre-service and in-service teacher education programmes are complementary to each other. However, pre-service programmes are not adequate to prepare teachers to meet up all the challenges they will face throughout their careers. Teacher education system therefore seeks to provide teachers with provisions continuous professional development during the whole tenure of in-service to sustain standard of teaching and quality workforce among the teachers.

OECD (2005) has rightly remarked that –

> Effective professional development is on-going, includes training, practice and feedback, and provides adequate time and follow-up support. Successful programmes involve teachers in learning activities that are similar to ones they will use with their students, and encourage the development of teachers' learning communities. There is growing interest in developing schools as learning organisations, and in ways for teachers to share their expertise and experience more systematically (p. 95).

The continuous development of teachers beyond their initial training can serve a number of objectives (OECD, 1998, p. 33), including:

- to update individuals' knowledge of a subject in light of recent advances in the area;
- to update individuals' skills, attitudes and approaches in light of the development of new teaching techniques and objectives, new circumstances and new educational research;
- to enable individuals to apply changes made to curricula or other aspects of teaching practice;
- to enable schools to develop and apply new strategies concerning the curriculum and other aspects of teaching practice;
- to exchange information and expertise among teachers and others, *e.g.* academics, industrialists; and
- to help weaker teachers become more effective.

OECD (1998; 2009) defined professional development "as activities that develop an individual's skills, knowledge, expertise and other characteristics as a teacher" (p. 18; 49). The development can be provided in many ways, ranging from the formal to the informal. It includes the following activities (OECD, 2009, p. 50):

- courses/workshops (*e.g.* on subject matter or methods and/or other education-related topics);
- education conferences or seminars (at which teachers and/or researchers present their research results and discuss education problems);
- qualification programme (*e.g.* a degree programme);
- observation visits to other schools;
- participation in a network of teachers formed specifically for the professional development of teachers;
- individual or collaborative research on a topic of professional interest; and
- mentoring and/or peer observation and coaching, as part of a formal school arrangement.

The NEP 2020 has also given due emphasis on the continuous professional development programmes for teachers and teacher educators. The recommendations include –

1) These programmes will be conducted in multiple modes, such as, workshops, online teacher development modules, etc.
2) Each teacher will participate in at least 50 hours of CPD programmes every year for their own professional development.
3) CPD opportunities will include the latest pedagogies regarding foundational literacy and numeracy, formative and adaptive assessment of learning outcomes, competency-based learning, and related pedagogies, such as experiential learning, arts-integrated, sports-integrated, and storytelling-based approaches, etc. (Government of India, 2020, p. 22, Para 5.15).
4) School Principals and school complex leaders will also participate in 50 hours or more of CPD modules per year, covering leadership and management, as well as content and pedagogy with a focus on preparing and implementing pedagogical plans based on competency-based education (Government of India, 2020, p. 22, Para 5.16).

Professional Standards for Teachers

The policy intended to introduce a common guiding set of National Professional Standards for Teachers (NPST) developed by the National Council for Teacher Education in its restructured new form as a Professional Standard Setting Body (PSSB) under the General Education Council (GEC), in consultation with NCERT, SCERTs, teachers at all levels and expert bodies in vocational education, and higher education institutions. The NPST entails the following issues –

1) The standards would cover expectations of the role of the teacher at different levels of expertise/stage, and the competencies required for that stage.
2) It will also comprise standards for performance appraisal of teachers.
3) The NPST will also inform the design of pre-service teacher education programmes.
4) This will determine all aspects of teacher career management, including tenure, professional development efforts, salary increases, promotions, etc.
5) The professional standards will be reviewed every ten years, on the basis of rigorous empirical analysis of the efficacy of the system (Government of India, 2020, pp. 22-23, Para 5.20).

Teachers' Recruitment and Deployment

The policy has proposed a number of guidelines for teachers' recruitment and their deployment. These include –

1) A large number of merit-based scholarships shall be provided across the country for studying quality 4-year integrated B.Ed. programmes to attract the outstanding students especially from rural areas into the teaching profession.

2) Incentives will be provided for teachers to take up teaching jobs in rural areas, especially in areas that are currently facing acute shortage of quality teachers (Government of India, 2020, p. 20, Para 5.2).
3) Teacher Eligibility Tests (TETs) will be strengthened both in terms of content and pedagogy.
4) The TETs will also be extended to cover teachers across all stages (Foundational, Preparatory, Middle and Secondary) of school education.
5) For subject teachers, suitable TET or NTA test scores in the corresponding subjects will also be taken into account for recruitment (Government of India, 2020, p. 20, Para 5.4).

Providing Quality Teachers in the School System

Teachers truly shape the future of our children – and, therefore, the future of our nation. It is because of this noblest role that the teacher in India was the most respected member of society. Only the very best and most learned became teachers. Society gave teachers, or gurus, what they needed to pass on their knowledge, skills, and ethics optimally to students. The quality of teacher education, recruitment, deployment, service conditions, and empowerment of teachers is not where it should be, and consequently the quality and motivation of teachers does not reach the desired standards. The high respect for teachers and the high status of the teaching profession must be restored so as to inspire the best to enter the teaching profession. The motivation and empowerment of teachers is required to ensure the best possible future for our children and our nation (Government of India, 2020, p. 20, Para 5.1).

The quality of training, recruitment, deployment, service conditions, and empowerment of teachers is not where it should be, and consequently the quality and motivation of teachers does not reach the standards where it could be. In order to ensure quality in learning, it has become imperative to prepare teachers to face the challenges of the dynamic society and impart quality education. The quality and excellence of the entire process of teacher education lie in its appropriateness of design, effectiveness of curriculum, soundness of structure, viability of organization, efficiency of transactional modes, appropriate integration of technology and above all its continuous commitment to meaningful research and innovation.

1) NCERT will study, research, document, and compile the varied international pedagogical approaches for teaching different subjects and make recommendations on what can be learnt and assimilated from these approaches into the pedagogies being practised in India (Government of India, 2020, p. 24, Para 5.27).
2) New and comprehensive National Curriculum Framework for Teacher Education (NCFTE) will be formulated by the NCTE in consultation with NCERT, based on the principles of this National Education Policy 2020 (Government of India, 2020, p. 24, Para 5.28).

3) Finally, to restore the integrity of the teacher education system, stringent action will be taken against substandard stand-alone Teacher Education Institutions (TEIs) running in the country, including shutting them down, if required (Government of India, 2020, p. 24, Para 5.29).

Systematic Policy Reforms in TE and Role of Teachers at a Glance

The whole spectrum of systematic policy reforms in teacher education and role of teachers in the light of the NEP 2020 can be summarised in the following way.

Table 12.3: *Systematic Policy Reforms in Teacher Education*

1.	All teacher education programmes to be conducted within composite multidisciplinary institutions.
2.	NPE 2020 proposed new 4-year Integrated B.Ed. course after completing XIIth Class, 1-year B.Ed. after Completing P.G. and 2-year B.Ed. after completing U.G.
3.	By 2030, the minimum degree qualification for teaching will be a 4-year integrated B.Ed. degree.
4.	All fresh PhD entrants, irrespective of discipline, will be required to take credit-based courses in teaching/education/pedagogy/writing related to their chosen Ph.D. subject.
5.	Stringent action will be taken against substandard stand-alone Teacher Education Institutions (TEIs).
6.	NTA testing for admission to B.Ed.
7.	Stringent action against substandard stand-alone Teacher Education Institutions (TEIs).
8.	Setting-up of National Mission for Mentoring with a large pool of outstanding senior/retired faculty
9.	National Higher Education Regulatory Council (NHERC) will function as single point regulator for higher education sector including teacher education.
10.	Restructuring the NCTE as a Professional Standard Setting Body under the General Education Council (GEC)
11.	Merit based scholarships for studying quality 4-Year Integrated B.Ed. programme.
12.	Teacher Eligibility Tests (TETs) for all teachers across Foundational, Preparatory, Middle and Secondary stage in both public and private schools.
13.	A common National Professional Standards for Teachers (NPST) will be developed for the country by NCTE in consultation with the NCERT, SCERTs, and other concerned institutions as well as with teachers.
14.	States /UTs/KVS/NVS will develop recruitment, deployment, transfer and recognition policy for teachers.
15.	Assessment of performance of teachers will be based on peer reviews, attendance, commitment, hours of CPD, and other forms of service to the school and the community developed by State/UT or based on National Professional Standard for Teachers (NPST) developed by NCTE.
16.	In-service teachers will participate in at least 50 hours of continuous professional development (CPD) every year.
17.	National Mission for Mentoring will be established, with a large pool of outstanding senior/retired faculty to provide mentoring/professional support to university/college teachers.

Source: Government of India, 2020 and Compiled by the Author

Challenges to Implementing the Policy Reforms Envisaged by the NEP 2020

Considering the policy recommendations related to teacher education and teachers, it can safely claimed that for the first time the NEP 2020 has envisioned a dynamic teacher education system to prepare the future teachers to the 21st century challenges. To raise some questions or to identify some weak propositions or to locate some daunting challenges to implementation doesn't mean to underestimate the strength of the policy reforms embedded in the NEP 2020. Few such areas are –

1) The policy prescribed 4-year integrated B.Ed. degree as minimum degree qualification for teaching by 2030 but didn't mention what will be the minimum qualification for teacher educators at multi-disciplinary TEIs. In addition to that, this policy is totally silent on specification of the training institutions for foundational, preparatory, middle and secondary levels. Moreover, when 4-year integrated B.Ed. will be compulsory for school education by 2030, what will be future of 2-year B.Ed. and 1-year B.Ed.?
2) One of the areas of concern towards transforming teacher education in India envisioned by the NEP 2020 is the scarce funding and budget on education. Union Budget for 2022-23 allocated around 1,04,278 crore to the education sector, which is an increase of 11.86, 12 per cent over the previous year. However, this figure is too little to actualise the aspirations embedded in the NEP 2020 and it is also far behind the recommended expenditure of six per cent of GDP on education. Until and unless the adequate budgetary allocation is ensured, the policy's vision of revamping TE will remain a distant dream (Hooda & Malik, 2022).
3) This policy has failed to address the issues of access, equity, and quality in TE. The policy makers are well informed of the fact that currently, 85 per cent of TEIs in India are in the private sector. That's why the policy has diplomatically dropped those issues.
4) The policy makes a provision for merit-based scholarships to attract talent from rural areas into the teaching profession (Government of India, p. 20). But strategy would not be effective. The problem is deeply rooted. With the passage of changing times, the willingness of students to opt teaching as profession has considerably reduced for various reasons of which economic benefits is a major reason (Yenugu, 2022).
5) Teachers are the key catalyst to revamp the entire gamut of TE in tune with aspirations envisaged by the policy. But the process of reconfiguration will be halted due to poor PTR in school sector across India. As per the report, titled "2021 State of the Education Report for India: No Teacher, No Class", there are 110,971 single-teacher schools in India, i.e. 7.15 per cent. 89 per cent of these single-teacher schools are in rural areas. Based on the PTR of 35:1, the total additional teacher requirement is found to be about 1,116,846. 69 per cent of total additional teacher requirement is in rural areas (Sarangapani et al., 2021, p. 33).

6) The policy has also failed to exempt teachers from the involvement with non-teaching activities in school. Today's teachers have to carry out mid-day meal scheme, distribution of free textbooks, dress and bicycle, entry of student data in the governmental portals, election, census, disaster management duties and others. The "2021 State of the Education Report for India: No Teacher, No Class" revealed that contrary to public perception, teacher workload is high although invisible, and a source of stress. Teachers prioritise professional autonomy, and disregard of this is a source of de-motivation and stress (Sarangapani et al., 2021, p. 75). The new policy has not only created provision of recognition and promotion of teachers on the basis of outstanding work but also suggested an array of means to revamp the service environment in school. Such provisions will not ultimately mitigate the invisible workload of teachers.
7) The policy has recommended taking stringent action against substandard stand-alone Teacher Education Institutions (TEIs). Code of professional ethics is one of the cardinal attributes of a profession. The new policy should have been proposed to formulate such code developed by the NCTE in consultation with NCERT, SCERTs and teachers' associations.
8) The practice of hiring contract/para teachers gained attractiveness since the launch of District Primary Education Programme (DPEP) in 1994. This practice continued under Sarva Shiksha Abhiyan (SSA), Rashtriya Madhyamik Shiksha Abhiyan (RMSA) and Samagra Shiksha Abhiyan (SSA). This gave rise to disparities in recruitment processes, service rules, tenure and payment. Their engagement was seen as an immediate measure to address teacher shortages by following a far simpler process of recruitment within a short time, without having to go through arduous processes of getting teacher posts sanctioned and adding to the state's/union territory's (UT's) financial burden. The idea of teachers on contract has also been seen as the panacea for teacher absence and teacher accountability. They could be deployed without long-term financial liability. Are contract/para teachers as qualified as regular teachers? The NEP 2020 is silent on contract teachers (Ramachandran et al., 2023). The policy endorsed provisions for recognition, promotion of teachers and enhancement of salary structure on the basis of their appraisal. Whether the para teachers be entitled to such opportunities? The policy has failed to answer to questions related to contract/para teachers.
9) The NPE 1968 stated that teachers' emoluments and other service conditions should be adequate and satisfactory having regard to their qualifications and responsibilities (Government of India, 1968, Para 4.2) and the NPE 1986 proposed that "efforts will be made to reach the desirable objective of uniform emoluments, service conditions and grievance-removal mechanisms for teachers throughout the country" (Government of India, 1986, Para 9.2). The new policy also endorsed provisions for recognition, promotion of teachers and enhancement of

salary structure on the basis of their appraisal. Like the previous policies, this new one will also fail to maintain due to multi-layered schooling system and varied recruitment bodies in India.

10) The Centrally Sponsored Scheme Pandit Madan Mohan Malaviya National Mission on Teachers and Teaching (PMMMNMTT) was launched in 2014 to address comprehensively all issues related to teacher training/ capacity building and professional development of teachers. Under this scheme, the total 95 centres were established across India. Presently, the Standing Finance Committee has appraised the Scheme and recommended for continuation till 2025-2026 with the total outlay of Rs. 493.68 crore (PIB, 2022). Probably due to ineffectiveness of such scheme, the NEP is silent on it. All the PMMMNMTT Centres have been organizing professional development programmes either in online or blended mode. If these centres receive financial assistance from the Government, collection of funds from the participating teachers by these centres in the name of registration is purely unethical and unprincipled. The aim of these centres is to collect revenue on the part of the Government. Besides, the quality of such professional programmes is also an area of concern. The policy of professional development of in-service teachers should be well-organized and State sponsored. Otherwise, the new policy on 50 hours of continuous professional development (CPD) every year will be fruitless.

Concluding Remarks

NEP 2020 is the first official national education policy in the 21st century and envisages much-needed changes in the way education is being delivered in India. NEP 2020 includes systematic reforms in education at all levels including teacher education and teachers. Whatever the reforms or changes have been prescribed in the policy, political commitment is highly necessitated for implementation. Since the approval of the policy by the Union Government, its tenure of implementation falls on the fourth year. But till now National Curriculum for Teacher Education or School Education has not been yet finalized. Consequently, the policy aspirations remain untested. For revamping teacher education in India, a robust state sponsored TE system should be structured. Adequate funding to TEIs and teacher recruitment in vacant post across India should be ensured. Too much dependence on the substandard private providers is detrimental to fulfilling the policy reforms envisioned by the NEP 2020. NCFs for school education and teacher education should reflect the changes in the techno-pedagogical era as well as emerging needs in the 21st century. There must be a link between the school education and teacher education curriculum frameworks and students' needs. All the TE programmes must cater to the diverse learning needs of 21st century learners. Access, equity and quality issues must be maintained in the domain of teacher education for attracting students to opt teaching as career.

References

Azim Premji University (2021). *Issues in Education: Teachers and Teacher Education (Volume)*. Bengaluru: Azim Premji University.

Government of India (1968). *National Policy on Education 1968*. New Delhi: Ministry of Education, Government of India.

Government of India (1986). *National Policy on Education 1986*. New Delhi: Ministry of Human Resource Development, Government of India.

Government of India (2020). *National Education Policy 2020*. New Delhi: Ministry of Education, Government of India.

Hooda, M. & Malik, V. (2022). Metamorphosing Teacher Education in India underneath NPE 2020. *Education India: A Quarterly Refereed Journal of Dialogues on Education*, 11(1): 1-12.

MHRD (2012). *Vision of Teacher Education in India: Quality and Regulatory Perspective — Report of the High-Powered Commission on Teacher Education Constituted by the Hon'ble Supreme Court of India*. New Delhi: MHRD, Government of India.

MHRD. (2012). *Vision of Teacher Education in India: Quality and Regulatory Perspective*. Report of the High-powered Commission on Teacher Education Constituted by the Hon'ble Supreme Court of India, Vol. I. New Delhi: MHRD.

NCERT (n.d.). *Teacher and Teacher Education: Background Paper for Teacher's Fest*. New Delhi: NCERT. Available at https://www.education.gov.in/shikshakparv/docs/background_note_NCF.pdf

NCTE (2016). *Upanishads: Messages for Teachers and Teacher Educators*. New Delhi: National Council for Teacher Education.

NCTE (2018). *NCTE (Recognition, Norms and Procedure) Amendment Regulations, 2018*. New Delhi: National Council for Teacher Education, Government of India.

NCTE (2019). *National Council for Teacher Education (Recognition Norms and procedure) Amendment Regulations 2019*. New Delhi: The Gazette of India Extraordinary.

OECD (1998). Staying Ahead: In-Service Training and Teacher Professional Development. Paris: OECD.

OECD (2005). *Teachers Matter: Attracting, Developing and Retaining Effective Teachers*. Paris: OECD.

OECD (2009). *Creating Effective Teaching and Learning Environments: First Results from TALIS*. Paris: OECD.

Pand, S. (2021). Indian National Education Policy 2020: Teacher Education as Part of University System, and Stand-Alone Institutions. *Staff and Educational Development International*, 24 (2): 51-65.

Ramachandran, V. (2023). *Persisting Challenge of Contract Teachers in Government Schools of India*. In Varghese, N.V., Mangalagiri, A. & Mathew, A. (Ed.). *Quality and Inclusion in Education: The Persisting Challenges*. New York: Routledge.

Sarangapani, P.M., Thirumalai, B., Ramanathan, A., Kumar, R. & Ramchand, M. (2021). *NO TEACHER, NO CLASS: State of the Education Report for India 2021*. New Delhi: UNESCO.

Yenugu, S. (2022). The new National Education Policy (NEP) of India: will it be a paradigm shift in Indian higher education? *Perspectives: Policy and Practice in Higher Education*. https://doi.org/10.1080/13603108.2022.2078901

PIB (2022). *Salient Features of NEP, 2020*. New Delhi: PIB, Ministry of Education, Government of India.

13

Intellectual Property Rights (IPRs)

NEP 2020 and Initiatives of UGC

Arindam Bhattacharyya
Aditi Ray

Introduction

Intellectual property is purely a creation of human mind and there is no sphere of life that is untouched by it. At present, global economy is rapidly transforming into knowledge economy and physical resources are being substituted into knowledge economy. Actually, wealth creation in the modern world is primarily based on Intellectual Property. Development, transmission and representation of knowledge should be supervised within the ethical and legal framework. It is only possible by proper implementation and incorporation of 'Intellectual Property Right' (IPR). Indian academic environment demands the practice of fearless true knowledge in every corner of the country. In this context, the protection of Intellectual property is conceived in the light of NEP 2020, where research and development are suggested to be one of the chief missions for the Indian Universities. NEP 2020 envisages the promotion of quality research within the higher education institutions (HEIs) and simultaneously the higher apex body of Indian higher education, the University Grants Commission (UGC) should play a significant role in implementing multidisciplinary research culture mandated in NEP 2020. It is important to promote more collaboration between HEI and industry through better clarity on IPR policy. IPR Cell is very important and also mandatory for all HEIs of India. UGC has taken several initiatives for the regular practice of IPR according to the vision of NEP 2020. Now it is expected that the higher education curriculum of different streams must include the discourse of Intellectual Property and Intellectual Property Right, both in the undergraduate (UG) and postgraduate (PG) level. Present paper is an attempt to investigate the vision of NEP 2020 on Intellectual Property and mission of the policy for the promotion of Intellectual Property Rights. UGC's several initiatives for the regular practice of intellectual property rights have also been addressed here for its better implementation.

Intellectual property rights (IPR) were first recognized in Paris Convention for the Protection of Industrial Property (1883) and in the Berne Convention for Protection of Literary and Artistic Work (1886). World Intellectual Property Organization (WIPO) mentioned that "Intellectual property (IP) refers to creations of the mind, such as inventions; literary and artistic works; designs;

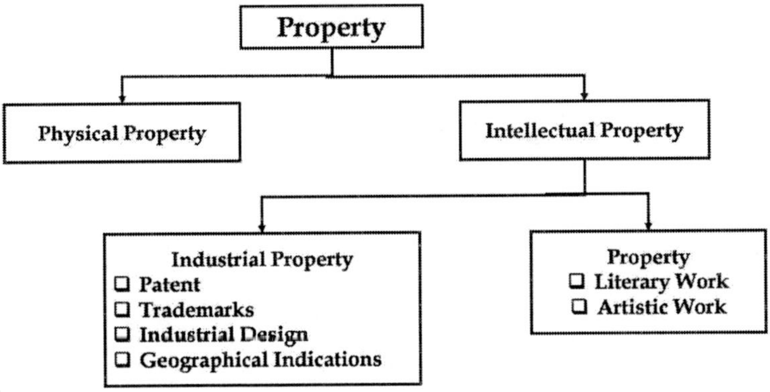

Figure 13.1: *Simple Classification of Intellectual Property*

and symbols, names and images used in commerce." On the other hand, World Trade Organization (WTO) stated that, "Intellectual property rights are the rights given to persons over the creations of their minds. They usually give the creator an exclusive right over the use of his/her creation for a certain period of time." In this context, UGC (2016) clearly stated that "Creations of mind such as inventions, designs for industrial articles, literary, artistic work, symbols, names and images etc. are protected by IPR".

Brief Description of Intellectual Property Rights

On the basis of type of invention and creation of human mind and their applications the intellectual property rights are classified (Jajpura et al., 2016). IPR is normally of two types:

1. Industrial Property Rights and
2. Copyright.

Industrial property rights include inventions (patents), trademarks, industrial designs and geographic indications of source. Copyright includes literary and artistic works like novels, poems and plays, films and motion pictures, musical works, artistic works such as drawings, paintings, photographs, sculptures, architectural designs, computer programmes and performing arts and broadcasting work. Intellectual property rights recognize the work of the creators and should protect them for flourish of their creativity. Therefore, the types of intellectual property rights are mainly Patents, Trademarks, Industrial Designs, and Geographic Indications of Source (GIS) and Copyright. A brief description of them is given below in tabular form.

National IPR Policy 2016

In this present scenario, the National Intellectual Property Rights (IPR) Policy 2016 was adopted on 12.5.2016 by Government of India, Ministry of

Table 13.1: *Brief Description of Intellectual Property Rights (IPR)*

Type	*Concept*	*Valid for*	*Related Indian Laws*
PATENT	Patent is a statutory right granted to the inventor for a limited period of time, excluding others from making, using, selling or importing any product covered by a patent. For the patent purpose, an invention is defined as a new product or process, involving with an Inventive Step, novelty and capable of Industrial application.	It is valid for 20 years from the date of filing or priority date	**1972**: The Patents Act 1970. The 1st, 2nd, 3rd amendment to the Patents Act in the year 1999, 2002, 2005 respectively.
TRADEMARKS	It means a mark capable of being represented graphically and which is capable of distinguishing the goods or services of one person from those of others. Trademark can be sign, words, letters, numbers, drawings, pictures, emblem, colours or combination of colours, shape of goods, packaging or sound or any other combination of the above.	It is valid for 10 years, but renewable perpetually for term of 10 years each	**1958:** Trade and Merchandise Act. **2002:** Trademark Act 1999 (as per TRIPS agreement) **2013:** Introduced provisions of Madrid Protocol.
DESIGNS	It means only the features of shape, configuration, pattern or ornament or composition of lines or colour or combination thereof applied to any article, whether two dimensional or three dimensional or in both forms, by any industrial process or means, whether manual, mechanical or chemical, separate or combined, which in the finished article appeal to and are judged solely by the eye.	Valid for 10 years, extendable by 5 more years only	**2001:** Design Act 2000. **2000:** Semiconductor Integrated Circuits Layout- Design Act.
GIS	It identifies agricultural or natural or manufactured goods for originating or manufactured in the territory of a country; or region or locality in that territory, where a given quality, reputation or other characteristics of such goods is essentially attributable to its geographical origin.	It always prevents unauthorised use of a registered Geographical Indication by others	**2002:** Geographical Indications of Goods (Registration & Protection) Act, 1999.
COPYRIGHT	It is an exclusive right given to the owner/author for an original work that he has created. Original works like literary, dramatic, musical, artistic, cinematograph films, sound recording etc. that are protected under Copyright.	Scope and duration vary with the nature of the protected work.	**1957: 1st** Copyright Act after Independence. **1994:** Some changes in the Copyright Act, 1957. **2012:** The copy Right (amendment) Act 2012.

Commerce and Industry as a vision document to guide future development of IPRs in India. The Policy has seven objectives which are mentioned below:

1) IPR Awareness: Outreach and Promotion (for creating public awareness about the economic, social and cultural benefits of IPRs);
2) Generation of IPRs (for stimulating the generation of IPRs);
3) Legal and Legislative Framework (for implementation of strong and effective IPR laws in context of the larger public interest);
4) Administration and Management (for the modernization and strengthening service oriented IPR administration);
5) Commercialization of IPR (Earn value for IPRs through commercialization);
6) Enforcement and Adjudication (to strengthen the enforcement and adjudicatory mechanisms for combating IPR infringements);
7) Human Capital Development (for strengthening and expanding human resources, institutions and capacities for teaching, training, research and skill building in IPRs);

The aim of the National Intellectual Property Rights (IPR) Policy 2016 is to integrate the intellectual property as a policy and strategic tool for national development of India. A holistic approach should be taken on IP legal, administrative, institutional and enforcement related matters. The main responsibility for the implementation of the plans of action will remain with the related Ministries / Departments concerned in their assigned sphere of work. Public and private sectors, institutions and State governments will also be involved in the implementation process.

National Education Policy 2020

After draft revision, finally 'The National Education Policy 2020' (NEP 2020) was published on 29.07.2020 by replacing '*NPE 1986*' (National Policy on Education, 1986). This new policy identifies a number of milestones for our education system. We hope that the NEP 2020 gives us revolutionary and qualitative changes in the Indian education system. The NEP 2020 "contributes directly to transforming our nation sustainably into an equitable and vibrant knowledge society, by providing high quality education to all" (Venkateshwarlu, 2021). The principal guidelines of this policy are based on *access, equity, quality, affordability* and *accountability*. The above guidelines of the policy have given emphasis on flexibility, multi-disciplinary approach, integrity and unity of knowledge, conceptual understanding, regular formative assessment, diversity, equity and inclusion, equality and quality, integrity and transparency, autonomy and empowerment, light but tight regulatory system, research and development, real policy-making, vibrant public education system, private participation etc. Sawant and Sankpal (2021) mentioned that the new policy strongly believes on the rational thought and action, scientific temper and creative imagination etc.

Vision of NEP 2020 on IPRs

Higher education is an important aspect of education system of a country. A well-structured education policy easily develops the economy, social stability, technology adoption, and human resource of a country. The National Education Policy 2020 essentially aims at increasing quality of Higher Education Institutions (HEIs) and positioning India as a Global Education Hub (GEH) by providing interdisciplinary approach and knowledge-based education. In this respect, NEP 2020 has declared the following points:

1) India moves towards becoming a knowledge economy and society, more and more young Indians are likely to aspire for higher education. (Para 9.1)
2) At the societal level, higher education must enable the development of an enlightened, socially conscious, knowledgeable, and skilled nation that can find and implement robust solutions to its own problems. Higher education must form the basis for knowledge creation and innovation thereby contributing to a growing national economy. (Para 9.1.3)
3) India will be promoted as a global study destination providing premium education at affordable costs thereby helping to restore its role as a Vishwa Guru. ... Research/teaching collaborations and faculty/student exchanges with high-quality foreign institutions will be facilitated, and relevant mutually beneficial MOUs with foreign countries will be signed. (Para 12.8)
4) Research and innovation at education institutions in India, particularly those that are engaged in higher education, is critical. Evidence from the world's best universities throughout history shows that the best teaching and learning processes at the higher education level occur in environments where there is also a strong culture of research and knowledge creation; conversely, much of the very best research in the world has occurred in multidisciplinary University settings. (Para 17.6)
5) India has a long historical tradition of research and knowledge creation, in disciplines ranging from science and mathematics to art and literature to phonetics and languages to medicine and agriculture. This needs to be further strengthened to make India lead research and innovation in the 21st century, as a strong and enlightened knowledge society and one of the three largest economies in the world. (Para 17.7)

Therefore, the present academic environment demands the practice of fearless true knowledge in our country. Development of knowledge, transmission of knowledge and representation of knowledge should be supervised within the ethical and legal framework and it can only be possible by proper implementation of 'Intellectual Property Right' (IPR). Indeed, the protection of intellectual property is conceived in the light of NEP 2020, where research and development are suggested to be one of the chief missions for the

Indian Universities. NEP 2020 envisages the promotion of quality research within the higher education institutions (HEIs) and IPR will play significant role in this context. Ganguli (2003) clearly stated that we "need realistic legal frameworks that would nurture innovation, provide for ownership of knowledge, facilitate fearless knowledge sharing / transfer / rejuvenation, encourage fair benefit distribution between the innovators and society resulting in enhanced trade and societal advancement. Appreciation of the issues of knowledge ownership and IPR linked issues are now beginning to take a centre stage in all knowledge linked activities." Sawant and Sankpal (2021) again mentioned that the "National Education Policy (NEP 2020) brings in ambitious changes that could transform the education system. But the key here is good implementation and execution".

Mission of NEP 2020 for the Promotion of IPRs

In the light of principal guidelines and chief aims of NEP 2020, certain salient features of higher education can be derived as follows:

- Increase GER in higher education including vocational education to reach at least 50 per cent by 2035;
- Arrangement of Holistic Multidisciplinary Higher Education;
- Opening the Multidisciplinary Education and Research Universities (MERUs);
- Preparation for optimal learning environments;
- High-quality support centres in HEIs;
- Professional, academic and career counselling for the students;
- Rationalised Institutional Architecture (HEIs will be transformed into large multidisciplinary Universities, Colleges, and HEI clusters/ Knowledge Hubs);
- Development of National Research Foundation (NRF);
- Financial support for meritorious students;
- Expanse of Open and distance learning;
- Internationalization of higher education;
- Recruitment of Motivated and Capable Faculty for HEIs;
- Effective Governance and leadership in HEIs;
- Single Umbrella Body for promotion of HEI;
- National Educational Technology Forum (NETF) for higher education (like DIKSHA/SWAYAM);
- Online Education and Digital Education as Alternative Modes;
- Creation of a Higher Education Commission of India (HECI);
- Exposure to Vocational Education through higher education and constitute a National Committee for the Integration of Vocational Education (NCIVE).

Thus, the new policy aims at making "India a global knowledge superpower". One of the significant aims of the NEP 2020 is to instil a "*deep-rooted pride*" in being Indian, not only in thought, but also in spirit, intellect, and deeds, as well as to develop knowledge, skills, values, and dispositions that support responsible commitment to human rights, sustainable development and living, and global well-being. NEP 2020 emphasized on interdisciplinary approach in the area of higher education. In this context, it is very important to explore NEP 2020 on the following issues, which are related directly or indirectly with intellectual property and intellectual property right:

- Identification of the innovative practices in NEP 2020 for knowledge development;
- Scope and provision of multidisciplinary research activities in NEP 2020;
- Knowledge creation through multidisciplinary research activities in NEP 2020;
- Outcomes of Multidisciplinary Education and Research Universities (MERUs);
- Activities of National Research Foundation (NRF) for IPR;
- Role of National Educational Technology Forum (NETF) for the Development, transmission and representation of knowledge.

UGC's Initiatives on Intellectual Property Rights (IPRs)

NEP 2020 has a normative vision and UGC has an operative mission for IPR. UGC (2016) already stated that the "IPRs should be protected to encourage the creator and also striking a balance between the innovators and public interest by creating an awareness where creativity can flourish". Sharma et al. (2022) advocated that proper dissemination of IPR knowledge and its execution is utmost significance in the context of NEP 2020. The following are the several initiatives of UGC towards IPRs:

a) *Awareness Program on Intellectual Property and Intellectual Property Rights (IPR):* On the occasion of 'Azadi ka Amrit Mahotsav', the Ministry of Education and UGC have jointly organized a "Launch of Online Workshop for Universities and Colleges on Intellectual Property Rights (IPR)" on 17.01.2022 with the collaboration of DPIIT & CGPDTM (Controller General of Patents, Designs and Trade Marks). After that, a number of online workshops on IPR were organized in India. On the other hand, the UGC has also asked all Universities and Higher Educational Institutions (HEI) to set up 'Intellectual Property Centres' and 'Innovation labs' in their institutions to promote a culture of innovation and entrepreneurship.
b) *Inclusion of the IPR as a generic elective subject under the CBCS*: The University Grants Commission has directed Indian Universities to include IPR as elective subject under the Choice Based Credit System (CBCS) to generate interest among students. The UGC ordered all Vice Chancellors to include IPR in UG and PG curriculum. The UGC Secretary, Jaspal S.

Sandhu wrote a letter on 15.07.2016 to the VCs of the various universities across India in this respect. The UGC secretary stated in his letter that, "Keeping in view the importance of IPR which recognizes the work of the creator, you are requested to devise, through academic council, inclusion of the IPR as a generic elective subject under the Choice Base Credit System (CBCS) in your esteemed university and the affiliated colleges." UGC also suggests that HEIs should boost the employability of graduates through curriculum reform like a Certificate Course in Intellectual Property Rights.

c) *Conduction of 'Lecture Series' throughout the country by eminent individuals*: The UGC was celebrating its Golden Jubilee Year during 2002-2003. On this occasion, the UGC conducted the 'Golden Jubilee Lecture Series' throughout the country by eminent individuals. These lecture series were organized in universities located in remote areas to bring UGC closer to students, teachers, educational administrators and local communities. As an example, Prof. P. Ganguli (2003) delivered a lecture entitled with "*Ad(d)venture with Knowledge....Stepping ahead with Intellectual Property Rights*" at the University of Bhavnagar, Gujarat, India on 13.11.2003. The UGC also published seven lectures in the form of Golden Jubilee Lecture Series Booklets for all.
d) *Launch of National Intellectual property Awareness Mission (NIPAM):* CGPDTM, Department for Promotion of Industry and Internal Trade, Ministry of Commerce and Industry, Government of India had launched a "National Intellectual Property Awareness Mission (NIPAM)" with an aim to impart IPR Awareness/Training to one million students. UGC has taken special initiatives in this respect.
e) *Offline / Online IPR Awareness/Training programme launched under the NIPAM:* Under the NIPAM, CGPDTM will provide resource persons for IPR Awareness / Training programme and also conduct separate training session for the Master Trainers (MTs) of IPRs.
f) *IPR Awareness/Training Programme in Universities and Colleges*: Vice Chancellor of universities and Principal of colleges are requested by UGC to organize IPR awareness/ training programme under NIPAM. They are further requested to nominate one faculty member from their own institution for the preparation of Master Trainers (MTs) in IPR.
g) *Publication of e-book on IPR:* The UGC is publishing various e-books in English & Hindi version on higher education from very beginning. More than 50 e-books are available in UGC Website. An important e-book related with IPR, viz. 'Academic Integrity and Research Quality' was published in December, 2021 by UGC.
h) *UGC and NAAC emphasized on opening IPR Cell in HEIs:* Indian government revised the National IPR policy in May 2016. All academic and research institutions are mainly concerned with managing projects

and research works successfully. The protection of their Intellectual Property Rights will benefit all stake holders. In this context, NAAC and UGC emphasized on opening IPR Cell in Higher Education Institutions of India. As per UGC's direction, HEIs initiated the formation of IPR Cell to encourage research and projects and provide proper environment to all researchers.

Concluding Remarks

In a nutshell, vision and mission of NEP 2020 on Intellectual Property Rights (IPR) is explored here. National Education Policy 2020 seeks to introduce intellectual property from a very young age to develop the scientific, creative, and innovative temper. Educational institutions should play a pivotal role in disseminating IP knowledge and creating IP professionals and policymakers. But NEP 2020 is theoretically sound, but its practical aspects are not well-rooted in this aspect. The policy has crafted the multidisciplinary approach to higher education without paying attention to the overall infrastructural conditions in the HEIs across India. In this context, Govinda (2020) remarked that it had been "transported into an ideational world of words, acronyms and prosaic imagination, away from the real educational world of people and institutions along with their handicaps and capabilities." Furthermore Batra (2020) also stated that the "measures suggested in the NEP indicate a lack of critical understanding of the ground realities of education in an unequal society". After 34 years, NEP 2020 replaces the previous NEP 1986. Therefore, the new policy demands the revision of the entire curriculum to fulfil the objectives of the NEP 2020. Hope that the new education policy will help to inculcate knowledge-based education with technological embedded which was missing in previous years. IPR has taken significant role in this context. The educational transformation has already started after the Covid-19 pandemic situation, and it will continue until the year 2050. NEP 2020 is expected to fulfil its objectives by 2030 and the first level of transformation is expected to be materialised by 2030. Establishment of IPR Cell and Research Promotion Cell in each higher education institute is highly necessitated to promote the culture of quality multidisciplinary research in the university. UGC must play a proactive role in promoting the scientific, creative, and innovative temper among the researchers and academicians.

References

Batra, P. (2020). NEP 2020: Undermining the Constitutional Education Agenda? *Social Change*. 50. 594-598. 10.1177/0049085720958809.

Ganguli, P. (2003). *Ad(d)venture with Knowledge.... Stepping ahead with Intellectual Property Rights*. New Delhi: University Grants Commission.

Government of India (2016). *National Intellectual Property Rights Policy 2016*. New Delhi: Ministry of Commerce and Industry, Government of India.

Government of India (2020). *National Education Policy 2020.* New Delhi: Ministry of Human Resource Development, Government of India.

Govinda, R. (2020). NEP 2020: A Critical Examination. *Social Change*, 50(4): pp 603-607.

Jajpura et al. (2016). An Introduction to Intellectual Property Rights and their Importance in Indian Context. *Journal of Intellectual Property Rights*: Vol. 22, January 2017, pp 32-41.

Sawant and Sankpal (2021). National Education Policy 2020 and Higher Education: A Brief Review. *International Journal of Creative Research Thoughts (IJCRT).* Vol. 9 (1), January 2021, pp 3456-3460.

Sharma et al. (2022). Intellectual Property Rights in Context of New Education Policy 2020. *Journal of Intellectual Property Rights*: Vol. 27, November 2022, pp 415-419. DOI: 10.56042/jipr.v27i6.66630

UGC (2016). Inclusion of the IPR as a generic elective subject under the Choice Based Credit System (CBCS) in University and the affiliated colleges (D.O.No.1 -1 /201 6 (Secy), dated 15th July, 2016). New Delhi: UGC. https://www.ugc.gov.in/pdfnews/4866021_IPR.pdf

Venkateshwarlu, B. (2021). A Critical Study of NEP 2020: Issues, Approaches, Challenges, Opportunities and Criticism. *International Journal of Multidisciplinary Educational Research.* Vol. 10 [2(5)], February 2021, pp 191-196.

14

Research and Publication Ethics in Social Sciences

Mousumi Boral

RESEARCH ETHICS

Introduction

The Indian higher education sector is undergoing a steady transformation and progress. To address the dynamic challenges such as population growth, unemployment, inclusivity, and brain-drain, it is crucial to revitalize and enhance the sector through academic and research innovation and excellence. Reassessing research policies, procedures, and practices, along with strategic measures, is urgently required to elevate research quality. A focused blueprint is essential to meet global standards and adapt to changing trends in community welfare.

Defining Research

Kerlinger (1964) defined research as a systematic, controlled, empirical, and critical investigation of hypothetical relations among natural phenomena. The term *research* itself delves into the processes of 'search' again and again. Research initiates knowledge building through the process of developing tools, concepts, and theories, and focuses on national development by formulating strategies and policies. Maintaining integrity in research is of paramount importance and therefore young researchers need to be imparted adequate education about related issues like plagiarism, duplication, gift and ghost authorships, salami publications, outsourced publishing, etc. at an appropriate level of their training. It is hard to achieve quality in research unless awareness about the importance of integrity, transparency, and accountability is promoted and incorporated as an inherent component of the research. But there is a need for ethics, to deal with the underlying unconformities in the diversity of complex human behaviour. Ethics encompasses rules, principles, and values that guide behaviour in society, institutions, and research. It promotes the right actions for ultimate happiness and is vital in all aspects of life. The most common way of defining "ethics" is the norms for conduct that distinguish between acceptable and unacceptable behaviour like the protection of the well-being, rights, and dignity of research participants, the trustworthiness of research findings, prevention of bias, manipulation, and selective reporting of research data, promotion of inclusivity and respect for diverse populations for imparting of social issues with justice. As good research adds knowledge to the existing body of knowledge, therefore should not transmit misleading information about reality (Bhashanjali, n.d.).

Ethics in Research

'The Guidelines for Research Ethics in the Social Sciences, Law and the Humanities' published by National Committees for Research Ethics in Norway (September 2006) refers to 'research ethics' as a complex set of values, standards, and institutional schemes that help to constitute and regulate scientific activity. Research ethics is based on general ethics of science which is eventually based on commonsense morality.

The Nuremburg trials in 1945-46 revealed the unethical experiments conducted by Nazi scientists, leading to the development of research ethics. The Nuremburg Code (1947), with principles emphasizing consent, avoiding harm, and prioritizing participant safety, serves as the foundation for subsequent ethical guidelines worldwide, including in India. It is important to mention that in India, two noteworthy ethical guidelines for research comprise the Ethical Guidelines for Biomedical Research on Human Participants (2006) issued by the Indian Council of Medical Research and the Ethics Guidelines for Social Science Research in Health (2000) issued by the National Committee for Social Science Research in Health. Ethics in research is a high-priority area for maintaining quality and high standards of research. Prime importance needs to be accorded to the issues like confidentiality, privacy, non-malfeasance, beneficence, autonomy, and justice without which no credible and substantive research is ever possible. Awareness about these components needs to be created from the very beginning of the research. Institutional Ethics' committees need to be vigilant, and proactive about any such malpractices in research and therefore be strict in ensuring full compliance with ethics in research. Unless integrity and ethics are maintained, no substantial gains can be made in achieving high standards of quality in research. It is universally agreed that high-quality research refers to a process that covers all aspects of the object of study by raising pertinent questions and arriving at reliable answers, which significantly enhance the prevailing knowledge base and create new knowledge.

Social Science Research

Social science is the science of people or collections of people (such as groups, firms, societies, and economies), and their individual and collective behaviours (Bhattacherjee, 2012). Social Sciences primarily deal with human behaviour which is dynamic in nature. Unlike Fundamental Sciences, social science researchers cannot investigate under strict guided conditions. This creates many problems for the researcher such as the problems of subjectivity and individualistic generalizations etc. To study social phenomena, a greater depth of knowledge, precision, and accuracy to arrive at valid generalizations is necessary. Social science research systematically explores, analyzes, and conceptualizes human life to enhance understanding and validate knowledge of behaviour and society. It seeks explanations, clarifies doubts, and corrects misconceptions through scientific methods.

Ethical research in social science is vital for community development as it protects the interests, rights, and well-being of individuals and communities. Upholds principles like autonomy, beneficence, and justice, establish trust and allows informed consent. Ethical research safeguards privacy, minimizes harm, and maintains dignity. It fosters inclusivity, diversity, and cultural sensitivity, ensuring unbiased research. By adhering to ethical standards, social science research informs evidence-based interventions that address societal challenges, community needs and promote social justice. Ethical research empowers communities to participate actively and contribute to their own time-bound implementation as per National Education Policy 2020 in a respectful, equitable, and sustainable manner. High-quality research involves raising significant questions, using objective approaches, employing appropriate methodologies, and engaging with intellectual networks. Comprehensive, contextual, and evidence-based research policies are needed at institutional, regional/state, and national levels.

Significance of Maintaining Ethical Standards in Social Science Research

Maintaining ethical standards in social science research is of utmost importance for several reasons. These ethical standards provide a foundation for conducting research that is responsible, respectful, and beneficial to both the participants and society. Maintaining ethical standards in social science research is crucial for protecting participants' rights, ensuring credibility and trustworthiness, enhancing the validity and reliability of research outcomes, avoiding harm and exploitation, complying with legal requirements, and achieving a positive long-term impact on society. By upholding ethical standards, researchers uphold the principles of integrity, respect, and responsibility in their pursuit of knowledge.

a) *Protection of Participants' Rights:* Ethical standards ensure the protection of participants' rights, including their autonomy, privacy, and confidentiality. Respecting participants' autonomy involves obtaining informed consent, allowing them to voluntarily participate or withdraw from the study, and ensuring their privacy is safeguarded. Ethical standards also require researchers to maintain confidentiality by protecting participants' personal information and ensuring that data cannot be linked back to individuals and that data remain confidential and are used only for the intended research purposes, like obtaining informed consent from participants in a study on mental health interventions.
b) *Credibility and Trustworthiness*: Adherence to ethical standards enhances the credibility and trustworthiness of social science research. By following ethical guidelines, researchers establish a foundation of integrity and honesty in their work. This increases the confidence that others, including fellow researchers, policymakers, and the general public, have in the

research findings and their potential impact. Like conducting a study on the efficacy of a new medical treatment with rigorous ethical practices and transparent reporting to ensure trust in the research outcomes.

c) *Validity and Reliability of Research*: Ethical standards contribute to the validity and reliability of research outcomes. By maintaining ethical practices, researchers ensure the accuracy and integrity of data collection, analysis, and interpretation. This leads to reliable research findings that can be replicated and verified by others and strengthens the overall body of knowledge in the field. Collaborative interdisciplinary research can be categorized into cross-disciplinary, pluri-disciplinary, and multi-disciplinary research based on the balance of influence among participating disciplines which helps to define the roles and levels of involvement of every discipline in a distinct manner. Like ensuring accurate data collection and analysis in a quantitative survey on educational outcomes.

d) *Avoiding Harm and Exploitation*: Ethical standards help researchers avoid causing harm or exploiting vulnerable populations. Researchers must carefully consider the potential risks and benefits of their studies and take steps to minimize any negative impact on participants such as children, prisoners, or individuals with cognitive impairments. Ethical guidelines also require researchers to be aware of power dynamics and potential conflicts of interest, ensuring that participants are not exploited for personal gain or agenda. Special considerations, such as obtaining informed consent from legal guardians or implementing additional safeguards, are necessary to protect the rights and well-being of these vulnerable populations. For example, implementing safeguards for vulnerable populations in a qualitative study on refugee experiences.

e) *Integrity in Data Analysis*: Ethical standards extend to data analysis, ensuring that researchers handle and interpret data with integrity. It involves employing appropriate statistical techniques, avoiding selective reporting of results, and refraining from manipulating data to fit preconceived notions or desired outcomes. Adhering to research ethics in data analysis enhances the credibility of research findings, as it demonstrates the researcher's commitment to unbiased and objective analysis. Over the past few years, the problem of predatory journals (under API pressure) that has alarmingly surfaced needs to be countered and controlled effectively and any cases of malpractices in research need to be dealt with severely to set an effective deterrent. Like applying transparent and unbiased data analysis techniques in a study on climate change perceptions.

f) *Ethical Review and Oversight*: Many research institutions and organizations require ethical review and oversight of research projects involving human participants. Institutional Review Boards (IRBs) or

Ethics Committees (IC) evaluate research proposals to ensure compliance with ethical guidelines. This review process serves as an additional layer of protection for participants' rights and promotes the integrity and credibility of research conducted within the institution. For instance, seeking approval from an IRB for a study investigating the effects of a new medical treatment.

g) *Compliance with Legal and Institutional Requirements*: Many research institutions and regulatory bodies have established ethical guidelines and regulations that researchers must adhere to for their purposes. Maintaining ethical standards ensures compliance with these legal and institutional requirements, preventing legal and professional repercussions. It also promotes consistency and accountability within the research community. Like following data protection regulations in a study on consumer behaviour.

h) *Long-term Impact on Society*: Ethical research practices have a long-term positive impact on society. Social science research provides insights into human behaviour, societal issues, and policy implications. By conducting research ethically, researchers contribute to the generation of knowledge that can inform evidence-based decision-making, policy development, and social change, ultimately benefiting individuals and communities. Like conducting research on sustainable development to inform policies promoting environmental conservation.

Exploring Ethical Issues Related to Data Collection in Social Science Research

Ethical issues related to data collection in social science research encompass a range of considerations that researchers must address to ensure the protection of participants and the integrity of the research process. Researchers can uphold the rights and well-being of participants, maintain the integrity of the research process, and produce reliable and meaningful findings. Adhering to ethical guidelines helps foster trust between researchers and participants, as well as ensures the ethical conduct of social science research overall.

a) *Informed Consent*: Obtaining informed consent is a fundamental ethical requirement in social science research. Researchers must ensure that participants have a clear understanding of the study's purpose, procedures, potential risks and benefits, and their rights before they agree to participate. Informed consent ensures that participants have the autonomy to make an informed decision about their involvement and helps to maintain the trust and voluntary nature of their participation.

b) *Privacy and Confidentiality*: Protecting participants' privacy and ensuring confidentiality are critical ethical considerations in data collection. Researchers must take measures to safeguard participants' personal information and ensure that data are anonymized or de-identified whenever possible. Confidentiality measures should be in place to prevent unauthorized access or disclosure of participants' data, providing them with the assurance that their information will be handled securely and used only for research purposes. Like individual or institutional confidentiality is adhered to with respect to research on social media and its impact on Artificial Intelligence (AI).

c) *Sensitive Topics and Emotional Well-being*: Some social science research may involve sensitive topics, such as trauma, mental health, or personal experiences. Researchers must be mindful of the potential emotional impact on participants and also implement appropriate measures to minimize any distress or harm. This may include offering support resources, debriefing sessions, or referrals to mental health professionals if needed.

d) *Power Dynamics and Coercion*: Researchers should be aware of power dynamics that may exist between themselves and participants, especially in studies involving vulnerable populations or hierarchical relationships (e.g., teacher-student, employer-employee). Ethical data collection requires ensuring that participants do not feel coerced or pressured to participate, share sensitive information, or provide certain responses. Maintaining a respectful and balanced power dynamic is crucial for upholding the rights and well-being of participants.

e) *Sampling and Representation*: Ethical considerations arise when determining the appropriate sampling techniques to ensure representative and diverse participant groups. Researchers should strive to include participants from different backgrounds, cultures, and demographics, aiming for inclusivity and avoiding the perpetuation of biases or marginalization. Transparent reporting of the sampling methods used helps ensure that research findings accurately reflect the broader population being studied.

f) *Data Ownership and Secondary Use*: Researchers should clarify the ownership and control of collected data with participants. Ethical practices involve informing participants about their rights regarding the use, storage, and dissemination of their data. Researchers should seek participants' consent if they plan to use the data for secondary analyses or share them with other researchers while preserving anonymity and confidentiality.

g) *Researcher Bias and Objectivity*: Researchers must be aware of their own biases and strive to maintain objectivity throughout the data collection process. Ethical research requires minimizing personal biases that could influence participant interactions, data collection techniques, or data interpretation. Transparency in reporting potential conflicts of interest or personal biases helps ensure the integrity and credibility of the research. For example, teachers as reflective practitioners should be aware of their own beliefs and biases to create an inclusive and unbiased learning environment for all students.

h) *Researcher-participant Relationship*: Ethical data collection involves establishing a respectful and professional relationship with participants. Researchers should ensure that participants feel comfortable asking questions, expressing concerns, or withdrawing from the study at any point. Clear communication and mutual respect contribute to a positive researcher-participant relationship and facilitate ethical data collection. Like maintaining open communication and respect in a study on community engagement for urban planning.

Informed Consent Process, Confidentiality and Privacy Concerns, and the Handling of Sensitive Information

By following robust processes for informed consent, addressing confidentiality and privacy concerns, and handling sensitive information ethically, researchers can protect participants' rights, maintain the trust of participants, and uphold the integrity of social science research. These practices are essential for ensuring the ethical conduct of research and fostering a positive relationship between researchers and participants.

Informed Consent Process: The informed consent process is a cornerstone of ethical data collection. It involves obtaining voluntary and informed agreement from participants to participate in the research study. The information sheet, given to participants in research studies, can be read out or conveyed through innovative methods like group meetings, films, posters, and role plays and through virtual mode also. Effective communication methods that allow participants to understand, seek clarification, and express their thoughts are considered suitable for conveying research information. Like obtaining written consent from participants in a study on educational interventions for children with disabilities.

***Key aspects of the informed consent process include*:**

a) *Providing Information:* Researchers must clearly explain the purpose, procedures, risks, benefits, and expected outcomes of the study to participants. This ensures that participants have a comprehensive understanding of what their participation entails.
b) *Voluntary Participation:* Participants should be aware that their involvement is entirely voluntary, and they have the right to withdraw at any point without any negative consequences.
c) *Capacity to Consent:* Researchers must ensure that participants have the cognitive ability to understand the provided information and make an informed decision. Special care should be taken when working with vulnerable populations, such as minors or individuals with cognitive impairments, to ensure appropriate consent processes are followed.
d) *Documentation*: Informed consent should be documented through written consent forms or electronic means, clearly indicating that participants have

understood the information and have given their voluntary consent. Care should be taken to use clear and understandable language, provide sufficient details about the study, and ensure participants have the opportunity to ask questions before signing or providing electronic consent.

Confidentiality and Privacy Concerns: Protecting participants' confidentiality and privacy is essential in social science research. Researchers must implement measures to safeguard the confidentiality of participants' personal information. To ensure data confidentiality, researchers must keep collected information secure and limit access to the research team. Paper records should be locked, while digital records should be password protected or encrypted. Data should be anonymized by removing identifying details to protect participant confidentiality. Reporting findings should avoid specifics that could lead to identification. Exceptions include publicly available information and explicit participant consent to disclose identities. Respecting dignity and preventing harm in research involves protecting confidential information and ensuring privacy. Data collection should occur in private settings to maintain participant privacy and anonymity. Researchers should also respect boundaries, refraining from intruding or gathering information outside the scope of the study. Information obtained through other sources should not be used as data or for interrogation. Example: safeguarding participants' personal information in a survey on sensitive topics like sexual health.

***Key aspects of confidentiality and privacy concerns include*:**

a) *Anonymity and Data De-identification*: Data should be collected in a manner that ensures participants' identities cannot be linked to their responses. This could involve assigning unique identifiers or removing identifying information from data sets.
b) *Data Storage and Security*: Researchers should store data securely, both during the data collection process and afterward. Adequate safeguards, such as password protection, encryption, and restricted access, should be in place to prevent unauthorized access to participants' data.
c) *Limited Access*: Researchers should limit access to participants' data only to those directly involved in the research. Data should be shared with others only after ensuring proper anonymization and with the explicit consent of participants.
d) *Reporting Aggregate Data*: When presenting research findings, researchers should report aggregated data rather than individual responses to further protect participants' identities.

Handling of Sensitive Information: Social science research often involves gathering sensitive information, such as personal experiences, health-related data, or information on sensitive topics. Research can lead to stigmatization, discrimination, and emotional risks for participants. Researchers should assess and minimize these risks through study design, data collection procedures, and proper training. Safeguards and remedial measures should be in place, including compensation, counselling, medical care, and support services. Harm, whether intentional or unintentional, should be acknowledged, and efforts made to alleviate suffering and compensate those affected. Participants' vulnerability and contributions should be respected and addressed ethically. Like providing psychological support for participants sharing traumatic experiences in a qualitative study.

***Handling sensitive information requires additional ethical considerations*:**

a) *Minimizing Emotional Distress:* Researchers should anticipate potential emotional distress that participants may experience when discussing sensitive topics. Clear guidelines and protocols should be in place to support participants and provide appropriate resources or referrals if needed. Like studies ensuring voluntary participation of employees in a workplace survey on job satisfaction.
b) *Privacy and Confidentiality*: Confidentiality refers to the control of access to information and privacy to a person's interest in controlling boundaries between self and others (Sieber and Stanley, 1988). Special care should be taken to ensure confidentiality and privacy, especially for sensitive information. Researchers must implement strict data security measures and anonymize data effectively to prevent inadvertent identification. In most research, ensuring the confidentiality of data is just plain good practice.
c) *Informed Consent for Sensitive Topics*: Researchers should provide comprehensive information about the nature of the study and the potential emotional impact of participating in research related to sensitive topics. Participants should have a clear understanding of the potential risks and benefits before giving their informed consent.
d) *Ethical Handling and Disposal*: Researchers should establish protocols for the ethical handling and disposal of sensitive information. This may include securely destroying physical documents or permanently deleting digital files after the research is completed. Example: In psychological counselling, maintaining client confidentiality is crucial. Ethical handling and disposal involve securely shredding therapy session notes or permanently deleting electronic files to safeguard the privacy and well-being of clients.

Need for Researchers to obtain Ethical Approval from Relevant Institutional Review Boards

By obtaining ethical approval from relevant Institutional Review Boards (IRBs), researchers demonstrate their commitment to ethical research conduct, participant protection, compliance with regulations, and the credibility of their research. Adequate funding is available at regional, national, and international levels through public institutions, private industries, NGOs, and public-private partnerships. National agencies like Department of Biotechnology (DBT), Department of Science and Technology (DST), University Grants Commission (UGC), Indian Council of Agricultural Research (ICAR), Science and Engineering Research Board (SERB), Indian Council of Medical Research (ICMR), along with industry, academia, and NGOs offer funding opportunities. In some cases, international agencies like World Health Organisation (WHO), World Trade Organisation (WTO), World Bank, United Nations Organisation (UNO) also provide research grants. These organisations offer funds after ensuring the ethical integrity of the research and its practices.

The several reasons crucial for researchers have been discussed in the following section:

a) *Protection of Participants:* Ethical approval ensures that research involving human participants is conducted in a manner that respects their rights, welfare, and well-being. IRBs assess research protocols to minimize potential harm or risks to participants, ensuring their protection by addressing conflicts of interest and upholding participant rights.
b) *Compliance with Ethical Standards*: Ethical approval from IRBs ensures that researchers adhere to established ethical standards and guidelines for conducting research. It demonstrates a commitment to upholding ethical principles, such as informed consent, privacy, confidentiality, and data protection. Moreover, timely, and regular communication about research output to the masses is equally important for greater transparency and establishing the spirit of entrepreneurship through research. These cells must provide sufficient startup grants as seed money to budding entrepreneurs for incubating their innovative ventures.
c) *Legal and Regulatory Requirements*: Many countries and institutions have legal and regulatory requirements in place that mandate ethical approval for research involving human participants. Researchers must obtain ethical clearance to comply with these requirements and avoid any legal or regulatory issues.
d) *Funding and Institutional Support*: Ethical approval is often a prerequisite for obtaining research funding from grant agencies and institutions. Funding bodies require evidence of ethical review and approval to ensure that research is conducted ethically and responsibly. Institutional support is also typically contingent upon obtaining ethical clearance. IRBs consist of multidisciplinary experts, including researchers, ethicists, legal professionals, and community representatives that provide invaluable oversight and collective expertise guidance on ethical considerations in research.
e) *Stakeholder and Public Trust and Credibility*: It provides assurance to participants, colleagues, and the wider community that the research has undergone rigorous ethical scrutiny, increasing confidence in the integrity

and validity of the research outcomes. Ethical oversight ensures that research is conducted with integrity, transparency, and respect for participants' rights. The involvement of an independent body, such as an IRB, in the ethical review process enhances the credibility and trustworthiness of the research findings and fosters public confidence in the research and its potential impact. In this context, the Buckley Amendment, also known as the Family Educational Rights and Privacy Act (FERPA), is a federal law that safeguards the privacy of students' educational records. It limits the disclosure of these records by the institution or an organisation, without the students' consent or permission of the guardian for accessing or using such data for conducting social research.

f) *Professional and Ethical Responsibility*: Researchers have a professional and ethical responsibility to conduct research in an ethical manner. Seeking ethical approval demonstrates a commitment to responsible research conduct and upholding the well-being and rights of research participants. Incentivizing good research is important, but using it in teacher appointments and promotions has sparked debate due to concerns about mechanization and a race for API points-based assessment of teachers by the University Grants Commission in 2010. Thereby different bodies have implemented measures such as revising assessment criteria, ensuring transparency, promoting quality teaching, and addressing concerns of bias and subjectivity.

g) *Peer Review and Publication*: Many peer-reviewed journals require evidence of ethical approval for studies involving human participants. Without ethical clearance, researchers may face difficulties in publishing their work or having it accepted by reputable journals. The research institutes and research centres need to be fully equipped with adequate, trained manpower, sophisticated instruments required to conduct high-end research, databases that are required to undertake systematic literature reviews, meta-analyses, access to literature through databases like Scopus, Science Direct, Pubmed, Medline, Toxline etc.

Integrity in Data Analysis and Reporting in Social Science Research

By upholding data integrity and transparency, researchers contribute to the advancement of knowledge, informed decision-making, and public engagement in social science research.

Fundamental principles of data analysis in social science research that contribute to the credibility, reliability, and replicability of research findings are as follows:

a) *Credibility of Research Findings*: Data integrity and transparency are essential for establishing the credibility of research findings. Maintaining data integrity involves ensuring that data collection, analysis, and reporting are conducted with rigor, accuracy, and consistency. By adhering to rigorous data collection methods, researchers can minimize errors, bias, and distortions in their findings, increasing the credibility and trustworthiness of their research.

b) *Replicability and Verification*: Transparency in data collection and analysis enables other researchers to replicate and verify the findings. When data and methodologies are transparently reported, other researchers can assess the validity and reliability of the results by conducting similar studies or re-analyzing the data. Replication of research findings strengthens the robustness and generalizability of social science research and helps build a cumulative body of knowledge.

c) *Avoiding Data Fabrication and Falsification*: Data integrity ensures that researchers do not engage in unethical practices such as data fabrication or falsification. These practices undermine the integrity and validity of research findings, leading to erroneous conclusions and misguiding subsequent research and decision-making. Transparent and rigorous data collection processes, combined with appropriate checks and balances, help prevent data manipulation and enhance the integrity of social science research. For instance, sampling and representation inferences including participants from diverse ethnic backgrounds in a study on healthcare access.

d) *Detection and Correction of Errors*: Data transparency facilitates the detection and correction of errors in research. When data and analytical procedures are transparently reported, researchers and peer reviewers can scrutinize the research process and identify any errors, inconsistencies, or methodological flaws. This feedback loop allows researchers to rectify errors, improve methodologies, and ensure the accuracy of their findings, ultimately enhancing the quality of social science research.

e) *Ethical Considerations*: Data integrity and transparency are closely linked to ethical considerations in social science research. By transparently reporting the data collection and analysis processes, researchers demonstrate their commitment to responsible research conduct. Ethical research practices require researchers to provide accurate and complete information to participants, ensuring their informed consent and protecting their rights. Transparency in reporting allows for the ethical review and oversight of research, promoting research integrity and accountability.

f) *Policy and Decision-making Implications*: Transparent and robust data contribute to evidence-based policy and decision-making processes. Policymakers, practitioners, and stakeholders rely on social science research findings to inform their decisions and develop effective interventions or policies. Data integrity and transparency play a critical role in providing reliable and valid evidence that can be used with confidence, leading to informed and impactful decision-making.

Example: In educational management, transparent and robust data on student performance can inform policymaking, enabling evidence-based decisions to improve educational practices, allocate resources effectively, and develop targeted interventions for student success.

g) *Building Trust and Public Engagement*: Data integrity and transparency are essential for building trust between researchers, participants and the public. Openly sharing data, methodologies, and research findings fosters transparency and allows for public engagement. When the research process is transparent and accessible, it enhances public understanding, facilitates informed discussions, and encourages collaboration between researchers and various stakeholders leading to improved educational practices.

Ethical Responsibilities of Researchers in Data Analysis and Reporting Findings

Researchers have significant ethical responsibilities when it comes to accurately analyzing data, avoiding biases, and honesty in social science research. Most disciplinary professional associations have developed a set of ethical standards for their field. Typical of these is Ethical Principles in the Conduct of Research with Human Participants by the Committee on Protection of Human Participants in Research of the American Psychological Association (APA) (1982). The code of ethics consists of 10 principles. "Each section begins with a review of the problem or issue that gives rise to the need for a guiding Principle. Then... a discussion relates the principle to various problems, research settings, and populations of research participants". In India, institutions conducting social science research are increasingly establishing Research Ethics Committees (RECs) or Institutional Review Boards (IRBs). These bodies should meet certain criteria, including being headed by an external person, having multidisciplinary members, including participant representation, and documenting and filing meeting proceedings. Decisions should be available to all in the organization, and conflicts of interest should be handled appropriately.

Responsibilities crucial for upholding the integrity of research and ensuring the validity and reliability of research findings have been discussed in the following section.

a) *Accurate Data Analysis*: Researchers have an ethical duty to conduct data analysis accurately and rigorously. This involves using appropriate statistical methods and analytical techniques to analyze the data in a reliable and valid manner. Accurate data analysis minimizes errors, enhances the credibility of research findings, and contributes to the generation of robust evidence.

b) *Minimizing Biases*: Researchers should be vigilant in identifying and minimizing biases that may affect data analysis and interpretation. Biases can arise from various sources, such as researcher bias, sampling bias, or response bias. Researchers must take proactive steps to minimize biases by employing rigorous research methodologies, ensuring representative sampling, using standardized measurement tools, and implementing strategies to mitigate potential biases.

c) *Transparency in Analytical Procedures*: Transparency in analytical procedures is an ethical responsibility of researchers. This involves clearly documenting and reporting the steps taken in data analysis, including any transformations, exclusions, or statistical tests applied. Transparent reporting enables other researchers to understand and evaluate the analytical process, promoting accountability, reproducibility, and trustworthiness of the research. Like seeking consent for sharing anonymized data from a longitudinal study with other researchers for improved research findings.

d) *Addressing Conflicts of Interest*: Researchers have an ethical obligation to disclose and manage any conflicts of interest that may arise during data analysis and reporting. Conflicts of interest can include financial interests, personal relationships, or affiliations that may influence the research process or bias the reporting of findings. Disclosing conflicts of interest allows for transparency and enables readers and reviewers to assess potential biases or influences on the research.

e) *Reporting Negative or Null Findings*: Researchers should report their findings honestly, including negative or null results. Ethical reporting requires avoiding the selective reporting of only positive or significant findings, as this can lead to publication bias and misrepresentation of the research landscape. Authentic reporting of all results, regardless of their statistical significance, contributes to a comprehensive understanding of the research topic and prevents the distortion of scientific knowledge.

f) *Protecting Participant Confidentiality*: Researchers have an ethical responsibility to protect participant confidentiality when reporting research findings. This includes ensuring that participants' identities are not revealed in any published materials. Researchers should adhere to strict confidentiality protocols and anonymize data to prevent the identification of individual participants. Respecting and safeguarding participant confidentiality maintains trust and upholds participants' rights.

g) *Interpreting Findings Objectively*: Researchers have an ethical duty to interpret research findings objectively and avoid overstating or misrepresenting the results. Findings should be presented accurately, without exaggeration or sensationalism, to prevent misleading interpretations. Researchers should acknowledge limitations and uncertainties in the research, providing a balanced and nuanced understanding of the findings. For example, addressing potential researcher bias in a study on political attitudes through rigorous methodology.

h) *Peer Review and Collaboration*: Researchers should actively engage in the peer review process, both as reviewers and authors. Peer review promotes ethical research by ensuring rigorous evaluation and feedback from experts in the field. Researchers should respond constructively to reviewer comments and suggestions, and collaborate with other researchers to enhance the quality, validity, and integrity of their work.

Addressing Issues such as Selective Reporting, Data Manipulation, and Plagiarism

For ensuring the advancement of knowledge in the social sciences selective reporting, data manipulation and plagiarism are serious ethical issues that can undermine the integrity and trustworthiness of social science research.

Selective Reporting: Selective reporting refers to the practice of reporting only a subset of collected data or emphasizing certain findings while neglecting others based on their significance or alignment with the researchers' expectations. Selective reporting can introduce bias and misrepresentation in research. It is important to address this issue by:

a) *Reporting all Findings:* Researchers have an ethical responsibility to report all findings, including negative or null results. By reporting the complete set of findings, researchers contribute to a comprehensive understanding of the research topic, avoid publication bias, and prevent the distortion of scientific knowledge.
b) *Pre-registration of Studies*: Pre-registering research studies, where researchers publicly declare their research plans and hypotheses before data collection, can help mitigate selective reporting. This practice promotes transparency and prevents researchers from changing their research questions or selectively reporting based on their findings.
c) *Transparent Reporting:* Researchers should provide a clear and transparent account of the research methods, data analysis procedures, and results. Detailed reporting helps ensure that readers can assess the validity and reliability of the findings and identify any potential selective reporting.

Data Manipulation: Data manipulation involves altering or misrepresenting data to support a desired outcome or to fit preconceived notions. Data manipulation seriously undermines the integrity and validity of research. To address this issue, researchers should:

a) Maintain Data Integrity: Researchers have an ethical responsibility to maintain the integrity of the collected data. This includes accurately recording, organizing, and storing data in a systematic and transparent manner. Data should be free from intentional or unintentional manipulation, fabrication, or falsification.
b) Use Reliable Analytical Procedures: Researchers should use valid and reliable analytical procedures when analyzing data. This involves applying appropriate statistical techniques and avoiding any data manipulation or selective exclusion that could lead to biased or misleading results.

c) Data Auditing and Replication: Researchers should encourage data auditing and replication by making their data available to other researchers. This practice allows for independent verification and increases confidence in the integrity of the research. Transparency and open data sharing help identify and prevent data manipulation.

Plagiarism: Plagiarism involves presenting someone else's work, ideas, or words as one's own without proper acknowledgment. Plagiarism is a severe ethical breach and undermines the principles of intellectual honesty and academic integrity. To prevent plagiarism, researchers should:

a) *Properly Attribute Sources:* Researchers must appropriately attribute and cite the works of the original author, using direct quotes or paraphrasing their ideas, or words of others used in their research. This includes citing relevant literature, acknowledging intellectual contributions, and providing proper references. The use of citation management tools can help researchers maintain accurate and consistent referencing.
b) *Understand Copyright and Intellectual Property*: Researchers should have a clear understanding of copyright laws and intellectual property rights. They should obtain permissions, when necessary, respect copyright restrictions, and avoid any unauthorized use or reproduction of copyrighted materials in images or excerpts.
c) *Use Plagiarism Detection Software*: Researchers and institutions can employ plagiarism detection software to identify instances of potential plagiarism to ensure originality and proper citation. These tools compare submitted work with a vast database of published materials to highlight similarities and potential instances of unacknowledged use.

Positivist and Non-positivist approaches related to Health Issues in Social Science Research

In social science research in health, ethical considerations play a crucial role regardless of whether a positivist or non-positivist approach is employed. Both approaches seek to expand our understanding of health-related phenomena, but they differ in their epistemological foundations and methodologies. Understanding the ethical implications of these approaches is essential to uphold the rights, well-being, and autonomy of participants involved in research.

Positivist approaches, rooted in a scientific and empirical worldview, prioritize objectivity and generalizability. They often employ quantitative methods and aim to uncover causal relationships through rigorous experimentation and measurement. In this context, ethical considerations revolve around ensuring informed consent, protecting privacy and confidentiality, minimizing harm, and ensuring the validity and reliability of data. Transparency in research design, rigorous data collection and analysis, and appropriate use of statistical techniques are essential to maintain ethical integrity. Like ensuring participant confidentiality in a large-scale survey on sensitive health issues.

Non-positivist approaches, on the other hand, such as qualitative or interpretive research, emphasize the subjective experiences, meanings, and social contexts surrounding health phenomena. Ethical considerations in these approaches extend beyond the traditional positivist framework. They encompass issues of power dynamics, researcher reflexivity, participant empowerment, and cultural sensitivity. Establishing trust, building rapport, and engaging in ethical dialogue become essential to ensure participant comfort and accurate representation of their experiences. Like recognizing the subjective experiences of patients with chronic illnesses through in-depth interviews to understand their unique perceptions of health and well-being.

Researchers employing non-positivist approaches must be aware of their own biases and preconceptions, actively work towards minimizing harm, and be transparent about their role in shaping the research process. They should also address issues of participant confidentiality, consent, and the potential impact of the research on marginalized communities. Additionally, the dissemination of findings should be approached ethically to respect the privacy and dignity of participants.

Ethical Challenges Specific to Research Methods: Quantitative and Qualitative Methods

Social science research methods, whether quantitative or qualitative, present distinct ethical challenges. In quantitative research, ensuring participant privacy and confidentiality is paramount due to the collection of identifiable data. Ethical dilemmas arise concerning informed consent, the potential for coercion, and minimizing harm while maintaining statistical rigor. Researchers must navigate issues of data protection, confidentiality, and secure storage. For example, in a large-scale survey study on sensitive topics such as mental health, researchers must carefully design their survey instruments to minimize potential harm, provide clear explanations of participant rights, and ensure data security to protect participant confidentiality.

In qualitative research, the ethical challenges centre around participant vulnerability, power dynamics, and researcher reflexivity. Respecting participant autonomy, ensuring voluntary participation, and obtaining informed consent are crucial. Maintaining confidentiality and anonymity becomes complex when rich, contextual details are shared. Researchers must address power imbalances, protect participants from harm, and respect cultural sensitivities during data collection, analysis, and interpretation. For instance, in ethnographic research conducted within marginalized communities, researchers must establish trust, respect cultural norms, and consider the potential impact of their presence on the community dynamics, while ensuring the protection of participant identities and maintaining confidentiality.

Both quantitative and qualitative methods require ethical considerations regarding potential biases, data integrity, and misrepresentation. Transparency, integrity, and accountability in data analysis and reporting are essential. Researcher's responsibilities include addressing conflicts of interest, protecting participants' rights and well-being, and maintaining trust throughout the research process.

Translating Ethics Concepts in Different Social Science Settings

Translating ethics concepts across diverse social science research settings requires contextual understanding and sensitivity. Concepts such as informed consent, confidentiality, and minimizing harm may vary in application. Cultural, social, and legal frameworks influence ethical considerations. Researchers must adapt principles to respect local norms, power dynamics, and community expectations. Collaboration with local stakeholders and ethical review boards enhances cross-cultural understanding. Effective translation of ethics concepts ensures the protection of participants' rights, welfare, and cultural values while upholding ethical standards in various social science research settings. Example: In a cross-cultural study on mental health and on end-of-life decisions, the concept of informed consent may need to be adapted to the concept of autonomy and accommodate cultural practices, values, and beliefs.

Research Ethics Governance

Adherence to research ethics governance in social science is achieved through ethical review boards, training programmes on education and training, promoting open dialogue and ethical discussions within research communities, and pursuing clear guidelines to foster a culture of ethical awareness and accountability. Its growing importance stems from increasing awareness of participant rights, evolving research practices, and the need to address ethical challenges in diverse settings. Observing ethical principles ensures participant protection, research credibility, and trustworthiness, and generates public confidence in social science research. Collaborative efforts among researchers, institutions, and policymakers are needed to adapt ethical guidelines to emerging technologies, data privacy concerns, and evolving societal contexts, ensuring continued ethical governance.

PUBLICATION ETHICS

Introduction

Publication ethics is a broad concept that deals with various issues, including statutory and ethics approval, informed consent, data manipulation, research fraud, plagiarism, simultaneous submission, duplicate publication, self-citation, consent to reproduce published material, ethics of authorship, conflicts of interest, etc. (Sengupta & Honavar, 2017). In a nutshell, it can be said that publication ethics is a bunch of rules which define a "code of conduct" and "best practice guideline" for publishing a research journal. To promote the highest standard in publication ethics, an international body named Committee on Publication Ethics (COPE) had been established in 1997.

A few codes of conduct to maintain the integrity of journals have been mentioned below:

Proper attribution of sources: During the time of publication of any research article it is important to give credit to all previous authors whose ideas, thinking, and words have been used in the present study. The use of research ideas of someone else without giving consent, credit, or acknowledgment to him is called Plagiarism. Acknowledging previous sources of the present research study raises the integrity of the research. According to Masic, 2013, referencing, is an indispensable part of any scientific work, which speaks about the sources used in the research study, and reflects the depth of information about the study. There may be various kinds of plagiarism, which are mentioned below:

a) *Direct Plagiarism*: It is a type of plagiarism where a researcher has directly copied someone else's writing without acknowledging him or her.
b) *Paraphrase Plagiarism*: When the researcher makes a few minor changes to someone's writing and passes it to his or her original work is called paraphrase plagiarism.
c) *Mosaic Plagiarism*: When a researcher borrows a few phrases from a particular source and does not use quotation marks and does not cite it, is called mosaic plagiarism.
d) *Accidental Plagiarism*: When the researcher skips giving a citation of a particular quotation or gives an incorrect citation due to lack of consciousness is called accidental plagiarism.

According to Katju (2011), plagiarism is a complex phenomenon that goes far beyond copying; it ranges from an innocuous and lazy kind of non-attribution to large-scale lifting of arguments and shreds of evidence. At present time these incidences are approaching the nature of the institutional structure of higher education including social science teaching.

Avoiding duplicate publications: Avoiding duplicate publications or self-plagiarism is another ethical consideration for a research study. Self-plagiarism is the practice of an author using portions of their previous writings on the same topic in their subsequent publications, without specifically citing it formally in quotes. In self-plagiarism, the author does not do any plagiarizing activity as he is not taking any words or ideas from someone else. Though it is treated offense as it is violating a publisher's copyright. According to Section 13 of the Copyright Act, of 1957 it is an intellectual property right vested in the owner of the property which helps to protect the original work that has not been published somewhere else (Menon, 2021). Multidisciplinary Digital Publishing Institute (MDPI, 1996) an open-access scientific journal has demarcated in their publication ethics guideline that a manuscript should not contain any information that has already been published. If one includes already published figures or images, he needs to obtain the necessary permission from the copyright holder to publish under the CC-BY license (Creative Commons Attribution (CC-BY) license grants permission to others to use, share, adapt, and distribute one's work if the researchers provide appropriate credit to the original creator or licensor).

Adherence to journal guidelines: According to the COPE Report, 1999 it is necessary for the author to obtain the guideline of the publishers, i.e., the work should be original, may not be published somewhere else; publication should be approved by all co-authors; the author should be accountable about the authenticity of the writing, etc. MDPI (1996) has depicted some guidelines to maintain publication ethics which have been discussed — a) any facts that might be perceived as a possible conflict of interest of the authors must be disclosed before submission of the paper, b) the author should accurately present their research findings and include an objective discussion of the significance of findings, c) data and methods used in the research need to be presented in sufficient detail so that other researcher can make it as a reference, d) raw data should preferably be publicly deposited by the author or at least be ready to submit to the editor of the journal if required, e) author cannot publish one particular manuscript to more than one publisher, f) if an image file or data which is included in the paper is identified as manipulated during the peer review process the paper will be rejected. These guidelines have depicted general publication ethics for a researcher that he/ she needs to obtain during the time of manuscript submission.

Peer reviewing: Peer review is a process of independent assessment of the submitted manuscript by a reviewer, applicable to all categories of articles. Peer reviewing has various types; among them, double-blind reviewing is a type of reviewing where the author as well as the reviewer could not get to know each other identity. Peer reviewing an article increases its transparency and can evaluate its quality which raises the integrity of research. The COPE Report 1999 have mentioned ethical consideration in the peer reviewing process — a) there should be no obligation on editors to obtain the suggestion of reviewers, b) the confidentiality of the assessment of the manuscript must be maintained, c) the submitted manuscript should not be retained or copied, the reviewer should provide a speedy, unbiased, justified review, etc. According to British Academy Review (2007), the peer review process should not be seen simply as a selection mechanism, but also as a way of improving the quality of the paper as well as it can help to improve the practicality of writing.

Reporting Ethics

A well-designed, rigorous, credible research study has the goal to publish the research finding in a good research journal. The findings and conclusions from one study or investigation may implicate the design of future studies.

According to Milton (2019), the quality, semantics, and coherency of research findings along with their depth and clarity are required for all scientific research studies. This is the basic ethical concern of any scientific research study and can be called reporting ethics. Some of the ethical issues related to reporting the research findings are mentioned below:

a) *Balanced Reporting*: To report the findings of any research work having a central idea, is called "Balanced Reporting". According to Gerken (2019) in the philosophy of science, there have been two central journalistic ideals — i) Balanced Reporting: resenting diverse points of view, ii) Reliable Reporting: presenting the most reliable testimony. In the case of any scientific research work it is important to evaluate every aspect of the research area and based on its accurate conclusion-making is the main concern of any research work. It should be straight-thinking conduct of the researcher; no vague documentation of the study would be there; as well as it should not be misleading and controversial for the readers. According to Berkeley University of California (n.d.), balanced reporting or justified reporting is such type of reporting that can balance every perspective of the issue. But it is seen that the judgement of any issue has become biased due to the impact of the previous report. For example, Scientific studies overwhelmingly support that global warming is primarily caused by human activities, with no credible evidence suggesting otherwise, this is the false balance situation.
b) *Avoid sensationalism*: According to Dempster et al., (2022), any journal article should not include a spin in its title, or in the article itself, as well as it should not include buzzwords, positive framing etc. It is called sensationalism in report writing. Sensationalism can operationalize exaggeration and can reduce the gap between "proper" and "entertaining" or generally attention-grabbing information (Mohanty & Kumar, 2022). As social science deals with social issues, the research findings should be appropriate not attention-seeking. Using exaggerated terminologies, and biased interpretations of research findings to get extra popularity may give a negative impact on some specific groups of people; they may suffer traumatic experiences in their social life. So, social science researchers should be careful to avoid sensationalism in their research study. Research studies on child abuse, violence, caste problem, a disease, and drug addiction are very sensitive issues. To get extra popularity exaggerating the interpretation of research findings may harm a particular community's social life, psychological state, and behavioural traits. In this regard, a researcher should be aware to choose words, phrases, etc. which may not spread negative viewpoint over some groups of people in society.
c) *Accurate interpretation of research outcomes*: In many cases, social science research is qualitative. Appropriate interpretation of research findings is a crucial aspect of this kind of research. According to

Willing (2017) interpretation is at the heart of qualitative research because qualitative research is concerned with meaning and the process of meaning-making. In qualitative research the data which is collected cannot speak for itself, it is interpreted by the researcher. So, it is an ethical consideration for a researcher to interpret the research data and its finding accurately. Misinterpretation of research findings may affect the social and psychological state of one or a group of people whose behaviour has been interpreted in a particular way. Thuy (2022) said that social science has always played an important role in the development of mankind, especially in the formation, promulgation, and implementation of development policies. So, it is obvious that the research findings and interpretation can set the future policy for a country. In this regard, a researcher must maintain the ethical concern to appropriately interpret the research findings.

d) *Engagement of the public*: In social science research people are the main source of information. But a researcher should not force anyone to participate in research. According to European Commission (2021), the person who is participating in the research work must have a fair chance to decide whether it is worthwhile taking the time and making the effort to share information with the researcher. It is an important ethical concern for a researcher to obtain participants' informed consent, and apprise them of the responsibilities and risks of research and telling the purpose of research. There should be no ambiguity between the researcher and participants in describing the purpose, benefits, and harms of the study. Nowadays, respondents do not hide their identities, especially when they see the project as an opportunity to gain empowerment through telling their stories and perhaps becoming a catalyst for social change. So, for a researcher, it is an ethical concern to transit the main purpose of the study to the research participants, so that they will be aware of the importance of the study and will support the researcher accordingly.

Ethical Dilemmas in Social Science Research

Every individual in their life faces the necessity to make decisions among two or more alternatives. Figar and Dordevic (2016) said that an ethical dilemma is a situation of choosing between two or more alternatives. It is a difficult situation for him/her to choose between ethical and unethical alternatives. This is called an ethical dilemma in a research study. According to Timothy & Thomas (2019) in social science research there may arise some ethical issues or dilemmas which can affect the research study, which are mentioned below:

a) *Informed Consent*: Informed consent is the willingness of an individual or group to participate in research work. This willingness must be based on the participants' full knowledge. No external pressure may be created on them. According to Mollet (n.d.) in some research studies, it is seen that seeking informed consent may change the attitude of research participants which may divert the research findings. Hiding the main purpose of the study is called covert research. Mollet also said that if the respondents have trust in the researcher there does not need to conduct this type of research. Research on "causes of people trafficking in the world" — may cause mental trauma to the research participants as they need to explore their socio-economic state and psychological experiences of that time. So, it is ethical for a researcher to inform all research participants about the benefits, and harms of participation, be empathetic to them during taking interview, take permission for them to use certain quotations from their interview as well as give an assurance not to reveal their identity.

b) *Deception*: The use of deception in research means that researchers deliberately lie or trick the participants in the research setting so that the true purpose of the study remains unknown to them (European Commission, 2021). Researchers have deception in the design of the study with the intention that if the real purpose is disclosed it would lead participants to modify their behaviour, thereby distorting the research objective. Though it may harm participants, researchers, research professionals, and society overall. According to the European Commission, it can be done if this activity may preserve the integrity of research or if there has been public interest. For example, during the time of research on how background noise affects the concentration of students, it is asked to take part in a quiz or to test the memory of students it is asked to read a list of words and write them accordingly (Oregon State University, 2022).

c) *Privacy*: In participatory research one of the important ethical principles is beneficence, no maleficence, justice, protection of an individual's identity and dignity as well as the truthful presentation of research results (Petrova et al., 2014). Maintaining the confidentiality of research participants' identity and sensitive information is the basic ethic of a researcher toward his research participants. But in various circumstances, this ethics may break. Bos (2020) explained the situation with an example. A researcher tried to research a topic namely, the attitude and experience of employees in a workplace about inclusion. After analysis, it is seen that the ethnic background of workers gave an impact on their experience at the workplace. Subsequently, to represent the result of the study it is an ethical dilemma whether to disclose workers' identity or not. A similar kind of situation may arise in various social science research which creates an ethical dilemma for a researcher.

d) *Physical or mental distress*: For any scientific research it is one of the most important ethical concerns is that it should not endanger research participants in any way. The risk may be varied kinds, for example, risk of life and health, risk of financial and material loss, risk of living in society, etc. In some research of social science, it is seen that the research study may create stigmatization and discrimination when it is known that a particular study involves only certain kinds of participants, e.g., those suffering from a certain disease, engaged in a certain activity, etc. can disclose their identity and exploit their social position. Not only that, certain research studies which focus on topics such as violence, abuse, or other traumatic experiences may compel participants to relive painful experiences. These studies may make a risk to the socio-emotional and psychological behaviour of participants. For example, a research study on the topic "Why do adolescents are committing suicide frequently in different countries" may raise the psychological distress level of research participants as the interview may reveal their past experiences and can make a negative impact on their behaviour, mental psychology, and social living.

e) *Conflict of interest*: According to Human Research Protection Program (2021) the term conflict of research interest refers to situations in which financial or other personal considerations may compromise or have the appearance of compromising an investigator's professional judgement in conducting or reporting research. George (2022) has identified two types of conflict of interest, i.e., i) tangible: connected with funding or financial influence, ii) intangible: relates with personal relationships or professional affiliations. This incident may introduce biases while reporting, publishing, or peer-reviewing the result of the study. Argandona (2004) said that it is ethically wrong to act against the interests of the principle in a de facto conflict of interest. Doing so causes injustice because the researcher has a moral obligation to act in the interest of the principal. But various reasons, like, financial issues, professional progress, funding, etc. may influence the researcher to manipulate the research findings according to the interest of the influencer. For example, in researching "how the caste system affects the psychology of people" — researchers' personal experience may influence the data collection, analysis, and interpretation. On the contrary, a researcher who is the head of any enterprise does not want to represent his research findings negatively exhibited towards his company for financial reasons.

f) *Scientific misconduct*: Manipulating the collected data in terms of fictitious data generation, selective recording of information, tapering test results and findings, etc. is collectively called scientific misconduct. It is ethically wrong to manipulate research findings due to any subjective reason of the researcher. According to Mollet (n.d.) in a research study, where the researcher acts as a research participant, it is difficult to make objective judgements due to the personal connection with the respondents. It also creates an ethical dilemma for the researcher.

Strategies to Combat the Ethical Dilemmas

To combat ethical dilemmas various kinds of strategies may be undertaken by a researcher. These strategies have been discussed in the following section:

a) *Pseudonyms*: Maintaining the confidentiality and autonomy of research participants is one of the most important ethical principles for a research study. Disclosing the identity and confidential information is an unethical treatment. But if the study is done over a small group of people, for example, cases of child abuse or elder abuse, HIV-affected people, drug-addicted people, etc. then his or her identity may be disclosed during the study. In such cases, pseudonyms can be used. It means that the real name of the participant shall not be used; some arbitrary identity will be used when it is necessary for research work. It is also advised that participants should be told how results will be published as well as before using the quotations or other data, from the participants which could reveal their identity, and prior approval of the participants is necessary before its publication (Orb et al., 2001). For example, differential experience at the workplace based on the ethnicity of the workers can be represented in the research study by using some arbitrary company and employee name and it can also be mentioned that the actual names are changed due to the reason of confidentiality.

b) *Moral obligation*: Sometimes research study may create mental distress for the research participant who has some painful experience regarding the research topic. Now this is a situation of moral dilemmas. In that situation, the researcher must stop the interview and search for possible solutions for the participants' distress (Orb et al., 2001). It indicates that researchers are aware of the vulnerability of participants and their rights. In the said situation, the researcher may refer participants to counselling or ensure that they have regained control of the situation by talking or catharsis. In some cases, a follow-up phone call or visit may be appropriate. For example, during the research study "The causes which tend adolescents to commit suicide" — the interviewer needs to be very empathetic and careful during the time of communication. She can use catharsis, and counselling strategies during the interview so that not only the research purpose will be fulfilled but also the morality toward the participants can be maintained.

c) *Maintaining objectivity:* Existing relationships with the participants or prior activities of the researcher can potentially create a conflict of interest which may affect the transparency of the research study. Flemming & Zegwaard (2018) have done a research study on ethical considerations for conducting research in work-integrated learning. It is common for researchers to conduct research around their institutional programs where the researcher may also have teaching responsibilities and management of staff who are participants in the research. Here it is difficult for the researcher to maintain the objectivity of the research study. In this situation, to maintain objectivity, a researcher can arrange a third party to collect data who has no direct connection with the research participants and who has no idea about the data before it is available to the researcher.

Conclusion

To transform Indian universities, focus on redesigning curriculum, improving academic and research infrastructure, restructuring human resources, restoring educational heritage, revamping organizational structure, reevaluating goals, revitalizing faculty development and student welfare, enhancing campus amenities, and realigning for growth and progress is indispensable. And herein, social science research must go beyond, generating evidence and actively contribute to policy formulation and implementation to address effectively, all these real-world issues. AI-based software aids in detecting unethical activities, and for improving research quality, it needs to be updated and active. Adequacy of funds is highly necessary for access, data collection, quality, collaboration, and dissemination especially in social science research. Currently, a gap exists between research and policy, with limited translation and implementation of research findings. To overcome the situation enhanced coordination between researchers and policymakers is necessary. Social science researchers need to be involved in policymaking processes to ensure the incorporation of research findings and recommendations. This collaboration will lead to more productive, effective, and robust government policies that have a tangible impact on society.

References

Book

Das, D.K.L. (2011). *Design of Social Research.* Rawat Publication.

Kerlinger, F.N. (1964). *Foundations in Behavioural Research.* Hilt Rinehart and Winston Inc.

Krathwohl, D.R. (1993). *Methods of Educational and Social Science Research.* Longman.

Ministry of Science and Technology. (2013). *The Science and Technology Innovation Policy.* Government of India, New Delhi.

Parashar, A.K., and Parashar, R. (2012). Innovations and Curriculum Development for Engineering Education and Research in India, Procedia. *Social and Behavioural Sciences*, 56, 685-90.

Sajchta, N. (2015). *Advanced Methodology of Social Research.* Delve Publishing LLC.

Sieber, J.E., & Stanley, B. (1988). Ethical and Professional Dimensions of Socially Sensitive Research. *American Psychologist*, 43, 49-55.

Ethical Guidelines for Social Science Research in Health. (2000). NCESSRH, CHEAT, Mumbai.

E-Book

Ahmad, T. (2020). *Measures to Promote Research and Innovation in Indian Universities*. Association of Indian University, New Delhi. Retrieved on 01/07/2023.

Chaddah, P. (2019). *Ethics in Competitive Research: do not get scooped, do not get plagiarized*. Research Gate, 1-127. Retrieved on 03/07/2023.

National Committees for Research Ethics in Norway. (2006). *Guidelines for Research Ethics in the Social Sciences, Law and the Humanities*. De nasjonale forskningsetiske komiteer, 4-40. http://www.etikkom.no/English/NESH/guidelines. Retrieved on 03/07/2023.

Timothy, H.P., & Thomas, S.J. (2019). *Ethical Issues in Social Science*. Applied Social Research: Springer Publishing Connect. DOI: 10.1891/9780826172846.0003. Retrieved on 07/07/2023.

Journal Article

Argandona, A. (2004). Conflicts of Interest: the Ethical Viewpoint. Chair of Economics and Ethics, working paper 58, 1-17. http://ssrn.com/abstract=683784. Retrieved on 08/07/2023.

Bhashanjali, S. (n.d.). Ethics in Social Research. IGNOU, 35-46. Retrieved on 01/07/2023.

Bhattacherjee, A. (2012). Social Science Research: Principles, Methods, and Practices. Textbooks Collection, 1-143. https://digitalcommons.usf.edu/oa_textbooks/3. Retrieved on 04/07/2023.

Bos, J. (2020). Confidentiality. Research Ethics for Students in the Social Sciences, 149-170. https://doi.org/10.1007/978-3-030-48415-6_7. Retrieved on 10/07/2023.

Committee on Publication Ethics. (1999). Guideline on Good Publication Ethics. COPE Report, 43-47. Retrieved on 08/07/2023.

Dempster, G., Sutherland, G., & Keogh, L. (2022). Scientific Research in News Media: A Case-study of Misrepresentation, Sensationalism and Harmful Recommendations. *Journal of Science Communication*, 21 (1), 1-23. DOI: https://doi.org/10.22323/2.21010206. Retrieved on 08/07/2023.

Figar, N., & Dordevic, B. (2016). Managing an Ethical Dilemma. Economics Themes, 54 (3), 345-362. DOI: 10.1515/ethemes-2016-0017. Retrieved on 09/07/2023.

Fleming, J., & Zegwaard, K.E. (2018). Methodologies, Methods and Ethical Considerations for Conducting Research in Work-integrated Learning. *International Journal of Work-Integrated Learning*, Special Issue, 19(3), 205-213. Retrieved on 09/07/2023.

Gallagher, B., Creighton, S., & Gibbons, J. (1995). Ethical Dilemmas in Social Research: No easy solutions. British Association of Social Workers, 25, 295-311. https://www.researchgate.net/publication/11694858. Retrieved on 08/07/2023.

Gerken, M. (2019). How to Balance Balanced Reporting and Reliable Reporting. *Philosophical Studies*, 177, 3117-3142. https://link.springer.com/article/10.1007/s11098-019-01362-5.

Harper, I. (2007). Translating Ethics: Researching Public Health and Medical Practices in Nepal. *Social Science and Med*, 65, 2235-2247.

Israel, M., & Hey, I. (2006). *Research Ethics for Social Scientists*. SAGE Publication. DOI: 10.4135/978184909779.

Katju, M. (2011). Plagiarism and Social Sciences. Plagiarism in Indian Academia, XLVI (9), 45-48. Retrieved on 10/07/2023.

Madhiwala, N. (2017). Ethical Issues in Research. IGNOU, 57-74. URI: https://hdl.handle.net/123456789/3949.

Masic, I. (2013). The Importance of Proper Citation of References in Biomedical Articles. ACTA Informed Med, 21 (3), 148-155. DOI: 10.5455/aim.2013.21. Retrieved on 03.07.2023.

Menon, R. (2021). Ethics in Publishing. IGNOU, 187-196. https://egyankosh.ac.in//handle/123456789/80478. Retrieved on 10/07/2023.

Milton, C.L. (2019). Ethics and the Reporting of Research Findings. *Nursing Science Quarterly*, 32 (1), 23-24. DOI: 10.1177/0894318418807934. Retrieved on 09/07/2023.

Mishra, K., & Dabas, A. (2021). Publication Ethics. *Indian Paediatrics*, 58, 781-785. Retrieved on 1/07/2023.

Mohanty, P., & Kumar, L. (2022). A Study to Measure the Effect of Sensationalism on Sensitive News Coverage. *International Journal of Creative Research Thought*, 10 (3), 395-426. Retrieved on 08/07/2023.

Mollet, J.A. (n.d). Ethical Issues in Social Science Research in Developing Countries: Useful or Symbolic. The Australian National University, 1-9. http://www.aust-neth.net/transmission_proceedings. Retrieved on 09/07/2023.

Nicolaisen, J. (2016). Citation Analysis. Annual Review of Information Science and Technology, 609-640. Retrieved on 03/07/2023.

Orb, A., Eisenhauer, L., & Wynaden, D. (2001). Ethics in Qualitative Research. *Journal of Nursing Scholarship*, 33 (1), 93-96. Retrieved on 09/07/2023.

Petrova, E., Dewing, J., & Camilleri, M. (2014). *Confidentiality in Participatory Research: Challenges from one study*. Sage Publication, 1-13. DOI: 10.1177/0969733014564909. Retrieved on 08/07/2023.

Wet, K.D. (2010). The Importance of Ethical Appraisal in Social Science Research: Reviewing a Faculty of Humanities Research Ethics Committee. Springer Science + Business Media, 301-314. DOI 10.1007/s10805-010-9118-8.

Willing, C. (2017). Interpretation in Qualitative Research. The SAGE Handbook of Qualitative Research in Psychology, 276-290. Retrieved on 08/07/2023.

Sengupta, S., & Honavar, S.G. (2017). Publication Ethics. *Indian Journal of Ophthalmology*, 65(6), 429-432. DOI: 10.4103/ijo.IJO_483_17. Retrieved on 03/07/2023.

Singhal, S., & Kalra, B.S. (2021). Publication Ethics: Roles and Responsibility of Authors. *Indian Journal of Gastroenterology*, 40 (1), 65-71. https://doi.org/10.1007/s12664-020-01129-5. Retrieved on 01/07/2023.

Thuy, P.T.T. (2022). The Role of Social Science Research: Some Requirements for Vietnam. *International Journal of Health Sciences*, 6(S4), 1166–1175. https://doi.org/10.53730/ijhs.v6nS4.6012. Retrieved on 11/07/2023.

Governmental Document

The British Academy. (2007). Peer Review: The Challenges for the Humanities and Social Sciences, 1-47. Retrieved on 09/07/2023.

European Commission. (2021). Ethics in Social Science and Humanities, 1-25. Retrieved on 08/07/2023.

National Committees for Research Ethics in Norway. (2006). Guideline for Research Ethics in the Social Sciences, Law and the Humanities, 4-37. Retrieved on 01/07/2023.

UNESCO. (1986). Interdisciplinarity in General Education: A Study by Louis d'Hainaut following an International Symposium on Interdisciplinarity in General Education held at UNESCO Headquarters. www.unesdoc.unesco.org.

University Grant Commission. (2019). Consortium for Academic Research and Ethics. Retrieved on 01/07/2023.

University Grant Commission. (2019). Improving the Quality of Research by Faculty and Creation of New Knowledge and Strategies for Improving Research Culture in Colleges and Universities Report.

Weblinks

Barkley University of California. (n.d.). Beware of False Balance: Are the views of the scientific community accurately portrayed. Understanding Science. https://undsci.berkeley.edu/understanding-science-101/a-scientific-approach-to-life-a-science-toolkit/beware-of-false-balance-are-the-views-of-the-scientific-community-accurately-portrayed/

George, E. (2022, 5th September). Conflicts of interest in research and why you should declare them. Researcher. Life Blog. https://researcher.life/blog/article/declaring-conflicts-of-interest-as-a-researcher/

Human Research Protection Program. (2021). Conflict of Interest (COI) in Research. University of California San Francisco. https://irb.ucsf.edu/conflicts-of-interest-research.

MDPI. (1996). Instructions to Authors. https://www.mdpi.com/journal/information/instructions.

Oregon State University. (2022). Research involving Deception. Human Research Protection Program and Institutional Review Board. https://research.oregonstate.edu/irb/research-involving-deception.

15

Catalysing Research and Innovation in 21st Century Indian Higher Education

Neeru Snehi

The higher education sector in the country is experiencing transition towards massification at an unprecedented rate in the present time. Though, the transition has further exacerbated the existing challenges of access, equity and inclusion, maintaining of quality higher education and research yet the major objective of achieving better student learning outcomes in higher education remains unchanged. Further, in the post COVID-19 pandemic period enabling the access and quality higher education has become a challenging task requiring earnest efforts in the direction. In this context, the aims and targets provided by the newly launched National Education Policy 2020 (NEP 2020) are highly relevant for achieving quality higher education. The Report observes that in world increasingly propelled by technology, university research and innovation is the foundation for national development and growth. In fact, the case for 21st century learning is becoming deeper and complex task as it is dependent not only on how the knowledge is generated, disseminated, applied and how it is transmitted to a student but also on producing employable graduates from universities and colleges. In this context, this paper focuses on one of the major aspects of improving quality namely enhancing of research and innovation in higher education institutions.

Impetus on Research in Higher Education

Higher education system in India constitutes 1113 universities, 43796 colleges, 11296 stand-alone institutions, 4.13 crore students, 1551070 teachers (AISHE, 2020-21) presently and is second only to China in the world. In fact, the last two decades have witnessed rapid change in the growth of this sector in comparison to before. This has not only presented with new challenges but also new opportunities. The challenges of access, equity, quality and relevance continue, at the same time the concerns arising from highly fragmented educational ecosystem, learning outcomes, skill development and employability issues, a rigid separation of disciplines, with early specialisation and streaming of students into narrow areas of study, inadequate mechanisms for merit-based career management and progression of faculty and institutional leaders, less emphasis on research at most universities and colleges, and lack of competitive peer-reviewed research funding across disciplines among others continue to nag the higher education institutions (GOI, NEP 2020).

Historically, the universities and colleges have been regarded as creators and disseminators of knowledge, and this role has gained high impetus in the 21st century education which is being transformed by the technology across the world. The research and innovation function of higher education institutions is now becoming backbone of the educational programmes being offered to the students. Along with promoting and fostering of manpower through research and innovation, the current emphasis is on enhancing its resource generation aspects so as to benefit the society and national economy. However, past efforts to upgrade the quality of higher education in the country could not make significant impact on teaching-learning and research. Due to segregation of teaching and research in the country, generations of students have graduated without the experience of research or without producing even a single original research. The policymakers and academia were not ignorant about the dismal status of research and questions have been raised about the quality and authenticity of research regularly.

During the last two decades, enhancing research capacity in the Indian Universities has been reiterated through the various documents, government portals as well as academia. Eleventh (2007-2012) and Twelfth five-year (2012-2017) plans document reiterated that research and innovation are now vital functions of higher education worldwide and placed priority on promotion of quality research in universities and colleges for establishing a knowledge society. Therefore, it was considered vital that the country promote a research culture across all institutions while ensuring special support for those able to engage in state-of-the-art research. At the same time, a number of initiatives were launched by the Government of India (GoI) to promote and boost the research and number of researchers in higher education. The Ministry of Human Resource Development (MHRD) launched the Rashtriya Uchchatar Shiksha Abhiyan or the National Higher Education Mission to strategically fund higher education institutes in the country in the year 2013. In 2015, the National Institutional Ranking Framework (NIRF) was launched to rank universities and institutes in various parameters, including research. Next came the 'Institutes of Eminence (IoE)' scheme, where GOI initially pledged to support 20 institutes to become world-class universities where teaching and research go hand-in-hand. In addition, a number of scholarships at the undergraduate and postgraduate level, fellowships for research in sciences and social sciences were introduced. However, these initiatives and schemes for funding institutions and scholars were restricted to a select few elite institutes that constitute only two per cent of student enrolment in higher education (Sengupta, 2018).

In recent times, National Education Policy 2020 document has also emphasised that universities and colleges should provide integrated education i.e., where research is an integral part of the discipline. According to UGC document too, "Research creates new knowledge, insights, and imparts excitement, vibrancy and dynamism in educational process. Research culture and academic integrity needs to be promoted among faculty and students from universities and colleges by creating conducive environment" (UGC, 2019). The NEP 2020 observes that "India has a long historical tradition of research and knowledge creation, in disciplines ranging from science and mathematics to art and literature to phonetics and languages to medicine and agriculture. This needs to be further strengthened to make India lead research and innovation in the 21st century, as a strong and enlightened knowledge society and one of the three largest economies in the world". The report further pointed out that "a robust ecosystem of research is perhaps more important than ever with the rapid changes occurring in the world today" and despite this critical importance of research, the research and innovation investment in India is, at the current time, only 0.69 per cent of GDP as compared to 2.8 per cent in the United States of America, 4.3 per cent in Israel and 4.2 per cent in South Korea. This implied that the research and innovation activities in the Indian universities and colleges need expansion.

In fact, earlier 12 FYP noted the reasons for limited research capacity in Indian higher education institutions as 'low levels of funding and segregation of the country's Research & Development institutions from universities and colleges have been responsible for the weak research capacity of Indian universities. The Report further highlighted the concerns regarding the country's top universities which have remained largely teaching-focused with limited research and doctoral education. Even though, there has been a remarkable turnaround in India's research performance over the last two decades, yet it is miniscule in comparison to China and USA. This lack of research orientation, even in the best of the Indian institutions, is reflected in their standing in global rankings, most of which rely heavily on measurable indices of research performance. The situation is not much different in case of filing of applications for patenting innovations and creation of intellectual property, no Indian academic institution figures in the list of top applicants for patent filing. Only few Indian universities secure place amongst the top 200 universities in the Times Higher Education (THE) Rankings or the Academic Ranking of World Universities (ARWU) or the QS World Rankings every year also makes it necessary to achieve high levels of research excellence as a natural pyramid of quality excellence suggests that, if the average quality improves, then the best will enter the top leagues of research-intensive universities.

The intent of NEP 2020 to promote quality research within the higher education system implies that the higher educational institutions, particularly the universities would bring back the research culture and becomes knowledge creation centres. A university as comprehended by the Policy would be a multidisciplinary institution of higher learning that offers undergraduate and graduate programmes, with high quality teaching, research, and community engagement. This definition of university will thus allow a spectrum of institutions that range from those that place equal emphasis on teaching and research i.e., Research-intensive Universities and the others i.e., Teaching-intensive Universities which place greater emphasis on teaching but still conduct significant research. Further, the 4-year undergraduate programme may also lead to a degree 'with Research' if the student completes a rigorous research project in their major area(s) of study as specified by the HEI. To provide support to the institutions, model public universities for holistic and multidisciplinary education, at par with IITs, IIMs, etc., called MERUs (Multidisciplinary Education and Research Universities) will be set up and will aim to attain the highest global standards in quality education. It is also envisaged that HEIs will focus on research and innovation by setting up start-up incubation centres, technology development centres, centres in frontier areas of research, greater industry academic linkages, and interdisciplinary research including humanities and social sciences research. At the same time to catalyse quality academic research in all fields, a new body namely National Research Foundation (NRF) would be established. The overarching goal of the NRF will be to enable a culture of research to permeate through our universities. The NRF will be governed, independently of the government, by a rotating Board of Governors consisting of the very best researchers and innovators across fields. Delineating the primary activities of the NRF, it was stated that its role will be to: fund competitive, peer-reviewed grant proposals of all types and across all disciplines; to seed, grow, and facilitate research at academic institutions to act as a liaison between researchers and relevant branches of government as well as industry; so as to allow breakthroughs to be optimally brought into policy and/ or implementation; and to recognise outstanding research and progress among others. In order to smoothly implement the recommendations of NEP 2020, UGC has brought out two documents namely 'Guidelines for Establishment of Research & Development Cell in Higher Education Institutions' and 'Operational Guidelines Scheme for Trans-disciplinary Research for India's Developing Economy (STRIDE)' — a new scheme to promote quality research by faculty and students. Initiatives for implementation of NEP 2020 recommendations are in full swing, and a steady pathway for enhancing research in higher education institutions is being developed.

Research: An Integral Function of Universities

Universities are spaces created for learning for the present and future generations. They provide platform for any generation of students to come together to debate, enter into dialogue, discuss, share, and roam into the world of ancient wisdom and old and new ideas (Parikh, 2017). In other words, it is implicit that pursuit of excellence in education and research are the fundamental goals of higher education institutions. The role of research i.e., production of knowledge is considered as a significant contribution of universities for societal and national development. It can also be said that universities contribute in developing new knowledge and skills, the ability to develop and exploit new technologies, as well as understanding how technology and society interact, and produce graduates which meet the needs of modern society and job markets.

Looking through the literature it is evident that universities and colleges engage in research as part of their mission i.e., pursuit of scholarship. Undertaking research by the university was considered its fundamental so that it generates and transforms knowledge for the benefit of society (Whitehead, 1967; Penfield et al., 2013). Research became an essential and increasingly important function of the universities during the 19th century (Buffo et al., 1999) and remained oriented towards academic disciplines. It has been observed that contribution of universities to society or economic progress can be direct or indirect for instance NTNU Study Report (2019) mentioned that universities contribute to value creation and impact in society through several research and innovation channels. Vessuri (2008) also reflected that universities should pursue scholarship and research, as higher education institutions have to support the needs of knowledge-based economy at the local, regional and national levels.

The extent of research activities undertaken and published determines the status and quality of the institution (Hazelkorn, 2004). According to him, there are differences among the universities which are late-developers and those who are newcomers and have adopted the polices and strategies of established universities. The newer universities face problems in development of research culture, lack of resources for research activities, institutional setup and management, lack of skills among faculty etc. Memon (2007) also cited factors that hinder the development of research culture, involvement of only specific group of people, lack of research funding and facilities in the sample of Pakistan's public universities he studied.

Research in Indian universities has also been studied and debated at different forums, Commission reports and in education policies. It was mentioned earlier that the research in Indian universities is of unsatisfactory quality and fragmented as most of the universities are still focusing on teaching function only (Tilak, 2018; Patel, 2017). The reasons for lack of research being carried out in the universities were highlighted by 12th FYP report. Shaw (2005) highlighted the declining standards of higher education and research in Indian universities and pointed out that paucity of governmental initiatives to address the systemic issues in the higher education institutions as the major reason. He suggested that the structural reforms, healthy university – government/state relationships are needed to improve the functioning of these institutions. Srivastava (2017) also pointed out that most research is carried out as a fulfilling requirement of career advancement purpose. Other important factors observed for lack of research included absence of research culture, lack/insufficient funding, inadequate socio-cultural support, other environmental and institutional factors, lack of scientific infrastructure-labs, libraries, equipment, insufficient time, teaching loads and other non-academic duties etc. (Patel, 2016; Iqbal et al., 2018; Sawyerr, 2004). Although, many public universities are under pressure to enhance their research activities and mobilise external fundings, yet they are not able to do so because of the conflicts arising due to university rules and regulations and or uneven distribution/ lack of clarity within the faculty roles (Huenneke, 2017).

Many researchers found that lack of availability of resources and institutional support in undertaking research, negligence of social science and humanities research has influenced the quality of research (Singh, 2015). In addition, literature also suggest political and bureaucratic factors have also led to unfavourable environments for doing good research (Venkataraman, 2016; Ramaswamy, 2017). Similarly, academic work on research quality in the Indian context is limited (Ray et al., 2016). They argued that research should be evaluated from both reader's and researchers' perspective and suggested two indices for quality — article index and journal index. Further, it is emphasised that research over the years has become increasingly more holistic and inter-disciplinary and trans-disciplinary, thereby opening up more dimensions for enhancing quality.

It is evident from this brief review of literature on research in higher education institutions that despite the continuing concerns on the factors influencing the extent and quality of research in universities, it is among the core functions of the universities and needs attention from all the stakeholders.

Research Capacity Building

Higher education institutions across the world are increasingly attempting to adapt themselves to face the pressures arising from the globalisation, internationalisation and increasing global ranking demands (Huenneke et al., 2017; Marginson, 2014). Apart from other initiatives, the universities have responded by enhancing the initiatives for improving quality and capacity of research. Hammad (2021) observes that "different approaches to capacity building have been adopted in the institutions, but they usually include elements such as establishing the infrastructure necessary for conducting research, recruiting, developing, and motivating staff members investing in affiliation and partnership programmes, promoting internal and external research collaboration, in addition to increasing research funding, and mapping out national research priorities. Further, capacity building in educational areas and institutions is considered very important as it proposes to address the shortcomings and gaps in educational research and help researchers to produce valid knowledge and respond to the needs of policymakers and practitioners.

In fact, research and capacity building for research is gaining significance due to the growing criticisms of the current educational research practices and outcomes (Cain & Allan, 2017; Hallinger, 2020; Jonbekova, 2020; Leitch, 2009; Lysenko et al., 2014). Although, there is no agreed definition of research capacity building or what it should entail. Researchers (Barrett et al., 2011; Rees et al., 2007; Ridley, 2011) view it as a process aimed at developing research skills and equipping researchers with sound research methodologies that enable them to carry out and produce high-quality research. In this context, in general the research capacity building implies a continuous process for developing and strengthening the skills of all the stakeholders in the institution, which will have impact on the institution. At the same time, Huenneke (2017) was of the view that "universities pursue specific strategies for building research capacity; expanding research, however, can cause tensions with traditional expectations for teaching, service, and outreach; increasing research focus also presents challenges in managing risk and regulatory compliance for institutions; positive outcomes of investment in building research capacity are by no means assured". Conventional approaches to increasing research activity in the institutions include engagement in research as a professional activity, critical reflection on professional experience, and interaction with fellow researchers, collaborative approach to capacity building has also been proposed where researchers and other concerned stakeholders collaborate during the research process and also international collaboration through North–South partnerships are also means for extending research activity. Further, it is apparent that the capacity building must become mandatory focus for every institution and its individuals. Therefore, higher education institutions require research capacity building at the individual researcher (faculty, student) and at the institution level.

Enhancing Research Capacity in Indian Universities and Colleges

Traditionally, in the post-independence period, the mechanism of expanding higher education included establishment of small stand-alone specialised institutions for areas like engineering (IITs), management (IIMs), medicine, law, social sciences, sciences etc. Thus, higher education system developed over the period of seven decades is highly fragmented. This fragmentation of the system leads directly to severe suboptimality on various fronts: resource utilisation, the range and number of programmes and disciplines, the range and number of faculty, and the ability to carry out high-quality multidisciplinary research (NEP, 2019). Reviewing the higher education system, it is evident that there is a dichotomy in the research sector vis-a-vis the large national research sector and the higher/university education sector. The major chunk of scientific research takes place in this large number of national research institutions which are outside the higher education sector. Higher/university education institutions play a limited role in producing research. This dichotomy gets further enhanced as only very small share of government funding goes to higher education while the national research institutions are largely supported. This is also reflected by the huge gap in terms of research contribution from the universities and specialised research and development (R&D) institutions. Consequently, universities and their affiliated colleges have largely remained teaching oriented (Snehi, 2013). This has impacted on two fronts, firstly, "so many members of the academic community of the country not conducting (and not incentivised to conduct) scholarly research is an enormous lost opportunity for research and innovation in the country. Secondly, on the education side, it is difficult to have outstanding higher education and teaching in an environment where knowledge creation is not taking place; indeed, how can students be taught to innovate in a location where innovation is not on the agenda" (NEP, 2019). The NEP 2020 clearly highlighted that there is "lesser emphasis on research at most universities and colleges, and lack of competitive peer reviewed research funding across disciplines". Therefore, the policy has recommended for institutional restructuring and consolidation envisioning a new conceptual perception/understanding for what constitutes a higher education institution i.e., a university or a college — allowing for research intensive universities and teaching incentive universities. It is expected that in 21st century, holistic and multidisciplinary education is the need and this approach will also improve and enhance the research. This is in keeping with the globally successful approach of setting up multidisciplinary research universities.

In this reference, expanding of research in the emerging multidisciplinary higher education institutions (as intended by NEP 2020) would propel it towards developing the capacities of research and innovation needed not only for India as knowledge economy but will also bring Indian institutions in the global arena. Enhancement and improvement in research in universities and colleges would require building of research capacity in these institutions. This in fact needs to be done for all the stakeholders of the institution so that it becomes an inbuilt process of functioning of the institution and is sustainable.

Enhancing Research at the Institutional Level

Developing of research-intensive university is not only significant for improving scholarly research but also provides a sound research base and informs policy and planning of the services in the country. There are several strategies that universities and colleges can use to increase their research capacity in India. These include:

Promote Research Culture: Universities and colleges need to promote a research culture to increase research capacity and output. Conducive research culture of an institution takes time, and it entails careful planning and constant process of development (Salazar-Clemna & Almonte-Acosta, 2007). The importance of developing research culture was recognised by the 12 FYP and it stated that "while all HEIs cannot be expected to become research-based institutions, it is vital that the country promote a research culture across all institutions while ensuring special support for those able to engage in state-of-the-art research". The research culture includes strategies such as providing incentives for researchers to conduct quality research, such as research grants, promotions, and recognition (by organising seminar, workshops, conferences). It also includes creating a culture of providing encouragement and time that enhances the research capacity of researcher and promotes research and innovation. Research culture is highly dependent on the administrative mechanism in the institution. The mindset of the personnel at the helm of providing infrastructural and financial support is very important for the smooth conduction of research activities. The institutions can take initiatives to provide research capacity building opportunities in diverse disciplines by mentoring, nurturing and supporting young talents.

Angom (2022) emphasised that very few higher education institutions have elements of research culture i.e., fairness, enquiry and conscientiousness. Other reasons cited for failing to promote good research culture were: faculty's emphasis on short term researches as it is now linked to academic promotion i.e., earning points for promotion/publication; institutions having few research projects/opportunities; inadequate infrastructural facilities; low motivation for research; inadequate fund/grants for research initiatives, lack of interdisciplinary research avenues and indifferent attitude and lack administrative support.

On the other hand, many institutions are able to create a strong research integrated education in their education programmes. For instance, OP Jindal Global university, declared Institution of Eminence by UGC has strengthened its research culture to meet the IOE's criteria of research and publication. OPJG University has developed a research ecosystem to become a world class university and achieve presence in rankings, the University has a strong focus on interdisciplinary research and an aggressive approach to be involved in cutting-edge and socially relevant research. It aims to not only contribute to ongoing disciplinary debates, but also to lead and shape debates on important national and global issues, including vulnerable subject areas that may not be prioritised for governmental and larger public attention such as their researchers have explored issues relating to the LGBT community in India, the right to contraceptive services and information in the state of Haryana, ethics in business etc. It has 60+ interdisciplinary research centres and three research and capacity building institutes. To develop a strong research ecosystem the University has adopted:

- Reward policy for Scopus-indexed publications in a peer-reviewed journals;
- Internal funding provision to support short- and long-term research projects;
- Financial support for conferences, FDPs and other research-related activities;
- Fostering international partnerships through interdisciplinary and high impact research;
- Motivate students to publish under guidance and active mentoring from faculty;
- Augment PhD programmes with research driven teaching agenda.

The university has built a research culture in their institution by setting up office of the Dean of Research which facilitates the faculty for publication, proposing and securing external funds and grants and promoting collaborative research projects with leading research organisations, experts and thinkers. At the institutional level, it would be a valuable strategy that every institution develops and implement a research excellence framework. Thus, it is of utmost significance to develop research environment/ research ecosystem in the institution for increasing research capacity.

Increase Funding for Research: Funding is cited by the institutions and researchers as the most significant aspect of the research support to the researchers. To increase research capacity, universities and colleges need to receive adequate funding for research. The government and private organizations need to invest more in research to provide universities and colleges with the necessary resources to conduct quality research. The financial support, research grants, incentives such as conference attendance grants, and publication rewards go a long way in motivating the researchers and contribute in developing of research culture in institutions. However, the researchers from universities and colleges reveal that funded projects help significantly in building capacity of researchers but delay in receiving funds from the agency and/or university administration hamper the research outcomes. Especially, colleges do not receive government grants for research, and carry out research if they get funds from industry or funding organisation for specific research.

Infrastructure Development: Universities and colleges need to invest in infrastructure development to provide researchers with the necessary facilities to conduct quality research. This includes well-equipped laboratories, libraries, and other ICT facilities required for research. Research literature reflects the inadequate availability of library, equipped laboratory facilities in the universities and colleges in a large number of institutions. On the contrary, many university departments, centrally funded institutions and colleges have cutting-edge, good and adequate resources for the research. Resources for developing the infrastructure need to be mobilised for enhancing research and innovation in the higher education institutions.

Building research capacity of faculty/researchers: Huenneke et al. (2017) observes that there is broad recognition that faculty members represent one of the most important elements of research capacity for an institution and that university policies, practices, and resources greatly shape the productivity of researchers. Universities and colleges need to invest in human resource development to enhance the research capacity of their faculty. This includes providing training and support for researchers to enhance their research skills. It also includes providing incentives for researchers to conduct quality research, such as research grants, promotions, and recognition. The strategies such as partnerships, research teams and collaborations for research capacity building have been utilised in many universities.

Collaboration between universities and colleges can help increase research capacity. This includes collaboration between universities and colleges within India and with other research institutions globally. Collaboration can help facilitate the exchange of ideas and resources, which can be beneficial to research capacity. These networks and collaboration with international scholars and established research networks can be carried out in the form of informal joint research projects initiated by the researchers themselves, or formal partnerships organized at the institutional level (Hammad et al., 2021; Griffioen, 2018) Many institutions, e.g., IITs, reputed central and state universities, the institutions of eminence are already using these initiatives. Another strategy is to encourage interdisciplinary research in universities and colleges to increase research capacity. This includes encouraging researchers from different disciplines to work together on research projects. Interdisciplinary research can lead to new insights and discoveries, which can contribute to the development of knowledge.

Capacity building activities, by and large, include the following: Periodical Training, Re-skilling and Upskilling, Continuous learning, relevant development activities, knowledge enhancement, coaching and teaching. Integrating the research-oriented activities with the above-mentioned set of attributes would enhance the research productivity of the faculty members (J. Meenakumari, 2022). Since NEP 2020 observes that revitalising research capacity in Indian higher education institutions is crucial for promoting quality research and contributes meaningfully towards the goal of a self-reliant India, there is need to rethink and adopt approaches to research that are more critical, relational and reflective.

Assessment of research management practices: Promoting research in the institution is not a singular activity, it includes planning the research agenda/ policy of the institution and its implementation. The management of the research going on in the institution involves decisions related to the kind of research projects and their approval process, the funding pathways, networking and collaboration, recruitment of research staff, laboratories, workload/time management and research output and its dissemination, patent etc. There is need to have a specialised cell/committee to look after these research practices introduced in the institution. Therefore, it is imperative to regularly assess the research management/ administrative practices in place for building research capacity in any institution. In order to implement the recommendations of NEP 2020, UGC has brought out e-Guidelines for Establishment of Research and Development Cell (RDC) in HEIs. It is expected that "the establishment of RDC in HEIs will enable attainment of targets of Atma-Nirbhar Bharat and is expected to play a pivotal role in catalysing research culture mandated in NEP 2020. The purpose of these guidelines is to put in place a robust mechanism for developing and strengthening the research ecosystem within HEIs, aligned with the provisions of NEP 2020. The essential elements of such an ecosystem, viz., generation of knowledge and facilitation of research, innovation and technology development for industrial and societal benefits, are addressed by human resource, intellectual capital, governance and financial resources, information management system, research promotion and guidance, integrity and ethics, capacity building and research monitoring. The Guidelines are to create a conducive environment for enhanced research productivity; to encourage collaboration across industry, government, community-based organizations, and agencies at the local, national, and international levels and to facilitate greater access to research through mobilization of resources and funding" (UGC, 2022).

Building research capacity of the undergraduate students: Zinjarde et al. (2020) emphasise that "the need for exposing undergraduate students to research and providing them with training in research-oriented scientific thought has been felt for quite some time in India". During the last few decades this has resulted in changes in the undergraduate research ecosystem. Interestingly, they pointed out that the undergraduate research ecosystem in India has improved since the late eighties, allowing more students to participate in research projects as part of the curriculum.

Sengupta (2019) in her study on improving undergraduate research reported that the Council on Undergraduate Research (CUR) defines "undergraduate research" (UR) as "an inquiry or investigation conducted by an undergraduate student that makes an original intellectual or creative contribution to the discipline." Typically, an undergraduate student in any discipline assists a faculty, researcher, graduate student and/or other undergraduates in research in areas of similar interests. Undergraduate students support collaborative research by either pursuing their own research ideas or joining established research projects. Resultantly, the Course-based Undergraduate Research Experiences (CURE) got integrated in undergraduate courses in the USA to enhance student learning. The institutions having research-supportive curricula expose students to the importance of research and even if they do not participate in research in the future, it helps them gain an "appreciation for research methodology in their area of study". Taking a cue from CURE, Sengupta (2019) opined that in India UG research needs to be embedded in programmes in such a way that it complements the current system of teaching, rather than disturbs it... Moreover, given the large number of students in the higher education institutes, CURE will offer a more inclusive system of research and education by giving opportunities to a larger group. Given the typical characteristics of a CURE, such courses will need capable instructors. In India, such instructors can be faculty, PhD students or post-doctoral students. A valuable way of involving external instructors is from specialised research institutes in India such as IISERs, IISc, Tata Institute of Fundamental Research (TIFR) among others.... this segregation of research and teaching institutes to fade out and make way for the blending of high-quality research in specialised institutes, and university teaching. The same has also been recommended by the 2009 Yashpal Committee Report on 'Renovation and rejuvenation of higher education'. However, it was reported that UG research is not completely absent in India. The problem is that it is not being practised in a structured, systematic way in universities and affiliated colleges thus far. These initiatives are taking place in sciences programme but research in social science is lacking (Sengupta, 2019).

In the present scenario, the impetus on research in undergraduate programmes has come through the NEP 2020 recommendation i.e., introduction of Four-Year Undergraduate Programme in Indian universities and colleges all over India. FYUP has been introduced in many universities, some did it in the last academic session, others are going to adopt in the current academic session 2023-24. The structure of FYUP as developed, makes the fourth year as the research-oriented year. Pursuing this course, the student will focus on research in the fourth year and will get the degree of BA/BSc Honors with research. Such students, on completion of their Graduation can join straight to doctoral programmes. In view of this, higher education institutions need to inculcate strong research culture that must be holistic, multidisciplinary along with the chosen major minor subjects.

Curriculum for the FYUP is the instrument through which inculcation of the research culture at the undergraduate level to be initiated. There is need to develop curriculum which includes research methodology. Other courses include — philosophy of research methods, Courses in the realm of Logic of reasoning and argument, Encouragement of reasoning, argument, and innovation, along with the scientific temper. Courses in History of Scientific Thought, Designing Research, Logic of Inquiry, Reasoning, Quantitative and Qualitative Research methods would allow for the researchers to hone their skills. This experience can be enhanced through starting student journals in the literary and scientific lone, creating student societies and equal assistance to all the courses undertaken. Further, provision of research to one and all should be made. Students can associate with the faculty in their research work to get the experience. Mentoring is another way through which research experiences can be transmitted to students.

All the undergraduate students want to experience internships and research opportunities with local industry as well as research internships with faculty and researchers at their own or other HEIs or research institutions. It is hoped that a multidisciplinary and liberal approach to higher education will serve to enhance not only undergraduate programmes but also graduate programmes and research in HEIs. This will make research by faculty and graduate students more interdisciplinary and locally relevant. It will encourage collaboration across departments and institutions to tackle issues relating to improvement of research performance at their institutions.

Way Forward

Higher education system in India is under transition and is attempting to align itself to the vision of NEP 2020. In the 21st century, research and innovation has emerged as a major driver of change, higher education institutions in the country are striving for improving the quality of research. The emphasis on international university rankings is influencing the way of functioning of universities too. This has given impetus to initiatives for promotion of research capacity and innovation in Indian universities and colleges so that they find their place in the rankings as well as continue to drive national economic development. Based on the earlier discussions, some of the strategies to enhance research in higher education institutions are summarised in the following lines:

- Every institution must develop its own framework for enhancing research capacity and output of the institution. The proper implementation of the developed strategies is also imperative.
- Management of research initiatives in the higher education institutions is very important for smooth implementation in the institute. UGC has made it mandatory for every institution to set up a Research Development Cell in every institution for managing the research activities being undertaken in the institution.
- Federal and state governments should continue to fund the research in the institutions. Both, research in liberal studies and sciences needs to be funded. Timely disbursement of research grants is essential for completing the research projects within the specified deadlines. Researchers need to be trained and motivated for applying grant proposals to other funding agencies.
- Investing in cutting-edge and or adequate research infrastructure, developing a healthy and vibrant research culture in the institution is highly desirable.
- Strengthening of networks, partnerships and collaborations for research work with other institutions, national as well as international would help in increasing research capacity, output and available funds.
- Mentoring programmes within and across institutions, investing on faculty and research students would lead to increasing not only research capacity but also the competitiveness of grant proposals developed and submitted by them.
- Another important strategy needs investing is preparing committed, involved institutional leadership at all levels. The role of institutional leaders i.e., academic and administrative leaders is important in order to ensure support and to overcome institutional barriers to continued research capacity development in the institutions.

Thus, enhancing the initiatives for research capacity building of all the stakeholders in the institution would enhance the quality of research output and teaching. This would contribute in accessing better research opportunities for development of national economy.

References

Angom, S. (2022). Improving Academic Research in Indian Higher Education Institutions: An enquiry into Teachers' Perspectives, *Journal of Educational Planning and Administration*, Vol. XXXVI, No.4., NIEPA.

Barrett, A., Crossley, M., & Dachi, H. (2011). International collaboration and research capacity building: Learning from the EdQual experience. *Comparative Education*, 47(1), 25–43.

Buffo, S., Daniel, C., Kaukonen, E., & Opdal, L.R. (1999). The evaluation of Research in European Universities, *European Journal of Education*, 34(3):325-334.

Cain, T., & Allan, D. (2017). The invisible impact of educational research. *Oxford Review of Education*, 43(6), 718–732.

Government of India (2012). Report of Twelfth Five Year Plan (2012-2017), Vol. 3, Planning Commission, 2012, New Delhi.

Government of India (2020) National Education Policy, final document, New Delhi.

Government of India (2022). *All India Survey on Higher Education, 2020-21*, New Delhi.

Government of India, (2019) Draft National Education Policy, New Delhi.

Griffioen, D. (2018). Building research capacity in new universities during times of academic drift: Lecturers professional profiles. *Higher Education Policy*, 33, 347–366.

Hallinger, P., & Hammad, W. (2019). Knowledge production on educational leadership and management in Arab societies: A systematic review of research. *Educational Management Administration & Leadership*, 47(1), 20–36.

Hammad, W. & Al-Ani, W. (2021). Building Educational Research Capacity: Challenges and Opportunities from the Perspectives of Faculty Members at a National University in Oman, SAGE Open, https://doi.org/10.1177/21582440211032668

Hazelkorn, E. (2004), Growing Research: Challenges for Late developers and New comers, *Higher Education Management and Policy*, Volume 16, No. 1, OECD 2004.

Huenneke, L.F., Stearns, D.M., Martinez, J.D., & Laurila, K. (2017). Key strategies for building research capacity of university faculty members. *Innovative Higher Education*, 42(5–6), 421–435.

Iqbal, M.; Jalal, S. & Mahmood, M.K. (2018), Factors influencing Research Culture in Public Universities of Punjab, Faculty Members Perspective, *Bulletin of Education and Research*, 40(3: 187-200).

J. Meenakumari, (2022). Research Capacity Building in Indian Higher Education Institutions – The Need and Way Forward, https://www.edtechreview.in/research/research-capacity-building-in-indian-higher-education-institutions-the-need-and-way-forward/.

Jonbekova, D. (2020). Educational research in Central Asia: Methodological and ethical dilemmas in Kazakhstan, Kyrgyzstan and Tajikistan. *Compare: A Journal of Comparative and International Education*, 50(3), 352–370.

Leitch, R. (2009). Harnessing the slipstream: Building educational research capacity in Northern Ireland. Size matters. *Journal of Education for Teaching*, 35(4), 355–371.

Lysenko, L.V., Abrami, P.C., Bernard, R.M., Dagenais, C. & Janosz, M. (2014). Educational research in educational practice: Predictors of use. *Canadian Journal of Education / Revue canadienne de l'éducation*, 37(2), 1–26.

Marginson, S. (2014). University rankings and social science. *European Journal of Education*, 49(1), 45–59.

Memon, A.M. (2007). An Event-Flow Model of GUI-Based Applications for Testing, Software Testing Verification and Reliability, 17(3): 137-157, https://doi.org/10.1002/stvr.364.

Parikh, Indira. J (2017), "The Future of Indian Universities: Voices from within Beckoning for The future" in the C. Raj Kumar (ed.) *The Future of Indian Universities: Comparative and International Perspectives*, Oxford University Press, New Delhi.

Patel, P.J. (2017). Research culture in Indian universities: The debate continues. *Social Change*, 47(1), 94–100.

Patel, P.J. (2016), Research Culture in Indian Universities, *Social Change*, 46(2) 238–259 SAGE Publications, DOI: 10.1177/0049085716635398

Penfield, T., Baker, M.J., Scoble, R & Wykes, M.C.(2014). Assessment, Evaluation and Definitions of Research Impact, Research Evaluation, 23: 21-32. Retrieved from https://doi.org/10.1093/reseval/rvt021.

Ramaswamy, E.A. 2017, "Why Higher Education is Devoid of Quality". *Business Line*.

Ray, Amit S., M. Parameshwaran, Man Mohan Agarwal, Sunandan Ghosh, Udya S. Mishra, Upasak Das and Vinoj Abraham.(2016), "Quality of Social Science Research in India," Working Paper, Centre for Development Studies, http://cds.edu/wp-content/uploads/2016/05/WP470.pdf

Rees, G., Baronb, S., Boyaskc, R., & Taylora, C. (2007). Research capacity building, professional learning and the social practices of educational research. *British Educational Research Journal*, 33(5), 761–779.

Ridley, B. (2011). Educational research culture and capacity building: The case of Addis Ababa University. *British Journal of Educational Studies*, 59(3), 285–302.

Salazar-Clemena, R.M. & Almonte-Acosta, S.A. (2007). Developing Research Culture in Philippine Higher Education Institutions: Perspectives of University Faculty, paper presented at the conference on "Competition, Cooperation, and Change in the Academic Profession: Shaping Higher Educations Contribution to Knowledge and Research". Accessed from: https://unesdoc.unesco.org/ark:/48223/pf0000157869.

Sawyerr, A. (2004) African Universities and the Challenge of Research Capacity development, *Journal of Higher Education in Africa / Revue de l'enseignement supérieur en Afrique*, Vol. 2, No. 1, Special Issue: African Higher Education: Implications for Development (2004), pp. 213-242 (30 pages)

Sengupta, A. (2018). "Budget for university education — More for less at the cost of more", Observer Research Foundation, February 9, 2018, https://www.orfonline.org/expert-speak/budgetuniversity-education-more-less-cost/

Sengupta, A. (2019). Improving Research in India: Introducing Undergraduate Research in Higher Education, *ORF Issue Brief, Issue No. 277*, February 2019, Observer Research Foundation.

Singh, R. (2015). Indian higher education and research ecosystem: Directions to a world class knowledge nation. In H. Chaturvedi (Ed.), *Transforming Indian Higher Education*. New Delhi: Bloomsbury Publishing.

Snehi, N. (2013), Sustaining Scientific Research at Tertiary level — A Challenge, *University News*, AIU, New Delhi.

Srivastava, V. K. (2017). The state of research culture in Indian universities. *Social Change*, 47(1), 101–107.

Tilak, J. B. G. (2018). On planning university development: Shibboleths versus stylized facts? *Social Change*, 48(1), 1–24

UGC (2019). *Guidelines for Establishment of Research and Development Cell (RDC) in HEIs*, New Delhi.

Venkataraman, Lakshmi Narayanan (2016) "Social Sciences in India: Premises and Promises of a Capability Approach", *Indian Journal of Human Development*, http://journals.sagepub.com/doi/pdf/10.1177/0973703016654560.

Vessuri, H. (2008) The Role of Research in Higher Education: Implications and Challenges for an Active Contribution to Human and Social Development in book *Higher Education in the World 3* (pp.119-141), DOI:10.1007/978-1-349-58169-6_6

Whitehead, A.N. (1967), Universities and Their Function, *The Aims of Education and Other Essays*, New York, Free Press, 1967, 91-101.

Zinjarde, S., Z. Kaushik, K., Kadam, S., & Majumdar, R. (2020). 'Four generations' of scientists discuss undergraduate research in India, Accessed at : https://indiabioscience.org/columns/education/four-generations-of-scientists-discuss-undergraduate-research-in-india

16

Social Science Research

Theories, Paradigms and Methodologies

Ujjwal Kumar Halder

Introduction

The field of social science is vast, aiming to comprehend how people and groups interact with one another and the societies in which they live. It uses empirical research, critical analysis, and systematic inquiry to explore various aspects of human culture and society. Social science comprises psychology, anthropology, sociology, economics, education, political science, history, communication studies, social work, and geography. Social scientists use several research methods like surveys, experiments, statistical analysis, observations, and interviews to collect data and draw conclusions about social phenomena. Their research helps us better understand human behaviour and societal trends and solve social issues.

Social Science Research

Social science research uses analytical and empirical techniques to systematically explore and examine various aspects of human behaviour and society. The primary objective is to understand social phenomena better, clarify human conduct, and enhance theories and knowledge in the social sciences. Here are some essential features and elements of social science research:

- The foundation of social science research is empirical evidence collected through systematic observations, surveys, experiments, interviews, and other methods. Researchers use this data to draw conclusions and make informed observations about the social world.
- Researchers develop and test theories and hypotheses, using data to refine them. The goal is to contribute to advancing theoretical frameworks within the field.
- Social science research is interdisciplinary, drawing from multiple disciplines such as sociology, psychology, economics, political science, and anthropology. Researchers apply insights from various fields to address complex social issues.
- Social scientists aim to maintain objectivity and rigour in their research, using systematic methods to ensure their findings are reliable and unbiased. This may involve careful study design, random sampling, statistical analysis, and peer review.
- Social science research involves qualitative and quantitative approaches. Qualitative research explores social phenomena through in-depth interviews

and content analysis, while quantitative research measures relationships between variables using numerical data and statistical analysis.
- Ethical principles and guidelines are essential in social science research. Researchers must ensure the well-being and confidentiality of participants, obtain informed consent, and follow ethical standards when conducting research involving human subjects.
- Social science research often has practical applications, influencing policy development, social programmes, and decision-making in various fields such as healthcare, education, economics, and governance.
- Social science researchers share their findings through academic journals, conferences, reports, and other forms of dissemination. This allows for peer review, replication of studies, and the integration of new knowledge into the broader academic and societal context.

Social science research covers an extensive range of topics, such as social behaviour, cultural dynamics, economic trends, and political processes. It plays a crucial role in comprehending and addressing intricate social issues and challenges, ultimately contributing to the betterment of society.

Theories

A theory is a structured and systematic collection of concepts, principles, or explanations that help us understand and clarify a particular phenomenon or set of related phenomena. This term is used in various fields of study, such as natural sciences, social sciences, mathematics, and philosophy. Although the features of a theory can differ depending on the discipline, some common elements include:

- A theory's primary objective is to provide a cause or framework for comprehending a phenomenon. It aims to answer questions about why and how something happens.
- Theories strive to generalise and apply their principles or concepts to various situations or cases. They are not limited to explaining a single occurrence but should have broader applicability.
- A solid theory should be testable or falsifiable, meaning it can be empirically tested and potentially proven wrong through observation or experimentation. This distinguishes it from mere speculation or opinion.
- Some theories go beyond explaining past or present phenomena and have predictive power. They can anticipate future events or outcomes based on the principles outlined in the theory.
- The elements of a theory should be logically consistent with one another, forming a coherent framework. Inconsistencies or contradictions within a theory are typically addressed and refined over time.
- The scope of a theory defines the range of phenomena it aims to explain. Some theories are comprehensive and encompass many phenomena, while others are more specific and focused.

- The development of theories is an ongoing process. As new evidence, observations, or insights emerge, theories evolve. The refinement and modification of theories are integral to the growth of knowledge in various fields.

Theories play a crucial role in advancing knowledge by offering a systematic and structured approach to understanding complex phenomena. They serve as a basis for research, experimentation, and the creation of practical applications across various fields of study. Nevertheless, it is essential to acknowledge that theories can change, be updated, or even replaced as new insights and evidence emerge, highlighting the constantly evolving nature of scientific and intellectual exploration.

Paradigms

A paradigm is a fundamental framework or model that serves as an example or pattern in various fields, including science, philosophy and thought. Paradigms shape our understanding of the world and guide our beliefs and actions. Here are some common uses of paradigms:

- A scientific paradigm represents a particular field's dominant theories, methods, and practices. These paradigms provide a framework for research. For example, the Copernican paradigm changed our understanding of the solar system from a geocentric to a heliocentric model.
- In linguistics, a paradigm refers to words with a common root but different grammatical forms. For instance, the verb "to be" has various forms like "am," "is," "are," "was," and "were," which make up its paradigm.
- In philosophy, paradigms can represent dominant worldviews, philosophical schools of thought, or foundational principles that guide thinking and discourse. For example, the empiricism paradigm emphasises sensory experience's role in acquiring knowledge.
- Cultural paradigms refer to shared beliefs, values, and practices within a society or culture. These paradigms shape how individuals within a culture perceive and interact with the world. For example, the cultural paradigm of individualism emphasises personal autonomy and self-reliance.
- A "paradigm shift" denotes a consequential alteration or shift in a field's dominant paradigm. This term, popularised by philosopher Thomas Kuhn, signifies a transformative change in the fundamental concepts and practices that govern discipline. For example, the shift from Newtonian physics to Einstein's theory of relativity marked a significant paradigm shift.
- According to Thomas Kuhn's philosophy of science, a paradigm encompasses theories and methods and shared assumptions and worldviews within a scientific community. Scientific progress often involves revolutionary shifts from one paradigm to another.

Paradigms structure thought, shape how we approach problems and influence our perceptions and interpretations of the world. They can evolve as new evidence, ideas, and perspectives emerge. Understanding paradigms is essential for comprehending how knowledge advances and how different fields of study develop and change over time.

Theories and Paradigms

The connection between theories and paradigms is complex, as paradigms often encompass multiple theories within a specific field or discipline. Understanding how theories and paradigms work together is crucial to comprehend this relationship.

- Paradigms serve as broad frameworks or worldviews within a specific discipline or field. These paradigms consist of shared beliefs, assumptions, and values. Within a given paradigm, numerous theories can fit within its framework and are consistent with its assumptions.
- Theories widely accepted and used within a paradigm are generally consistent with that paradigm's fundamental assumptions and principles. They align with the paradigm's worldview and contribute to knowledge development. For instance, in psychology, the behaviourist paradigm includes various theories (e.g., classical conditioning, operant conditioning) that align with its focus on observable behaviours and stimulus-response relationships. In economics, the neoclassical paradigm encompasses supply and demand, utility, and cost-benefit analysis theories.
- At times, new theories or evidence challenge the established paradigms. These challenges can lead to debates and discussions within a discipline as researchers question whether the existing paradigm can adequately explain new findings. Such challenges may eventually lead to paradigm shifts.
- A paradigm shift occurs when the dominant framework within a discipline undergoes a significant change due to the emergence of new theories, concepts, or perspectives that challenge the existing paradigm's fundamental assumptions. In his famous book, *The Structure of Scientific Revolutions*, Thomas Kuhn explores this phenomenon.
- In some fields, multiple paradigms may coexist simultaneously. Researchers operating within different paradigms may develop distinct theories aligning with their worldviews. These competing paradigms may offer various explanations for the same phenomena.
- Interdisciplinary research often involves the integration of theories from multiple paradigms. Researchers draw on theories and frameworks from various disciplines to gain a more inclusive understanding of intricate issues.

In summary, theories and paradigms are interconnected components of the intellectual landscape within a particular discipline or field. Paradigms provide the overarching framework, assumptions, and worldview within which theories operate. Theories, in turn, are specific explanations, models, or frameworks that fit within a given paradigm, contributing to the accumulation of knowledge and the development of the field. However, the relationship between theories and paradigms is dynamic, as paradigms can evolve, be challenged, or even replaced over time due to changes in theories and evidence.

Theories and Paradigms in Social Science Research

In social science research, theories and paradigms are important as they offer explanatory frameworks to understand human behaviour and society. They help researchers identify patterns, relationships, and underlying mechanisms to make sense of complex social phenomena. Theories are the basis for hypothesis development, forming empirical research's foundation. For instance, social theories about crime may lead to hypotheses about the factors influencing criminal behaviour. They also guide research design and methodology, informing researchers about the types of data to collect, methods to use, and variables to measure to investigate specific social phenomena. Additionally, theories enable comparative analysis by offering a common framework for comparing different cases, contexts, or groups. Social theories inform policy development and practice. Policymakers and practitioners rely on them to understand social issues and design effective interventions. Economic theories guide taxation and welfare policies. Paradigms play a crucial role in social science research as they determine the orientation and philosophy of the study. They influence the researcher's perspective on key issues such as objectivity, subjectivity, and the significance of values in research. Paradigms have a considerable impact on the selection of research methods. For instance, a positivist paradigm may prioritise quantitative methods and stress empirical data collection, while an interpretive paradigm may emphasise qualitative approaches and the exploration of meaning. These deal with epistemology (how knowledge is obtained) and ontology (what exists or can be known). Different paradigms offer different answers to these philosophical questions, affecting the research process and outcomes. Paradigms encompass a worldview and a set of assumptions about human behaviour and society. Researchers within a particular paradigm share common beliefs and perspectives that inform their research questions and interpretations. Social science paradigms can also intersect with other disciplines, such as philosophy, psychology, and economics. Researchers may adopt multiple paradigms to gain a more comprehensive understanding of complex social phenomena. Paradigms encourage critical evaluation of existing theories and methodologies. Researchers within a paradigm may challenge dominant theories and paradigms if they believe they do not adequately address the issues at hand.

In social science research, theories and paradigms play crucial roles. Theories offer explanations and hypotheses for social phenomena, while paradigms provide philosophical frameworks that guide the entire research process, from selecting methods to interpreting results. Researchers typically work within a specific paradigm while utilising relevant theories to deepen our understanding of the intricate social world.

Significant Theories and Paradigms in Social Science Research

Social science research encompasses various disciplines with paradigms, perspectives, and approaches. Here are some significant paradigms or schools of thought in social science research:

Positivism: Positivism is a philosophical and epistemological approach that originated in the 19th century, primarily associated with the French philosopher Auguste Comte (1798-1857). Positivism uses empirical observation and measurement to study social phenomena and uncover objective, law — like relationships and causal explanations. It emphasises the importance of empirical observation and scientific methods as the primary means of acquiring knowledge about the world. Positivism has significantly influenced various fields, including philosophy, sociology, psychology, and the natural sciences.

The fundamental principles of positivism include the belief that knowledge should be derived from sensory experience and empirical observations. Positivists advocate using the scientific method, which involves systematic observation, hypothesis testing, experimentation, and accumulating empirical data. They view science as the most reliable and objective way of understanding the world. Positivism also strives for objectivity in pursuing knowledge, seeking to minimise personal biases, emotions, and subjective interpretations in favour of objective, verifiable facts and data. Positivist research commonly employs quantitative methods like surveys, experiments, and statistical analysis. Positivist research might use large-scale surveys and statistical analysis to explore the correlation between socio-economic status and crime rates in sociology. Positivism rejects metaphysical or speculative inquiries about the nature of reality that cannot be empirically tested and often dismisses metaphysical questions as meaningless or unanswerable. In the philosophy of language, positivists introduced the verification principle, which suggests that a statement or proposition is meaningful only if it can be empirically verified or is logically necessary.

Positivism is often associated with naturalism, which is the belief that the natural sciences provide the most reliable and comprehensive understanding of the world, and other fields should strive to emulate their methods. Positivists typically reject metaphysical or speculative inquiries about the ultimate nature of reality, such as questions about the existence of God or the soul, as unverifiable and outside the scope of scientific inquiry.

It is worth noting that positivism has evolved and has been subject to criticism and refinement by various philosophers and scholars. Some complaints include concerns about its limited scope in explaining complex social and human phenomena and its potential to overlook important aspects of human experience that cannot be reduced to empirical observations alone. Contemporary positivist philosophy has incorporated some of these criticisms and has adapted to accommodate a broader range of perspectives, including developments in the philosophy of science and the social sciences.

***Post-positivism*:** Post-positivism is a philosophical and epistemological viewpoint that arose in response to the limitations and criticisms of classical positivism. While empirical observation and scientific methods are valuable, post-positivism acknowledges that they have limitations and that there is no purely objective or value-neutral way to acquire knowledge. Post-positivism combines elements of both positivism and interpretivism while recognising the complexity and subjectivity of human experience. Post-positivism often adopts a critical realist stance, which acknowledges an objective reality that exists independently of our perceptions but recognises that our subjective experiences and interpretations mediate our understanding of this reality. They are typically epistemic relativists, meaning they recognise that human perspectives and subjectivity shape knowledge. They argue that objectivity is an ideal to strive for but may never be fully attainable.

Post-positivists embrace fallibilism, the idea that scientific knowledge is always tentative and subject to revision. They reject the notion of absolute certainty and acknowledge the possibility of errors and corrections in scientific theories. Post-positivists emphasise the importance of contextual analysis in understanding social phenomena. It is conceded that events and behaviours hold meaning shaped by the historical, cultural, and social context in which they occur. While post-positivism is more open to qualitative and interpretive research methods, it does not reject quantitative methods. Researchers in this paradigm may use qualitative and quantitative approaches to gain a more comprehensive understanding of complex phenomena. Post-positivism acknowledges that values and ethical considerations play a role in the research process. Researchers are encouraged to be transparent about their values and consider their potential impact on research outcomes. Post-positivist researchers engage in reflexivity, acknowledging their biases and perspectives and how they may influence the research process.

Post-positivists recognise that theories and conceptual frameworks shape how we observe and interpret the world. They argue that scientific theories are not entirely theory-neutral and can influence the collection and interpretation of data. Some post-positivist perspectives draw from social constructivism, which emphasises the role of language, discourse, and social interactions in shaping reality. This theory suggests that social and cultural factors shape reality and can differ based on historical context. Post-positivism promotes pluralism in research approaches, acknowledging that different research methods and paradigms may be appropriate for further research questions and contexts.

Post-positivism represents a more nuanced and flexible approach to knowledge acquisition than classical positivism. It seeks to address some of the critiques of positivism while retaining a commitment to empirical investigation and the scientific method. Researchers adopting a post-positivist stance aim to balance objectivity and subjectivity, recognising that knowledge is a complex interplay between the two.

***Interpretivism*:** Interpretivism is an approach used in social sciences and humanities, including sociology, anthropology, psychology, and cultural studies. It differs from positivism, which focuses on empirical observation and natural science methods. Interpretivism concentrates on comprehending social phenomena from the viewpoint of those being studied, highlighting meaning, context, and subjective experiences. Its fundamental principles and characteristics include:

Interpretivists believe that the social world differs fundamentally from the natural world, with subjective meanings, intentions, and perceptions shaping human actions and behaviours. Therefore, it's crucial to consider individuals' and groups' personal perspectives to understand social phenomena. Interpretivism emphasises the importance of studying social phenomena within their specific cultural, historical, and social contexts, as context provides the framework for understanding the meanings attached to actions and behaviours. Interpretive research methods are usually qualitative, including interviews, participant observation, content analysis, and textual analysis. Anthropologists also conduct ethnographic research to understand specific groups' cultural practices and beliefs.

Hermeneutics is a key component of interpretive research, focusing on understanding and interpreting written, spoken, or symbolic communication, such as texts, narratives, or symbols. Interpretive researchers recognise that multiple interpretations and realities may exist, varying across individuals and cultures. They argue against a single objective reality discovered through scientific methods. Interpretive research frequently engages in reflexivity, acknowledging and critically examining biases, assumptions, and perspectives that may influence data interpretation. Interpretive research often uses case studies to explore specific social phenomena in-depth, allowing researchers to comprehensively understand a particular situation's complexities and nuances. Interpretive research uses inductive reasoning, starting with specific observations or data and developing broader theories or generalisations based on those observations. Interpretivists acknowledge that complete value neutrality in research is challenging because researchers' values and perspectives inevitably influence their interpretations. However, they strive to be aware of and transparent about their values and how they may impact the research process.

Interpretivism aims to uncover people's subjective meanings and interpretations of their actions and behaviours, including their cultural, historical, and social significance. In summary, interpretivism is a research paradigm that focuses on interpreting subjective meanings to comprehend social phenomena in context. It is ideal for studying complex and context-dependent aspects of human behaviour and society.

***Anti-positivism*:** Anti-positivism, also called non-positivism, is a philosophical and epistemological position that opposes the principles and methods of positivism. While positivism prioritises empirical observation, scientific techniques, and the pursuit of objective knowledge, anti-positivism challenges these notions and often advocates for a more interpretive, subjective, and context-dependent approach to comprehending the world. The following are some key features and principles of anti-positivism:

Anti-positivism asserts that human experience and comprehension are inherently subjective and cannot be reduced to purely objective observations. It acknowledges that individual and cultural perspectives shape how people perceive and interpret the world. Anti-positivists emphasise the importance of understanding phenomena within their specific social, cultural, and historical contexts. Context is essential for grasping the meaning and significance of human actions and behaviours. Anti-positivism often favours qualitative research methods, such as interviews, participant observation, ethnography, and textual analysis, which allow researchers to explore the nuances of human experience and meaning. Hermeneutics, the art of interpretation, plays a central role in anti-positivist research. Researchers engage in a deep and reflective analysis of texts, narratives, symbols, and cultural artefacts to uncover their underlying meanings.

Anti-positivism draws from social constructionism, which posits that reality is not an objective, pre-existing entity but is constructed through social and linguistic processes. It highlights the role of language, discourse, and social interactions in shaping reality. Anti-positivism acknowledges that values, ideologies, and ethical considerations are integral to the research process. Researchers are encouraged to be transparent about their values and consider their influence on research outcomes. Rather than seeking universal laws or causal relationships, anti-positivism aims to understand better individuals' and groups' motivations, intentions, and perspectives. Anti-positivists are sceptical of grand or overarching theories that claim to provide a one-size-fits-all explanation for complex social phenomena. They prefer more context-specific and nuanced answers.

Like interpretivists and post-positivists, anti-positivist researchers engage in reflexivity, recognising and critically examining their biases and perspectives and how they may influence the research process. Some anti-positivist views are influenced by critical theory, which seeks to identify and challenge structures of power, inequality, and oppression in society. Critical theorists often employ a normative and value-laden approach to research. Hence, anti-positivism encompasses diverse philosophical and methodological approaches that reject the positivist emphasis on objectivity and empirical observation in favour of a more interpretive, context-dependent, and subjective understanding of the social world. Researchers adopting an anti-positivist stance aim to capture the richness and complexity of human experience and meaning, recognising that the social sciences require approaches beyond traditional positivist methodologies.

***Critical Theory*:** Critical theory is a framework of thought that emerged in the mid-20th century, associated with the Frankfurt School of Social Research in Germany. It aims to critically examine society, culture, and power structures to understand and transform them. Critical theorists analyse and critique the dominant ideologies and belief systems that shape society, uncover hidden power dynamics, and question the status quo in areas such as politics, economics, culture, media, and education.

Some forms of critical theory draw on Marxist ideas, emphasising the role of economic factors and class struggle in shaping society. Critical theorists also explore modern capitalist society's alienating and dehumanising effects, where individuals may feel disconnected from their work, themselves, and others. They seek to promote social justice, equality, and the empowerment of marginalised communities through hermeneutics of suspicion, where they approach texts, institutions, and social practices with scepticism, questioning the hidden motives and power structures behind them.

Critical theory emphasises the importance of praxis, which integrates theory and practice. It encourages individuals and groups to apply essential insights to everyday life and work toward social change. Critical theory has influenced sociology, political science, philosophy, cultural studies, and literature. It continues to evolve and adapt to contemporary challenges, addressing power, inequality, and social justice issues. Scholars and schools of thought within critical theory may emphasise different aspects and approaches, but they all commit to critical inquiry and social transformation.

***Structural Functionalism*:** Structural functionalism perceives society as a complex system of interrelated parts, each with a specific function contributing to overall stability and equilibrium. This perspective emerged in the early 20th century and influenced sociology during the mid-20th century. Structural functionalists focus on how social institutions, norms, and roles serve specific functions that help maintain social order and stability. Education, for example, socialises individuals and prepares them for societal positions.

Structural functionalists believe that societies tend to seek equilibrium or balance. When a part of the social system becomes dysfunctional or experiences a breakdown, other factors will adjust to restore stability. This perspective emphasises the importance of social integration and cohesion. It argues that shared values, norms, and institutions create a sense of solidarity and social order. Structural functionalists distinguish between manifest functions and latent functions. For example, a religious institution may provide spiritual guidance as its manifest function but also create social cohesion and community as its latent function. Structural functionalists acknowledge that dysfunctions such as crime disrupt the smooth functioning of society as a threat to social stability.

Critics argue that structural functionalism may not adequately address conflict, inequality, and social change issues. It is sometimes criticised for being overly conservative and justifying the status quo. Prominent sociologists associated with structural functionalism include Emile Durkheim, Talcott

Parsons, Robert K. Merton, and Herbert Spencer. While it faced criticism and gave way to other sociological paradigms, elements of structural functionalism continue to influence sociological thinking and research today.

***Conflict Theory*:** The sociological perspective and theoretical framework known as conflict theory emphasises the role of power, inequality, and conflict in shaping society and driving social change. According to conflict theory, society comprises competing groups and individuals vying for scarce resources like power, wealth, and social status. This theory is rooted in the works of sociologists, including Karl Marx, Max Weber, and Ralf Dahrendorf. Conflict theory examines social inequality in terms of economic disparities and disparities in power and privilege. It argues that those in positions of power intentionally perpetuate these inequalities to maintain their advantage. Karl Marx, a founder of conflict theory, emphasised the significance of class conflict in society. He argued that a fundamental conflict between the bourgeoisie and the proletariat characterises capitalist societies. Conflict theory posits that struggles for power and resource control mark society. These struggles can occur between social classes, ethnic groups, genders, and other social categories.

Social change is viewed as a product of conflict and tension in conflict theory. When groups with differing interests and goals clash, it can lead to social change and the restructuring of society. For example, labour and civil rights movements are often seen as products of social conflict. Conflict theory also highlights the role of ideology in perpetuating and justifying social inequality. Dominant groups often create and promote ideologies that justify their privileged position and maintain the status quo.

French sociologist Pierre Bourdieu introduced the concept of symbolic violence, which refers to how dominant groups impose their values, norms, and cultural practices on subordinate groups, often without physical force. Conflict theory examines how structural factors such as laws, policies, and institutions contribute to and perpetuate inequality. These structural elements can favour certain groups while disadvantaging others.

Conflict theory provides insights into the formation and actions of social movements. It suggests social movements arise when marginalised or oppressed groups challenge the status quo and seek social change. While conflict theory offers valuable insights into power dynamics, inequality, and social change, it is not without its criticisms. Some critics argue that it oversimplifies complex social phenomena and may not adequately account for societal cooperation, stability, and shared values. Nonetheless, conflict theory remains a central and influential perspective within sociology and continues to inform research on social issues and social justice.

***Symbolic Interactionism*:** Symbolic interactionism is a sociological perspective and theoretical framework that focuses on the subjective meanings and symbols that people attach to their actions, interactions, and the world around them. This viewpoint emphasises the importance of understanding how individuals and groups create and interpret symbols and meanings in everyday social interactions. Symbolic interactionism is often associated with the work of American sociologists such as George Herbert Mead, Herbert Blumer, and Erving Goffman. Symbolic interactionism emphasises the significance of symbols and signs in human communication and interaction. Symbols can be words, gestures, objects, or any other shared representations that carry meaning. The meaning of a symbol is not inherent but is socially constructed through interaction.

Symbolic interactionism is particularly interested in studying face-to-face social interactions and how individuals engage in various social contexts. It examines the micro-level processes of communication and social exchange. The development of self-concept and identity is a central theme in symbolic interactionism. George Herbert Mead introduced the idea of the "self" as a product of social interaction. Individuals develop a sense of self through the process of taking on the perspectives of others, known as "role-taking" or "the generalised other". Symbolic interactionists explore how individuals play different roles in various social situations. Roles are sets of behaviours and expectations associated with particular social positions. Negotiating roles and role expectations is a fundamental aspect of social interaction.

Erving Goffman's dramaturgical approach likens social interaction to a theatrical performance. He introduced the concept of "impression management," which refers to people's conscious or subconscious efforts to shape how others perceive them in social situations. While symbolic interactionism primarily focuses on the micro-level interactions of individuals, it also considers how these interactions contribute to the construction of larger social structures and institutions. Social order and norms emerge from patterns of interaction. Labelling theory, a symbolic interactionist perspective, examines the consequences of societal labels and how they can shape an individual's self-identity and future behaviour. It highlights the impact of social judgements and stereotypes. Symbolic interactionists argue that reality is socially constructed through shared meanings and interpretations. What is considered authentic or significant is contingent on the meanings assigned to it by individuals and groups. Symbolic interactionists often use qualitative research methods like participant observation and ethnography to study social interaction in natural settings. They aim to understand how people create and interpret symbols daily.

Symbolic interactionism is particularly valuable for studying the nuances of human communication and social behaviour. It offers insights into how people make sense of their experiences, negotiate their identities, and create social realities through interactions. This perspective has applications in various fields, including sociology, psychology, communication studies, and anthropology. It continues to influence research on interpersonal relationships, identity formation, and socialisation processes.

***Rational Choice Theory*:** Rational choice theory is a theoretical framework used in various fields, such as economics, sociology, political science, and criminology, to comprehend human behaviour and decision-making. This theory views individuals as rational actors who make decisions by considering the costs and benefits of their actions.

According to rational choice theory, individuals aim to maximise their utility or satisfaction when making decisions. Utility is the satisfaction or happiness individuals derive from different choices or outcomes. Rational choice theorists assume that individuals make decisions to maximise their utility. Individuals often weigh the potential costs and benefits of various courses of action before deciding based on a cost-benefit analysis. Rational choice theory assumes individuals make decisions that serve their well-being and utility. This theory acknowledges that individuals have preferences or desires for specific outcomes but are subject to limited resources, information, and time constraints. Individuals base their decisions on their expectations of the utility they will gain from different choices. This requires estimating the probabilities of various outcomes and their associated utilities. Rational choice theory is often applied to social contexts, such as voting behaviour, criminal behaviour, and organisational decision-making. Game theory, a branch of sound choice theory, focuses on interactions between rational actors and helps study strategic decision-making in situations where the outcome depends on the choices of multiple individuals or parties.

Critics argue that rational choice theory oversimplifies decision-making by assuming perfect rationality and complete information. They also contend that emotions and social norms play a significant role in decision-making. Therefore, it is essential to recognise the limitations of rational choice theory and consider the role of psychological, cultural, and social factors in decision-making. In summary, the logical choice theory provides a valuable framework for analysing and predicting human behaviour in various contexts. However, integrating this theory with other perspectives can provide a more comprehensive understanding of human behaviour.

***Feminist Theory*:** Feminist theory emerged in the late 19th and early 20th centuries. It focuses on issues related to gender inequality and women's rights and analyses societal power dynamics. Feminist theory aims to comprehend and contest the societal, political, and economic systems that result in gender-based disparities and demand for women's rights and authority. It includes various perspectives and approaches that have evolved.

Feminist theory challenges the idea that gender is a natural or biological category. Instead, it argues that gender is socially constructed, created and reinforced by societal norms, expectations, and institutions. This perspective highlights that gender roles and identities are not fixed but shaped by culture and society. One of the central concepts in feminist theory is patriarchy, referring to a social system where men hold primary power and dominance over women. Feminist theorists analyse how patriarchy operates in various spheres of life, including politics, economics, and culture. Intersectionality is a key concept within feminist theory that recognises that individuals experience multiple intersecting forms of oppression and privilege, including those related to race, class, sexuality, and more. Intersectional feminism emphasises the interconnected nature of various social inequalities. Feminist theory advocates for the empowerment of women and the achievement of gender equality. It challenges and dismantles the barriers restricting women's opportunities, rights, and social roles. Feminist theorists challenge traditional gender roles and stereotypes that limit women's and men's potential. They analyse how these stereotypes reinforce and perpetuate gender inequality.

Feminist theory is often categorised into waves, each associated with particular historical periods and emphases. The first wave of feminism focused on women's suffrage and legal rights in the late 19th and early 20th centuries. The second wave, in the 1960s and 1970s, addressed broader issues such as reproductive rights, workplace discrimination, and sexual liberation. The third wave, emerging in the 1990s, emphasises the diversity of women's experiences. Some feminist theorists explore how gender and power dynamics influence knowledge production. They question traditional knowledge systems and advocate for more inclusive and diverse perspectives. Feminist theory often intersects with feminist activism and social movements. Many feminists work to effect social change through political advocacy, grassroots organising, and awareness-raising campaigns. Contemporary feminist theory has expanded to include discussions of gender diversity and the experiences of transgender and gender-nonconforming individuals. Queer and trans feminists advocate for the rights and recognition of all gender identities and sexual orientations. Feminist theory continues to evolve and adapt to address contemporary issues and challenges. It has significantly contributed to academic scholarship, social policy, and cultural critique, and it remains a vital force in advocating for gender equity and social justice.

***Social Learning Theory*:** The social learning theory, propounded by Albert Bandura in the 1960s, is a well-known and influential concept in social science research, particularly in psychology, sociology, and education. This theory proposes that individuals learn by observing others' behaviour and the results of that behaviour and then imitating or avoiding those behaviours based on their observations. Some of the key components and principles of the social learning theory include the emphasis on observational learning, which highlights the role of observation in the learning process. According to this theory, individuals acquire new knowledge, skills, and behaviours by watching others, especially role models or influential figures. The theory also suggests that people are more likely to imitate behaviours they observe if they perceive the model as attractive, credible, or similar to themselves. Furthermore, observational learning is influenced by the consequences of behaviour.

Individuals may adopt a behaviour if they see it being rewarded and may avoid it if they see it being punished. This is known as vicarious reinforcement or punishment. In addition, the social learning theory highlights the importance of self-regulation and self-control. Individuals learn from external consequences and the intrinsic satisfaction or discomfort they experience when adopting certain behaviours. Bandura introduced the concept of reciprocal determinism, which suggests that behaviour, environment, and personal factors all interact with and influence each other.

Over time, the social learning theory has evolved into the social cognitive theory, which incorporates cognitive processes, such as attention, memory, and problem-solving, into understanding how individuals learn from their social environment. This theory has been applied to various areas of social science research, including education, with implications for teaching methods and classroom management. Researchers have also used the theory to study how exposure to violent or aggressive behaviours in the media or from peers can influence individuals' behaviour. Additionally, the theory has been applied to understand how observing others' health practices can influence health-related behaviours, such as smoking cessation or exercise adoption. Social learning theory has been used to analyse how criminal behaviour can be learned and passed down through generations and how interventions can prevent such learning. Researchers have also explored how social learning processes affect workplace behaviours, leadership development, and organisational culture. In summary, the social learning theory is a crucial framework in social science research for understanding how individuals acquire new behaviours and knowledge through observation, imitation, and the influence of their social environment. Its practical implications can be seen in education, psychology, sociology, and other fields.

***Human Capital Theory*:** The term "human capital" refers to individuals' combined knowledge, skills, education, training, experience, and health, which can improve their productivity and contribute to their economic and social well-being. According to this theory, investment in education and skill advancement is wise because it yields returns. This theory is a significant area of research in social sciences, mainly in economics and sociology, and was primarily developed by Gary Becker and Theodore Schultz in the 1960s and 1970s. It focuses on the idea that individuals are investments in themselves, with the knowledge, skills, and abilities they acquire being considered forms of capital with economic value.

Investing in education and training is crucial, as emphasised by human capital theory. Such investments benefit individuals and society, leading to higher earning potential and economic growth. According to this theory, individuals with more human capital enjoy better job prospects and higher incomes. Education and skill development enhance an individual's productivity and desirability to employers. Human capital is not a fixed entity, as it can be accumulated over time through formal education, on-the-job training, and experiential learning. The theory suggests that individuals and society should capitalise on incessant learning and skill advancement to promote economic prosperity. When investing in human capital, individuals weigh the expected returns against the opportunity cost of education (income forgone while studying) and potential future earnings gains. Human capital theory can be used to analyse and explain income and wealth disparities resulting from differences in education and training opportunities. As such, it has influenced policy decisions concerning education, workforce development, and labour market policies, emphasising the importance of investing in education, job training programmes, and policies promoting equal access to human capital development opportunities.

However, despite its influence, human capital theory has faced criticism. Some argue that it oversimplifies the complex process of skill development and may not account fully for factors such as discrimination, social networks, and other non-educational determinants of earnings. Nonetheless, in social science research, human capital theory provides a framework for understanding how education, training, and skill development contribute to economic and social outcomes, enabling researchers to investigate topics such as the impact of education on income, the role of workforce development programmes, and the relationship between human capital and economic growth. It has also helped analyse the effects of educational policies and design interventions to improve access to education and skills training, particularly among marginalised populations.

***Social Exchange Theory*:** Social exchange theory is crucial in social science research, particularly sociology, psychology, and economics. It provides a framework for understanding social interactions and relationships based on the idea that individuals engage in these interactions to maximise rewards and minimise costs. Early sociologists like George Homans and Peter Blau developed social exchange theory, which has since been expanded upon and applied in various social science disciplines. Social exchange theory assumes that individuals decide on the basis of a cost-benefit analysis. They seek to maximise their gains and minimise their losses in social interactions. The theory emphasises the principle of reciprocity, where individuals expect their actions to be met with equivalent responses from others. Individuals wish to receive positive outcomes or benefits from their interactions or relationships, such as love, companionship, material support, or emotional support. They should also be aware of negative aspects or sacrifices associated with exchanges, including time, effort, resources, or emotional distress. Individuals evaluate the relationship based on whether the actual rewards exceed or fall short of the comparison level, representing their expectations regarding the outcomes they should receive. Individuals also consider what they could achieve in alternative relationships or situations. If the rewards in the current relationship are higher than the potential rewards elsewhere, they are more likely to stay in the current relationship. Equity Theory is a related concept within social exchange theory. It suggests that individuals are most satisfied in relationships with a fair balance between their contributions and what they receive. Inequity, where one person perceives an unfair distribution of rewards and costs, can lead to dissatisfaction and potentially affect the relationship. Relationships are seen as dynamic processes where exchanges of rewards and costs continuously occur. Over time, individuals may adjust their behaviours, renegotiate terms, or terminate relationships if they perceive inequity or dissatisfaction. Social exchange theory is applied in various areas of social science research, such as family dynamics, workplace relationships, friendships, romantic relationships, and economic transactions.

It has practical applications in understanding factors that affect relationship satisfaction, commitment, and stability. However, some critics argue that social exchange theory oversimplifies human relationships by reducing them to economic transactions. It may not fully capture the complexity of social interactions, emotions, and cultural influences. Others contend that it doesn't adequately address altruistic behaviour and actions motivated by a sense of duty or social norms. Social exchange theory delivers an essential outline for studying social interactions, relationships, and decision-making in social science research. Researchers use this theory to investigate the dynamics of trust in relationships, the impact of economic factors on social interactions, and the negotiation of social norms and expectations in various contexts. It has practical implications for understanding why people engage in certain social behaviours and how relationships develop and change over time.

These above theories and paradigms are just a few significant theories and paradigms used in social science research, providing different lenses through which social scientists examine and understand complex social phenomena. Researchers may draw from multiple theories and paradigms or combine approaches to address complex research questions and gain a more comprehensive understanding of social phenomena. Choosing theories and paradigms often depends on the researcher's research question, objectives, and philosophical orientation.

Contribution of Theories and Paradigms in Social Science Research

The role of theories and paradigms in social science research is crucial in many ways. They offer frameworks, explanations, and tools that researchers use to understand social phenomena, generate hypotheses, and conduct empirical studies. Here are some keyways that theories and paradigms contribute to social science research:

Researchers use theories and paradigms to provide structured frameworks for understanding complex social phenomena. These frameworks guide researchers in generating hypotheses, formulating specific questions, and making predictions to test through empirical research. The choice of theory or paradigm informs research design, including selecting research methods, data collection techniques, and measuring variables.

Theories and paradigms provide a basis for interpreting data, making sense of findings, identifying patterns, and drawing meaningful conclusions. They also enable researchers to explain why certain social phenomena occur and predict future behaviour or outcomes, having practical applications in fields like policy development and planning.

Moreover, theories and paradigms help integrate knowledge across different studies and disciplines, providing a common language and conceptual framework for researchers to communicate and build upon each other's work. Researchers often seek to advance existing theories or develop new ones to better adapt to changing contexts or explain social phenomena.

Social science theories and paradigms have practical implications, informing policy development, interventions, and strategies for addressing social matters such as poverty, discrimination, and health disproportions. However, ethical questions may arise, and researchers must consider the ethical dimensions of their work within the theoretical and paradigmatic context.

Over time, social science research may give rise to new paradigms or perspectives that challenge existing theories and paradigms, leading to innovative approaches and insights. Theories and paradigms encourage critical thinking and analysis, judging the strengths and weaknesses of diverse clarifications for social phenomena and leading to a deeper understanding of the issues under investigation.

Hence, theories and paradigms are the groundwork for social science research. They offer a structured approach to examine, comprehend, and clarify social phenomena. They aid in the progress of knowledge, the creation of policies, and the betterment of society by assisting researchers in understanding the social world and tackling crucial problems.

Contribution of Social Science Research in Developing Theories and Paradigms

The significance of social science research in shaping theories and frameworks cannot be overstated. Collecting empirical evidence, analysing data, and accumulating knowledge are essential to social science research. This research contributes significantly to the advancement of theories and the emergence of new paradigms. There are several keyways in which social science research achieves this:

- Firstly, social science research tests the validity and applicability of existing theories by collecting and analysing data. Researchers confirm whether a theory accurately explains or predicts social phenomena through empirical studies. If the evidence supports the theory, it reinforces its validity. If not, it may lead to revisions.
- Secondly, research provides opportunities to test hypotheses and propositions derived from existing theories. Researchers can determine whether theories hold in real-world contexts by subjecting theories to empirical scrutiny, thereby contributing to theory refinement or rejection.

- Thirdly, social science research often leads to the generation of new theories or the modification of existing ones. Observations, patterns, and relationships discovered during empirical investigations can inspire the development of novel conceptual frameworks.
- Fourthly, systematic research helps scholars identify gaps in existing theories and paradigms. Identifying gaps can spur the development of new theories or the expansion of existing ones.
- Fifthly, social science research can facilitate the integration of diverse perspectives and theories. Scholars often draw from multiple theoretical frameworks to comprehensively understand complex social phenomena, creating interdisciplinary paradigms.
- Sixthly, as social science research accumulates, theories may evolve to account for changing societal norms, technological advancements, and cultural shifts.
- Seventhly, groundbreaking research findings can challenge existing paradigms and lead to paradigm shifts. Such shifts can revolutionise entire fields of study.
- Eighthly, social science research informs policy development, intervention strategies, and practical applications. Research demonstrating the effectiveness of specific theories or interventions can influence public policies and lead to real-world changes.
- Ninthly, research may uncover ethical dilemmas or raise moral questions related to theories and paradigms. This can lead to discussions and refinements in ethical frameworks and guidelines.
- Tenthly, long-term research projects allow for tracking social trends and changes over time. This longitudinal data can lead to new insights, refine existing theories, and help predict future societal developments.
- Lastly, comparative research across different cultures and societies can challenge ethnocentrism and lead to more universal theories that apply across diverse contexts. Social science research often intersects with other disciplines, synthesising theories and paradigms and enriching the understanding of complex issues.

Social science research is pivotal in developing, refining, and expanding theories and paradigms. Through systematic investigation, critical evaluation, and the pursuit of new knowledge, social scientists continually contribute to understanding the world and developing theories that shape our thinking and inform our actions.

Methodologies of Social Science Research

Social science research incorporates a varied range of methodologies, each tailored to the study's specific research questions, goals, and contexts. These diverse methodologies range from quantitative methods involving numerical data analysis to qualitative methods focusing on understanding the social context and human experiences. Social science research employs a variety of methodologies to investigate and understand social phenomena. The choice of methods depends on the research question, the phenomenon being studied, and the researcher's philosophical and practical considerations. Here are some standard methodologies used in social science research:

1) *Surveys*: Surveys include gathering data from a sample of people through questionnaires or interviews. These often gather information on attitudes, beliefs, behaviours, and demographics. They can be conducted in person, over the phone, online, or via mailed questionnaires.
2) *Experiments*: Experimental research involves manipulating one or more independent variables to observe their effects on dependent variables. Controlled experiments are often used to establish cause-and-effect relationships and test hypotheses. This methodology is common in psychology and economics.
3) *Observational Studies*: Observational research involves systematically observing and recording behaviour or events in their natural settings. This approach is used to study behaviours that cannot be manipulated or controlled. Observatory methodologies include ethnographic research, participant observation, and content analysis.
4) *Content Analysis*: Content analysis involves analysing text, audio, video, or visual materials to identify patterns, themes, and trends. It is commonly used in media studies, communication research, and textual analysis of documents and archives.
5) *Case Studies*: Case studies comprise an in-depth examination of a single individual, group, organisation, or event. Researchers collect and analyse detailed data to comprehensively understand the specific case. Case studies are often used in sociology, psychology, and business studies.
6) *Longitudinal Studies*: Longitudinal research involves gathering data from identical individuals or groups for a long period. This approach allows researchers to track changes, developments, and trends over time and is valuable for studying processes like ageing, human development, and social change.
7) *Cross-sectional Studies*: Cross-sectional research collects data from individuals or groups simultaneously. It helps study population characteristics, attitudes, and behaviours across different segments of society.
8) *Meta-analysis*: Meta-analysis involves the systematic review and synthesis of findings from multiple studies on a particular topic. It provides a way to quantify and aggregate the results of individual studies to draw broader conclusions.
9) *Grounded Theory*: Grounded theory is a qualitative investigative technique that focuses on developing theories or concepts based on data collected through interviews or observations. It is often used in sociology and other social sciences to explore and generate new theoretical insights.

10) *Action Research*: Action research involves collaboration between researchers and practitioners to address practical problems and improve real-world situations. It is common in fields like education and community development.
11) *Mixed-methods Research*: Mixed-methods research combines qualitative and quantitative data gathering and investigation within a single study. This approach allows researchers to gain a more comprehensive understanding of complex social phenomena.
12) *Interviews*: Interviews involve conducting structured or semi-structured conversations with individuals or groups to collect qualitative data. Interviews are used to gather in-depth information, perspectives, and narratives on various fields such as sociology, anthropology, and qualitative psychology.
13) *Secondary Data Analysis*: Secondary data analysis involves using existing data sources, such as government records, surveys, or databases, to answer research questions. Researchers use secondary data to analyse trends, patterns, or relationships, often when primary data collection is not feasible.
14) *Network Analysis*: To study social networks and structures, network analysis examines relationships and interactions among individuals, organisations, or entities. This methodology is applied in sociology, communication studies, and organisational research to analyse social connections and influence patterns.
15) *Simulation and Modeling*: Simulation and modelling involve creating mathematical or computational models to simulate and understand complex social systems or behaviours. This methodology is used in economics, political science, and sociology to study emergent properties and interactions within social systems.

These methodologies represent a range of approaches to studying social phenomena, and researchers often choose the methodology that best aligns with their research objectives, research questions, the available resources, ethical considerations, the most appropriate approach for their study's goals and the nature of the phenomenon under investigation. Additionally, interdisciplinary research often combines multiple methodologies to expand a more inclusive understanding of multifaceted social issues. Researchers often combine multiple methods to triangulate findings and enhance the robustness of their conclusions.

Conclusion

The chapter describes the various theories, paradigms and methodologies influencing social science research; and only major theories, paradigms and methods have been included. However, numerous theories and paradigms not included here are used in some special research. Again, beyond the familiarity of the predetermined methodologies in general, numerous methods are mainly used in specific types of research. Countless fundamental studies have given rise to and will continue to give rise to, many new theories, paradigms and methods. Therefore, research methods and contexts are not confined to a limited number of theories and paradigms; rather, some fundamental studies have introduced new theories, paradigms and methods. It would not be superfluous to say that if the researcher's personal knowledge and impartiality or unbiasedness are the heart of social science research, then theories and paradigms are the brain (head), and methodologies are the hand of that research.

References

Babbie, E. (2007). *The Practice of Social Research*. Belmont: Thomson Wadsworth.

Bhattacherjee, A. (2012). *Social Science Research: Principles, Methods, and Practices*. Textbooks Collection 3.

Bryant, C.G. (1985). *Positivism in Social Theory and Research*. Basingstoke: Macmillan.

Carnap, R. (1952). *The Continuum of Inductive Methods*. Chicago, IL: University of Chicago Press.

Comte, A. (1851). *The Philosophy of Mathematics*. New York: Harper and Brothers.

Comte, A. (1891). *The Catechism of Positivism*. London: Trubner.

Comte, A. (1970). *Introduction to Positive Philosophy*. Indianapolis, IN: Bobbs Merrill.

Comte, A. (1974). *The Positive Philosophy*. New York: AMS Press.

Crano, W.D., & Brewer, M.B. (2002). *Principles and methods of social research* (2nd ed.). Mahwah, NJ: Lawrence Erlbaum Associates.

Crano, William D. & Lac, A. (2011). The Evolution of Research Methodologies in Social Psychology: A Historical Analysis, in Arie W. Kruglanski and Wolfgang Stroebe (ed.). *Handbook of the History of Social Psychology,* Abingdon: Routledge.

Delgado, Richard & Jean, S. (2001). *Critical Race Theory. An Introduction.* New York: New York University Press.

Gane, M. (2006). *Auguste Comte*. New York: Routledge.

Glass, G.V., McGaw, B., & Smith, M.L. (1981). *Meta-analysis in social research*. Newbury Park, CA: Sage.

Heilbron, J. (1995). *The Rise of Social Theory*. Oxford: Polity Press.

Horkheimer, M. (1972). *Critical Theory*. New York: Continuum.

Kuhn, Thomas (1970). *The Structure of Scientific Revolutions*. Chicago: University of Chicago Press.

Kuntz, M. (2012). *The postmodern assault on science*. EMBO Reports. https://doi.org/10.1038/embor.2012.130

Reinharz, Shulamit (1992). *Feminist Methods in Social Research*. New York: Oxford University Press.

Ritzer, George (1988). *Sociological Theory*. New York: Knopf.

Contributors

Dr Ajit Mondal is an Assistant Professor, at the Department of Education, West Bengal State University, Barasat, Kolkata. Formerly he was associated with the Department of Education, Surendranath College for Women, Kolkata. He has to his credit more than 35 papers in peer-reviewed journals and five books. He has also edited fifteen books on different aspects of education. Policymaking, historical development of education in India, social issues, child rights and right to education fall under the areas of his interest.

Professor (Dr) Madhumita Bandyopadhyay is with Department of School and Non-Formal Education at National Institute of Educational Planning and Administration (NIEPA). Her areas of interests include policy analysis, decentralised planning and management, education of girls and deprived groups. She has contributed papers to many national and international conferences and published papers in many journals and books.

Professor (Dr) Neeru Snehi is with Department of Higher and Professional Education at National Institute of Educational Planning and Administration (NIEPA), New Delhi. She is engaged in educational research, teaching, guidance and training activities of the Institute. Her research interests are governance of higher education, internationalization-student and faculty mobility, teaching-learning in higher education.

Professor (Dr) Bijan Sarkar is with the Department of Education, University of Kalyani, Kalyani, West Bengal since 2002. His research and teaching areas include Environmental Education, Educational Psychology, Educational Technology, and Research Methodology. He has presented more than thirty research papers in National and International Seminars and published more than fifty papers in reputed journals and ten books.

Professor (Dr) K.N. Chattopadhyay is former Head, Department of Education, University of Burdwan, West Bengal. His current research areas are Physics Education, Science Education, Educational Technology, Teacher Education etc. With over fifteen years of teaching experience in the Department of Education, University of Burdwan. He has to his credit more than fifty research articles in the SCOPUS-indexed journals and also authored many books of education. He has visited several countries to extend research work.

Professor (Dr) Ujjwal Kumar Halder is with the Department of Education at the University of Gour Banga, Malda, West Bengal. He has contributed more than fifty research papers in various peer reviewed journals and more than fifteen numbers of chapters in various edited books. Research Methodology, Statistics in Education, Educational Technology, Measurement and Evaluation and Application of Social Media in Education are his major areas of interest for study and research.

Dr Abhijit Guha is Associate Professor at Ramakrishna Mission Sikshanamandira, Belur Math, Howrah, West Bengal. He has experience of more than twenty years in Teacher Education College, five years in Secondary School. He has been acting as convener of PhD Research Advisory Committee, Swami Vivekananda Centre for Multidisciplinary Research in Educational Studies (Department of Educational Studies, Calcutta University).

Dr Sangeeta Angom is an Associate Professor, Department of Higher and Professional Education, NIEPA, New Delhi. She has contributed various research papers on areas relating to Indian higher education at seminars/ conferences conducted at national, international, and regional levels.

Dr Mousumi Boral is an Associate Professor in the Department of Geography at Satyapriya Roy College of Education, Kolkata. With a teaching experience over 25 years, she specializes in various subjects such as Geography, Science Education, Population and Environmental Education, Educational Management, Educational Psychology, Education in Special Needs, and Guidance and Counselling.

Dr Shnaoli Chakraborty Acharya is an Assistant Professor in the Department of Education at West Bengal State University, with fifteen years of teaching experience. Her interest areas comprise Psycho-variables in Education, Leadership and Management in Education, Women's Studies, Lifelong Learning, and Techno-pedagogy. She has presented papers and addressed over 40 international, national, and state conferences, published research papers in international and national journals, and contributed chapters in different edited volumes and modules.

Dr Swati Gupta is an Assistant Professor in Department of Teacher Education, Central University of South Bihar, Gaya Her major area of teaching and research are Language Education, Creativity Enhancement among learners, Psychological and Social issues. She has participated in several national and international conferences and seminars. She has published 14 research papers in journals of national and international repute.

Dr Smritikana Ghosh currently holds the positions of an academic counselor and an approved project guide at IGNOU. She has an extensive publication record, including contributions to psychology magazines, e-magazines, books, and numerous articles in both international and national journals. She has demonstrated a strong professional presence in the field of psychology, and a significant number of presentations at both national and international conferences and seminars.

Dr Arindam Bhattacharyya is presently working as an Assistant Professor. He is former HoD, Department of Education, Serampore Girls' College, University of Calcutta. He has more than 16 years teaching experience. He has published over 25 papers in national and international journals and authored ten edited volumes/ books or chapters.

Parnab Ghosh is an Assistant Professor at the Department of Education, Panskura Banamali College, Panskura, Purba Medinipur, West Bengal and has more than 15 years of teaching experience. His areas of interest include Educational Psychology, Educational Technology and ICT in Education, Social Issues, Inclusive Education, Policy Perspectives in Education and Teacher Education.

Basanti Mahanta is a Research Scholar at the Department of Education, University of Kalyani, Kalyani, West Bengal. She has published several research papers in various national and international journals.

Dr Puja Sarkar (Bal) has currently been working as Assistant Professor in the Department of Education, University of Burdwan, Burdwan, West Bengal. Earlier she served in BHU as a teaching faculty. She has six years of teaching experience. She has specialization in Inclusive Education, Educational Psychology and Guidance and Counselling.

Dr Rajab Ali Biswas has been presently working as Assistant Professor, Department of Education at Narajole Raj College, Narajole, West Medinipur, West Bengal. He is an author of three books on educational subjects and published 10 papers in research journals and presented more than fifteen papers in national and international level seminars and conferences.

Nassif Muhammed Ali is a researcher working at NIEPA, New Delhi. Dr Ali's primary area of research is history. His works have been published in journals like *Indian Historical Review*, South Asian Popular Culture, Proceedings of the Indian History Congress, Pratimaan, etc.

Anupam Gupta is a researcher in the Department of School and Non-Formal Education, NIEPA. His areas of interest include health and nutrition, natural sciences, learning and assessment, and participation of children at different levels. He has to his credit many published work.

Meenakshi Khandari is a Senior Consultant at Technical Support Group, EdCIL, New Delhi. She has been engaged in various research studies in the area of school education She has also published several articles and chapters in books and reputed journals.

Anupriya Kholia is a researcher and also engaged in various organizations such as Amity University and NIEPA. She has been also associated with various projects at NIEPA. Her areas of interest include management and administration and school education.

Partha Roy is currently pursuing his education at Ramakrishna Mission Sikshanamandira, Belur Math, Howrah. He was attached with Netaji Satabarshiki Mahavidyalaya as Lecturer. He published several articles in various reputed UGC listed journals including UGC-CARE and authored a textbook on Pedagogy in Bengali.

Aditi Ray has been associated with teaching institutions such as H.GL. High School, Kalna, Bardhaman, JRSET College of Education, Nadia, Institute of Education for Women, Hastings House (CTE), Kolkata. She is co-author of four books. She has written many articles and chapters in national journals and books. She attended over 40 International, National and State Level Seminars, Webinars and Conferences.

Azharuddin Molla is presently pursuing Doctorate Programme. He has also been working as Assistant professor in a Teacher Education Institute (BEd). He authored a book and has published a number of research papers in peer reviewed journals and presented papers in seminars and conferences in national and international levels.

Nilay Mondal is currently pursuing PhD. He published three articles in the UGC-CARE listed journals and five articles in national and international journals. He has also participated in several workshops and presented research papers in various national and international seminars.

Susanta Rajbanshi is a PhD Research Scholar. His research interest areas are Curriculum and Evaluation, Educational Psychology, Educational Planning and Policies.-He has presented several papers in conferences and participated more than fifteen national and international conferences, seminars and Webinars.

Swarup Chandi is currently been working as Junior Research Fellow (JRF) and pursuing PhD. He has published six research articles and also presented a number of research papers in national and international level seminars and conferences. His areas of Research are Metacognitive Awareness, Soft Skills, and Self-Regulated Learning.